50 HIKES
IN CENTRAL FLORIDA

OTHER BOOKS IN THE 50 HIKES SERIES

50 HIKES
IN CENTRAL FLORIDA

THIRD EDITION

Sandra Friend &
John Keatley

THE COUNTRYMAN PRESS

A division of W. W. Norton & Company

Independent Publishers Since 1923

For Jim and Ginny Owen,
for setting an example of a life made richer
with time in the woods.

"I go to Nature to be soothed and healed,
and to have my senses put in tune once more."
—John Burroughs

AN INVITATION TO THE READER

Over time trails can be rerouted and signs and landmarks altered. If you find that changes have occurred on the routes described in this book, please let us know so that corrections may be made in future editions. The author and publisher also welcome other comments and suggestions. Address all correspondence to:

Editor, 50 Hikes Series
The Countryman Press
500 Fifth Avenue
New York, NY 10110

For information about permission to reproduce selections from this book, write to Permissions, The Countryman Press, 500 Fifth Avenue, New York, NY 10110

For information about special discounts for bulk purchases, please contact W. W. Norton Special Sales at specialsales@wwnorton.com or 800-233-4830

Manufacturing by Versa Press
Book design by Chris Welch
Production manager: Lauren Abbate

The Countryman Press
www.countrymanpress.com

A division of W. W. Norton & Company, Inc.
500 Fifth Avenue, New York, NY 10110
www.wwnorton.com

978-1-68268-213-5 (pbk.)

10 9 8 7 6 5 4 3 2 1

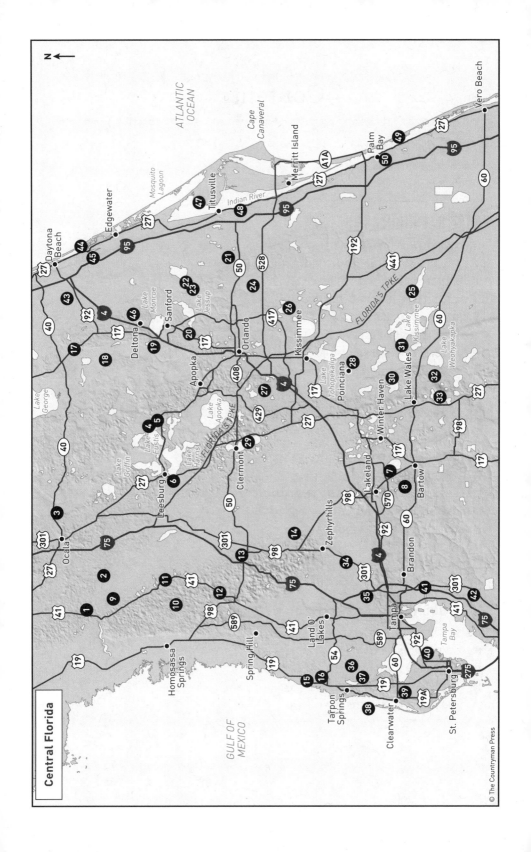

Contents

Hikes at a Glance

Hike	Location	Distance	Entrance fee	Dog friendly
1. Rainbow Springs State Park	Dunnellon	2.7	$	✓
2. Holly Hammock Hiking Trail	Ocala	2.4		✓
3. Silver Springs State Park	Silver Springs	8.7	$	✓
4. Trout Lake Nature Center	Eustis	1.4		✓
5. Hidden Waters Preserve	Eustis	1		
6. Flat Island Preserve	Leesburg	3.7		
7. Circle B Bar Reserve	Lakeland	4.4		
8. Lakeland Highlands Scrub	Lakeland	2.8		✓
9. Johnson Pond Trail	Citrus Springs	2.7		✓
10. Citrus Trail	Inverness	39.1		✓
11. Fort Cooper State Park	Inverness	5	$	✓
12. Chinsegut Wildlife and Environmental Area	Brooksville	5.6		
13. Croom River Trail Loop	Ridge Manor	3.9		✓
14. Withlacoochee River Park	Dade City	6.8		✓
15. Werner-Boyce Salt Springs State Park	Port Richey	1.9	$	✓
16. James E. Grey Preserve	New Port Richey	1.3		
17. De Leon Springs State Park	De Leon Springs	5.1	$	✓
18. St. Francis Trail	Ocala National Forest	7.9		✓
19. Black Bear Wilderness Area	Sanford	7.1		✓
20. Spring Hammock Preserve	Winter Springs	3		✓

Best views	Best for kids	Camp-ground	Primitive camping	Special Features	Note
✓	✓	✓		FGH	Spectacular springs and historic gardens en route to trails
	✓	✓	✓	F	Habitat diversity along the rim of Ross Prairie
✓	✓	✓		FGHW	Two parks in one: wild and tamed, seeing the spring a must
	✓			W	Delightful narrow boardwalks through swamps along lake
				G	Splashing cascades accompany elevation changes
			✓	F	Botanically-rich forest surrounded by swamps
✓	✓			W	One of Florida's don't-miss wildlife watching sites
				FGW	Ancient sands cradle an oasis of wetlands at their center
				FW	Birding on a flatwoods pond in scrubby flatwoods
	✓		✓	FGHW	Florida's longest backpacking loop in a single forest
	✓		✓	H	Second Seminole War historic site with good wildlife watching
	✓			FHW	Outstanding forest of ancient longleaf pine
				FW	Giant trees and cypress knees along a scenic river basin
	✓	✓	✓	FW	Mild and wild options for loop hikes in the Green Swamp
✓	✓			GW	Unusual collection of salt springs along a Gulf Coast estuary
✓	✓			FW	Accessible boardwalk showcases the Pithlachascotee River
				FGHW	Make your own pancakes after this wild walk in the woods
✓			✓	FHW	Riverfront ghost town west of Deland
✓			✓	FW	One of our favorite loop hikes for scenery and wildlife
	✓			FGW	Ancient cypress tower over other tall trees along Lake Jesup

Hike	Location	Distance	Entrance fee	Dog friendly
21. Orlando Wetlands Park	Christmas	6.2		
22. Lake Proctor Wilderness Area	Geneva	4		✓
23. Geneva Wilderness Area	Geneva	1.9		✓
24. Hal Scott Preserve	Bithlo	5.9		✓
25. Prairie Lakes Loop	Kenansville	11.4	$	✓
26. Split Oak Forest Wildlife and Environmental Area	Orlando	6.4		
27. Tibet-Butler Preserve	Windemere	3.5		
28. Disney Wilderness Preserve	Poinciana	2.5		
29. Crooked River Preserve	Clermont	1.7		
30. Allen David Broussard Catfish Creek Preserve State Park	Haines City	3.5		
31. Lake Kissimmee State Park	Lake Wales	15.6	$	✓
32. Tiger Creek Preserve	Babson Park	11.8		
33. Crooked Lake Prairie	Frostproof	2.3		✓
34. Hillsborough River State Park	Tampa	6.7	$	✓
35. Lettuce Lake Park	Temple Terrace	1.8	$	
36. Brooker Creek Preserve	Tarpon Springs	2		
37. John Chesnut Sr. Park	Palm Harbor	3.3		
38. Honeymoon Island State Park	Dunedin	2.5	$	✓
39. Eagle Lake Park	Largo	3		✓
40. Weedon Island Preserve	St. Petersburg	4.6		
41. Alafia Scrub Nature Preserve	Riverview	1.4		✓

Best views	Best for kids	Camp-ground	Primitive camping	Special Features	Note
✓				W	Superb birding along extensive man-made marshes
				W	Scenic walk along Lake Proctor and upland habitats nearby
	✓			FHW	Turpentine and railroad history in a former Boy Scout camp
✓			✓	FW	Sweeping views of pine flatwoods near historic Curry Ford
✓		✓	✓	FW	Backpacking loop on an isthmus in the Kissimmee basin
		✓		FW	Sandhill crane habitat that's home to unusual oak trees
	✓			FW	Popular nature center near Walt Disney World
✓	✓			FW	Carefully restored pine flatwoods along scenic Lake Russell
	✓			FGW	A compact beauty spot along the Palatlakaha River
✓			✓	FGW	Strenuous climbs and serious elevation changes on the ridge
		✓	✓	HW	Well-established loop trails showcase lakeside habitats
✓				FW	Extensive footpaths across hills and valleys on the ridge
✓				FW	An outstanding example of Lake Wales Ridge scrub
	✓	✓	✓	FGHW	Central Florida's most showy set of rapids
✓	✓			FW	Boardwalks along the Hillsborough River and its swamps
	✓			FW	Excellent intepretive stations along the Education Center Trail
✓	✓			FW	Boardwalks along Lake Tarpon showcase the shoreline
✓	✓			FW	A significant nesting ground for osprey in coastal pine flatwoods
	✓			W	Pleasant urban park with great birding and local history
✓	✓			FHW	Interpreting an ancient civilization along Tampa Bay
				F	Last remnant of a scrub ridge along the Alafia River

Hike	Location	Distance	Entrance fee	Dog friendly
42. Little Manatee River Trail	Wimauma	6.5	$	✓
43. Tiger Bay State Forest	Daytona Beach	4.1		✓
44. Ponce Preserve	Ponce Inlet	1.6		✓
45. Doris Leeper Spruce Creek Preserve	New Smyrna Beach	8.2		✓
46. Lyonia Preserve	Deltona	2.1		
47. Merritt Island National Wildlife Refuge	Titusville	12.2	$	
48. Enchanted Forest Sanctuary	Titusville	3		
49. Maritime Hammock Sanctuary	Melbourne Beach	2.8		
50. Turkey Creek Sanctuary	Palm Bay	3.1		

Best views	Best for kids	Camp- ground	Primitive camping	Special Features	Note
✓		✓	✓	FW	Outstanding loop hike along the Little Manatee River
				FH	A forgotten highway and a beauty spot in a swamp forest
✓	✓			FHW	Stretches from the Atlantic Ocean to the Halifax River
✓				FGHW	Hike on high bluffs where a prehistoric village once stood
	✓			FW	One of the best places to see a Florida scrub-jay
✓	✓			WH	Fabulous birding adjoins rocket launches
	✓			FGHW	A mosaic of habitats surround the Atlantic Coastal Ridge
				FW	Tropical forest on the Indian River Lagoon
✓	✓			FW	Family-friendly nature center on a scenic creek

Acknowledgments

Although we tackled most of the re-exploration of our home region on our own, we are grateful to those who joined us for some of the adventures in this book. Thanks to Morena Cameron, Bob Eggleston, Yvonne Entingh, Joan Jarvis, Phyllis Malinski, Mary McKinley, Vera Hurst, Melissa Bruneau and David Waldrop, Sandy Yates, and Sandra's sister Sally White for putting in the miles with us. Ed and Pat Riskosky encouraged us to include Doris Leeper Spruce Creek Preserve, guiding us down their favorite trails. Rachael Augspurg didn't mind us crashing her group hike at the St. Francis Trail, always a favorite, and we thank her for that.

Off the trail, others contributed to making this an outstanding collection of hikes. Richard Durr and Jim Duby of Seminole County Leisure Services filled us in on future plans for Spring Hammock Preserve. Ranger Allen Miller and Park Manager Adam Belden were eager to show us around beautiful Werner-Boyce Salt Springs State Park and share future plans for the park. Cheryl Millett, Tiger Creek Preserve Manager, helped us with mapping changes to the trails in the preserve. Florida Trail Association volunteers Bill Alexander, Linda Taylor, and David Waldrop kept us updated on changes to regional trails originally established by FTA, while FTA Regional Representative Kelly Wiener kept us in the loop on future plans for Split Oak Forest and Hal Scott Preserve. FTA section leader Joe Dabes helped us update backpacking information for the Citrus Hiking Trail. Terrance Wilson posted details online about Alafia Scrub Nature Preserve, which piqued our interest enough to visit.

We appreciated the support of several regional tourism bureaus—including Florida's Adventure Coast, the Ocala Marion County Visitors and Convention Bureau, and West Volusia—during our research and photography trips. Thank you to Kimberly Popke of Florida's Adventure Coast for arranging a stay for us at the unique Chinsegut Hill Retreat in Brooksville, and to the staff at Chinsegut Hill Manor for showing us around the historic estate.

OPPOSITE: HIKING THE ST. FRANCIS TRAIL

SUNSET AT HAL SCOTT PRESERVE

Introduction

If you think theme parks and beaches define Central Florida, think again. It's nature that makes Florida truly unique. Botanical diversity thrives throughout Florida, and it's in Central Florida that tropical forests meet northern hardwoods. Trails pass through desert-like scrub islands, jungle-like hydric hammocks, and deep, dark swamps where giant cypress trees rise out of inky water. Trails cross through salt marshes, river floodplains, and along coastal dunes and beaches with sparkling white sand. Trails scramble over and into karst landforms, big limestone boulders, bluffs, and deep sinkholes lush with ferns, and lead you along the edges of springs that gush billions of gallons of crystal-clear water from the Floridan Aquifer.

Along the trails of Central Florida, each elevation gain or loss of only a few inches leads to an entirely new ecosystem. It's why not every trail leads to a panorama, as many are an immersion in the little things that make each moment in nature special. Shoestring ferns wrap the trunk of a cabbage palm in ribbons of green. Hooded pitcher plants cluster around a seep spring on a hillside. Sundews glisten with sticky jelly-like droplets. Spiderwebs glimmer in the afternoon sun. Sea oats sprout from windswept dunes. White ibises silently pick their way across the blackwater swamp of a cypress dome.

As longtime Central Florida residents—John is a native of Brevard County, while Sandra came to Ocala as a teenager—we've watched our region radically change from a sleepy, wild place to a sprawling sea of subdivisions washing up to the edges of metro areas and smaller towns. But it's in the woods where we learned to love our state, and it's by continuing to spend time in our wild places that we stay connected with what's most worthwhile about our home.

THE REGIONS

We've divided Central Florida into seven geographic regions. **Central Highlands** refers to the higher elevations between Ocala, Leesburg, Mount Dora, and Lakeland, covering Marion, Lake, Sumter, and the western side of Polk County. **Nature Coast** encompasses the coastal counties north of Tampa Bay between Inverness and New Port Richey, including Citrus, Hernando, and Pasco. **St. Johns River** focuses on hikes along the vast floodplain of Florida's longest river, which forms county lines between Lake and Volusia as well as Orange, Seminole, and Brevard, with Deland, Sanford, and Winter Springs as focal points. **Orlando Metro** sweeps up all remaining hikes within Orange, Seminole, and Osceola counties. The **Lake Wales Ridge** is a notable landform stretching south from Clermont through Polk County, with Frostproof being the southernmost point along it in Central Florida. It is one of the oldest pieces of land in Florida, an ancient island when the rest of the state was beneath the sea. **Tampa Bay** includes hikes in the two counties that share this major body of water, Hillsborough and Pinellas. **Atlantic Coast** covers Volusia and Brevard, the two counties that stretch the length of Central Florida between Ormond Beach and Melbourne.

THE HIKES

As the publishers of FloridaHikes.com, we're always out hiking, and Central Florida is our home. We're fortunate that the counties in Central Florida have extensive conservation programs in place to preserve land for wildlife habitat and public recreation. Since the first edition of this book, we've watched hiking opportunities expand dramatically, and the public respond accordingly. We're meeting more outdoor enthusiasts out on the trails than ever before.

While this edition is built on the framework of prior editions, we've revisited all of the trails in the guide, updated those we kept, and changed out a dozen chapters from the previous edition. Hikes in this book run the spectrum from a short and scenic 1-mile loop to a backpacking loop of 39 miles. While we prefer narrow footpaths through the woods over paved trails and forest roads, we provide a mix in this book. Pets are welcome at more than half of the hikes in this guidebook. We've also noted which of these trails are open to cyclists.

At many of the public lands we visit, there are multiple places to hike. Given the popularity of Central Florida as a tourist destination, we include family-friendly options along with places that are at least partially wheelchair accessible. In each chapter, we focus on one piece of public land, even if it has multiple trails on it. Where possible, we combine these into our preferred route through a network of trails. Where trails are not contiguous, we sometimes list multiple hikes—up to four or five—to tally a full day of hiking on one piece of public land. In this edition, we also added *Other Hiking Options* near the end of each chapter. These include alternative routes (shorter and longer) as well as other nearby public lands with hikes. Between the 50 chapters and the other options we provide, you have more than 150 public lands to visit and over 200 possible hikes just within the pages of this guidebook.

Our maps are based on GPS tracks we collected, with supplementing information from land managers on some of the alternate routes. All attempts at habitat and plant identification are our own, using a variety of references.

USING THIS BOOK

Each chapter follows the same structure. There is a map of the hike, and sometimes an inset map or two showing different trails on the same piece of public land. Our route is highlighted, but alternative routes are also shown. We list the *Total Distance* covered by the chapter, the *Hiking Time* based on an estimated 2 mph pace on easy terrain (more time added for tougher terrain), and a *Difficulty* rating of easy, moderate, or difficult. A difficult hike in Florida is very different from one in North Carolina—we're rating against other hikes in Florida. Here, difficult means hilly, muddy, deep soft sand, wading in swamps, or a combination of these conditions in one hike. Under *Usage*, we list entry fees if applicable, hours open, and any regulations regarding pets or bicycle use of the trails. *Trailhead GPS Coordinates* are the latitude and longitude to plug into a map app or your onboard GPS system to find the hike. *Contact Information* includes the street address and the land manager's phone number and URL. An overview of the hike follows.

The descriptive portion of the chapter starts with *Getting There*, with directions from the nearest major highway or interstate exit. *The Hike* (sometimes *The Hikes*) covers the step-by-step details of the route(s). *Other Hiking Options* offers you other routes (if available) on the trail described as The Hike. If those options are limited or unavailable, we send you to other nearby places to hike, along with trailhead GPS coordinates to get you there.

As travel writers, we know you may be planning a vacation in Florida's great outdoors. So at the end of each chapter is *Camping and Lodging*, a short list of campgrounds and hotels you'll find nearby. These are not comprehensive lists, and none of these listings were paid for in any way. They come from our personal knowledge of the region.

SPECIAL FEATURES

As noted in the *At A Glance* chart, our hikes include one or more special features—flora, geology, history, or wildlife. **Flora** is perhaps what Florida is best known for—for both diversity and beauty. Of more than 4,000 types of plants found in Florida, 3,600 are native to the state. Only California and Texas surpass Florida in botanical diversity. **Geology** calls attention to landforms, from ridges and rocky terrain to our bubbling springs. **History** notes locations where human activities shaped the landscape, from prehistoric villages to war memorials to America's space program. **Wildlife** notes the best hikes for wildlife watching and birding.

FLORIDA'S HABITATS

As we mention them throughout our hike descriptions, you may want to know what we mean by terms like *scrub*, *pine flatwoods*, and *oak hammock*. Florida has 81 distinct natural communities, some of which you will encounter far more often than others. They are characterized by certain groupings of plants. The word *hammock* in Florida means forest, so a *palm hammock* is a dense cluster of cabbage palms. Some of the rarer habitats you'll encounter in Central Florida include bluff forest, mangrove forest, and rosemary scrub. For an explanation of Florida's habitats with photos that illustrate each one, visit floridahikes.com/habitats.

HIKING IN FLORIDA

If you haven't hiked in Florida before, our state is unlike any other when it comes to hiking. We are a winter destination, with optimal months for day hikes being October—April, and the best backpacking being in January and February. Our hiking calendar is flip-flopped from the rest of the United States. Winter tends to be dry, and once we have at least one good freeze in late fall, insects aren't a problem. However, don't assume it doesn't get cold in Florida. During hiking season, Central Florida temperatures can drop into the 20s, although balmy days in the 70s are more common. It can also suddenly rise to 80°F.

During the summer months, heat and insects, along with frequent thunderstorms, make hiking unappealing. If you hike in summer, start early, use lots of insect repellent, and plan to be done before noon. Short hikes are best for summer excursions.

Getting damp is a part of hiking in Florida. It's not uncommon to find standing water on some trails, especially after a few days of rain, as not all soils drain well. Some habitats are always wet, but trails will lead you right into them. We note these usually-wet places in our hike details. Plan to wear shoes that drain water if you do those hikes. It's always humid here, even in winter, so your tent will be damp after an overnight in the woods. Dry it out later in the day by staking it out in the sun. Layering your clothing is a smart idea, so you don't get cold by getting damp.

Because Florida's terrain is often sandy or wet, your footwear need not be rugged. Avoid heavy leather boots. If you wear waterproof boots, be aware that if you walk into a place where the water goes over the top of your shoe, it won't be able to get back out. We prefer lightweight hiking shoes and trail runners. When your shoes get waterlogged, you want them to be able to dry out.

Spiders can be annoying between March and November, as they build large webs across trails. The large golden orb spider makes a sticky yellow web. The smaller crab spider has a shell on its back. Try to duck under webs, as a spider's web is a masterpiece of nature—and the spider is helping to rid the forest of other pesky bugs. But if you find yourself getting a face full of spiderwebs, pick up a stick (the stalk of a saw palmetto frond works well) and hold it tilted in front of you to catch any human-height webs.

Are there alligators? You bet. When we were kids they were an endangered species; now you'll find them in almost every body of water. As long as no one has fed them—and it's against the law to do so in the wild—they should be skittish when you approach. But if they don't move, keep at least 20 feet away.

Many trails are not maintained between April and September, since most hiking occurs in the fall and winter. An overgrown trail can be painful when sandspurs dig into your socks. We wear low gaiters to cover our socks and shoes. Wearing lightweight nylon hiking pants year-round helps protect you from insect bites and poison ivy.

Learn more about hiking in Florida: dig through floridahikes.com.

SAFETY ON THE TRAIL

If you haven't hiked before, it's important to know the basics. First, you need to **know what you are physically capable of doing.** Don't take on a 10-mile loop if you've never hiked a 2-mile loop. Get to know your pace and ability by starting small and working up to longer mileages. As mentioned above, **be aware of hiking season.** Just as you wouldn't plunge into the Alaska woods in December, you shouldn't take on more than a very short walk in Florida in August. Wear clothing that will keep you warm and dry (or will help you cool down on a hot day). Use sun protection (sunscreen, hat, and sunglasses as needed) and insect repellent.

What's in your daypack? A trail map is essential, a compass or GPS worthwhile on longer treks. Snacks are a smart idea. **Always carry more water with you than you think you need,** as it is easy to dehydrate without realizing it. The warm temperatures and sunshine will sometimes prompt you to drink, but not often enough. We carry at least one liter per 4 miles, and twice that when temperatures are over 80°F.

Dehydration and long exposure to the sun can lead to **heat exhaustion,** which starts with nausea, chills, and dizziness, and can lead to deadly heatstroke. If you feel any of these symptoms, stop hiking. Drink as much fluid as possible. Rest a while before attempting any further exertion.

It's always smart to check the **weather** forecast before you take a Central Florida hike, not just to select the right clothing but also to select the right hike. You don't want to be scrambling over sand ridges or crossing open prairies or wetlands if there's a chance of bad weather approaching. Packing a **rain jacket or poncho** is a good idea on overcast days or on longer hikes.

Florida's prime hiking season is also prime **hunting season**. During deer season, which usually occurs between October and January in Central Florida, wear a lightweight, bright orange vest when hiking in areas posted for hunting. These are noted in the text and include Florida State Forests, many water management lands, and all wildlife management areas. For full details on hunting dates and restrictions in specific state lands, check online with the Florida Fish and Wildlife Conservation Commission at myfwc.com.

Don't mess with **wildlife**. Don't walk up to an alligator, and make sure you take the long way around any snake you don't recognize. We have six kinds of **venomous snakes** in Central Florida, with the water moccasin the most aggressive and the pygmy rattlesnake the most often seen. Diamondback rattlesnakes can be 5 feet long or more. Black racers aren't venomous, but they can be aggressive. Avoid overgrown trails and be cautious stepping over logs. If you backpack or camp, be aware that our bear population is growing and—especially near urban areas—bears are getting savvier about grabbing food bags. Know how to bear bag (it's required in the Ocala National Forest) or carry a bear canister to protect your food, not just from bears but thieving raccoons that hang out around campgrounds.

Thanks to our warm weather, Florida's **insects** enjoy longer lives than in most states. Nylon hiking pants help protect your legs from bug bites. As for exposed body parts, use a long-lasting insect repellent to keep the insects off of you. Mosquitoes can be vectors for a number of tropical diseases that have snuck back into Florida. Ticks may carry Lyme disease. To keep ticks and chiggers (also known as "red bugs") off you, spray your hiking clothing beforehand with permethrin. To minimize bug problems when you take a break on your hike, carry a plastic garbage bag to sit on.

Poisonous plants are as common here as in other states, particularly poison ivy. It grows in clumps on forest floors and also as a vine climbing up trees and over boardwalks; its large leaves mimic hickory leaves. While poison ivy can be almost anywhere, poison oak and poison sumac are mainly found in sandhill habitats. Tread softly, also known as bull nettle, has a beautiful white flower atop a tall stem; its leaves are covered with tiny stinging nettles. Avoid brushing bare skin against it.

Use common sense when **leaving your vehicle at a trailhead**. Don't leave valuables in plain sight, and lock the vehicle. If a permit was required to enter the land or to hike the trail, make sure the permit is showing inside the front windshield.

PERMITS AND FEES

Access to most of Florida's public lands are free, although camping may require a free permit. We explain those details in each hike description. The main exceptions to this rule at a federal level are National Parks, National Wildlife Refuges, and National Forests, which may choose to collect a fee at some recreation areas. Some wildlife management areas and county parks also charge an entrance fee. Only 12 hikes in this book will cost you when you visit.

Most **Florida State Parks** have an entrance fee. We've found the purchase of an annual pass to Florida State Parks to be a worthwhile investment if you plan to visit a dozen or more in any given year. An individual pass costs $60, and a family pass covering up to eight people costs $120. Passes cover entrance fees only, not the costs of guided tours or camping. Obtain one at any staffed ranger station or online at floridastateparks.org/AnnualPass.

Florida State Forests often charge an entrance fee. Their Annual Day Use Entrance Pass costs $45 and covers entrance fees for up to six people. Costs of camping are extra. Their pass can be purchased at any state forest office or online at floridastateforests.org/memberships.

Entrance fees are charged at some **Wildlife Management Areas** overseen by the Florida Fish and Wildlife Conservation Commission. An annual permit is available for $30. It can be purchased through any tax collector's office or online at gooutdoorsflorida.com.

CAMPING

October through March is our season for **tent camping**, with January and February best for backpacking. Florida State Parks and Florida State Forests have outsourced camping reservations to Reserve America, which socks you with a non-refundable reservation fee on top of the campsite cost. Competition for these campsites is tough as Florida is flooded with RV snowbirds who spend their winter months living in state-run campgrounds. A few sites are held for walk-ins at each park and recreation area. County park campsites tend to be less busy and don't require reservations, with sites first-come, first-served.

When **backpacking**, use a camp stove for cooking, as many of Florida's habitats are quite flammable. Use privies when available, otherwise dig a hole at least 400 feet from all campsites and water sources. Follow Leave No Trace ethics: use established campsites. Leave the site as pristine as you found it, and pack out your trash. Consider bear bagging or using a bear canister to protect your food from all thieving creatures. It's required along St. Francis Trail (Hike 18) and smart along the Citrus Trail (Hike 10), Black Bear Wilderness Area (Hike 19), Hal Scott Preserve (Hike 24), and Prairie Lakes Loop (Hike 25). Some backcountry sites require permits; you'll find those details in the overview for the hike.

HIKING PROGRAMS

Local chapters of the **Florida Trail Association** offer guided hikes, beginner backpacking trips, and other outdoor activities on a regular basis. Find a chapter near you at floridatrail.org.

Florida State Forests were the first to encourage you to take a hike by getting you to log your miles. Their **Trailwalker Program** awards patches and certificates based on the number of different trails completed in the state forests. Learn more at freshfromflorida.com.

More than a decade ago, Friends of the Parks launched **Trek Ten Trails** in Polk County, which combines hiking with geocaching to encourage residents to explore their local trails. Optional hosted hikes are offered November–April. Collect ten stamps on your game card to receive a certificate of completion and a souvenir token. Game cards are available at Circle B Bar Reserve (Hike 7). Program information at friends oftheparks.net.

Hillsborough County has launched an annual **Hiking Spree** to encourage hikers to explore the county's growing network of trails across natural lands and county parks. Join a guided hike or hike on your own, completing 8 of 20 trails during hiking season to receive a medallion. Search for details at hillsborough county.org.

GIVING BACK

Founded in 1966, the **Florida Trail Association** is the oldest and most highly regarded trail maintaining organization in Florida. While their primary focus is the care of the 1,400-mile Florida National Scenic Trail, local FTA chapters built many of the longer trails featured in this guidebook and still maintain some of them. Join a volunteer work party during hiking season, or get involved with a local chapter through floridatrail.org.

Most **Florida State Parks** rely on volunteers for maintenance and daily operations through Citizen Support Organizations (CSOs), typically known as "friends" groups. If you live near a state park and would like to help maintain trails, look into their local volunteer group by checking with the park or through friendsoffloridastateparks.org.

Similarly, **Friends of Florida State Forests** seeks volunteers for our state forests, which tend to have more mileage in their trails and more backcountry: floridastateforests.org.

WHAT'S NEW IN THE THIRD EDITION

All trails have been updated, with mileages recalculated from our new GPS tracks. We hope that the new-to-this-edition *Other Hiking Options* and *Camping and Lodging* information will enhance your trip planning. We've also provided previews of each of these hikes on our YouTube channel at youtube. com/floridahikes.

You'll find 12 new hikes in this edition, plus expanded trail networks at Silver Springs State Park (Hike 3), Lake Kissimmee State Park (Hike 31), Tiger Creek Preserve (Hike 32), Merritt Island National Wildlife Refuge (Hike 47) and Turkey Creek Sanctuary (Hike 50). As the authors of *The Florida Trail Guide*, we've included some segments of our 1,400-mile statewide National Scenic Trail in this book: Citrus Trail (Hike 10) and Chinsegut Hill WEA (Hike 12), as well as the new Croom River Trail Loop (Hike 13) and Prairie Lakes Loop (Hike 25). More Florida Trail segments are referenced under *Other Hiking Options*. In addition, the Florida Trail is being routed into Split Oak Forest WEA (Hike 26) and Hal Scott Preserve (Hike 24) over the next year, so we've shared what we know about those routes.

Trout Lake Nature Center (Hike 4) is an endearing private preserve established by an Audubon Society chapter in Eustis in 1988. It's a perfect place to take the kids to have fun in nature, and you'll find yourself acting like a kid on the boardwalks and swinging bridge, too.

Lakeland Highlands Scrub (Hike 8) caught our attention because of its boardwalk across a flatwoods pond and the expansion of its trail system since our initial visit there 15 years ago. As it is dog-friendly and on the edge of suburbia, it's become a popular destination.

Werner-Boyce Salt Springs State Park (Hike 15) is our newest state park added to the book. We were impressed by the updates to the park, as it now showcases its namesake springs and stunning coastal views. The trail system here will expand.

Black Bear Wilderness Area (Hike 19) and Orlando Wetlands Park (Hike 21) are personal favorites of ours along the St. Johns River basin. Each has a very different feel, but they are both fabulous destinations for spotting wildlife, from box turtles to roseate spoonbills to black bears.

With the increasing challenges of traffic in the Tampa Bay area, we decided to shift focus to easier-to-reach nature preserves. Brooker Creek Preserve (Hike 36) and Weedon Island Preserve (Hike 40) are Pinellas County preserves that offer extensive hiking trail networks based around interpretive centers. Alafia Scrub Nature Preserve (Hike 41) is a pleasant loop on one of Hillsborough County's Environmentally Sensitive Lands, right off I-75.

Revisiting a hike that was in the first edition, we found it worth adding back: the Buncombe Hill Hiking Trail. Tiger Bay State Forest (Hike 43) now also includes an interpretive trail on a fascinating piece of automobile history in Daytona Beach.

When friends pointed out just how much the trail system at Doris Leeper Spruce Creek Preserve (Hike 45) had grown, we knew it was a must-add. We think you'll find it as enjoyable and unique as we did while standing on the tall bluffs upriver from Ponce Inlet.

As Central Florida becomes more urban, more trails we've been visiting for years have been intentionally widened,

especially around the Orlando metro area and in many Florida State Parks. We don't know whether this is for ease of trail maintenance or to prevent hikers from being surprised by wildlife. While a trail the width of a road removes the wilderness feel of a walk in the woods, we also have seen more families walking together enjoying those trails.

Many natural lands no longer allow dogs, to protect the wildlife that has been squeezed more tightly into those wild spaces. Some urban parks have closed to dogs because of issues with owners ignoring leash requirements and poop-scooping. We note dog-friendly hikes in the *At a Glance* chart, but as we've learned, that access can change overnight. Even in parks where dogs are permitted at campgrounds and on trails, such as the state parks with springs, they are not allowed around swimming areas and beaches for sanitation reasons. Honeymoon Island State Park (Hike 38) offers a dog beach.

Rising access fees had us replace several hikes with nearby alternatives. When the cost of a hike rises to $8 or more, we think that's a bit much. We definitely encourage the purchase of park passes for frequent visitors to Florida State Parks and Florida State Forests.

Land equals politics in Florida, and with every change of elected leaders, public lands become a political football. One disturbing trend in the past decade is the taking of conservation lands for highway projects. We had to drop a second edition favorite, Lower Wekiva Preserve State Park, due to toll road construction right through the trailhead. Other nearby preserves are also affected. Split Oak Forest Wildlife and Environmental Area (Hike 26) is threatened with being bisected by a toll road; local residents are fighting it. Another troubling trend is political pressure to sell off public lands. Management plans for public lands now include a "surplus lands" section where land managers are asked to identify what portion of their park or preserve could be sold off. Knowing the intrinsic value of having vast wild spaces for both wildlife and recreational use, these trends are very frustrating. Our advice: get out there and enjoy your public lands now.

AUTHORS' NOTE

While we've walked every step of these trails, your experience may not match what we describe. Trails change over time, as do our forest habitats. Hiking is an activity that involves personal risk. You need to be aware of your surroundings in both rural and urban settings, both at the trailhead and in the woods. Following our advice and descriptions does not guarantee your safety. Know your limits: turn back if you are tired or uncomfortable with what you find, like a flooded or burned-over trail. Always let the land manager know about problems with trail maintenance, missing signs or blazing, aggressive wildlife, and non-hikers loitering at trailheads. We list contact information for each land manager at the beginning of every chapter.

We encourage you to learn more about Florida hiking by digging into our extensive website and following us on Instagram and Facebook, where it's our goal to both educate and inspire you to enjoy Florida's outdoors. We also appreciate it when you inform us of any changes to the trails in this guidebook. Visit us at floridahikes.com.

MAP LEGEND

———	Described trail	═══	Interstate highway
- - - -	Important trail	══	Secondary highway
◀———	Hike direction arrow	———	Minor highway, road, street
———	Perennial stream	- - - -	Unpaved road, trail
- - - -	Intermittent stream	+—+—+	Railroad
———	Major contour line	—··—	International border
········	Minor contour line	—·—··	State border
▮	National/state park, wilderness	🅿	Parking area
▯	National/state forest, wildlife refuge	🚶	Trailhead
▯	Perennial body of water	•	City, town
▯	Intermittent body of water	≪	Overlook, scenic view
▭	Swamp, marsh	⋏	Campground, campsite
▮	Wooded area	⋔	Shelter
		✕	Mountain peak
		▪	Place of interest

SINKHOLE TRAIL, SILVER SPRINGS STATE PARK

I.

CENTRAL HIGHLANDS

Rainbow Springs State Park

TOTAL DISTANCE: 2.7 miles in two loops	

TOTAL DISTANCE: 2.7 miles in two loops

HIKING TIME: 1.5 hours

DIFFICULTY: Easy to moderate

USAGE: Entrance fee. Open 8 AM–5 PM. Leashed pets welcome.

TRAILHEAD GPS COORDINATES: 29.104404, -82.438669

CONTACT INFORMATION: Rainbow Springs State Park, 19158 SW 81st Place Road, Dunnellon, FL 34432 (352-465-8555, floridastateparks.org/park/Rainbow-Springs)

A panorama of timeless beauty opens as you step onto the terrace and look out at the Rainbow River flowing away in full force from the clear, chalky blue first-magnitude spring at the bottom of the hill. It's hard to imagine a day when this was a hillside ravaged by mining, but that's part of the legacy of Rainbow Springs State Park. In the 1930s, private reclamation efforts turned the steep hills and deep pits into a stunning public garden with waterfalls, a rarity in Florida. Never mind that they poured from pools created by water pumped uphill out of the river—it was the illusion that mattered. A popular Florida attraction when we were kids, the park once boasted several boat rides—including a boat with underwater portholes where you could look out into the crystalline waters face-to-face with fish—along with a rodeo, aviary, zoo, and a monorail.

In addition to the hike and water activities at the headspring, Rainbow Springs State Park also has a campground connected by the river but detached by road. Offering tent and trailer camping, it has full hookups, special spots set aside for fishing and swimming along the river, and a canoe rental. Just 1.4 miles south of the campground on the same side of the river is the destination for one of Dunnellon's most popular summer activities—tubing the Rainbow River.

GETTING THERE

From I-75, take exit 352, Ocala, and follow FL 40 west for 19 miles to US 41 north of Dunnellon. Turn left and drive 0.8 mile. The park entrance is on the left. Follow the winding park road 0.8 mile back to the parking area. The campground (29.086746, -82.417124) is along SW 180th Avenue Road, 2 miles south of

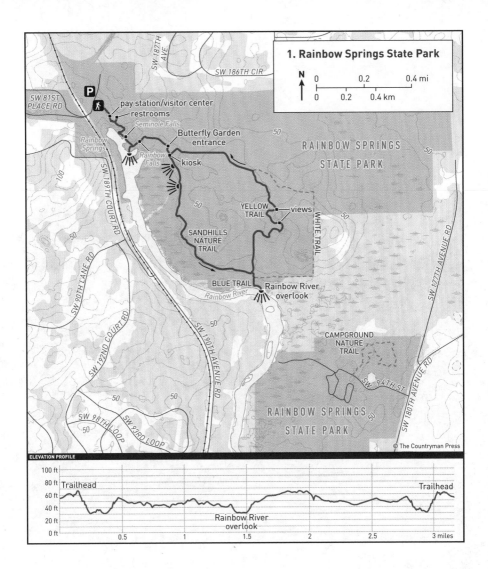

1. Rainbow Springs State Park

FL 40, on the east side of the river, and the tubing entrance is 1.4 miles south of the campground along SW 180th Avenue Road.

THE HIKE

Although the hiking trail at Rainbow Springs focuses on the natural habitats downriver, to get there you must roam through the historic gardens. From the terrace with its National Natural Land-mark memorial, walk down the path to the right and take the next left. This lower path provides a better view of the spring itself. First known as Blue Spring (there are many Blue Springs in Florida), it was later dubbed Rainbow Springs to sell the attraction. In addition to the lovely springs and gardens, it offered submarine boat rides where you would stare right out the portholes at fish and turtles swimming past in the clear water.

As the lower path joins into the

larger path coming downhill, take a right. Arrive in February for one of the showiest displays of azaleas and camellias in Florida. The path leads to a four-way junction. Turn right to continue downhill. A cove bubbles with dozens of tiny springs. Keep right at the fork to walk out between the cove and a glassy spring on your left. The path converges with the wide trail to bring you up to Seminole Falls, the first of the two waterfalls splashing down the steep hillside. Passing the pump house, take the next right down a long boardwalk. It ends at the mouth of a larger cove along the river. These shallows are busy—look for wading birds of all types amid the clumps of lance-leafed arrowhead.

Returning to the main path, turn right. Another cluster of tiny bubbling springs are in the shallows. Grains of sand churn up like fountains as striped fish swim through these miniature sandstorms. Well-shaded by the live oak canopy, it's a mesmerizing spot. As the path swings left, you see Rainbow Falls, which looks like a scene out of Hawaii. Tropical plantings crowd the outflow from the falls, which tumble down a moss-covered limestone wall. The zigzagging path to the right leads to another waterfall.

The main path continues up the hill to enter the area that was once a small zoo. The former rodeo grounds lie just beyond it. The remains of the bleacher posts are here, and the foundation of the horse stalls. Despite the natural environment and these man-made enhancements, it wasn't enough to keep the public interested in Rainbow Springs after I-75—and Walt Disney World—arrived on the scene, and travelers started bypassing Dunnellon. The attraction closed in 1974, and almost became a subdivision. It was through the unrelenting efforts of concerned citizens that the springs and gardens were purchased as a county park. Much volunteer cleanup was required before it opened as a state park in 1995.

After you enter the butterfly garden, turn right and walk to the old access road. There you'll find the Nature Trail trailhead (29.100980, -82.433454) with a large kiosk and map of the trail. The broad, well-trodden Sandhills Trail leads you through the pines to the edge of a man-made ravine reclaimed by the forest. This is the first of several former mining pits along this hike. Emerging into an open meadow where cattle grazed once upon a time, the trail follows the edge of the meadow, sticking to the shade beneath the trees. At a well-marked trail intersection, three blaze colors are shown on the post: yellow, white, and blue.

To see the Rainbow River, head downhill along the blue blazes on a spur trail that reaches a spot with a bench at the river. The trail extends a little ways downriver through the cypresses for another glimpse. Returning along the blue trail, you see a white-blazed trail to the right. That's the perimeter trail, which gives you a 2.1-mile loop. It's a beautiful option in the fall when the sandhill wildflowers are in bloom, but it hugs closely to a fence line for a portion of the hike. Follow the yellow blazes for a more interesting route, continuing up the hill. The trail follows a forest road briefly before it enters the forest, leading past a limestone cistern at the site of a homestead. That strong tapping at the top of a longleaf pine is a pileated woodpecker, Florida's largest, distinguished

OPPOSITE: LOOKING UP AT THE TERRACE
SLOPES ACROSS THE RAINBOW RIVER

by its size and its bright red crown. Pine flatwoods are its domain, where it ranges over a wide area and announces its arrival by pounding on hollow trees.

Deeper into the forest, the trail undulates up and over mounds, and the forest grows on these mounds—they are leftover diggings from the phosphate pits. You encounter the extremely deep pits, each with a fence along the edge, where the forest has filled in. Slash and loblolly pines reach for the sky, as tall above the pits as they are below. Albertus Vogt struck it rich with a find of high-grade phosphate ore. Florida's mining boom was on. Hard rock mining was an expensive process, however. As higher-grade phosphate ore was discovered near Lakeland, the mining industry tapped out its Dunnellon resources. The last mines here closed in 1965.

The yellow blazes once again intersect with the white blazes. Turn left and follow them across the meadow, where a bench sits in the shade of a large cedar tree. Plum trees show their bright white blooms in February. Entering a stand of regularly spaced planted pines, the

HIKING THROUGH THE SANDHILLS OF RAINBOW SPRINGS STATE PARK

trail crosses a park road and returns you to the butterfly garden, completing a 2-mile circuit. To return to the park entrance, walk back through the gardens. This time, take the right fork before the path makes the steep descent down to the waterfall. This upper trail leads you around and over the pools of water that feed the two waterfalls. After you cross the second bridge, follow the winding path down to the junction of pathways at the base of the hill below the terrace. Head back to the terrace, where you'll find restrooms, a small snack bar and picnic tables, interpretive displays, and the gift shop on your way out.

OTHER HIKING OPTIONS

1. **The Gardens**. For a quick and easy stroll with some serious terrain and elevation changes, stick with a circuit of the paved and bricked trails throughout the gardens and along the swimming/paddlesports area on the opposite side of the spring. Ramble almost two miles on the park's walkways without ever stepping off the paved paths.

2. **Campground Nature Trail** (29. 087954, -82.420877). If you're staying at the Rainbow Springs State Park campground, there is a 0.25-mile family-friendly nature trail to ramble. The trailhead is along the entrance road.

3. **Blue Run Park** (29.049374, -82.446673). Where the Rainbow River flows into the Withlacoochee River, Blue Run Park offers access to more than four miles of gentle trails, paved and unpaved. Paved trails are open to bicycles. The primary trailhead is along CR 484 at the bridge over the Rainbow River, with a secondary trailhead (29.048086, -82.444214) off San Jose Boulevard a little farther east.

CAMPING AND LODGING

Rainbow Springs State Park (1-800-326-3521, floridastateparks.reserve america.com)

Comfort Suites, 20052 Brooks Street, Dunnellon, FL 34432 (352-533-5234, dunnellonhotel.com)

Two Rivers Inn, 20814 W Pennsylvania Avenue, Dunnellon, FL 34431 (352-489-2300, tworiversinn.com)

Holly Hammock Hiking Trail

TOTAL DISTANCE: 2.4-mile loop and spur to campsite

HIKING TIME: 1.5 hours

DIFFICULTY: Easy

USAGE: Free. Open sunrise to sunset. Call ahead for a free permit for primitive camping. Leashed pets welcome.

TRAILHEAD GPS COORDINATES: 29.037983, -82.295851

CONTACT INFORMATION: Ross Prairie State Forest, 10660 SW SR 200, Dunnellon FL 34432 (352-732-1201, freshfromflorida.com)

Peeking out of a mature forest to ramble along the edges of one of the region's largest natural grasslands, the Holly Hammock Hiking Trail provides an outstanding amount of habitat diversity on a relatively short hike. Ross Prairie is a landform that folks driving from Ocala to the Gulf Coast zip right by and hardly notice. It's the only significant remaining natural prairie west of Ocala, draining toward the Withlacoochee River. In the wet seasons, the prairie teems with aquatic life, hosting ponds where American lotus bloom on the surface and purple pickerelweed creates natural bouquets. During the dry seasons, the prairie grasses grow tall and colorful, waving in sheets of golden and orange hues. Ross Prairie State Forest protects more than 3,500 acres surrounding this beautiful spot.

GETTING THERE

From exit 350 on I-75, Dunnellon/Hernando, follow FL 200 south from Ocala, crossing CR 484 after 9 miles. After another 1.5 miles, look for the Ross Prairie Trailhead on the left, and turn left. Follow the entrance road around to park near the restrooms. If the gates are closed, park at the Ross Prairie State Forest sign and hike the dirt road from that parking area to the trailhead kiosk (29.037083, -82.295833).

THE HIKE

Start your hike at the sign near the parking area. It's well marked with a trailhead sign, so you shouldn't miss the gap in the fence that leads you into the deep shade of an old oak hammock along the blue-blazed trail. The narrow footpath emerges through another gap in a fence marking the boundary between the

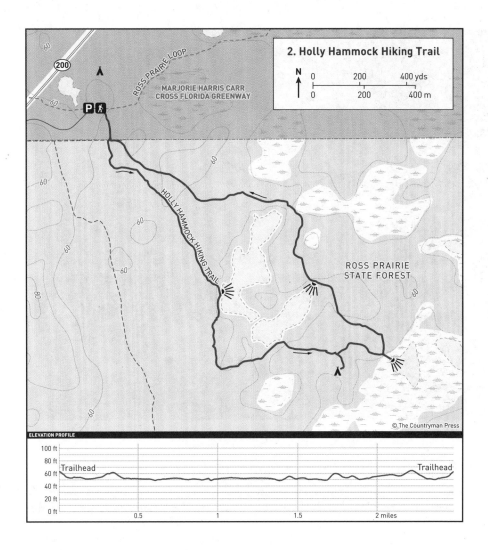

2. Holly Hammock Hiking Trail

ROSS PRAIRIE LOOP

MARJORIE HARRIS CARR
CROSS FLORIDA GREENWAY

HOLLY HAMMOCK HIKING TRAIL

ROSS PRAIRIE
STATE FOREST

© The Countryman Press

ELEVATION PROFILE

Trailhead   Trailhead

100 ft
80 ft
60 ft
40 ft
20 ft
0 ft

0.5   1   1.5   2 miles

Cross Florida Greenway (where you're parked) and Ross Prairie State Forest. A kiosk shows the trail map and may have trail brochures available. This trail is part of the statewide Florida State Forests Trailwalker Program, so on your way out pick up a postcard to send in.

Cross the firebreak—which serves as part of the larger equestrian trail system in this forest—and follow the blue blazes into a very dense oak hammock. Per the name, American holly is a major component of this hammock, as is spar-

kleberry. A little elevation makes a big difference in habitat as the trail rises into the sandhills, where young longleaf pines rise above a sea of wiregrass. The understory is very open, the better to showcase colorful wildflowers, including pawpaw and blazing star, in spring and fall. In the winter, the winged sumac turns a bright crimson.

As you descend back into the hammock, the elevation change is obvious, and you enter a mix of sandhills and scrub, where sand live oaks shade the

SANDHILL HABITAT ALONG THE HOLLY HAMMOCK HIKING TRAIL

trail and silk bay grows next to holly. Look for red blanket lichen on the holly trunks—it almost looks like blazes! Colorful lichens are a major component of this hammock. The sand live oaks get very large here, and typically have lush gardens of resurrection ferns in the crooks of their branches. Look closely, and in summer, you may notice greenfly orchids in bloom, hidden amid the profusion of resurrection ferns.

After 0.5 mile, the trail emerges along what looks like a retention pond, but is in fact an arm of Ross Prairie, diked by a rancher who once owned this land. In the early morning, you may see sandhill cranes or herons here. Turn right and walk to the next HIKING TRAIL sign, which steers you back into the forest through a thick carpet of deer moss and reindeer lichen. Back in the shade, the trail passes more massive oaks with ferns and orchids. Fungi grows in leaf litter and on rotting logs. After making a sharp turn at a bed of moss, the trail ambles around large trees to emerge again along the prairie arm. It turns right and passes a large sand pine that sits low to the ground. Along the trail's edge, purple blooms of spiderwort delight the eye and attract the showy tiger swallowtail butterfly.

Turning right, the trail reenters the shady hammock. After 0.9 mile, a sign marks the side trail to the campsite. Lime green blazes lead right, snaking through a patch of deer moss to emerge in an open spot beneath the oaks. A picnic table and fire ring are at the center of the camping area, with places to pitch your tent nearby. Returning to the main trail, turn right. You see light through the trees, as you're approaching one of the larger expanses of Ross Prairie. As the trail slips into the open, you're greeted with a panorama of grassland and a distant tree line. Walk into the prairie to savor the view. American lotuses decorate a pond just down the slope. It's a beauty spot, but be cautious of alligators sunning along the water's edge. In Ross Prairie, they generally don't have many opportunities to find a body of water this big.

The trail returns to the shade of the hammock, meandering past more large oaks. As the footpath winds through the woods past sentinels of sand live oaks, it passes through an oak portal before emerging at the end of a prairie arm. The bright pink blooms of pale meadow beauty lend color to the landscape as you cross a firebreak and reenter the forest. It doesn't take long for the elevation to rise again, and you enter the sandhills, with longleaf pines all around. Delicate wildflowers peep out of the wiregrass. Descending again, you're greeted with patches of saw palmetto along the sides of the trail and can see patches of prairie through the understory. The trail weaves its way around

POND IN ROSS PRAIRIE

one patch to emerge into the sun within sight of a fence line. Turn left and head down the straightaway to the kiosk. At the kiosk, turn right to exit.

OTHER HIKING OPTIONS

1. **Florida Trail** (29.038822, -82.295425) **to Spring Park**. As this trailhead is shared with the Cross Florida Greenway, it provides access to a segment of the statewide Florida National Scenic Trail. Follow the blue blazes (from the other gap farther down the fence near the campground) to the orange blazes of the Florida Trail, and turn right at the junction. Continue another 0.25 mile to a clearing with a picnic table and a SPRING PARK sign, where there is a spring (which barely flows) in the bottom of a deep sinkhole. An out-and-back hike is 3.3 miles.

2. **Florida Trail to SW 49th Avenue**. Follow the blue blazes to the Florida Trail per above and head east from Spring Park. The terrain is varied and often hilly, and no road crossings are required as there are underpasses under the roads. A hike from the Ross Prairie Trailhead to the SW 49th Avenue trailhead (29.040043, -82.202006) is 6.9 miles each way.

3. **SW 49th Avenue to Land Bridge**. Hike east on the Florida Trail from the SW 49th Avenue trailhead to the Land Bridge, a giant planter over I-75 filled with forest. When it opened in 2000, it was the first one ever built in the United States. A round-trip is 5 miles.

CAMPING AND LODGING

Ross Prairie Campground/Cross Florida Greenway, 10660 SW SR 200, Dunnellon, FL 34432 (1-800-326-3521, floridastateparks.reserveamerica.com)

Shangri-La Campground/Cross Florida Greenway, 12788 SW 69th Court, Ocala, FL 34473 (1-800-326-3521, floridastateparks.reserveamerica.com)

Hampton Inn & Suites Ocala-Belleview, 2075 SW CR 484, Ocala, FL 34473 (352-347-1600, hilton.com)

Silver Springs State Park

TOTAL DISTANCE: 8.7 miles; 7.3 miles along a network of five interconnected trails inside the camping entrance, plus 1.4 miles at the main entrance to see the springs.

HIKING TIME: 4–5 hours

DIFFICULTY: Easy

USAGE: Admission $5–8 per vehicle. Open 8 AM to sunset. Leashed pets welcome. Bicycles permitted on camping entrance trails.

TRAILHEAD GPS COORDINATES: 29.200899, -82.034505

CONTACT INFORMATION: Silver Springs State Park, 1425 NE 58th Avenue, Ocala, FL 34470 (352-236-7148, floridastateparks .org/park/Silver-Springs)

Pouring from one of the world's largest springs, the transparent waters of the Silver River meander 7 miles through a jungle-like setting to merge with the Ocklawaha, the largest tributary of the St. Johns River. Since the late 1800s, the Silver River has attracted tourists, with visitors climbing aboard glass-bottomed boats to see the river's many springs. Now a Florida State Park, the former attraction has been merged with the pre-existing state park along the river. The complex is now known as Silver Springs State Park.

The campground, a good base camp for exploring the park, has cabins and spaces for trailers and tents. Open to the public on weekends, the Silver River Museum presents in-depth information on geology, paleontology, and archaeology. Many important finds have been made along the river, from mastodon skeletons to artifacts from Florida's aboriginal cultures. The Cracker Village shows off buildings found on an 1800s Florida homestead and hosts living history demonstrations, with the park's signature event, Ocali Country Days, held in November. Additional fees apply for canoe rentals, museum, and boat rides.

GETTING THERE

From exit 352 on I-75 in Ocala, follow FL 40 for 8.4 miles through the city of Ocala to Silver Springs. Turn right on CR 35 (Baseline Road/NE 58th Avenue) and drive another 1.1 miles to the Camping Entrance (29.2011, -82.0534) on the left, gateway to most recreational activities. Ask for a trail map at the entrance station. Follow the entrance road 1.3 miles to the main parking area, flanked by the Cracker Village, the Silver River Museum, the Environmental Education

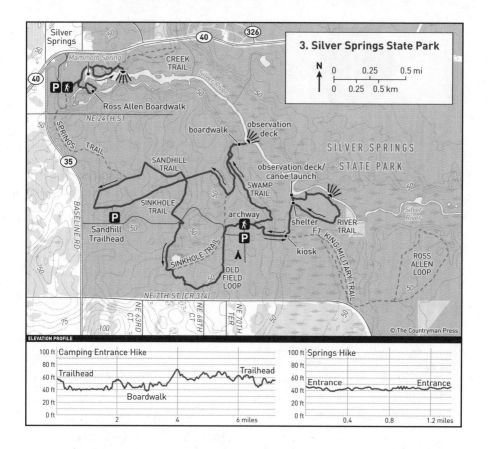

3. Silver Springs State Park

N

| 0 | 0.25 | 0.5 mi |
| 0 | 0.25 | 0.5 km |

Silver Springs

CREEK TRAIL

Mammoth Spring

Silver River

Ross Allen Boardwalk

NE 24TH ST

boardwalk

observation deck

SPRINGS TRAIL

SANDHILL TRAIL

observation deck/ canoe launch

SWAMP TRAIL

SILVER SPRINGS STATE PARK

Silver River

SINKHOLE TRAIL

archway

shelter

RIVER TRAIL

BASELINE RD

Sandhill Trailhead

kiosk

FT. KING MILITARY TRAIL

ROSS ALLEN LOOP

SINKHOLE TRAIL

OLD FIELD LOOP

NE 7TH ST (CR 314)

© The Countryman Press

ELEVATION PROFILE

Camping Entrance Hike

100 ft	
80 ft	
60 ft	Trailhead ... Trailhead
40 ft	
20 ft	Boardwalk
0 ft	2 4 6 miles

Springs Hike

100 ft	
80 ft	
60 ft	
40 ft	Entrance ... Entrance
20 ft	
0 ft	0.4 0.8 1.2 miles

Center, and two arched trailheads—Sinkhole Trail and River Trails.

CAMPING ENTRANCE HIKE

Begin your hike at the RIVER TRAILS archway. At the first junction, take the right fork. The trail wanders through hickories and oaks, past a low depression and over a grassy levee, emptying out onto a forest road. Turn left, downhill into dense hardwood hammock. Make a left onto another road at the bottom of the hill, where a kiosk for the bike trails sits straight ahead. Elevated slightly above a portion of Marshall Swamp, the trail rises into an open field with scattered sweetgum and then drops into a hydric hammock, dense with cabbage palms and bald cypresses. Passing a rain shelter, it emerges into an open area along the Silver River at 0.6 mile. Walk down to the canoe launch and its adjacent observation deck with its view of the river bend. Alligators drift through mats of pennywort, and ibises flutter up to the trees.

Turn around and take the trail to your left along the river, following the floodplain forest on the river's edge. Scattered cedars, cabbage palms, and groundsel bushes grow amid tall grasses. Watch for a rough trail leading into the floodplain forest, affording a view of the river from beneath the cypress trees. Return to the main trail, where there is a bench with a river view at 0.9 mile.

GLASS-BOTTOMED BOATS GLIDING ACROSS THE SURFACE OF THE SPRING-FED SILVER RIVER

VIEW OF THE SILVER RIVER FROM THE RIVER TRAIL

The glittering blue bottom of the river hides more small springs. Purple asters cascade down the riverbanks.

The River Trail loops back toward its beginning, through stands of tall wax myrtle, cedars, and cabbage palms, returning to the main trail near the rain shelter. Turn left, following the old road back through the floodplain forest. Turn right at the T intersection with the bike trail kiosk, retracing your steps up to the footpath that turns right within sight of the park cabins. Ramble beneath the hickories and oaks to the trail junction just before the parking area. You've walked 2 miles. Turn right to start the Swamp Trail. Rounding a yaupon holly hugging a laurel oak firm in its grip,

notice the bat boxes up in the lofty trees of this hardwood hammock.

The trail turns to follow the edge of the floodplain forest, a dense stand of cypresses leading off toward the river. You walk beneath tall southern magnolias and under hickory trees furry with wild pine. A swamp chestnut oak drops enormous leaves on the footpath. At the T intersection, turn right (left leads to the Environmental Center). This trail has a layer of crushed lime rock beneath the leaves. It winds through live oaks, red bay, and tall slash pines, with cinnamon fern and gallberry in the understory. Where a trail comes in from the left, turn right. There are many trails from the Environmental Center that join the Swamp Trail, so Marion County schoolchildren can investigate the forest as part of their environmental curriculum. The twists and turns may seem confusing, but as long as you follow the sporadic SWAMP TRAIL arrows, you'll make your way to the river.

After a short stretch on the tram road, follow the trail into the floodplain forest to join a boardwalk. At 3 miles, the boardwalk ends at a dock and observation deck on the Silver River. A purple gallinule floats across the glassy surface. Watch the three-dimensional world below, where bluegill hang in crystalline suspension and a mud turtle moves in slow motion across the river bottom just a few feet offshore. The Silver River has dozens of smaller springs like this adding more than 200 million gallons of water to the daily outflow of Mammoth Spring at its headwaters.

Take the boardwalk back to the tram road, looking for orange-tipped SWAMP TRAIL markers that lead you to a second opening in the forest on the left. The trail ducks into a tunnel of sand live oaks knitting a dense canopy overhead, their twisting trunks covered in a thick blanket of lichens. As the trail gains elevation, it enters a pine flatwoods with a thick understory of saw palmetto. Beyond a tunnel of oaks with squiggly-looking trunks, the trail crosses the tram road and enters a scrub forest with fluffy sand pines. You pass a bench before reaching another tunnel of oaks, where the Swamp Trail comes to an end as it reaches the intersection with the Sinkhole Trail at 3.5 miles. Turn right.

Red-tipped markers guide you along the Sinkhole Trail into a sand pine scrub, with the footpath ahead a blinding white. At the junction of the Sinkhole and the Sandhill Trail, 3.7 miles into the hike, there's a picnic bench and a kiosk.

Turn right to start the Sandhill Trail. Continue down the forest road until you reach the yellow-tipped posts and yellow arrow markers that usher you left into a longleaf pine forest with a very open understory beneath the pines and turkey oaks. Sandhill wireweed, with its spiky blooms, emerges from the wiregrass. At the next T intersection, turn left to follow a forest road. Where longleaf pines dominate the forest, notice the change in the understory. Blueberries take root in the acidic soil, as do winged sumac, which rises above the saw palmetto.

Reaching the junction with the light blue-blazed Springs Trail at 4.2 miles, you have a decision point. Using this trail—a round-trip connector of two miles through the sandhills and pine forest—link this 7.3-mile circuit hike with the 1.4-mile circuit described below as the Springs Hike for a total trek of 10.7 miles. The Springs Trail is an easy walk, following blue-tipped posts through the woods before emerging on little-used roads to end at the canoe launch at the springs, and then along the Fort King Waterway into the former attraction grounds.

Assuming you'll return to your car and drive over to the springs for the Springs Hike, keep following the yellow blazes. They lead you on a mowed path into the forest, away from the SERVICE ROAD sign. In early morning, birds flutter about, especially woodpeckers. Listen and watch for the pileated woodpecker, high up in a longleaf pine. Its large size and distinctive red crest make it hard to miss. You'll more commonly see the red-bellied woodpecker, pecking at rotten wood. Although it is only nine inches tall, its zebra-striped wings and red-crowned head make it easy to pick out amid the greenery.

After 5.2 miles, you return to the

junction of the Sandhill and Sinkhole Trails. Take a moment to relax and hydrate, then turn right to resume the Sinkhole Trail. The trail makes a sharp right, and a red-tipped post confirms you're on the right path. Passing through a junction of unmarked trails, you cross the park entrance road at 5.6 miles. Continue into the laurel oak forest on the other side. The trail reaches a T intersection, jogs right, and then left at the fence line. Deep shade is a welcome relief after walking through the open scrub and sandhill habitats. Florida dogwood grows along this section of the trail; look for its white blooms in spring.

The trail follows the edge of a large, forest-filled sinkhole, noticeable because of the saw palmetto slope dropping off to the left. A vantage point before an interpretive kiosk lets you look down into the sinkhole, which is filled with red maples, sweetgum, and live oaks. Turn right at 6 miles to follow the Old Field Loop, an interpretive side trail. Yellow-tipped posts lead the way. Winding through the turkey oaks, you pass a solution hole, a sinkhole caused by gradual erosion. Sand pines and longleaf pines have reclaimed the old field. An eastern fence lizard scurries up the side of a turkey oak trunk, blending in well with the bark.

As the trail swings into the oak hammock, it rounds a fallen live oak that continues to grow, sending up trunk-like branches from its prone trunk, thick with resurrection fern. The transition from the old field into the dark, mossy hammock isn't as jarring as it used to be. The trail drops through a stand of loblolly pine and into a hammock of ancient live oaks along the back fence of the campground, rejoining the Sinkhole Trail after 6.9 miles. Continue along the campground fence to reach the park entrance road again, crossing it to meet the trail junction. Turn right to follow the footpath past the picnic area and restrooms and the Cracker Village to finish under the SINKHOLE TRAIL arch at the parking lot, completing a 7.3-mile walk.

SPRINGS HIKE

To get to the Springs Hike, either use the Springs Trail (as described along the Sandhill Trail) or drive to the main entrance (29.214635, -82.055296) off FL 40, east of the traffic light with CR 35. Once you've parked and walked in the grand entrance on the boardwalk through a stand of ancient cypress trees, you'll need to show the attendant your receipt or state park pass to enter this portion of the park. Long before Walt Disney World came along, we both spent many happy childhood visits here roaming the park and gardens and riding the glass-bottomed boats.

Turn right to find the blue-tipped posts of the Springs Trail ending at the base of a boardwalk. Originally constructed in the 1970s, the boardwalk provided access to Ross Allen Island, a zoological park with a focus on reptiles. It was a successor to the Ross Allen Reptile Institute, which once stood where you just entered the park. A noted herpetologist, Ross Allen came to Silver Springs in 1929 and started milking rattlesnakes for their venom. He assisted movie crews by providing local knowledge and live animals. By the 1960s, he was a Boy Scout leader and a founding board member of the Florida Trail Association. The Ross Allen Boardwalk honors his legacy. Crossing the Fort King Waterway, it does a 0.5-mile loop around this natural island, showing off the spring-fed waters at Fort King Landing (where the Jungle Cruise once docked) and views across the Silver River by the amphitheater used for reptile shows.

After you complete the boardwalk loop, follow the sidewalks toward the spring basin, the headwaters of the Silver River. It's evident this was a Florida attraction not just from the architecture of the former shops but by the glass-bottomed boats themselves. Their route takes you across a dozen or more springs in the Silver River. Continue by foot to see the biggest of them all, Mammoth Spring. Just follow the walkways around the boat docks. Depending on the angle of the sun, there are times when the bottom of this cavernous spring is visible. It pumps out more than 500 million gallons of water a day from two spring vents 30 feet deep.

Continue from this observation deck into the gardens, where meander-ing pathways provide excellent panoramas across the Silver River while fencing keeps visitors separated from sunning alligators. As the attraction was established more than a century ago, the pines, cypresses, and oaks in the gardens are enormous. Make a loop through the gardens. Take a side trail off the main trail to a showy spring basin that sits next to what was once a boat dock. At what's now a picnic pavilion, a Jeep Safari ride drove visitors into the floodplain forest, a route that is now the (optional) Creek Trail along the old roads.

Return to the entrance gate at your leisure, taking time to learn about the history of Silver Springs from the interpretive information sprinkled throughout the park. Opened in 1878, it was one of Florida's first tourist attractions, and it's always been nature—the springs, the alligators, the enormous trees—

BOARDWALK ON ROSS ALLEN ISLAND

that drew visitors here. By the time you return to your car, you've walked at least 1.4 miles around the park.

OTHER HIKING OPTIONS

1. **Springs Hike**. Follow just the Springs Hike above for an easy 1.4-mile walk along the main basin of Silver Springs. Shorten it to less than a mile by skipping the Ross Allen Island Boardwalk and just focusing on the gardens. Or do 2.1 miles by adding on the Creek Trail, which starts at the far end of the gardens. It is noisy since it's near FL 40. It follows the former route of the Jeep Safari Ride through what were animal pens in the floodplain forest.

2. **River Ramble**. The beauty of the Silver River is the main reason most people come to this park. For a hike that highlights the best overlooks, follow only the first part of the Camping Area Hike: take the 2.1-mile River Trail, and add on a walk out and back to the boardwalk on the Swamp Trail for a comfortable 4.2-mile hike.

3. **Bike Loops**. Immerse yourself in the jungle-like floodplain forest on foot or by bike for 4.5 miles by following the River Trail to the bike trails kiosk. The first loop, along the Fort King Military Trail, rambles close to the edge of Marshall Swamp. The second loop, the Ross Allen Loop, is a technical, twisty, windy singletrack that works its way towards the Silver River. Walk in the opposite direction of bike traffic.

CAMPING AND LODGING

Silver Springs State Park (1-800-326-3521, floridastateparks.reserve america.com)

Wilderness RV Resort, 2771 NE 102nd Avenue, Silver Springs, FL 34488 (352-625-1122, wildernessrvpark estates.com), no tents.

Sun Plaza Motel, 5461 E Silver Springs Boulevard, Silver Springs, FL 34488 (352-236-2343, bgsunplaza.com)

Trout Lake Nature Center

TOTAL DISTANCE: 1.4-mile circuit

HIKING TIME: 1.5–2 hours

DIFFICULTY: Easy

USAGE: Free. Open Tuesday to Saturday 9 AM–4 PM, Sunday 1-4 PM. Trails are not suited for bicycles. Leashed pets welcome.

TRAILHEAD GPS COORDINATES: 28.872238, -81.681494

CONTACT INFORMATION: Trout Lake Nature Center, 520 E CR 44, Eustis, FL 32736 (352-357-7536, troutlakenaturecenter.org)

Established by the Oklawaha Valley Audubon Society in 1988, Trout Lake Nature Center provides a place for cormorants to gather in a grand colony among the tall cypresses along an unspoiled shoreline of Trout Lake. Encompassing 230 acres, this privately owned conservation complex offers gentle family-friendly interpretive trails through floodplain forests, pine flatwoods, and oak hammocks, with old-fashioned catwalk-style boardwalks.

Inside the Environmental Education Center you'll find restrooms, exhibits, and a library. Evening classes are offered here; check their calendar in advance. Take a peek in the Charles Newell Hall and Museum—the nature center on the other side of the parking area—for an overview of native flora and fauna before you wander down the trails. On weekdays, you may see busloads of children roaming the trails under supervision, as this is a popular destination for field trips.

GETTING THERE

From the cloverleaf at FL 19 and US 441, where Eustis and Mount Dora meet, drive north through downtown Eustis on FL 19. After 3.6 miles, you reach CR 44 (not to be confused with FL 44) at an intersection with a CVS and Walgreens on the right. Turn right and continue 0.4 mile to the entrance on the right. Follow the narrow entrance road deep into the woods to reach the parking loop in front of the Environmental Education Center.

THE HIKE

Start your hike next to the trailhead kiosk at the LAZY OAK TRAIL sign, but put the bug spray on before you begin. The marshy habitats around Trout Lake

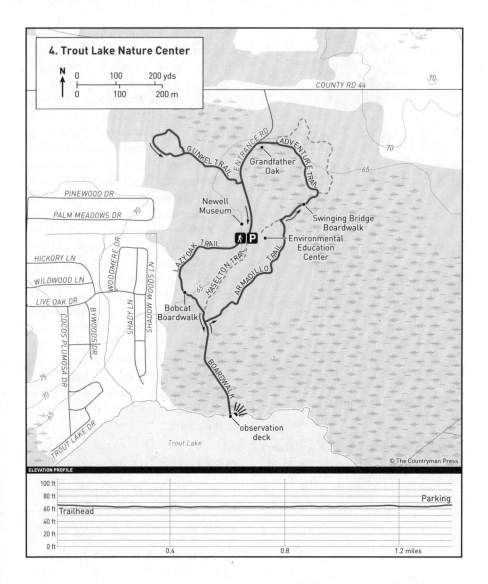

4. Trout Lake Nature Center

mean the mosquitoes can be mean at certain times of the year. Walking beneath oaks and cabbage palms, you come around a sharp turn to start the Bobcat Boardwalk. It's a narrow catwalk. There are times of year when you'll wonder why it's here, but the floodplain nature of these habitats make it important to elevate this walk. Soon after the boardwalk ends you meet the Haselton Trail at a kiosk. Turn right.

Walk past the entrance to the Armadillo Trail to join a broad boardwalk that leads you through the marshes that fringe the edges of Trout Lake. It meanders past a covered rain shelter before making another turn to a straightaway towards the open waters of the lake. After 0.4 mile, a covered observation deck provides a protected spot for wildlife observation. While the entire lake isn't a conservation area, this portion is. To your left are the tall cypresses where the cormorants roost, swooping and diving into the lake for their meals. That bellow below might be an alligator seeking a mate.

Returning along the boardwalk, pay attention when you step back off of it. If the Armadillo Trail is under water, which it often is, pass it by and continue up the Haselton Trail on slightly higher ground under the oaks. The Little Armadillo Trail provides a drier connector to the Armadillo Trail, which winds beneath slash pine and cabbage palms. You'll hardly notice that it passes right behind the Environmental Education Center, meeting a T intersection with a boardwalk. A left returns you to the parking lot. Turn right.

You're now on the Adventure Trail, and it is true to its name. Like the Bobcat Boardwalk, it is a narrow catwalk, but it is definitely keeping your feet dry as you walk into a cypress strand. A rope provides a handhold on one side. Reaching the middle of the strand, the trail crosses a swinging bridge, where it's hard to resist making it bounce as you step across. The boardwalk curves through this jungle-like habitat until it gets out of the floodplain. It ends at an intersection with the Grandfather Oak Trail at 0.8 mile. The Adventure Trail continues right, but we found it too much of an adventure to follow as it was still roughed up from hurricane damage. Take a left to walk to the Grandfather Oak, which you saw along the entrance

NARROW BOARDWALK ALONG THE ADVENTURE TRAIL

CORMORANTS ROOSTING IN THE CYPRESSES ALONG TROUT LAKE

road to the park. It's a sizable live oak, with a picnic table inviting you to stop and stay a while. The swooping loop of the Adventure Trail ends here at the Grandfather Oak too.

To continue your loop, turn left and walk the entrance road towards the nature center. There is one more side loop to explore: the 0.25-mile long Gunkel Trail, which starts on the right just after you cross the culverts over the cypress strand. When you reach it, you've walked a mile. Turn right to tunnel beneath the tall slash pines and cabbage palms. At the Y intersection, stay right. The trail leads you through a loop past more large

OTHER HIKING OPTIONS

1. **Haselton Trail.** On the left-hand side of the trailhead kiosk is the Haselton Trail, which makes a beeline for the boardwalk to Trout Lake. This is the quickest route for birders and photographers to see the roosting cormorants, a 0.5-mile round-trip.

2. **Adventure Trail-Grandfather Oak Loop.** Park just inside the preserve gates at the first parking area on the right. Walk over to the picnic table under the Grandfather Oak to follow the Adventure Trail towards the northeast property boundary. After less than 0.5 mile, it loops through the woods to a junction with the Grandfather Oak Trail. Return along that route or go for more adventure along the Adventure Trail boardwalk and swinging bridge, returning to the parking area via the park entrance road.

3. **Lake May Reserve** (28.872458, -81.629856). At 3.4 miles east along CR 44/44A (Burlington Avenue), this Lake County Preserve provides access to a 1.6-mile loop hike around a lake and former orange grove. Pets are not permitted.

CAMPING AND LODGING

Lake Dorr Campground, Ocala National Forest (29.012542, -81.639965), FL 19, Altoona, FL 32702 (352-669-3153, fs.usda.gov/ocala), tent or RV.

Southern Palms RV Resort, 1 Avocado Lane, Eustis, FL 32726 (352-357-8882, rvonthego.com/florida/southern-palms-rv-resort), no tents.

Fox Den Country Inn, 27 S Central Avenue, Umatilla, FL 32784 (352-669-2151, foxdencountryinn.com)

live oaks, crossing an easement twice. When the loop ends, follow the Gunkel Trail back to the entrance road and turn right. It doesn't take long to get back to the Newell Hall and Museum, and the parking area between it and the Environmental Education Center, wrapping up this 1.4-mile hike.

5

Hidden Waters Preserve

TOTAL DISTANCE: 1-mile loop along a network of trails

HIKING TIME: 30–45 minutes

DIFFICULTY: Easy to moderate

USAGE: Free. Open 8 AM to sunset. No pets or bicycles permitted.

TRAILHEAD GPS COORDINATES: 28.838570, -81.660787

CONTACT INFORMATION: Hidden Waters Preserve, 2121 Country Club Road, Eustis FL 32726 (352-324-6141, lcwa.org/open-preserves)

Tucked away inside a residential area not far from Mount Dora, Hidden Waters Preserve is one of those small but special places in Florida that inspire surprise upon discovery: this hike includes more than 105 feet of elevation change! A network of short trails form a loop in and around the park's main feature—the Eichelberger Sink, an enormous sinkhole containing Lake Alfred. The "lake" (more properly a wetland area) can't flow out of the sinkhole, so it slowly seeps through the bottom of the sinkhole into the Floridan Aquifer. The damp north slope of the sinkhole shelters an Appalachian-like forest, while the south slope hosts a drier sandhill environment, with abundant prickly pear cactus and the signs of a healthy gopher tortoise community. The preserve is managed by the Lake County Water Authority.

GETTING THERE

From the cloverleaf at FL 19 and US 441, where Eustis and Mount Dora meet, drive south for 1.7 miles on US 441. Turn left at the light onto E Crooked Lake Drive. Continue 0.4 mile to Country Club Road. Turn right. Drive 0.7 mile to the grassy parking area and trailhead on the right.

THE HIKE

Pick up a map at the trail kiosk and sign in. Dropping steeply downhill from a grassy hillside into the forest, you'll come to the first intersection of the Lake Alfred Trail, the loop into and around the sinkhole. Stay left, following the blue-tipped posts beneath tall laurel oaks. Before becoming a preserve in 1996, this property was a golf course in the 1950s and a citrus grove until the killer freezes of the 1980s. As a

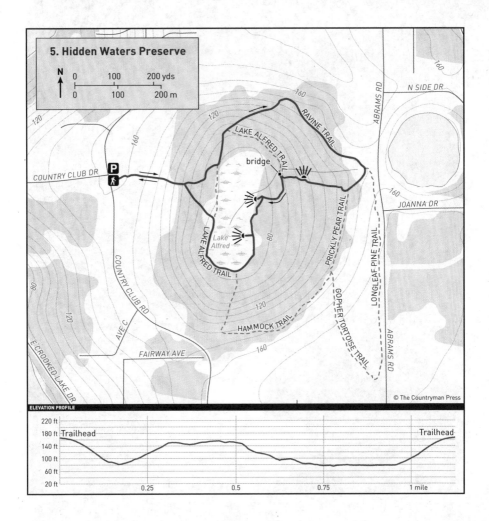

5. Hidden Waters Preserve

ELEVATION PROFILE

220 ft				
180 ft Trailhead				Trailhead
140 ft				
100 ft				
60 ft				
20 ft	0.25	0.5	0.75	1 mile

result, the natural forest community has been severely altered from its original state—a sandhill community dense with longleaf pine. Reforestation efforts are slowly bringing this landscape back to its natural state.

After crossing over some dike-like structures, possibly from the old golf course, the trail swings around the edge of the deeply forested sinkhole, climbing the steep slope. The blue blazes of the Lake Alfred Trail go to the right. Continue straight ahead to follow the red-tipped posts marking the Ravine Trail, which provides the steepest climb

out of and back into the sinkhole. Tall sweetgum and laurel oak shade the trail until it emerges at the top of the hill. At a T intersection, stay right to follow a sweeping curve towards the fence line around a stormwater drainage area. Passionflower blooms on an opportunistic trellis of wire fence. Intersecting briefly with the Longleaf Pine Trail, the Ravine Trail curves back around the drainage to an old gate and a junction with the Prickly Pear Trail. Walk past the gate to follow the red-tipped posts.

The sound of running water reaches your ears. The trail descends steeply as

A SERIES OF CASCADES LEADS TO THE BOTTOM OF THE EICHELBERGER SINK

WETLANDS AT THE BOTTOM OF THE EICHELBERGER SINK

water splashes nearby. As the ravine has eroded substantially since we first hiked here, there is now a fence between the trail and the ravine. A short loop leads to a view. No matter the time of year, water flows into this ravine, cutting deeper and broader channels. Normally, groundwater seeps into a sinkhole from beneath a cap of clay, below where the formation of the sinkhole cut through the earth. Most of the water flowing into this sink is stormwater drainage from above, which is why the ravine keeps growing.

These splashing waters are a delight for waterfall-starved Florida residents, as the steady, clear flow meanders down a series of deep ravines edged by a dense growth of ferns. Sinkholes provide a cooler environment for plants than the surrounding forest, encouraging a unique habitat. The broad leaves of elephant ears bow their heads over the

water. As you descend, thickets of sword fern give way to a mix of bracken, netted chain, and cinnamon fern. Royal fern and elderberries grow under a canopy of water oak. You reach the Lake Alfred Trail again at a bridge. Turn left before the bridge to follow that trail deeper into the sinkhole, enjoying the stairstep of cascades that parallel the footpath.

As the elevation evens out, the splashing stream spreads out across the sand, accelerating downhill until it reaches the marshy edge of Lake Alfred. Perpetual dampness along the eastern edge of the lake encourages sundew, a tiny carnivorous plant, to flourish. Home to a variety of turtles and small fish, these wetlands attract passing waterfowl like great egrets, little blue herons, and cattle egrets. A short side trail provides a closer view of the wetland.

At the junction with the purple-blazed Hammock Trail at 0.7 mile, keep right along the wetland to stay with the blue blazes. The area opens into the edge of the upland forest. Local birders have spotted a Cooper's hawk here, a threatened species in Florida. The Cooper's hawk has short wings and a long gray-and-white striped tail, with a red-brown breast and wingtips in black and white.

As you loop around the wetland, you return to the mixed forest of live oak, laurel oak, and open areas with prickly pear cactus. The Lake Alfred Trail steers you up the steep hill out of the sinkhole. Your legs will notice the climb of more than 100 feet of elevation to the trailhead kiosk as you finish the mile-long circuit. Sign out of the trail register before leaving.

OTHER HIKING OPTIONS

1. **Perimeter Walk.** Since this preserve offers a network of hiking trails, use those trails to expand upon the scenic circuit we described. If you want to more than double your mileage, the 1.5-mile Longleaf Pine Trail, blazed green, provides a walk around the perimeter, hugging the fence in most spots.
2. **Open Space.** Add an extra loop of

almost a mile—in the open meadow above the sinkhole before you plunge down the Ravine Trail—by following the Prickly Pear Trail to the Longleaf Pine Trail. Turn left and take that perimeter trail back to the Gopher Tortoise Trail, which merges back into the Prickly Pear Trail and leads you back to the junction with the Ravine Trail.

3. **Palm Island Park** (28.793528, -81.642427). In nearby Mount Dora, go birding along a mile of boardwalks along Lake Dora under ancient cypress trees.
4. **Trimble Park** (28.765101, -81.651324). On a breezy peninsula between lakes south of Mount Dora, enjoy a nicely shaded 1.2-mile loop with great views and a campground.

CAMPING AND LODGING

Trimble Park, 5802 Trimble Park Road, Mt. Dora, FL 32757 (407-254-1982, ocfl .net), tent and RV.

Woods-N-Water Trails, 1325 Bay Road, Mt. Dora, FL 32757 (352-735-1009, woods-n-watertrails.com), no tents.

Lakeside Inn, 100 Alexander Street, Mt. Dora, FL 32757 (352-383-4101, lakeside -inn.com)

6

Flat Island Preserve

TOTAL DISTANCE: 3.7-mile loop along a trail system

HIKING TIME: 2 hours

DIFFICULTY: Easy to moderate

USAGE: Free. Open 8 AM to sunset. No pets or bicycles permitted.

TRAILHEAD GPS COORDINATES: 28.778544, -81.900365

CONTACT INFORMATION: Flat Island Preserve, 2388 Owens Road, Leesburg FL 34748 (352-324-6141, lcwa.org/open-preserves)

Surrounded by the vast Okahumpa Marsh, the forests of Flat Island shelter an interesting mix of flora—more than 110 species, including rare trees, unusual wildflowers, and colorful mushrooms. Dedicated to Rexford and Jean Daubenmire, botanists who retired to Leesburg and fought for the preservation of this land, the well-engineered trail follows a circuit around the edge of the island's high ground. Built and maintained by the local Highlanders Chapter of the Florida Trail Association, the trail is clearly blazed and signposted at every cross-trail.

For avid canoeists who want to try the canoe trail—a series of narrow old canals through the Okahumpa Marsh—the Lake County Water Authority provides canoes. Call ahead and plunk down a refundable deposit to pick up your paddles and safety gear before you start hiking to the canoes, which are stored along this hiking loop. If you'd like to stay overnight along the trail—an easy backpacking trip for newbies—call the number above in advance of your hike for a free camping permit.

GETTING THERE

From the junction of US 441 and US 27 in Leesburg, follow US 27 south for 2.3 miles. Turn right onto CR 25A and follow it 1.1 miles. Turn right onto Owens Road, a narrow dirt road. After 0.6 mile, it ends at the parking area, with its large trail kiosk and restrooms.

THE HIKE

Unless you're hiking after the first winter frost, apply your strongest insect repellent before setting out on the trail. Okahumpa Marsh is a breeding ground for insects, so clouds of mosquitoes will

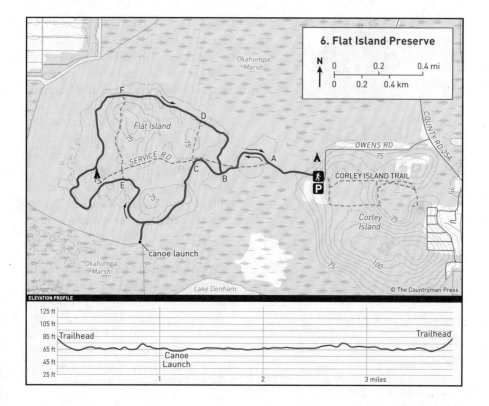

6. Flat Island Preserve

dog your steps most of the year. Starting your hike at the trail kiosk, sign in and follow the orange blazes. A large group campsite sits under the oaks, beyond the picnic table. Fresh water is available from a spigot behind the kiosk. Past the memorial to the Daubenmires, these trappings of civilization fall behind as you enter the deep shade of an oak hammock beneath a tall canopy of oaks and cabbage palms. Monkeyflowers crowd the sides of the footpath. The trail turns into a causeway, barely above the tannic waters of the surrounding hydric hammock.

The Island Hammock Trail starts at Signpost A, where a stone memorial pays homage to the late John Weary, a tireless trail maintainer responsible for many of the Florida Trail Association's best efforts in Central Florida. Veer

right, away from the service road, following the well-established tread into a forest of southern magnolia and young laurel oaks. Look up and down—greenfly orchids cling to the trees, and *collybia* mushrooms grow in crowded groups, like miniature forests.

Crossing the service road, the trail continues through younger oaks along the edge of a palm hammock. Roots break through the hard-packed dirt of the trail. At 0.5 mile, Signpost B marks the beginning of the outer loop. Continue straight ahead to walk the trail clockwise under the lofty live oaks. At Signpost C, pass the junction with that cross-trail as the oak forest yields to a hydric hammock. Around you, moss glows green on the trunks of cabbage palms. An earthy scent rises from the swamp as you first encounter the needle

58 | CENTRAL HIGHLANDS

FLOODPLAIN FOREST ALONG THE BOARDWALK

LUSH HARDWOOD HAMMOCK ALONG THE ISLAND HAMMOCK TRAIL

palm, which thrives along the boundary between wetlands and uplands. Yellow-eyed grass and the bright purple berries of the American beautyberry lend contrast to the deep green landscape. A slight elevation returns the trail to the hardwood forest, with its sandy floor and tall oaks. The bark of a southern magnolia hides under an array of air plants. The canopy opens, allowing more sunlight to the forest floor and encouraging the understory to grow. Wild coffee, winged sumac, and green-brier compete for the spaces between the saw palmettos.

After 1.1 miles, you'll reach a sign with a canoe symbol. That side trail leads to where the rental canoes are stored. Continue along the main trail,

and you'll reach the boardwalk that leads to the canoe launch. It's worth the side trip. Interpretive signs point out many of the typical flora in the swamp, including bald cypress, cinnamon ferns, and royal ferns. The trail ends on the floating launch above the dark waters of the canal. Walk back to the main trail and turn left.

The trail continues through oak and palm hammocks. Downed palm fronds can sometimes obscure the footpath. At 1.6 miles, Signpost E marks the final cross-trail. Continue past it into a thicket of needle palms, royal ferns, and marsh ferns. The trail is prone to flooding in this section, as the swamp creeps up close on both sides.

Reaching the western edge of Flat

Island, the trail veers right. Mosses and lichens cover the trees, whose roots are frequently flooded. The tall rotting stump covered with blue patches is the remains of a bluejack oak. Patches of lichen cover the bark of the water oaks and magnolias. The trail veer rights, now following the north edge of the island. Crossing a 1-foot-wide ditch lined with cabbage palms, it returns to higher ground, carpeted with the fallen needles of tall slash pines. In the moist earth, mushrooms abound, including clusters of jack o'lantern mushrooms. The turnoff to the primitive campsite is at 2.1 miles. Sheltered by a canopy of oaks and magnolias, the campsite provides benches and a pitcher pump.

As the trail elevation drops slightly, the scenery changes. The sparse understory gives way to dense saw palmetto and the canopy shifts to cabbage palms and laurel oaks. Needle palms rise along both sides of the trail. At Signpost F, you pass the cross-trail from Signpost E. Continue straight ahead, entering a forest of younger live oaks, sweetgum, and southern magnolia. Their supple limbs braid an arbor over the trail. A little farther along, hickory trees drop their bounty of nuts onto the trail. Each nut consists of two layers—a soft exterior skin and a tough, thick inner shell that hides the nutmeat.

When you reach Signpost D, you've hiked 2.9 miles. The cross-trail from Signpost C meets up with the main trail. Pass it by as the trail stays close to the edge of the island, skirting a broad expanse of swamp dense with bald cypress and cabbage palms. The trail crosses the service road, returning to the end of the loop at Signpost B.

Turn left to retrace your incoming route across the causeway to the entrance, past Signpost A. Ending your 3.7-mile hike at the trail kiosk, sign the trail register before you leave.

OTHER HIKING OPTIONS

1. **C–D or E–F Loop.** Instead of following the full perimeter of the trail around Flat Island, shorten the hike by taking either of the cross-trails to make loops of 1.5 or 2.5 miles.
2. **Restoration Area.** Adjacent to the restrooms at the trailhead is a marked path into a habitat restoration area. It's not a long walk, but showcases some excellent fall wildflowers.
3. **Corley Island Trail.** At the opposite end of the parking lot from the main trailhead, the Corley Island Trail provides a loop hike of less than a mile through lush hardwood hammocks surrounding a marsh. A spur trail off of it leads to a local neighborhood.
4. **PEAR Park** (28.735116, -81.869879). Less than 4 miles south along US 27 is Palatlakaha Environmental and Agricultural Reserve Park. A pleasant nature trail follows the historic watershed of the Palatlakaha River through old-growth oak hammocks along the park's northern edge.

CAMPING AND LODGING

Lake Griffin State Park, 3089 US 441, Fruitland Park, FL 34731 (1-800-326-3521, floridastateparks.reserveamer ica.com)

Mission Inn Resort, 10400 SR 48, Howey-In-The-Hills, FL 34737 (352-324-3101, missioninnresort.com)

7

Circle B Bar Reserve

TOTAL DISTANCE: 4.4-mile perimeter loop with many shorter options available

HIKING TIME: 2–3 hours

DIFFICULTY: Easy

USAGE: Free. Open sunrise to sunset. No pets permitted. Bicycles are welcome; in fact, the trail system now connects to the Fort Fraser Trail, a lengthy paved bike path in Lakeland, through a back gate. The Discovery Center is closed on Mondays.

TRAILHEAD GPS COORDINATES:
27.989618, -81.857654

CONTACT INFORMATION: Circle B Bar Reserve, 4399 Winter Lake Road, Lakeland FL 33803 (863-668-4673, polknature.com/explore/circle-b-bar-reserve)

A gem of the Polk County Environmental Lands system, Circle B Bar Reserve was a cattle ranch between Lakeland and Bartow. It's now home to the Polk Nature Discovery Center and one of the best places to go birding in the Lakeland area, and one of the best destinations for wildlife watching in Florida. Along the shores of Lake Hancock, this former ranch has undergone extensive restoration to bring back the wetlands that originally filled the low-lying areas closest to the lake. Trails with benches and covered shelters top the berms. Enjoy a relaxed pace around this loop to appreciate the diversity of wildlife that depends on the marshes for survival.

GETTING THERE

From I-4, take the Polk Parkway to exit at FL 540 (Winter Lake Road). Follow FL 540 west. It zigzags and turns near the municipal dump before entering a tunnel of forests and swamps. Watch for the park entrance on the left. Follow the entrance road deep into the preserve to the large parking area at the Nature Discovery Center, home to the main trailhead from which the trail system radiates. Two smaller parking areas also provide access to the Treefrog Trail (27.995025, -81.865039) and the Lost Bridge Trail (27.991597, -81.860553).

THE HIKE

If the Nature Discovery Center is open, stop in to acquaint yourself with the habitats and their inhabitants before you start your hike. The trail begins at the TRAIL STARTS HERE sign just past the kiosk, which has maps. Meet a T intersection with a sidewalk for the Shady Oak Trail and turn left. The sidewalk ends, but the trail continues, becoming a natural

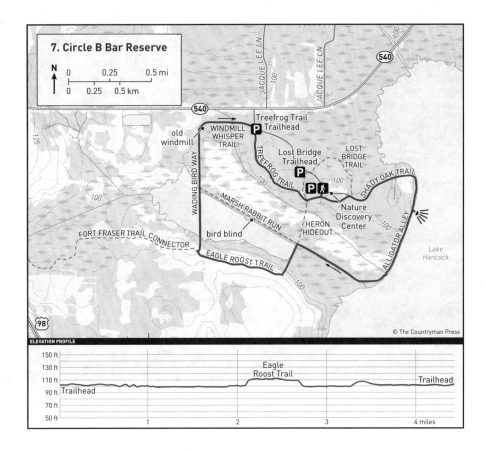

7. Circle B Bar Reserve

N
| 0 | 0.25 | 0.5 mi |
| 0 | 0.25 | 0.5 km |

ELEVATION PROFILE

footpath near an interpretive sign about the wetlands. One of the more misunderstood habitats in Florida—or so it would seem given the green light to destroy them for development—wetlands serve as natural filtration systems, with grasses and algae that can chemically break down substances like cow patties (or the outflow of a sewage treatment plant) and render them less harmful.

In the early morning hours, the sun streams through live oaks draped in Spanish moss, the grass below making you feel like you're walking in a park instead of a forest. Such is the nature of reclaiming natural habitats. Past a connector with the Lost Trail, there is a bench. Circle B Bar Reserve does an excellent job of education, from the markers you'll find along all the trails to the top-notch nature center, so this is a great destination for homeschoolers and families, in general, to gently immerse their children in Florida's native habitats. It's very much an outdoor classroom, as may be seen from the groupings of benches where a small field trip group can sit down and talk about what they see around them.

After you cross the footbridge, the trail intersects with a crushed-shell road and becomes Alligator Alley at 0.5 mile. Paying homage to one of the well-known crossings of the Everglades, this footpath leads you through a shady tunnel of moss-laden oaks and red maples along the shore of Lake Hancock. Measuring equipment monitors the health

ANHINGA SWALLOWING ITS FRESH CATCH

and depth of the lake. A wooden walkway leads left to a canopied observation deck on the lake. Sit still and watch, and you may see alligators cruising offshore. More benches provide places to pause and enjoy the view, most notably a very open spot at 1.2 miles next to a little cove. As the trail leaves the lakeshore, it continues along restored marshes on a narrow berm with a canal. Cypress rise from the shallows to your right. A Florida cooter turtle basks on a fallen log while a great egret spears a small fish. Moss-draped trees still provide patches of shade.

The trail comes to a four-way intersection at 1.8 miles. To stay to the perimeter, take a left to follow the Eagle Roost Trail. The open water here is a prime birding spot. Look for purple gallinules and coots, and wading birds along the edges. Passing a concrete water trough, the trail enters an open field under restoration to scrubby flatwoods. An eagle nest is clearly visible in the top of a tall longleaf pine. It's the main reason for walking along this loop, along with the extensive views across the marshes.

At 2.6 miles, the trail curves past a junction with a 0.8-mile side trail leading to the paved Fort Fraser Trail, a bike path between Bartow and Lakeland that's part of a larger network of paved trails through Polk County. This entrance provides cyclists with an easy way to come in and explore the wetlands. Past this junction, the trail heads through the middle of the wetlands on a berm, providing magnificent views across the open water along Wading Bird Way.

As it passes Marsh Rabbit Run coming in from the left, Wading Bird Way continues along another stretch of open wetlands. A cormorant rests on the shore, drying its wings in the morning sun to the delight of a flock of photographers. At 3.3 miles, you see an old windmill and reach the junction with the Windmill Whisper Trail. Turn right and walk down the oak-lined path through the uplands. The entrance road is straight ahead when you reach the Treefrog Trail. Make a right at that kiosk to walk beneath the shade of the live oaks, their curved limbs hosting thick jungles of resurrection fern. Reaching the junction with the Heron Hideout Trail, continue straight back onto the Shady Oak Trail to return to the beginning of the loop, where the recycled-surface footpath comes in from the left. Turn left to exit and complete this 4.4-mile hike.

OTHER HIKING OPTIONS

1. **Marsh Rabbit Run**. By far, the quickest and easiest opportunity for birders and photographers to focus on wildlife is to follow the Shady Oak Trail west to the Heron Hideout Trail, which crosses the marsh to the four-way intersection of Alligator Alley, Eagle Roost Trail, and Marsh Rabbit Run. Turn right to follow Marsh Rabbit Run, which is entirely surrounded by the marshes and has a bird blind less than 0.25 mile along the route.

MARSHES IN BLOOM ALONG THE EAGLE ROOST TRAIL

Expect to see a broad variety of wading birds in Banana Creek Marsh to the north of the trail, including rarer varieties like wood storks and roseate spoonbills.

2. **Lost Bridge Loop**. Following the Shady Oak Trail north, turn right at the Heron Hideout Trail, using Acorn Pass to connect to the opposite side of the park entrance road for the Lost Bridge Trail, a mile-long hike that showcases the grand live oaks that grow in that part of the preserve. It returns back around to the Nature Discovery Center.

3. **Marshall Hampton Reserve** (28.007846, -81.821038). Less than 4 miles away via FL 540, this sister preserve to Circle B Bar sits along the northeast shore of Lake Hancock and offers 12 miles of multi-use trails from a trailhead off Thornhill Road, with the new Panther Point Trail along the lake being the most popular destination.

CAMPING AND LODGING

Saddle Creek Campground, 3716 Morgan Combee Road, Lakeland, FL 33801 (863-413-2399, polk-county.net)

Best Western Auburndale Inn & Suites, 1008 US 92 W, Auburndale, FL 33823 (863-551-3400, bestwestern.com)

Lakeland Highlands Scrub

TOTAL DISTANCE: 2.8-mile perimeter loop with shorter options available

HIKING TIME: 1.5–2 hours

DIFFICULTY: Easy to difficult

USAGE: Free. Open 6 AM–6:30 PM during standard time, 5:30 AM–8 PM during daylight savings time. Leashed pets welcome. Bicycles permitted but not recommended.

TRAILHEAD GPS COORDINATES: 27.9367, -81.9235

CONTACT INFORMATION: Lakeland Highlands Scrub, 6998 Lakeland Highlands Road, Lakeland, FL 33813 (863-534-7377, polknature.com/explore/lakeland-highlands-scrub)

One of the original Polk County Environmental Lands, Lakeland Highlands Scrub offers a close-up look at a scrub ridge in the Central Highlands. Parallel to the Lake Wales Ridge but shorter and much farther west, the Lakeland Ridge boasts some serious elevation for the Florida peninsula, with portions of this 551-acre preserve sitting around 230 feet above sea level. An island of natural habitats surrounded by shuttered phosphate mines and subdivisions, it offers a boardwalk across a large flatwoods pond as a delightful surprise amid its otherwise dry habitats.

GETTING THERE

From downtown Lakeland, follow US 98 south towards Bartow for 2.5 miles. Turn right onto E Edgewood Drive. Continue for 0.7 mile and make a left onto Lakeland Highlands Road (CR 37B). Drive straight south on this road for 5.2 miles. It ends at the preserve. As the parking area is sandwiched between a fenced-off, water-filled, abandoned phosphate pit and a nondescript wall around a compound of nicer homes, it's not a very appealing entrance. But once you park and walk over to the preserve itself, you're in a different world.

THE HIKE

Leaving the parking area, walk through the pass-through stile in the wooden fence to enter Lakeland Highlands Scrub. Passing the entrance to the Scrub Flatwoods Trail—where you'll exit when you complete this clockwise loop around the perimeter of the preserve—walk to the kiosk by the picnic shelter to take a look at the map of Florida's ancient islands. Pick up a map of

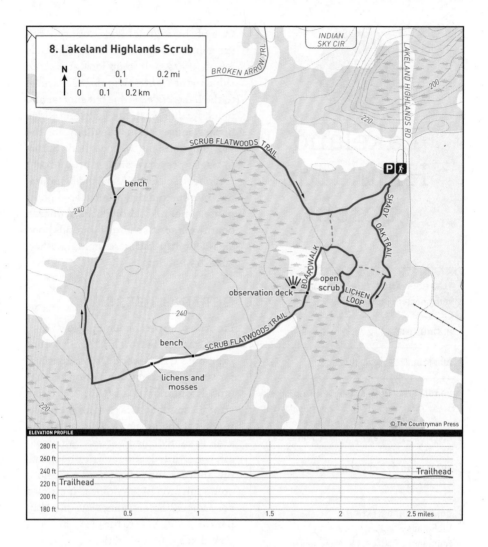

8. Lakeland Highlands Scrub

N

| 0 | 0.1 | 0.2 mi |
| 0 | 0.1 | 0.2 km |

INDIAN SKY CIR

BROKEN ARROW TRL

LAKELAND HIGHLANDS RD

SCRUB FLATWOODS TRAIL

bench

240

SHADY OAK TRAIL

BOARDWALK

open scrub

observation deck

LICHEN LOOP

240

bench

SCRUB FLATWOODS TRAIL

lichens and mosses

220

© The Countryman Press

ELEVATION PROFILE

280 ft				
260 ft				
240 ft				Trailhead
220 ft Trailhead				
200 ft				
180 ft	0.5	1	1.5	2	2.5 miles

the trails in the BROCHURES box. Beyond the kiosk is the SHADY OAK TRAIL sign. The trail immediately leads you into a *xeric* hammock, an evergreen forest on well-drained sandy soils. Before these rolling hills between Lakeland and Mulberry became ranches, phosphate mines, and subdivisions, islands of sandhill forest rich with longleaf pine and wiregrass sat among ancient scrubs and prairies, much like what is seen in the Ocala National Forest today. But a century's worth of human activity means this habitat has been isolated. A climax forest

of oak hammock has taken over. Sand live oaks thrive in scrub habitats. They also provide shady tunnels for the trail to lead you through.

As the forest floor is covered in oak leaves, the footpath can be indistinct. Look for trail markers and be cautious of where fallen trees might block the path and send you in an incorrect direction as you walk beneath the curving, lichen-studded limbs of the sand live oaks. Scattered saw palmetto grow throughout the understory. In one open spot, you see a clue as to the sandhill habitat that's no longer dominant: tufts of wiregrass and prickly pear cactus.

After 0.3 mile, you reach the junction with the Lichen Loop Trail. Turn left to follow this fascinating loop. It crosses a grassy path that was an old railroad line before it enters deep shade under the moss-draped sand live oaks. Beyond a stand of pines, the trail bisects dense beds of lichens adapted to the harshness of this fine-grained sand, including *Cladonia evansii*, the red-tipped lichen known as reindeer lichen or "British soldiers." Among them are clusters of slender green fingers of sand spike-moss, a fascinating lichen that reproduces by spores. The trail continues as a narrow tunnel beneath a low canopy of sand live oaks, with cushion-like mats of deep green *Leucobryum albidum* padding the edges of the footpath.

Leaving the shade of the oaks, the trail pops into an area with a panoramic sweep of sky over a dense understory of saw palmetto and other scrub shrubs like shiny lyonia. Follow the signs and watch the footpath so as not to lose your way in this open space with its nice views of the scrub forest. Zigzagging towards a cluster of oaks thickly draped in Spanish moss, the trail turns sharply left to cross the old railroad grade again. In this spot, the trail sits on a bed of the bright white sand you've started to see underfoot.

Reaching the end of the Lichen Loop Trail after 0.6 mile, turn left to resume the Shady Oak Trail, which continues under a low canopy of oaks, the understory open except for clusters of saw palmetto. Taller oaks form the canopy and pines tower overhead as the trail meets a junction with the Scrub Flatwoods Trail. Turn left and join the old railroad

DENSE BED OF LICHENS ALONG THE LICHEN LOOP

grade at a four-way intersection. You see the start of the boardwalk nearby. The boardwalk leads across a large open basin in the scrub, a flatwoods pond, and the wet prairie that surrounds its edges. It provides scenic views across the water as it guides you towards a covered observation deck. Take a break on the benches and listen to the frogs croaking; watch ibis wheel across the sky and land in formation. This is an oasis in a dry landscape, the observation deck ideal for wildlife watching.

Leaving the boardwalk, you've completed the easy part of this hike. If you're wondering why we rated such a broad spectrum of difficulty for this trail, you may not be familiar with walking across Florida's ancient sands. Just beyond the boardwalk, a mile into your hike, you'll

ground, and the sun reflects brightly back at you from underfoot. It's easy to get dehydrated in this open habitat, so keep drinking your water regularly as you walk. The dense oak scrub is short and does not cast shade across the trail. Prairie grasses wave in the sun.

Patches of scrub mint grow atop the bright white sand, looking like cushions. After you pass a bench at 1.2 miles, look closely at the lichens growing on the white sand. *Cladonia prostrata* is a crispy-looking, silvery lichen. When this lichen becomes damp, the crispy edges unfurl like a miniature staghorn fern, exposing a greenish interior. The rounded puffy lichens are lumped under the colloquial name of deer moss. Like the smaller lichens, these plants become brittle when dry, and soft and spongy when wet. *Cladonia perforata*, or perforate reindeer lichen, is a rare species only found in the ancient scrubs like the one that this preserve protects. You'll need to look closely at the lichen patches along this section of the trail to identify it: look for natural holes (perforations) in the stems. There are many thick beds of lichens in this area.

While the trail primarily stays to the broad sandy patches between the hammocks, it passes through an island of pines in the scrub at 1.4 miles. The change to pine needles and leaves underfoot makes for much easier walking, and there are patches of shade. As the trail makes a sharp turn, it emerges into another stretch of deep, soft ancient sands. Watch for trail markers. Oak scrub presses in from both sides before the landscape opens again. The divots

note a distinct cutoff between soil and sand. Once you step across it, footing becomes uneven and sand sneaks into your shoes from every direction. You may even break through a crust on the top. Walking through what we call "sugar sand" is quite strenuous, especially when you add in the lack of shade in the open scrub. The scrub is Florida's desert. Rainfall quickly soaks into the

BRIGHT WHITE SANDS OF THE LAKELAND RIDGE

of thousands of footprints in the bright sand look like suncups on a snowy slope.

Don't be surprised to see a flash of blue as a Florida scrub-jay settles into the top of a myrtle oak. Found only in Florida, these curious birds live in family groups, so when you see or hear one, others may appear. They keep their distance as they scurry beneath the diminutive oaks in search of acorns. This is one of the better places in the region to see them. Notice how the pines are draped in Spanish moss? It's not uncommon to see a scrub-jay perched on one of the lower limbs. A warning *shrweep* from this lookout sends the others for cover.

At 1.7 miles, the landscape opens into a prairie. A bench provides a rare break in a patch of shade. The soft white sand vanishes as low grasses swarm across the footpath. Note a slow transition of habitat back to xeric hammock, as the oaks are taller and the increased number of leaves on the ground decay into soil. Crossing the old grass-covered railroad line once again after 2 miles, the trail curves right to parallel it. As the trail draws close to the fence line of the preserve, you catch glimpses of homes and paddocks. The habitat is shifting again, this time into pine flatwoods. Passing a bench beneath a pine, the trail continues down a straightaway under the pines. A mowed area with prairie grasses can become soggy after a rain. As the footpath becomes grassy, settle in for a comfortable stretch between the scattered pines.

Passing the corner of the property line at 2.4 miles, the trail curves through an oak hammock to emerge into another prairie area where rangers' vehicles often leave deep ruts because of the soft earth underneath. Water collects in this area at times, draining off the prairie to the low spots. Saw palmetto competes with the grasses to create an impenetrable understory. Reaching the next SCRUB FLATWOODS TRAIL sign, the trail merges in with the Shady Oak Trail. Turn left to walk through the last stretch of oak hammock to the trailhead. By the time you get to the parking area, you've completed a 2.8-mile hike.

OTHER HIKING OPTIONS

1. **Shady Oak Trail**. Sticking to the Shady Oak Trail, walk an easy 0.7-mile circuit beneath the oak hammocks closest to the park entrance. Simply skip the turnoff for the Lichen Loop Trail and turn right when you reach the T intersection with the Scrub Flatwoods Loop.
2. **Shady Lichen & Wetlands**. For a scenic and easy walk, follow the first portion of our hike route around the Shady Oak Trail and Lichen Loop and to the Flatwoods Pond boardwalk. Enjoy the view from the observation deck. Use this as your turnaround point and head back towards the trailhead on the remainder of the Shady Oak Trail for a 1.3-mile hike.
3. **Wetlands Walk**. If your focus is birding, head straight to the Flatwoods Pond boardwalk. Do so by following the Scrub Flatwoods Trail backward to the Shady Oak Trail, then over to the Scrub Flatwoods Trail to get to the boardwalk. A round-trip from the parking area to the observation deck and back is 1 mile. Add an extra ramble into the scrub beyond the boardwalk if you're looking for Florida scrub-jays.

CAMPING AND LODGING

Saddle Creek Campground, 3716 Morgan Combee Road, Lakeland, FL 33801 (863-413-2399, polk-county.net)
Holiday Inn Express Bartow, 1565 N Broadway Avenue, Bartow, FL 33830 (863-533-8070, ihg.com)

BOARDWALK OVER NEEDLERUSH MARSH,
WERNER-BOYCE SALT SPRINGS STATE PARK

II.

NATURE COAST

9

Johnson Pond Trail

TOTAL DISTANCE: 2.7-mile loop that crosses and briefly joins trails shared with equestrians and cyclists

HIKING TIME: 1–1.5 hours

DIFFICULTY: Easy to moderate

USAGE: Free. Open sunrise to sunset. Leashed pets welcome.

TRAILHEAD GPS COORDINATES: 29.005133, -82.384067

CONTACT INFORMATION: Withlacoochee State Forest/Two Mile Prairie Tract, 3033 E Withlacoochee Trail, Dunnellon, FL 34434 (352-797-4140, freshfromflorida.com or www.swfwmd.state.fl.us)

Flowing north towards the Gulf of Mexico, the Withlacoochee River defines the boundary between Citrus and Marion counties. Just south of the river lies the Two Mile Prairie Tract of Withlacoochee State Forest, where the Johnson Pond Trail provides a walk through sandhills and oak scrub, touching on prairies along the way. The most notable stop is the trail's namesake, Johnson Pond, a birder's delight. Watch for the yellow flash of the palm warbler; listen for the languid warble of the warbling vireo. Great blue herons step gracefully through the shallow waters of Johnson Pond, and bluebirds are encouraged to nest nearby.

GETTING THERE

From I-75, take exit 350, Ocala (southbound) or exit 341, Belleview (northbound) and go west on either FL 200 or CR 484 for about 10 miles, where the two roads intersect. From the intersection, follow FL 200 west for 6.2 miles to the Withlacoochee River bridge, turning right onto CR 39, between the two gas stations. Drive 2.6 miles to the trailhead on the left side of the road, which has the sign JOHNSON POND RECREATIONAL TRAILHEAD. The trail starts at a kiosk with a map of the trail.

THE HIKE

From the trailhead kiosk, pass through the split-rail fence. Follow the trail as it swings left onto a forest road into the sandhill habitat, where young longleaf pines rise to touch the sky. Eruptions of orange sand along the trail mark the underground paths of pocket gophers. Loblolly and sand pines intersperse with the longleaf pines; the scent of pine rises

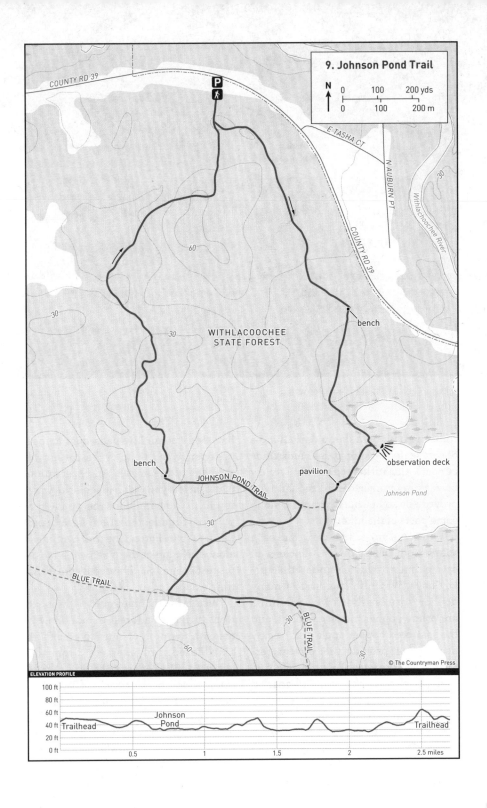

9. Johnson Pond Trail

N

| 0 | 100 | 200 yds |
| 0 | 100 | 200 m |

COUNTY RD 39

E TASHA CT

N AUBURN PT

COUNTY RD 39

Withlachoochee River

WITHLACOOCHEE
STATE FOREST

60

30

30

30

bench

bench

JOHNSON POND TRAIL

pavilion

observation deck

Johnson Pond

BLUE TRAIL

30

BLUE TRAIL

60

30

© The Countryman Press

ELEVATION PROFILE

100 ft					
80 ft					
60 ft					
40 ft	Trailhead	Johnson Pond			Trailhead
20 ft					
0 ft	0.5	1	1.5	2	2.5 miles

JOHNSON POND, AT THE HEART OF ITS PRAIRIE

from the path on a damp day. Clumps of soft seafoam-colored deer moss hide beneath the turkey oaks. The yellow blazes are oversized and frequent and prove to be somewhat distracting along some parts of the hike.

After 0.5 mile, the trail makes a sharp right past a bench. Thickets of saw palmetto cluster under the turkey oaks. Watch for the first of many gopher tortoise burrows. Sandhills are prime gopher tortoise habitat, and the scattered gopher apple and prickly pear cactus provide fuel for the tortoise's wanderings. Turning left, the trail passes through a stand of gnarled sand live oaks, past a prairie edged by longleaf pines. This is one of the few remaining spots along the trail with a mat of *Cladonia* lichens, commonly called reindeer lichen. By 0.7 mile, you reach Johnson Pond, a broad, marshy flatwoods pond. Lily pads float across the open water; pond cypresses crowd the edge of the marsh. An observation platform lets you watch for colorful wading birds that frequent the pond—the purple gallinule, the green heron, and the great blue heron. The trail continues along the edge of the lake past a set of picnic benches. Songbirds flit across the trail, small blurs in motion.

Watch for the markers for the next right turn onto a forest road. Follow it beneath the arch of sand live oaks. A blue-blazed trail intersects from the left at 1.2 miles—one of the horse trails from the southern extreme of Two Mile Prairie. It shares the hiking trail for the next 0.2 mile, so expect the footpath to be rough, especially if it's deeply rutted by fat-tire enthusiasts. In the soft sand along both sides of the road, look for sand pine whitlow-wort. These

FLORIDA ROSEMARY IN THE SCRUBBY FLATWOODS

endangered wildflowers grow only in a limited region of Florida's sand pine scrub, and have dense square flower clusters of pale pink or white, blooming through the summer and into October.

After you pass a barbed-wire fence, the hiking trail turns away from the horse trail. It makes a sharp right and descends through a live oak hammock to what once was a rosemary scrub. Perhaps prescribed burns caused its demise, or a change in how water flows across the landscape. Only a couple of Florida rosemary plants remain in this once-thriving spot, and the dense carpet of deer moss found beneath the oaks has vanished entirely.

The trail parallels a dry streambed, then veers left into the slash pines before rising into an oak hammock. Bright pink red blanket lichen livens up the live oak trunks. Southern red cedars are scattered amid the oaks. An American holly shades a small limestone outcrop at 1.9 miles. A shaded bench sits at the upper end of a steep karst valley; the trail swings right, climbing up between live oaks to work its way back into the sandhills. Turkey oak and longleaf pine dominate the canopy. The grassy understory hosts a parade of fall wildflowers— blazing star, deer's tongue, and yellow buttons.

The pines show burn scars as you climb a long uphill through turkey oaks, which in fall are dressed in crimson and brown. More than any other Florida habitat, the sandhill shows the change of the season. Winged sumacs turn a deep, dark crimson, while the wiregrass fades to straw. Swinging left around a short stand of wax myrtle, the trail plunges downhill under the long-leaf pines to complete the loop. Continue straight ahead to return to the parking area, completing the 2.7-mile loop.

OTHER HIKING OPTIONS

1. **Short Loop.** After you pass the pavilion beyond the observation platform on Johnson Pond, look for an obvious forest road on the right. It's not blazed at first, but it quickly connects you with the other side of the loop. Continue straight ahead along the blazes to make a 2-mile loop.
2. **Oxbow Nature Trail** (29.005623, -82.387915). North about 0.25 mile along CR 39 is a separate 1.2-mile loop within Withlacoochee State Forest. This trail tunnels through oak scrub similar to what you see on the Johnson Pond Trail, but also follows the banks of the Withlacoochee River for a short stretch.
3. **Bear Head Hammock** (28.966384, -82.401349). At the south end of Two Mile Prairie, a trailhead off CR 491 provides access to the 8.3-mile equestrian loop inside the forest, which intersects with the Johnson Pond Trail.

CAMPING AND LODGING

Ross Prairie Campground, 10660 SW SR 200, Dunnellon, FL 34432 (1-800-326-3521, floridastateparks.reserve america.com)

Angler's Resort, 12189 S Williams Street, Dunnellon, FL 34432 (352-489-2397, anglersresort.us)

Dinner Bell Motel, 12094 S Williams Street, Dunnellon, FL 34432 (352-489-2550, dunnellonmotels.com)

Citrus Trail

TOTAL DISTANCE: A 39.1-mile hike along the perimeter of a trail system made up of four stacked loop trails, broken into segments of 11.1, 13.9, and 14.1 miles. Segments are based on the locations of designated primitive campsites along the loop.

HIKING TIME: 3 days

DIFFICULTY: Moderate to difficult

USAGE: Free. Open 24 hours. Hunting season precautions must be taken. Leashed pets welcome.

TRAILHEAD GPS COORDINATES: 28.799305, -82.384676

CONTACT INFORMATION: Withlacoochee State Forest/Citrus Tract, 4399 Trail 10, Inverness, FL 34452 (352-797-4140, freshfromflorida.com)

With nearly 158,000 acres spread over four counties, Withlacoochee State Forest is Florida's third largest state forest, and arguably the most popular for outdoor recreation. Its largest tract, Citrus, contains the state's longest backpacking loop trail in a single contiguous forest. This is Central Florida's most rugged backpacking trail, with aggressively rolling sandhills, steep descents into sinkholes, and rock-strewn footpaths providing a stunning array of contrasting habitats. It is a well-groomed trail, easily followed, with a clearly defined footpath and signposts at trail junctions. Established in the 1970s by the Suncoast Chapter of the Florida Trail Association, it remains a premier backpacking destination thanks to their ongoing care of the trail. A portion of the statewide Florida National Scenic Trail follows the east side of the loop.

Backpacking the Citrus Trail takes some logistical planning because water sources are at a premium. There are no surface streams. Karst features—sinkholes and solution holes—seasonally retain rainfall, as do flatwoods ponds. The recreation areas have tap water, plus there are a couple of horse watering cisterns that can be used to filter water in a pinch. Finalize your route beforehand if you need to cache water jugs at forest road crossings before you start hiking.

No permits are required, but check your hiking schedule against the hunting dates posted by the Florida Fish and Wildlife Conservation Commission on their website. The Citrus Tract is one of the region's most popular deer hunting grounds, so hiking is not recommended during deer season in the fall and winter. Always wear an orange safety vest if any type of hunting is going on along the Citrus Trail. If you modify this hike to fit an easier daily mileage for yourself,

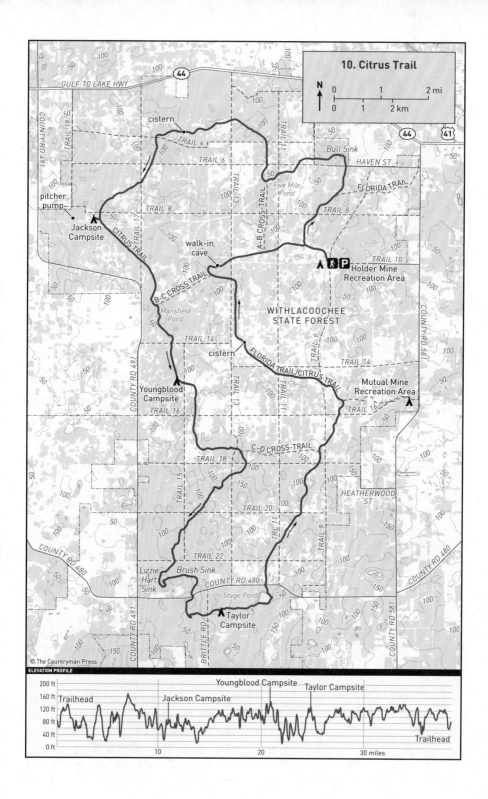

10. Citrus Trail

N

0   1   2 mi

0   1   2 km

GULF TO LAKE HWY

44

44

41

cistern

TRAIL 19

TRAIL 4

TRAIL 6

TRAIL 11

Bull Sink

HAVEN ST

Five Mile Pond

FLORIDA TRAIL

COUNTY RD 491

TRAIL 17

TRAIL 8

TRAIL 13

A–B CROSS-TRAIL

TRAIL 8

pitcher pump

CITRUS TRAIL

Jackson Campsite

walk-in cave

Holder Mine Recreation Area

TRAIL 10

B–C CROSS-TRAIL

Mansfield Pond

WITHLACOOCHEE STATE FOREST

TRAIL 9

TRAIL 14

cistern

FLORIDA TRAIL/CITRUS TRAIL

TRAIL 14

Youngblood Campsite

TRAIL 13

TRAIL 11

Mutual Mine Recreation Area

TRAIL 16

TRAIL 16

COUNTY RD 491

COUNTY RD 581

C–D CROSS-TRAIL

TRAIL 18

TRAIL 15

TRAIL 20

HEATHERWOOD ST

TRL 21

TRAIL 9

TRAIL 22

Lizzie Hart Sink

Brush Sink

COUNTY RD 480

COUNTY RD 480

Stage Pond

Taylor Campsite

BRITTLE RD

COUNTY RD 491

COUNTY RD 581

© The Countryman Press

ELEVATION PROFILE

200 ft
160 ft
120 ft
80 ft
40 ft
0 ft

Trailhead

Jackson Campsite

Youngblood Campsite

Taylor Campsite

Trailhead

10   20   30 miles

PRIMARY TRAILHEAD AT HOLDER MINE RECREATION AREA

you'll probably need to reserve a camp-site at either Mutual Mine or Holder Mine Recreation Area. A camping fee applies at those sites.

GETTING THERE

From I-75, take exit 329, Wildwood. Turn west on FL 44, driving 11 miles to Inverness. Continue west on FL 44 into Inverness to CR 581, located opposite Whispering Pines Park. Turn left. Drive 2.5 miles, passing the fire tower, to the sign for HOLDER MINE RECREATION AREA. Turn right. The road becomes sand after the first mile and continues for another mile as FR 10 into Holder Mine Recreation Area. Pass the hunt check station and campground. The trailhead is on the left at the kiosk. Note that signs inside Withlacoochee State Forest, as well as online maps, refer to Trail 10, Trail 13, and the like; all of these are forest roads, most of them very rough and some not open to vehicles. The land was initially managed by the US Forest Service between 1936 and 1958. Only Trail 10 and Trail 13, both of which can be rough in places, do not require a high-clear-ance vehicle and/or four-wheel drive for access.

THE HIKE

DAY ONE (11.1 MILES)

Start and end your backpacking loop at Holder Mine Recreation Area, but fill up on potable water first. When you sign in at the kiosk, specify how long you plan to be on the trail. Walk over to the road and turn left, following the blue blazes until they veer right, into the forest. After you pass a low depression, you cross two horse trails. The Citrus Tract has separate sets of trails for hikers, cyclists, and equestrians. A color band around the trees designates horse trails. Florida rosemary forms neat patches under the sand pines. Reindeer lichen blankets the glittering white sand. As the trail ascends sharply, it enters a for-est of turkey oaks and sand live oaks with scattered wiregrass, which gives way to oak scrub.

The blue-blazed connector trail ends after 0.8 mile, at the LOOP A sign. Turn right to begin following the orange blazes of the statewide Florida Trail, our National Scenic Trail in Florida. Only a portion of the 39-mile loop is painted in orange blazes, and that's the portion that's officially part of the linear Florida Trail. The rest of the loop's blazes are painted yellow.

Oak scrub gives way to sandhills. Be alert as the trail veers right after crossing a track, rising into a forest of longleaf, slash, and sand pines. Gopher apple grows in shady spots. You pass a longleaf snag heavy with resin—lighter pine, the heartwood of a dead longleaf pine, is a perfect fire-starter.

The open understory impresses upon you the size of this forest as the wiregrass fades into the distance, a taupe fog. You start a long, slow descent down the sandhill. When you reach Trail 8 at 1.6 miles, there are trail signs on both sides of the road. Usually, these signs indicate on the back which road you're crossing, which makes it easy to find your place on the map. Descending under the longleaf pines, you enter a grove of sand live oaks, with their trunks and branches all swept toward the left. The orange eruptions of pocket gophers pockmark the footpath. As you climb up and down the sandhills, watch for gopher tortoise

SAND LIVE OAKS UNDER THE PINES NORTH OF THE FLORIDA TRAIL CONNECTOR JUNCTION (LOOP A)

burrows and rounded armadillo holes. At 2.1 miles, the Florida Trail leaves the Citrus Trail on its way north into Inverness. Continue along the yellow blazes to stay on the loop.

At 2.9 miles, you cross Haven Street, a paved road. After climbing up and over a ridge, the trail drops around Bull Sink, a prairie that hosts an ephemeral pond. Forest roads crisscross the trail as it winds through the dense shade of an oak hammock. The trail starts a long uphill, crossing Trail 6 up into a longleaf forest, through a narrow corridor of dense sand live oak, until it emerges in a clearing along the bottom of a steep sandhill, nearly 100 feet high. Returning to the woods, the trail turns right and climbs the sandhill, reaching an open forest of turkey oaks at the top. Oaks yield to pines as the trail descends, crossing Trail 11 and continuing to descend through a hunt camp into an oak hammock, where Five Mile Pond lies in the open prairie. It's another ephemeral pond, so don't count on it as a water source.

After 5 miles, you reach the A–B Cross-Trail junction. Turn right to remain on the outer loop. The trail makes a long slow climb through the sandhill before crossing Trail 6, rising into a mix of turkey oaks and longleaf pine. On the downhill, the trail passes tightly between two longleaf pines; one sports a catface, a deep cut in the trunk that is now healed, from tapping its sap for turpentine. Watch for scattered clay pots, relics of the turpentine era in Florida, a century or more ago. Undulating over the sandhills, the trail drops through a longleaf forest on a needle carpet so thick that it buries the wiregrass.

At the bottom of the hill, the trail winds through an oak hammock, then rises into the sandhills, meeting Trail 13 at 6.8 miles. Trail 13 is the most accessible road through the forest, and the trail crosses it six times over the course of the loop—use it as your water drop point if you opt to cache water. Just beyond Trail 13 is the first permanent water source along the trail, a massive concrete cistern for watering horses. Because of its proximity to the road, it isn't a great water source. Be sure to strain and filter the water if you use it.

The habitat changes from sandhills to sand pine scrub as the trail crosses Trail 2 and enters an oak scrub, where you might see a Florida scrub-jay. You're on the extreme northern edge of the forest, so traffic noise from FL 44 filters in. After crossing an oak scrub, you reenter a stand of tall sand pines, its understory dense with myrtle oaks. The trail meanders through stands of saw palmetto under the longleaf pines, the habitat shifting to scrubby flatwoods as it crosses Trail 4 and Trail 4A in quick succession.

Climbing up through the pines, the trail crosses Trail 6 at 9.1 miles. Expect wildlife sightings in this remote corner of the forest, as you spy the white flags of two retreating white-tailed deer. Look for bobcat tracks along the footpath. Trail 17 sits in a deep ditch, making the crossing a little tricky. The trail continues downhill under the longleaf pines into a dense corridor of sand live oaks, making a long, slow descent to Trail 8. Just after you cross Trail 8, start watching for the campsite sign, at 10.9 miles. Follow the blue blaze right for 0.2 mile as it jogs through the forest to the Jackson Campsite (PCZ-B), an open spot under a gnarled live oak. Set up your tent, pull up a log, and enjoy the serenity of an evening away from the sounds of civilization. Need water? There is a pitcher pump 0.5 mile due west (28.812750,

-82.475017) of the campsite along the Dixie Land Trail, an equestrian trail, and it's painted orange, so it's visible from a distance. It can be reached via Trail 8 or Trail 10A too.

DAY TWO (13.9 MILES)

After packing up your gear, follow the blue blazes for 0.2 mile to return to the yellow-blazed loop trail. Turn right. As the trail descends through scrubby flatwoods, blueberry bushes crowd the forest floor, a perfect feeding ground for bears or for your breakfast, if you hike through here in April or May. Where the understory opens, yucca grows in scattered clumps between the wiregrass. Crossing Trail 10A, the trail veers left to parallel the road briefly. Climbing uphill, you cross two narrow tracks in quick succession. The trail goes downhill. After crossing Trail 3, the trail veers left, reaching a power line, then crosses Trail 17 at 1.3 miles. Most of the older longleaf pines along this section of the trail bear the scars of catfaces, some embedded with metal shaped like a broad V to channel the resin into the turpentine cup. As the trail drifts west towards the community of Lecanto, you hear traffic on CR 491. The trail climbs a steep sand slope. At the top of the hill, take in the view of longleaf forest stretching off on both sides.

You reach the signpost for the B–C Cross-Trail junction after 2.7 miles. Continue straight ahead through a stand of southern magnolias. Descending steeply into an oak hammock, the trail makes a sudden sharp left. Watch the blazes carefully through this section, as the trail zigzags through the forest on and off forest roads. Pass a giant split oak, its trunk cleaved in three sections, sprawling across the ground, sending up limbs as thick as trunks themselves.

Skirt around Mansfield Pond when you reach it. Because of its size and location, it's not a reliable water source, as it can go dry. As the trail veers from the pond, it passes under a canopy of tall live oaks, climbing back into the scrubby flatwoods. Crossing Trail 14, the trail continues past the Youngblood Campsite (PCZ-C) at 4.5 miles. When you approach the edge of the meadow, walk softly. It's an ideal place to watch for deer. The trail crosses Trail 16, paralleling a longleaf pine forest.

Two live oaks form a gateway into the pine forest, where maidencane bamboo grows tall in damp spots along the trail. The forest becomes a dense mix of oaks and pines as the trail twists and turns through a corridor of saw palmetto. When rocks appear in the footpath, you've reached the rolling karst hills of the central forest. Limestone outcrops appear on the surface as small rocks and large boulders. Look for a dark pit, an entrance to a cave. Karst is a landscape shaped by the action of water on rock, where rainfall trickling through tannic oak leaves becomes an acidic solution that etches pathways through soft bedrock. Karst features in this forest include caverns and sinkholes, and rough exposed limestone along the trail. In karst, water flows down instead of out, so what few seasonal streams flow through the Withlacoochee State Forest are gobbled up into sinkholes.

You cross Trail 13 at 7 miles, dropping down into a karst valley, which drains into a plugged-up cave entrance. Limestone-loving spleenwort grows in clusters on the bare rock. Climbing up into an oak hammock, the trail reaches the signpost for the C–D Cross-Trail junction. Turn right to stay with the yellow blazes, climbing up through the scrubby flatwoods to cross Trail 18A

RUGGED KARST BLUFF ALONG LIZZIE HART SINK, LOOP D

and Trail 18 in quick succession. The trail merges onto a forest road, veering left through the flatwoods before rising through an oak hammock to cross Trail 13 again. As you cross an old railroad bed and then descend a rocky slope, you're back in a karst valley. Sweetgum and American holly crowd the trail. There is an open area with a depression. If you leave the trail and walk through the depressions, you'll find a sinkhole that sometimes holds water, a duck-weed-choked pond.

Watch for two sharp turns as the trail ascends out of the valley into scrubby flatwoods. You continue uphill through a low oak understory, with bracken ferns spilling across the forest floor. After crossing Trail 20 at 9.1 miles, a divided road with a power line, the trail descends under the pines. The flower-ing plants with waxy green leaves and ivory blossoms are sandhill milkweed, attracting dozens of colorful butterflies,

including the long-tailed skipper. In this section of the trail, you'll cross over numerous horse trails, each marked with a different-colored band. After the trail rises through a stand of tall pines, it crosses Trail 15 down in a deep ditch. Pines yield to sandhills—in this part of the forest, many of the sandhills were planted over with longleaf pines after the original forest was logged, so it's difficult to determine the habitat.

Where the trail descends a steep grade into an older forest of pines, keep alert, as needles obscure the footpath, making it easy to miss where the trail veers right. Rocks come to the surface again in a cedar grove, where the trail passes through dense pines and oaks before reaching Trail 22 at 10.4 miles. From here, the trail drops steeply down-hill past a deep gully into a mixed forest of elms, hickory, southern magnolias, and cedar. Look over the rocky lip of Lizzie Hart Sink, a massive depression cradling numerous caves. Because of the rocky terrain, the footpath becomes indistinct. Follow the orange blazes carefully, watching your footing, and be respectful of this fragile, unusual terrain. The trail twists and turns around obstacles, including a colossal swamp chestnut oak and a rocky bluff with a cave.

When the trail leaves Lizzie Hart Sink, it crosses a forest road and descends into a forest of oaks and sweetgum. Brush Sink, swampy and water-filled, hides behind the bushes on the right, another potential water source. The trail rises steeply, reaching the CR 480 crossing at 12.5 miles. Carefully cross the highway, then head into the rolling sandhills. The trail turns to follow a dry streambed, then turns to cross it. This seasonal stream flows a significant distance, cutting a deep ravine along the trail's edge until it plunges into a large sinkhole fed by several similar streams.

Stay right at the fork. At the top of the hill, the trail turns right, crossing Trail 13. You wind through a rocky forest of oaks and hickories to reach the campsite sign at 13.8 miles. Turn right and follow the blue blaze for 0.1 mile to select your spot at the Taylor Campsite (PCZ-D). After this interesting but tiring hike, it won't be long before you're sleeping soundly.

DAY THREE (14.1 MILES)

After packing up, return up the blue blaze to the main trail and turn right. Rocks poke out of the footpath. Descending into the sweetgum forest, the trail becomes a narrow track. A marsh lies to the right, surrounded by dense forest. After a forest road, a large open area looms—Stage Pond, a permanent and reliable water source about a mile into your hike. Netted chain fern grows

along its edge. The trail follows an old track along the eastern edge of the lake, with two good access points for filtering water. After the trail turns right, it veers through an oak hammock to cross CR 480 again at 1.6 miles. This is where you rejoin the orange blazes of the Florida Trail.

Cross the road and enter a forest of scattered sand pines, longleaf pines, and scrub oaks. In the early morning, the sandhills are alive with the furious activities of birds darting between the trees—blue-gray gnatcatchers, yellow vireos, cedar waxwings, and downy woodpeckers. Crossing Trail 22, you pass between two live oaks, and the trail veers right, flanked by the profuse blooms of sandhill milkweed. Crossing Trail 11, the trail descends beneath sand live oaks, continuing an undulating route over the sandhills. After you cross Trail 20 at 3.4 miles, keep alert for several sharp turns as the trail enters an extensive laurel oak forest. Emerging into the sandhills, the trail jumps on and off old roads before reaching Trail 18. Blue flag iris bloom in a damp area along a seepage slope.

At 4.9 miles, you meet the sign for the C–D Cross-Trail. Turn right to stay with the orange blazes. The landscape opens into scattered longleaf pines. Icicles of hardened amber resin drip from one catfaced pine. Crossing a dry, windy hilltop, you reach Trail 18A and discover another old railroad bed, this one still decorated with the ballast used under the rails. Beyond Trail 9A, Trail 16 runs in a deep ditch. Cross Trail 7 and enter a stand of longleaf pines. The trail rises to a bench and the sign for the connector trail to Mutual Mine at 6.4 miles. This developed campground sits along the edge of one of the phosphate pits dug during the early 1900s and offers potable water, picnic tables, restrooms, and grills. It's a pleasant place to camp, and you may want to adjust your hike to start and end here. Today's trek, however, continues on to finish the full Citrus Hiking Trail loop.

Rising through a young longleaf forest on the sandhills, the trail traverses open grassland replanted with longleaf pines before crossing Trail 7. Beyond Trail 9, prickly pear grows in the open spaces between myrtle oaks and Chapman oaks. Watch for gopher tortoises browsing through the underbrush, and fox squirrels scampering up the trees. The habitat yields to a more mature forest on the sandhills, with wiregrass and scattered oaks underneath a tall canopy of longleaf pine. You cross Trail 11, then Trail 14, climbing up into the pine-forest sandhills.

You see your first saw palmettos of the day just before crossing Trail 14A, where a square, concrete-block water cis-

tern shimmers along the side of the trail at 9 miles. This is the last water source you will encounter before returning to Holder Mine. Take a moment and sit on the broad wall, watching for eastern bluebirds in the surrounding oaks. The trail continues through large clumps of saw palmetto under a dense pine understory with plenty of blueberry bushes. To the west you see an orange gash, a break in the trees—the trail now parallels Trail 13. Longleaf pines and wiregrass stretch east. You cross Trail 13 at 10.7 miles and reach the junction with the B–C Cross-Trail within the next 0.25 mile. Continue straight along the orange blazes.

As the trail descends into an oak hammock, the vegetation suddenly becomes unusually lush. At the bottom of the hill, look left—it's the biggest cave yet along this trail, with a walk-in opening flooded with sunlight. Drop your pack and take a few minutes to explore. Ladder brake and spleenwort ferns decorate crevices

A HAZE OF WIREGRASS UNDER THE LONGLEAF PINES ALONG LOOP C

in the limestone. As you continue down the trail, notice the tall southern woods fern growing out of a sinkhole. Limestone breaks up the footpath. The trail veers left, down into an oak hammock in a vast karst bowl. Crossing Trail 13 for the final time at 11.6 miles, the trail rises through a blueberry patch to meet the A–B Cross-Trail. Continue straight, walking through a scrubby hammock under the longleaf pines. After you cross Trail 11, the trail rises into scrub, with sugary white sand underfoot, tall rosemary bushes, and dense patches of reindeer moss.

Beyond two horse trails, you enter a narrow path through a dense oak scrub. Watch for Florida scrub-jays here, as they prefer a habitat dense with these short myrtle oaks and Chapman oaks. At 13.3 miles, you reach the end of the loop at the LOOP A sign. Continue straight along the blue blaze to reach your car at Holder Mine Recreation Area, wrapping a 14.1-mile day and a 39.1-mile three-day journey.

OTHER HIKING OPTIONS

Because the loops provide so many different ways to tackle the Citrus Hiking Trail, the perimeter hike is only one option for hiking here. Use any of the cross-trails to create overnight or two-night hikes: the A–B and B–C Cross-Trails are each 1.6 miles long; the C–D Cross-Trail is 1.8 miles long. Parking areas are limited for day hikes on this big loop, but here are a few of our favorite options.

1. **Loop A**. Because it starts and ends at the Holder Mine trailhead, Loop A is the most popular day hike within the Citrus Tract, treating hikers to mature scrub forest and sandhills along its 8.3 miles. It is part of the Florida State Forests Trailwalker Program.

2. **Walk-In Cave**. From Holder Mine, follow the connector trail to Loop A. Turn left and follow the Florida Trail's orange blazes south, passing the A–B Cross-Trail and crossing Trail 13. After 2.9 miles, you reach the walk-in cave. Round-trip is 5.8 miles.

3. **Lizzie Hart Sink**. Tackle the "karst corner" of Loop D, the most fascinating part of the Citrus Tract, on a day hike featuring Lizzie Hart Sink, surface limestone features, sinkholes, and rocky crevices leading to caves. Follow Trail 13 south of CR 480 to a parking area at the trail crossing. Hike west on Loop D past the deep sinkhole and intermittent stream, crossing CR 480 to continue past Brush Sink up to Lizzie Hart Sink. A round-trip to Lizzie Hart Sink from the parking area is 4.8 miles; if you pull off on CR 480 and hike in instead, it's 2.6 miles.

CAMPING AND LODGING

If you tackle this trail as a series of day hikes instead of a backpacking trip, base camp at either **Holder Mine** or **Mutual Mine**. Each holds a site or two for walk-ins, but to guarantee a spot, reserve ahead at 1-877-879-3859, floridastate forests.reserveamerica.com. Lodgings in Inverness include **Holiday Inn Express** (903 E Gulf to Lake Highway, Lecanto, FL 34461; 352-341-3515) ihg.com; and **Central Motel** (721 US 41 S, Inverness, FL 34450; 352-726-4515, centralmotel.com).

Fort Cooper State Park

TOTAL DISTANCE: 5 miles in a network of three interconnected loops. Longer and shorter options are possible.

HIKING TIME: 2–2.5 hours

DIFFICULTY: Easy to moderate

USAGE: $2–3 per vehicle. Open 8 AM to sunset. Leashed pets welcome.

TRAILHEAD GPS COORDINATES:
28.8089, -82.3039

CONTACT INFORMATION: Fort Cooper State Park, 3100 S Old Floral City Road, Inverness, FL 34450 (352-726-0315, floridastateparks.org/park/Fort-Cooper)

With a picnic area and playground along Lake Holathlikaha, and gentle trails winding through the woods, Fort Cooper State Park is a great place for a family outing, but the reason for this state park isn't as pleasant. The park preserves a chapter of Florida history from the Second Seminole War, when more than 300 sick and injured soldiers stopped to regroup and recuperate after a month-long battle at the Cove of the Withlacoochee. A hastily built log fort protected the men when the Seminole laid siege several days later. Named for Major Mark Anthony Cooper, who was charged with protecting the soldiers, the fort was later abandoned. The military road from Fort King in Ocala to Fort Brooke in Tampa passes through the park and is incorporated into two of the hiking trails.

GETTING THERE

From I-75, take exit 329, Wildwood. Turn west on FL 44, driving 11 miles to Inverness. Take US 41 south to Old Floral City Road; turn left at the light. Cross the Withlacoochee State Trail, a popular biking trail. Turn right, following the signs 1.6 miles to the park entrance. After paying your Florida State Parks entrance fee, follow the winding road back into the woods. Pass by the grassy parking area at the Sandhill Trail Loop and continue on to the paved parking area. Take the first paved turn to loop back and park near the entrance sidewalk down to the Lake Holathlikaha picnic area.

THE HIKE

Start your hike of the park's trail network by walking down the paved path to the picnic area along the marshy lake.

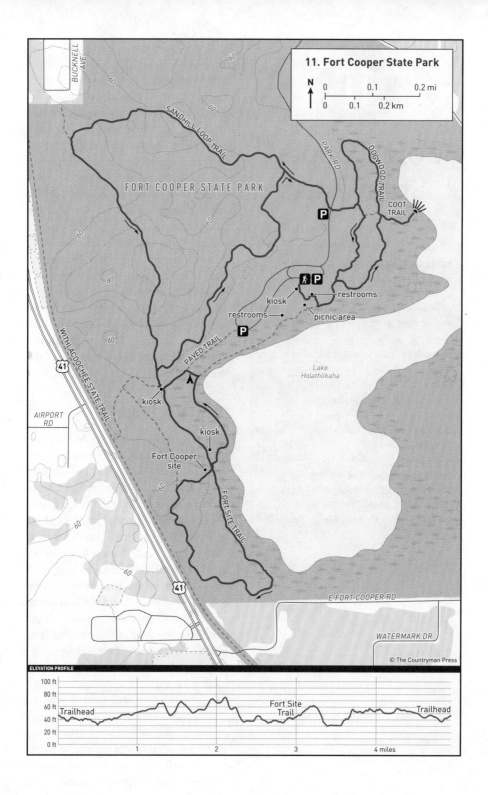

11. Fort Cooper State Park

N
0   0.1   0.2 mi
0   0.1   0.2 km

BUCKNELL AVE

60

60

SANDHILL LOOP TRAIL

FORT COOPER STATE PARK

PARK RD

DOGWOOD TRAIL

COOT TRAIL

P

60

60

80

P

kiosk

restrooms

P

restrooms

picnic area

PAVED TRAIL

60

WITHLACOOCHEE STATE TRAIL

41

AIRPORT RD

kiosk

Lake Holathlikaha

kiosk

Fort Cooper site

FORT SITE TRAIL

60

60

60

E FORT COOPER RD

41

WATERMARK DR

© The Countryman Press

ELEVATION PROFILE

100 ft
80 ft
60 ft
40 ft
20 ft
0 ft

Trailhead

Fort Site Trail

Trailhead

1   2   3   4 miles

LAKE HOLATHLIKAHA

You'll pass an interpretive kiosk with an overview of the historical significance of Fort Cooper, followed by a picnic pavilion and the main restrooms. Where the paved path comes to a T intersection, turn left and look for the large DOGWOOD TRAIL sign. This easy interpretive loop shows off a mesic hammock, the climax community that takes over when pine flatwoods aren't subject to regular wildfires. Hardwood trees dominate the forest. Loblolly bay and southern magnolia compete for space, both showing off their glossy leaves. Frequent benches allow for quiet moments of reflection along the trail.

The first bench sits just before a four-way junction of trails. Turn right. Soon after is the first of many trail maps along the park's trails with YOU ARE HERE symbols on them to help you navigate the trail system. The landscape is a little odd and undulating—a reshaping of the forest by phosphate pits. Saw palmettos, sweetgum, and live oak cling to the mis-

shapen hills. Florida's phosphate boom started in the late 1890s, just after a big freeze killed off the commercial citrus industry. Miners came from all over the south, digging small claim stake pits such as these or working in larger operations such as the ones at Rainbow Springs (Hike 1).

The Short Loop junction joins in from the left. Turn right, following the brief Coot Trail spur toward the marshy shore of Lake Holathlikaha, winding through a forest of laurel oak past moss-covered limestone outcroppings. The trail ends along the edge of the marsh, where herons, coots, and egrets browse the grassy wetlands. You've walked 0.5 mile. Return to the trail junction. Turn right to continue on the Dogwood Trail. A NATURE TRAIL sign points you down the Long Loop. The hardwood forest is primarily a climax forest, with many laurel oaks. Four-inch-wide specimens of shelf fungus grow like steps along the trunks of some of the oak trees. As you get deeper into the hardwood hammock, the forest becomes more lush, the canopy interwoven by tree limbs high above. Saw palmetto grows in clumps throughout the understory.

The trail narrows to a footpath—most of the trails at Fort Cooper State Park have been widened to the width of a road, but not this one—and is covered with fallen oak leaves. You pass another locator map before the trail veers left, turning back on itself to make the loop. Notice the many weathered stumps half-hidden by the undergrowth, the remains of a virgin oak forest that covered these hills. They were cut by hand in the 1930s after the phosphate boom subsided.

At a junction with a side trail at 0.9 mile, turn right. This footpath leads to the park road and across it to reach the kiosk at the Sandhill Loop Trail. Pick up a map here. A nice narrow connector trail leads you to a forest road. Turn left. Although the Sandhill Loop Trail is an excellent destination for wildlife watching—we came across at least a dozen deer and a flock of turkeys along it—it is entirely on forest roads. You reach the main junction at the top of the loop, where piles of dirt are currently stored in an open area. Turn right. This is an upland trail, focused on the highest, driest habitat in the park. This loop also has its own set of locator maps. Side roads that are not a part of the route are marked with DO NOT ENTER or SERVICE ROAD signs. You may see heavy equipment or piles of brush along this walk, as we did since restoration is still ongoing to return this portion of the park to the longleaf forest that stood here when Fort Cooper was built. A thicket of lowbush blueberries tops one of the hills, where pawpaw also blooms in late spring.

After a long, curving and slow descent among the oaks and pines, the Sandhill Loop comes to a T with a service road, 1.7 miles into your hike. There is a locator map soon after, and you hear the sounds of traffic along US 41. Continuing down the moderate grade, you see young candle-stage longleaf pines rising from the wiregrass, and clumps of saw palmetto in the open understory. Spanish moss hangs in heavy draperies on some of the taller oaks. A gopher tortoise browses in a healthy patch of sandhill. In late spring, the gopher apple—a favorite food of the gopher tortoise—blooms here. Winding up and over and down again along gently undulating hills, the sandy road has deer tracks, fox tracks, and raccoon tracks to follow. When you get to the SANDHILL LOOP TRAIL sign, you've hiked 2.3 miles. Pass by the return loop at this junction and walk straight ahead, coming out at a four-way intersection of trails with a sign that indicates that the path you've been on is a part of the Old Military Road between Fort King and Fort Brooke, a route which soldiers began to construct in 1825. The kiosk at this intersection explains the timeline of the Second Seminole War, which began in December 1835 farther south along this road, on a site now protected as Dade Battlefield State Park in Bushnell.

At this junction, walk straight ahead past the kiosk (with it to your right) along the Old Military Road to start a loop along the Fort Site Trail. The road winds through the forest past a bench and emerges at a clearing, where the next kiosk details the siege of Fort Cooper. Under the direction of General Winfield Scott, more than 5,000 soldiers were marching to Fort Brooke after a pitched battle with the Seminole at the Cove of the Withlacoochee. They camped on the bluffs overlooking spring-fed Lake

Holathlikaha. General Scott decided to leave the sick and wounded with Major Mark Anthony Cooper, and promised to return in nine days. Major Cooper had the men build a log fort for their protection. Within days, the Seminole attacked, drove off the cattle, and held the soldiers under siege. The siege did not break until the relief soldiers that General Scott had promised returned and drove them off. The fort remained in use on and off through the remainder of the war.

The bleachers are here for the annual reenactment that occurs during Fort Cooper Days each spring. Walk past them for the panorama of Lake Holathlikaha, and to see a picket wall that illustrates how Fort Cooper would have been built of pine logs pointed at the ends

and buried closely together. Continue straight ahead along the Old Military Road, leaving the clearing to enter the shade of ancient oaks on the bluff above the lake. Passing a couple of benches, you come to a FORT SITE TRAIL sign at 2.8 miles. Turn right to follow the footpath into the shady hardwood hammock. Removal of hurricane-damaged trees means the park boundary fence is visible as the trail curves right, and traffic noise echoes in off US 41.

Along a bend in the trail, you reach a FORT SITE sign. Follow the arrow. The path leads to the picket wall and the view of Lake Holathlikaha. Walk towards the lake, where a forest road from the left leads downhill at an angle. To the right is an opening in the marsh that might be the spring the soldiers used. The for-

RECONSTRUCTION OF A PORTION OF THE PICKETS OF FORT COOPER

est road guides you down to the sandy lakeshore of this broad lake, a low spot surrounded by prairie grasses. Follow the track along the sandy shore of the lake. At 3.6 miles, there is a right curve along the lake. Benches sit in the shade of the oaks on the bluff, a primitive campsite. It's mainly in place for long distance cyclists on the Withlacoochee State Trail: call ahead to reserve, and there's a $5 per night fee. This is a decision point for the rest of your hike. If you continue following the lakeshore, you end up right back at the picnic area and can call this a 4-mile hike. To add on another mile and see more of the park's trails, turn left and walk up past the benches to meet a paved path. This accessible path leads to the parking area to the right. Turn left.

It doesn't take long to return to the kiosk at the Old Military Road junction. Straight ahead, the paved path leads to the Withlacoochee State Trail, one of Florida's premier bike paths. Walk in that direction very briefly to the OLD MILITARY ROAD sign. Turn right to rejoin the Sandhill Loop Trail, and stay right at the next Y intersection to follow the east side of the loop. This side is shorter than the west side you traversed earlier. The trail sticks to the ecotone between sandhill and hardwood forest, so it's much shadier. The hardwood forest descends the hills towards the lake, and the sandhill forest is on your left, topped with longleaf pine and wiregrass in places. Occasionally the path veers into the hardwood forest. Around 4 miles, there is a depression in the forest, a large sinkhole. After you pass the next locator map, it only takes a few more minutes to reach the top of the loop. At this T intersection, turn right. Watch for the footpath that tunnels through the forest and back to the Sandhill Loop

Trail kiosk and parking area. Cross the park road to follow the connector trail back to the Dogwood Trail. Turn right when you reach it. You've walked 4.6 miles.

The Dogwood Trail is both familiar-feeling and new as you walk this final stretch around its loop. At the SHORT LOOP sign, keep right to stay on the outer loop. Continue straight through the oak forest. The trail veers left around a small solution sinkhole, a deep depression filled with leaves and saw palmetto. Arriving back at the original four-way junction of trails, continue straight ahead, passing the PICNIC AREA sign on your right. You emerge out at the big DOGWOOD TRAIL sign and the view of Lake Holathlikaha. Continue along the paved path back to the parking area to complete a 5-mile hike.

OTHER HIKING OPTIONS

1. **Fort Site Trail**. Focus your visit on a walk to the fort site, with a wander along the shore of Lake Holathlikaha. Starting at the first of the Seminole War interpretive kiosks near the main recreation area restrooms—Fort Cooper Latrine—continue down to and along the lakeshore in the opposite direction from the Dogwood Trail, following the shoreline curve until it leads you up a forest road to the fort site. Walk back along the Old Military Trail for additional interpretive stations. When you get to the 4-way junction, use the paved path to the right to reach the far end of the parking area (28.807342, -82.306062). Take a side path down to the lake and walk back along it to the main recreation area for a 1.1-mile walk. Extend this by taking the Long and Short Loops instead of the

Old Military Trail, making for a 2-mile hike.

2. **Sandhill Loop**. Of all of the trails in the park, the Sandhill Loop Trail is the best one for spotting wildlife, especially gopher tortoises, woodpeckers, and fox squirrels. Park at the grassy Sandhill Loop Trail parking area near the trailhead kiosk and follow the signs around the loop for a 2-mile hike.

3. **Dogwood Trail**. The most natural-feeling of the hiking trails at this state park, this interpretive trail stays in the shade for most of its 1-mile loop. Be sure to take the Coot Trail spur trail to the marsh (adding another 0.25 mile). Using the Short Loop, cut this walk down to less than 0.75 mile.

4. **Accessible Trail**. Follow the park drive through the parking areas to where it curves past the entrance to the paved bike path (28.807342, -82.306062) and park in one of the nearby spaces. From here, follow the paved portion of the Fort Site Trail connector to the paved Withlacoochee State Trail. While this route doesn't take you to the fort, it does meander through habitats representative of the park as a whole. A round-trip to the Withlacoochee State Trail is 0.9 mile. There are many benches along the route.

CAMPING AND LODGING

Central Motel, 721 US 41 S, Inverness, FL 34450 (352-726-4515, centralmotel.com)

Moonrise Resort, 8801 E Moonrise Lane, Lot 18, Floral City, FL 34436 (352-726-2553, moonriseresort.com)

Chinsegut Wildlife and Environmental Area

Tempted by free land from the Armed Occupation Act of 1842—one of the tools the US Government used to force Native Americans out of Florida—Colonel Bird M. Pearson came from South Carolina in the late 1840s to the high rolling hills north of what would become Brooksville. Bringing his family and slaves, he staked his claim for 160 acres and established a plantation on the highest hill in the region. He called it Mt. Airy. After the Civil War, the Ederington family purchased the estate and expanded the home into a grand manor before abandoning it.

In 1904, when author Elizabeth Robins bought the property with her brother Raymond, much work had to be put into the ruined manor and its grounds. Colonel Raymond Robins called it Chinsegut (chin-SEE-gut) after the Inuit word for "spirit of lost things." Raymond, his sister, and his wife were activists, involved in politics and business worldwide. They lectured for peace, protested for voting rights for women, worked with the International Red Cross, and championed the causes of laborers. As a result, many prominent people visited them at Chinsegut Hill, including Thomas Edison, J. C. Penney, and Helen Keller.

By 1932, the Robins had donated their Chinsegut Hill Sanctuary to the US Department of Agriculture. They were allowed to live in the manor for the rest of their lives. Much of the property was used as an experimental station to grow plants and trees from around the world, but wooded portions were largely left untouched. Among the Sanctuary's treasures were 400 acres of virgin longleaf pine, broad open prairies, and hardwood forests that had never seen an ax. After the Robins' deaths in the 1950s, Lisa von Borowsky, the Robins' gardener since 1924, advocated for the property

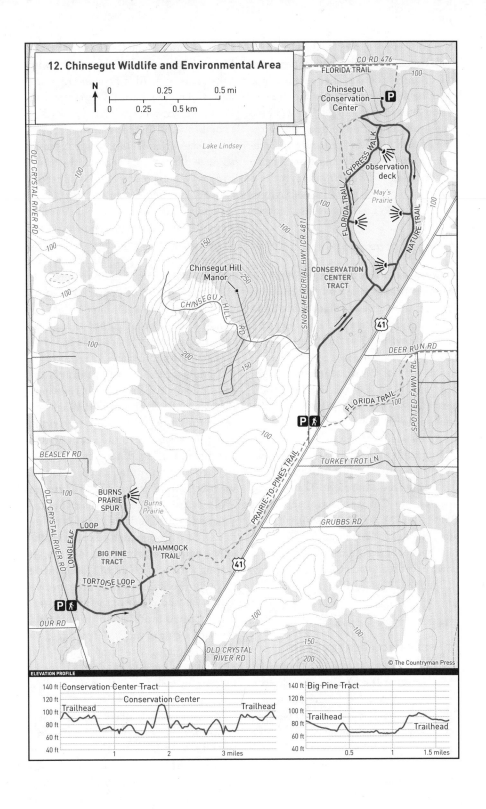

12. Chinsegut Wildlife and Environmental Area

N

0   0.25   0.5 mi
0   0.25   0.5 km

CO RD 476
FLORIDA TRAIL
100

Chinsegut
Conservation
Center — P

observation
deck

FLORIDA TRAIL / CYPRESS WALK

May's
Prairie

NATURE TRAIL

100

CONSERVATION
CENTER
TRACT

Lake Lindsey

100

150

Chinsegut Hill
Manor

250

CHINSEGUT HILL RD

200

150

SNOW MEMORIAL HWY (CR 481)

41

DEER RUN RD

SPOTTED FAWN TRL

FLORIDA TRAIL

100

P 🚶

TURKEY TROT LN

BEASLEY RD

100

BURNS
PRARIE
SPUR

Burns
Prairie

LOOP

LONGLEAF

BIG PINE
TRACT

HAMMOCK
TRAIL

TORTOISE LOOP

P 🚶

OUR RD

OLD CRYSTAL RIVER RD

PRAIRIE-TO-PINES TRAIL

41

GRUBBS RD

OLD CRYSTAL
RIVER RD

150
200

0

100

© The Countryman Press

ELEVATION PROFILE

Conservation Center Tract

140 ft
120 ft
100 ft — Trailhead   Conservation Center   Trailhead
80 ft
60 ft
40 ft
            1   2   3 miles

Big Pine Tract

140 ft
120 ft
100 ft — Trailhead
80 ft   Trailhead
60 ft
40 ft
            0.5   1   1.5 miles

to become a permanent nature reserve. She'd become a leading environmentalist in Florida. She donated her own funds to open the nature center (now the Conservation Center) in the 1970s. The Big Pine Tract was transferred to the FWC (Florida Fish and Wildlife Conservation Commission) in 1989. With their special focus on education and conservation, the two tracts of Chinsegut Wildlife and Environmental Area (WEA) are closed to hunting.

GETTING THERE

Both tracts of the Chinsegut WEA lie between Brooksville and Nobleton off US 41, south of the Withlacoochee State Forest headquarters and 6 miles north of Brooksville. The Prairie-to-Pines trailhead is the easiest one to find, at the corner of Snow Memorial Highway and US 41. For the Big Pine trailhead (28.599042, -82.377272), as you're headed north from Brooksville on US 41, make a left onto Crystal River Road and continue along this narrow, winding road for about 2 miles until you reach the trailhead on the right. The parking area at the Chinsegut Conservation Center (28.631216, -82.353559), which is along Lake Lindsey Road (CR 476) 0.5 mile east of Snow Memorial Highway, is down a dirt road and is only open Friday to Saturday, 8 AM–2 PM.

THE HIKES

CONSERVATION CENTER TRACT

Starting from the May's Prairie parking corral, stop at the kiosk and pick up a trail map. A portion of the statewide Florida National Scenic Trail (FNST) is routed through the Conservation Center Tract, so you will see orange blazes and FNST symbols along the first part of this loop. Walking past the sign, head into the pine forest along the broad path. The forest road is marked with posts with hiker markers. At a fork in the path, keep right and head up the grassy path. Passing a marker beneath the pines dedicated to A. B. Tucker, the trail continues past a series of sinkholes at 0.5 mile, shallow depressions beneath the forest canopy. When you reach the Chinsegut Nature Trail at 0.75 mile, turn left to walk clockwise along the loop. Passing a maintenance shed, you come up to the first of several scenic overlooks along May's Prairie. At 1.1 miles, a boardwalk leads to a wildlife blind on the prairie's rim, where you'll find yourself spending quite a bit of time watching the flocks of sandhill cranes that gather among the tall grasses. Nicely shaded, it's an excellent spot for photography.

Longleaf pines rise tall through the sandhill habitat as the terrain rises gently toward the Cypress Walk. When you reach the CYPRESS WALK sign, turn right. A sinkhole sits off to the north, with a short side trail leading to it and looping around it, pointed out by a small wooden SINKHOLE sign. The Cypress Walk is much narrower than the forest road you've followed to this point, and winds through lush oak hammocks dense with saw palmetto and ferns. At a spot with a view across the prairie through the live oaks, an interpretive sign talks about one of the more interesting inhabitants of Chinsegut Hill, the tiger salamander. Growing 6 to 8 inches long, these "tiny tigers" live along the boggy edge of the prairie, feeding on earthworms, slugs, snails, and other invertebrates.

As you reach a narrow boardwalk, continue into a cypress dome along the edge of May's Prairie, zigzagging through the trees to turn right onto an overlook along the prairie's edge.

LOOKING OUT OVER MAY'S PRAIRIE FROM THE CYPRESS WALK

Crickets and frogs add to the chorus of songbirds along the grassy fringe. The Cypress Walk emerges at the outer loop at a set of benches. Turn left. Continue up through the pine woods to the trail junction. Turn right to walk uphill to the Conservation Center, which you reach at 2 miles. Open only on weekends, it's an interesting spot, with a short interpretive loop around the old Bishop Homestead, and the nature center with its many native creatures.

After you visit the homestead site, head back down the hill to the loop trail. Turn left and continue past the Cypress Walk. The broad forest road continues through the pine woods down to another excellent view over May's Prairie from the Hammock Spur Trail, looking across to the wildlife blind. Watch the edge of the prairie for wading birds. Reaching the Big Hickory Spur after 2.9 miles,

take a wander down this narrow path to a view across the wet prairie covered in American lotus, with cypress trees outlined against the far shore. As you leave, turn right. Head on down the broad forest road to complete the Nature Trail Loop at 3.2 miles, backtracking along the Prairie-to-Pines Trail to the trailhead for a 4-mile hike.

BIG PINE TRACT

A rare example of a virgin longleaf pine forest in Central Florida, the Big Pine Tract was preserved by the Robins family for future generations to visit. You'll thank their foresight as you walk the loop through this towering pine forest. Starting at the kiosk, turn right to follow the Longleaf Loop. Although the hike is along forest roads, the trees make it worth the visit. Instead of a dark, dense forest, the Big Pine Tract is open,

BENEATH ANCIENT LONGLEAF PINES ON THE BIG PINE TRACT

undergoing sandhill restoration as the understory is managed to cull out the thickets that cropped up from too many years without a prescribed burn. Walking counterclockwise, you pass a shed and enter the forest of giant trees after 0.25 mile. Since the pines are extremely tall and skinny, it almost seems like they aren't as large as they actually are. Step back and look up. It helps to have a friend along to put it all in perspective. Many of the pines show catfaces from the turpentine industry, but these are true giants, some growing with unusual curved trunks and spreading crowns.

As you continue along the loop, the scent of pine fills the air, compliments of the many small longleaf pines in their grass stage, distinguishable from wiregrass only by the deep green of their needles. These seedlings germinate in the winter. Passing a sinkhole full of forest debris, you come up to an intersection with the Hammock Trail and the

Tortoise Loop after 0.5 mile. Turn right and take a short jog down the Hammock Trail. It connects with the Prairie-to-Pines Trail almost immediately along a bayhead. Turn left and follow the narrow path, which follows the ecotone between sandhills and hardwood hammock. After the Hammock Trail drops you back on the main Longleaf Loop, turn right and continue down to the Burns Prairie Spur, which heads down a shady path through grand old live oaks to the edge of a large, sometimes-wet prairie. The trail becomes indistinct as you come to the overlook along the water, so turn around and retrace your steps. Returning to the Longleaf Loop, you've hiked a mile. Turn right, and make a sharp left at the next intersection so you don't wander off on a perimeter trail.

The remainder of the hike loops through the pine forest—younger pines, not the old-growth ones at the beginning of the hike—with little change in landscape along the way. The understory is dense, but here and there you see colorful aster and phlox. At the next trail junction, make a sharp left and continue down a long straightaway, partially shaded by the pines. You pass a forest road. Continue past the incoming Tortoise Loop to complete the 1.6-mile hike at the trailhead kiosk.

OTHER HIKING OPTIONS

1. **Nature Center Loop**. Chinsegut Conservation Center and its parking area are open on Friday and Saturday mornings, providing a 1.8-mile loop down to May's Prairie for small children and those who can't walk as far. The kids will love the terrariums and aquariums filled with native wildlife inside the conservation center.

2. **Prairie-to-Pines Connector**. The two major loop trail systems at this preserve—Nature Center Tract and Big Pine Tract—are joined together by a linear trail, the 1.1-mile Prairie -to-Pines Trail. It passes through the May's Prairie trailhead at US 41 and Snow Memorial Highway, so it's possible to make one long day hike (7.8 miles total) out of the above two loops and the connector. However, the Prairie-to-Pines Trail is a fence line trail—out in the open with a lot of cows nearby—and gets into some seriously soggy terrain as it connects with the Big Pine Tract, although it does showcase the historic FL 5 highway bridge as it nears that loop.

3. **Chinsegut Hill Retreat** (28.618894, -82.365058). It's a short drive from the Prairie-to-Pines trailhead up Snow Hill. Follow the signs that lead you up to the restored manor house and its gardens. Sitting atop the highest hill in the region, at 274 feet above sea level, the Manor House is a Florida treasure, its earliest foundation dat-

MANOR HOUSE AT CHINSEGUT HILL

ing back to the 1840s. Surrounding it are grand old live oaks and gardens that grew out of plantings started by Lisa von Borowsky in 1925 under Margaret Robins' direction. Lisa cultivated the grounds, planting azaleas, camellias, and roses, and planted 13 different varieties of bamboo; the thick stand behind the manor is said to have started with cuttings from Thomas Edison. Once the land was transferred to the USDA, CCC Camp A-1 undertook a beautification project throughout the manor grounds under the coordination of a landscape architect and Ms. von Borowsky's watchful eye. Although the trails built in the 1930s have mostly been swallowed up by vegetation, a meander around the manor grounds, down to the CCC buildings, and around the retreat center cottages will net a pleasant walk of at least a mile with outstanding views from the hilltop. Museum tours are offered Monday to Friday 10–4, Saturday 10–5, and Sunday 12–6; details at chinseguthillmuseum.com. Ramble through the gardens is on your own; the cottages are available for overnight stays.

CAMPING AND LODGING

Chinsegut Hill Retreat, 22495 Chinsegut Hill Road, Brooksville, FL 34601 (352-799-5400, chinseguthillretreat .com)

Hog Island Recreation Area/Withlacoochee State Forest, 9274 CR 635, Bushnell, FL 33513 (1-877-879-3859, floridastateforests.reserveamerica .com)

Croom River Trail Loop

TOTAL DISTANCE: A 3.9-mile loop using the Blue Loop Trail and a portion of the Florida Trail through the southern section of the Croom Tract of Withlacoochee State Forest.

HIKING TIME: 1.5–2 hours

DIFFICULTY: Easy to moderate

USAGE: Free. Open sunrise to sunset. Leashed pets welcome.

TRAILHEAD GPS COORDINATES: 28.526801, -82.218817

CONTACT INFORMATION: Withlacoochee State Forest, Recreation/Visitor Center, 15003 Broad Street, Brooksville, FL 34601-4201 (352-797-4140, freshfromflorida.com)

Occupying one tiny corner of the 20,000-acre Croom Tract of Withlacoochee State Forest, the Croom River Trail Loop is only a small piece of the larger puzzle of Florida's largest state forest, which draws a steady stream of outdoors enthusiasts to its many campgrounds, equestrian and biking trails, paddling routes, motorcycle trails, and of course plenty of hiking. Easily accessed from major highways and pleasant to hike, this trail treats you to the shade of ancient live oak trees, the haunting beauty of cypress swamps, and the lazy curves of the Withlacoochee River flowing north. It's on those river bluffs where you walk a portion of Florida's greatest hiking treasure, the statewide Florida Trail, first established in 1966. One of eleven National Scenic Trails in the United States, it connects beauty spots like this from one end of Florida to the other. Consider this short hike an introduction, a gateway to exploring more of the Florida Trail through this region.

GETTING THERE

From exit 301 (Brooksville/Ridge Manor) on I-75, drive east on FL 50 for 1 mile to the traffic light at Croom-Rital Road, just before the big bicycle bridge over the highway. Turn left. The road curves around and, after 0.25 mile, comes to an entrance for the Ridge Manor trailhead on the right, with a long stretch of parking adjoining the paved Withlacoochee State Trail, a popular bicycle path.

THE HIKE

From the parking area, walk up to the picnic area on the opposite side of the trail, and continue through it to the

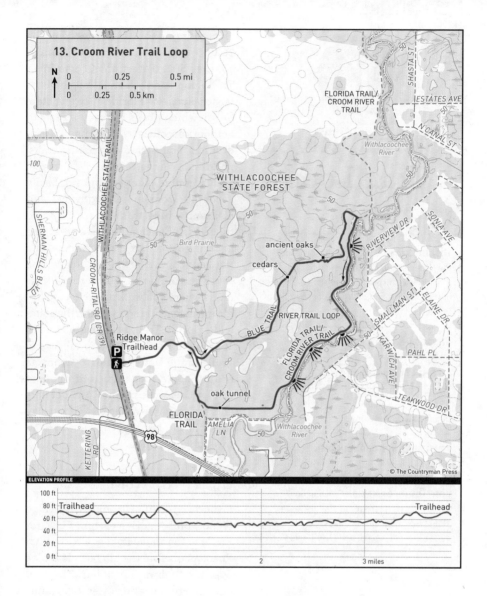

13. Croom River Trail Loop

N

| 0 | | 0.25 | | 0.5 mi |
| 0 | 0.25 | | 0.5 km | |

SHASTA ST

FLORIDA TRAIL/
CROOM RIVER
TRAIL

ESTATES AVE

N CANAL ST

Withlacoochee
River

WITHLACOOCHEE
STATE FOREST

SHERMAN HILLS BLVD

WITHLACOOCHEE STATE TRAIL

CROOM-RITAL RD (CR 39)

100

50

Bird Prairie

50

50

ancient oaks

cedars

RIVERVIEW DR

SONIA AVE

SMALLMAN ST

ELAINE DR

KARWICH AVE

PAHL PL

RIVER TRAIL LOOP

BLUE TRAIL

FLORIDA TRAIL/
CROOM RIVER TRAIL

50

Ridge Manor
Trailhead

P

oak tunnel

TEAKWOOD DR

FLORIDA
TRAIL

AMELIA
LN

Withlacoochee
River

50

KETTERING RD

98

© The Countryman Press

ELEVATION PROFILE

100 ft
80 ft Trailhead   Trailhead
60 ft
40 ft
20 ft
0 ft
            1   2   3 miles

fence line in the distance. A grand old live oak arches over the picnic table adjoining the kiosk at the entrance sign that says RIVER TRAIL. Sign in at the trail register and start your hike. The trail quickly transitions out of an oak hammock and into a pine plantation, where the footpath is softly carpeted in pine needles. As the landscape opens into sandhill habitat, you pass a Chickasaw plum, draped in bright white blooms in

February. At a double blaze, it's necessary to check and double-check the turn: at the time of our hike, these blazes were mirror-image of what they should be. Keep curving right.

After 0.5 mile, in an old pasture studded with blackberry bushes, you reach the first BLUE LOOP TRAIL sign. Turn left and follow the trail as it descends down to the tree line. Slipping through an oak hammock, it reaches a junction with an

SCENIC STOP ON THE WITHLACOOCHEE RIVER

old track. A swale—a marshy depression between ridges—may cradle a pond. Limestone boulders sit along its edge. This is a karst area that the Withlacoochee River meanders through, so there are few surface streams, but plenty of underground connections between the river and basins like these. Water marks on the trunks of trees bear witness to the fact that a rising river can seep up from underground and inundate this low area. The Withlacoochee rises from the Green Swamp and flows northward, with only a few minor tributaries feeding it to the south of here.

Climbing out of the¨ basin, the trail follows the blue blazes through the sandhill forest, where a haze of grasses blurs the open hilltops between stretches of oak hammocks. Live oaks dominate the canopy, their thick limbs draped in stringers of Spanish moss

atop a bed of lichens and resurrection ferns. The green leaves of butterfly orchids are high overhead; they bloom in the summer months, when you're less likely to hike. Even in winter, the tangle of oak limbs above casts a fair amount of shade. Live oaks generally do not drop their leaves until the new growth emerges, typically in early March.

When you start seeing cedar trees in the forest, things are about to change. Rounding a curve on a slight downhill at 1.2 miles, you circle an enormous live oak that sits across from an extensive cypress swamp. There are times when this swamp will be dry. If it is not, and the water is flowing, you should turn around and return to the trailhead. You've reached a chain of cypress swamps that are hydrologically connected to the river and will be walking along and between their basins

CYPRESS FLOODPLAIN ALONG THE BLUE LOOP

over the next 0.5 mile. They are hauntingly beautiful, especially when there is just enough water in them to reflect the trees. When they're dry, the forest of cypress knees in the grass—and the terrifying heights of the watermarks on the trunks—are fascinating.

Soon after the trail makes a sharp left turn, you pass a sinkhole. Just beyond it is a curious signpost that says WILD PIG WALLER, amid a stand of laurel oaks at 1.5 miles. The forest becomes denser around the next curve, with laurel oaks, water oaks, and slash pines intermingled. If the river has flooded in recent history, there will be a persistent shadow of watermarks across all of the vegetation. The unparalleled rains of Hurricane Irma in 2017 caused widespread flooding through this area, which is why there are watermarks most of the way along this hike, some well over our heads.

After 1.7 miles, the orange blazes of the Florida Trail are just ahead as the Blue Trail comes to a T intersection on the bluffs above the river. To continue along the loop, turn right. A few minutes later you arrive at a bench with a panorama of a bend in the Withlacoochee River. For more than a mile, the Florida Trail stays atop the sandy river bluff as you walk southbound, upstream to the river's flow. Old barbed wire fencing blocks river access in some places, the legacy of the former landowner. Through the vegetation, peek at towering cypresses on the river's far shore, and the occasional cabin. The bluff narrows for a stretch, dropping steeply off into cypress swamps, their swales receding into the distance. When the river floods, it fills these old channels. At a sandy curve on the river, it's tempting to slip down to the water's edge where the cypresses are particularly picturesque. Around the bend, the oxbow pond of cypresses sports some knees that rise 5 feet tall, worth a close look.

By the time you reach the next bench,

you've walked 2.6 miles. It doesn't have a great view, but it's a place to take a break. By now you have noticed the occasional wooden mile marker along this hike. We haven't mentioned them before because we can't figure out what they correspond to, other than to let you know you've walked another mile. Perhaps the countdown starts at Crooked River Campground (see *Other Hiking Options*). The MILE 4 sign is soon after this bench.

Vegetation crowds out the views of the river. Fenceposts used to hold up the old barbed wire fence almost look like railroad ties, and there is a good chance they were. In addition to the main rail line that once ran where the Withlacoochee State Trail is now, there were hundreds of narrow gauge rail line spurs through the cypress swamps along the river, the better for Lacoochee-based Cummer Sons Cypress Company, operating from 1922 to 1959, to strip the old-growth trees from this region. The only survivors were those unfit to go through the sawmill because of odd shapes, galls, and hollows within.

When the trail makes a final sharp right away from the river at 2.9 miles, it heads straight up a corridor that feels like a railroad grade. Sand live oaks form a tunnel effect down this straight and narrow section, which ends when the trail reaches an open grassy area in the sandhills. At this junction, which was not marked on our visit, the southbound Florida Trail turns sharply left to head for the forest's boundary gate. You do not. Stay right to curve around the grassy area and into the pines. By 3.4 miles, you've completed the loop, passing by the BLUE

GIANT CYPRESS KNEES IN AN OXBOW POND

LOOP TRAIL sign. Note the MILE 5 sign in this direction as you approach the Ridge Manor trailhead. Be sure to sign out at the trail register as you finish up.

OTHER HIKING OPTIONS

1. **Blue Trail Yoyo**. Cut 0.5 mile off the loop by taking the Blue Trail to the Withlacoochee River and returning on the same route for a 3.4-mile round-trip.

2. **Crooked River Trek**. Extend your hike by taking the Blue Trail and turning left instead of right onto the Florida Trail at the Withlacoochee River to follow it northbound to the trailhead at Crooked River Campground (28.5657, -82.2075). If you arrange for a pick-up (or a drop-off at Ridge Manor trailhead), do a 4.9-mile linear hike. Or hike up to the campground, take a break there and return around the loop for a 10.3-mile hike.

3. **Withlacoochee State Trail**. The Ridge Manor trailhead was originally built to provide access to this 46-mile paved bicycle path that stretches from Dade City towards Dunnellon on a former rail line. While the pavement isn't compelling to hike when you have footpaths to choose from, it's worth bringing your bicycle for a ride through the forest to Nobleton, an 18-mile round-trip.

4. **Cypress Lakes Preserve** (28.5186, -82.2069). On the other side of the Withlacoochee River, the Florida Trail meanders around cypress-lined lakes at this scenic county-managed preserve. Turn off FL 50 eastbound after you cross the Withlacoochee River onto a piece of the old highway behind Hernando County Fire Rescue Station 8. Park near the preserve sign and walk in for up to a 3-mile round-trip to see the ancient cypresses and wildflowers.

CAMPING AND LODGING

Half a dozen hotels are at the nearby junction of I-75 and FL 50, including **Holiday Inn Express Brooksville I-75** (30455 Cortez Boulevard, Brooksville, FL 34602; 352-796-0455, ihg.com). There are three Withlacoochee State Forest campgrounds 3.1 miles north of this trailhead off Croom-Rital Road, all along Silver Lake Road, all with access to the Withlacoochee River. A few walk-in sites are held. Reservations at 1-877-879-3859, floridastateforests .reserveamerica.com. Silver Lake is most popular for RVs. The campgrounds are: **Silver Lake Campground** (28.575042, -82.218751), **Cypress Glen Campground** (28.568133, -82.211348), and **Crooked River Campground** (28.565876, -82.206699).

14

Withlacoochee River Park

TOTAL DISTANCE: 6.8 miles on a route along a network of hiking trails, forest roads, and nature trails, with shorter options available.

HIKING TIME: 3–3.5 hours

DIFFICULTY: Easy to moderate

USAGE: Free. Open dawn to dusk. Leashed pets welcome on trails, but not at campsites or cabins.

TRAILHEAD GPS COORDINATES: 28.3447, -82.1205 (canoe landing parking), 28.3389, -82.1211 (south parking lot)

CONTACT INFORMATION: Withlacoochee River Park, 12449 Withlacoochee Boulevard, Dade City, FL 33525 (352-567-0264, pascocountyfl.net)

Along the Withlacoochee River Trail, dip a toe into one of Florida's largest and most important floodplains—the Green Swamp. It's the headwaters of four of Central Florida's largest rivers—the Hillsborough, the Ocklawaha, the Peace, and the Withlacoochee. The Green Swamp is no ordinary wetland. Instead of a vast sheet of water covering thousands of acres of floodplain forest, the Green Swamp is a patchwork of flatwoods, sandhills, and cypress domes, uplands and lowlands covering more than 860 square miles to the northeast of metropolitan Tampa. Showcasing a series of outstanding ancient oak hammocks and prairies, this hike follows both the Withlacoochee River Trail, built by the Florida Trail Association in the Green Swamp Wilderness, and a portion of the Withlacoochee River Park, a network of nature trails through an adjacent county park with camping, cabins, and plenty of activities for families.

GETTING THERE

Follow US 301 south from FL 50 (or I-75 exit 301, Brooksville/Ridge Manor, heading east) to the northern edge of Dade City. Turn left onto Truck Route US 301, making the immediate second left onto River Road. Follow the twisting, winding River Road 4.5 miles to its junction with Auton Road, just before the bridge. Turn right on Auton Road, then make the first left into the park. Stop at the kiosk at the park entrance for a trail map and an interpretive guide. Pull into the first parking lot on the left (28.3447, -82.1205) to start your loop hike.

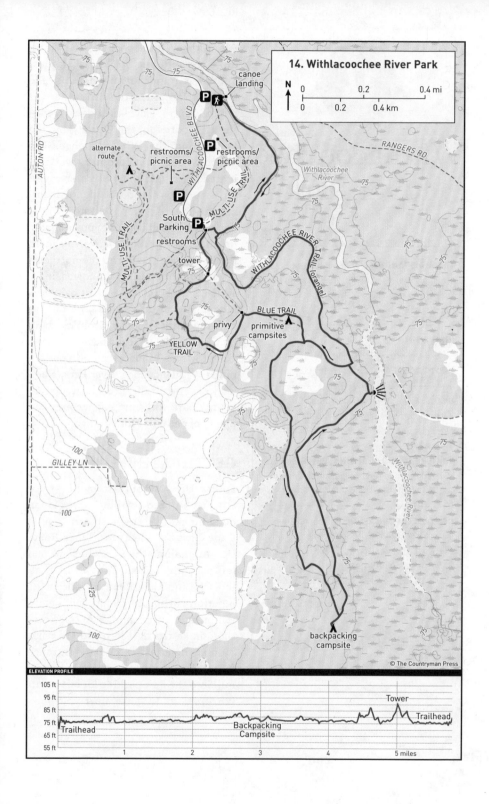

14. Withlacoochee River Park

N

| 0 | | 0.2 | | 0.4 mi |
| 0 | 0.2 | | 0.4 km | |

AUTON RD

RANGERS RD

canoe landing

alternate route

restrooms/ picnic area

restrooms/ picnic area

WITHLACOOCHEE BLVD

Withlacoochee River

South Parking

restrooms

MULTI-USE TRAIL

MULTI-USE TRAIL

tower

WITHLACOOCHEE RIVER TRAIL (orange)

75

BLUE TRAIL

privy

primitive campsites

YELLOW TRAIL

GILLEY LN

100

100

125

100

Withlacoochee River

backpacking campsite

© The Countryman Press

ELEVATION PROFILE

105 ft						Tower	
95 ft							
85 ft							Trailhead
75 ft	Trailhead						
65 ft				Backpacking			
55 ft				Campsite			
	1	2	3	4		5 miles	

HIKING ALONG THE WITHLACOOCHEE RIVER SOUTH OF THE CANOE LANDING

THE HIKE

Walk down to the canoe landing to take in the view of the Withlacoochee River, where its dark waters swirl mysteriously around cypress knees. The trailhead for the Withlacoochee River Trail starts to the right of the landing. Sign in at the trail register, where a memorial plaque in the box recalls the dedication of FTA volunteer Virginia Edwards, who participated in designing and building the Withlacoochee River Trail in the 1980s. Follow the orange blazes upriver as you enjoy the river views. Greatly aged interpretive signs appear along the first mile of trail, pointing out specific trees and shrubs. Live oaks swaddled in resurrection fern and lichens arch overhead as the trail cuts a broad corridor through the saw palmetto. At 0.4 mile, you'll cross a sand road. A prairie meadow stretches into the distance, a wide-open area sparkling with the lavender blooms of blazing star.

The trail reaches its first important junction at 0.6 mile, with blue blazes leading through a gap in the boundary fence between the water management land and the county park to the southernmost parking lot and restrooms. Stay with the orange blazes. The trail veers left beneath an ancient live oak with limbs that reach towards the ground, and turns to follow an outstanding corridor of live oak hammock, a ribbon dividing the open sandhill habitat from the wet prairie. Brilliant red and pink splotches of red blanket lichen cover the gnarled oak limbs that shelter the trail. Watch for telltale signs of armadillo: small holes dug into the sand at your feet. These shy armored creatures will jump more than a foot in the air if you startle them!

The trail veers left again at 0.8 mile, away from the tree line and into a low, open area of slash pine and damp ground, edging along the east side of the prairie. After crossing an area of tall grass, you emerge on a more distinct footpath, a mile into the hike. It crosses a sand road. Sweetgum trees share the forest with live oaks, laurel oaks, and dahoon holly. Ancient saw palmetto grows in clusters. Passing under a series of spreading live oaks, the trail gains a little elevation, and the habitat changes to pine flatwoods, with part of the river floodplain—a cypress swamp—to the left. Cross the sand road twice more, meandering back into an oak hammock.

After 1.6 miles, you'll reach the first junction of the orange-blazed loop trail. Turn right, crossing an open area and entering the forest just to the left of a large water oak into a pine hammock. For the next 0.25 mile, a wet prairie stretches to the left. Sandhill cranes pick their way through the tall grass. The trail becomes rough underfoot in places, thanks to the feeding activities of feral hogs. Like armadillos, they root up the ground—but they do it in a big way. Crossing over a forest road and through an opening in the fence, you reenter the park.

At 1.8 miles, a blue-blazed trail leads

BENEATH THE ANCIENT OAKS ALONG THE ORANGE-BLAZED LOOP

right to the primitive camping area inside the county park. Turn left and follow the orange blazes around the prairie, wandering past the knees of pond cypress, trees that permanently depend on the moisture from this low area to survive. The trail enters a grove of tall slash pine, then turns abruptly. Passing through the fence again to leave the park boundary, the trail crosses the sand road again and heads into an oak hammock. Black-eyed Susan lends a dash of color to the leaf-strewn forest floor. After

crossing an open meadow, the trail veers left along the tree line, meandering on a narrow dry strip between cypress swamp and wet prairie.

Crossing a forest road at 2.3 miles, you'll catch a glimpse of a large wet prairie along the boundary of this public land. Back in the oak hammock, sword ferns cluster alongside chunks of rounded limestone. An open area with tall dog fennel can provide a challenge—watch the footpath closely. It emerges into an area of tall laurel oak, where bracken fern grows in an open understory. At 2.9 miles, you reach a short blue-blazed trail that leads to a primitive campsite for backpackers. Pause to enjoy a break at the picnic table before you turn left, following the orange blazes into the pine flatwoods, where tall goldenrod provides splashes of bright color. Crossing the forest road yet again, the trail runs along the edge of a cypress swamp, part of the Withlacoochee River floodplain. You cross the forest road twice more, spending a short stretch in a narrow corridor of laurel oak paralleling the road. After the second crossing, the trail meanders down the line of where the pine flatwoods and the cypress swamp meet. You catch a glimpse of the open river, with a Boy Scout cabin on the far shore. The trail joins up with the forest road briefly before returning to the original loop junction at 4 miles.

Turn left to repeat a short stretch back through the pines along a prairie and through the gap in the fence. It's time to start rambling through the trail network at Withlacoochee River Park. Unlike the orange-blazed Withlacoochee River Trail, the trail network through the county park is primarily made up of forest roads. Turn right to follow the blue blazes towards the primitive campground. The trail gains a little elevation as it approaches the camping area. Keep right at the fork where both directions are blazed blue. Set in a mature live oak hammock, this primitive campground is a destination for family camping on the weekends, since it's a short enough distance from the south parking lot that backpacks aren't necessary to haul in your gear, yet it still allows families to rough it in this beauty spot in the woods, with a vault toilet set far enough but not too far away for comfort. As the loop comes back together (most campsites were on the other side of the loop), you walk beneath an archway of oaks, with a view of a prairie. At the next junction, at 4.5 miles, the vault toilet is straight ahead, as is a shortcut to the tower that shaves 0.4 mile off the rambling route along the prairies. If you don't need to hurry back, turn left to start walking along the yellow-blazed trail.

As the yellow blazes lead you down the forest road, the trail provides views through the oaks of the open prairie. The rattle-like calls of sandhill cranes rises from where they browse through the tall grasses, answered by a flock cruising overhead. The trail turns away from the prairie, entering an open sandhill habitat with small patches of scrub forest. Keep right at the next two trail intersections to head towards the observation tower; signs point the way. The trail pops into an open prairie and leads to a boardwalk, which was boarded over with a CLOSED sign on our visit. Instead, a mowed path paralleled it. Pass the red-blazed trail leading to Boardwalk #1 on the way to the tower, which becomes obvious as you leave the shade of the oaks and climb the sandhills. At 5.1 miles, rising several stories high, the tower does not—as most visitors expect—provide a view of the Withlacoochee River. The best view of the river is at the canoe launch and along this start of this hike. Instead, the view is more of an overview of habitats in this 406-acre county park, the sandhills and prairies and oak hammocks as viewed from above.

As a significant landmark, the tower is a good decision point on your hike. Follow the dirt road, blazed with blue-and-yellow-tipped posts, downhill towards the restrooms and south parking area, where the trail connects with the orange blazes just outside the fence line, allowing you to return to your car at the canoe launch parking area for a 5.8-mile hike.

Alternately, continue along the network of nature trails to loop around the west side of Withlacoochee River Park back to the canoe launch parking area. To do so, return the way you came up to the tower. Follow the yellow-tipped posts, descending off the sandhill and into the live oak hammock. Keep right at the fork into the shaded hammock, turning right to follow the yellow-and-red tipped posts from the bench at the Y intersection. Keep right at the next junction. Low prairie stretches out from both sides of the hammock as the trail emerges to cross Boardwalk #1, the showiest of the three at the park. A slight rise changes the habitat back to sandhill. Cross the paved multi-use path, paralleling it for a short stretch.

At 5.5 miles, you reach a junction with the trail coming in from the primitive camping area. Turn right and continue through the oak hammock, passing an unusually tall specimen of gopher apple. The roots of this small shrub stabilize the sandhill, and its fruits are delectable to the gopher tortoise. Rising back through sandhill, the trail veers into the forest. It circles around a low, broad sink-

MULTI-USE PATH IN THE CENTER OF THE PARK

hole pond before it approaches the camp-ground set beneath the canopy of oaks. As you pass a tent camping area, you find the nature trail frequently paralleled by the paved multi-use trail, which is open to cyclists. Crossing the paved road through the park, the nature trail joins the other branch of the yellow trail. Turn left. The last 0.25-mile of trail passes by picnic pavilions and restrooms. The nature trail ends at Pavilion 1. Join the multi-use trail for the last short stretch back to the canoe launch parking area, completing your 6.8-mile hike.

OTHER HIKING OPTIONS

1. **Nature Trail Loop**. For the younger set, the Nature Trail through Withla-coochee River Park hits the high-lights of the park while providing access to popular destinations like the observation tower, boardwalks, playgrounds, and restrooms. Follow the NATURE TRAIL signs and the yellow blazes for an easy 2.5-mile loop.
2. **Multipurpose Trail**. This paved trail allows families to bike through the park while enjoying the live oak can-opy and views of prairies that are also seen from the hiking trails. Including a paved spur to the canoe launch, a must for views of the Withlacoochee River, it is 2 miles in length.
3. **Withlacoochee River Trail**. While the orange-blazed Withlacoochee River Trail makes up most of the mileage of this hike, it is also a stun-ning destination in itself, thanks to being a narrow footpath through sce-nic places that sit outside the county park, closer to the river. Hiking out and back from the canoe launch trail-head to the primitive campsite at the far end of the loop and back nets you a respectable 5.6-mile hike.

CAMPING AND LODGING

Withlacoochee River Park, 12449 Withlacoochee Boulevard, Dade City, FL 33525 (352-567-0264, pasco countyfl.net)

Hampton Inn Dade City, 13215 US 301, Dade City, FL 33525 (352-567-5277, hilton.com)

Werner-Boyce Salt Springs State Park

TOTAL DISTANCE: 1.9 miles in two loops at two separate trailheads: the 0.6-mile habitat-focused Scenic Drive Trail, and the geologic wonders of the 1.3-mile Springs Trail.

HIKING TIME: 2–2.5 hours

DIFFICULTY: Easy

USAGE: $3 per vehicle. Open 8 AM to sunset. Leashed pets welcome.

TRAILHEAD GPS COORDINATES:
28.3072, -82.7057 (Scenic Trail),
28.2881, -82.7190 (Springs Trail)

CONTACT INFORMATION: Werner-Boyce Salt Springs State Park, 8737 US 19 N, Port Richey, FL 34668 (727-816-1890, floridastateparks.org/park/werner-boyce)

During the Ice Age, Florida was a balmy place and twice as broad as it is today. Megafauna roamed palmetto prairies and marshes. Giant armadillos as big as trucks shared the landscape with saber-toothed cats, mastodons and mammoths, and beavers the size of black bears. When the seas rose again, Florida's coastal plains were inundated. The Gulf Coast shoreline north of Anclote Key is a special place, the southernmost reach of a terrace of Suwannee limestone underlying salt marshes and seagrass beds that nurture marine life. Encompassing 4,000 mostly submerged acres along four miles of coastline in a densely populated region, Werner-Boyce Salt Springs State Park protects this rich estuary, the nesting grounds of two life-list birds for birders: the black rail and the endemic Scott's seaside sparrow.

You expect marshes and mudflats along Florida's Gulf Coast, along with maritime hammocks and palm hammocks, bayheads, and pine flatwoods. All of these can be sampled along the park's nature trails, with the Scenic Drive Trail providing a primer on forested coastal habitats. But what makes Werner-Boyce Salt Springs State Park special is its unusual collection of artesian salt springs. They rise up through tidal basins and marshes, pouring forth spring runs that make their way to the Gulf of Mexico. Two of the springs—Cauldron Spring and Salt Spring—are more than 300 feet deep. In all, there are eight named springs in the park. Five are along the aptly named Springs Trail, showcasing a scenic sweep of estuary north of Tampa Bay.

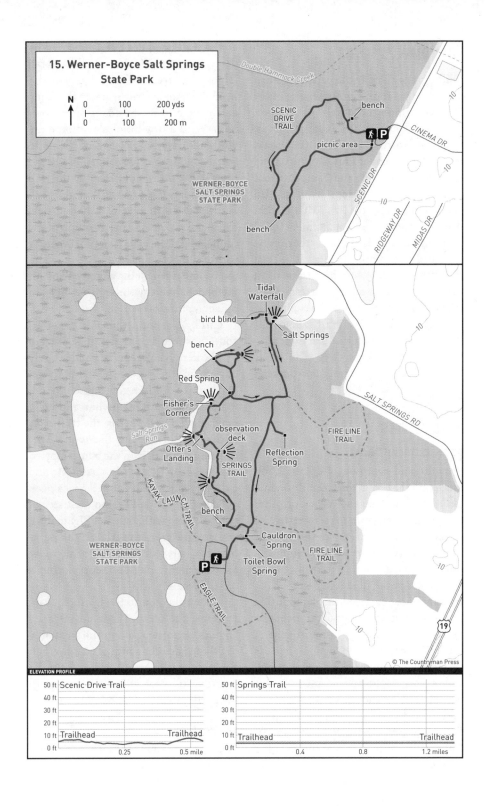

15. Werner-Boyce Salt Springs State Park

N
0   100   200 yds
0   100   200 m

Double Hammock Creek

SCENIC DRIVE TRAIL

bench

picnic area

CINEMA DR

SCENIC DR

RIDGEWAY DR

MIDAS DR

10

WERNER-BOYCE SALT SPRINGS STATE PARK

bench

Tidal Waterfall

bird blind

Salt Springs

bench

Red Spring

Fisher's Corner

observation deck

Salt Springs Run

Otter's Landing

SPRINGS TRAIL

Reflection Spring

SALT SPRINGS RD

FIRE LINE TRAIL

KAYAK LAUNCH TRAIL

bench

Cauldron Spring

WERNER-BOYCE SALT SPRINGS STATE PARK

Toilet Bowl Spring

FIRE LINE TRAIL

EAGLE TRAIL

19

10

© The Countryman Press

ELEVATION PROFILE

Scenic Drive Trail
50 ft
40 ft
30 ft
20 ft
10 ft Trailhead   Trailhead
0 ft
          0.25   0.5 mile

Springs Trail
50 ft
40 ft
30 ft
20 ft
10 ft Trailhead   Trailhead
0 ft
          0.4   0.8   1.2 miles

GETTING THERE

Finding the park is surprisingly easy once you've found your way to Port Richey, which is north of Tarpon Springs along US 19. From the east, your most direct access to this coast is via the Suncoast Parkway (toll road between Brooksville and Tampa) to exit 27. Follow FL 52 west for 9.2 miles to US 19. Alternatively, use I-75 exit 285, San Antonio, and drive west 23 miles to US 19. FL 52 dead-ends at the northernmost trailhead of the park, the Black Rail Trail (28.3313, -82.7074), but the best trails in the park are to the south. Turn south on US 19 off FL 52 and get in the right lane. For the Scenic Drive Trail (28.3072, -82.7057), drive 1.8 miles. Turn right onto Cinema Drive. After 0.25 mile cross Scenic Drive into the trailhead parking area.

THE HIKES

SCENIC DRIVE TRAIL

Providing an overview of upland habitats along the coast, the 0.6-mile Scenic Drive Trail is also the park's original footpath. Start your hike next to the kiosk and pay station at the NATURE TRAIL sign. A grassy path through the pine flatwoods, the trail passes a bench overlooking a small marsh pond. While the pines are scattered throughout this patch of flatwoods, the understory of saw palmetto and gallberry is quite dense. A side trail tempts you to explore: it leads to another overlook on the marsh pond, where you might spy a marsh rabbit half-hidden by undergrowth. It doesn't take long to transition from the pine flatwoods into a hardwood hammock. Habitat diversity is one of the delights of this loop.

The grass underfoot yields to soil as the trail becomes deeply shaded by young red maples, dahoon holly, and tall loblolly bay trees on the edge of a bayhead. Cinnamon fern thrives in the damp earth and crowds the edges of the footpath. With a tiny bit of elevation gain, you walk past an ancient saw palmetto with a long trunk. Towering loblolly bay trees and ferns remind you that the trail still parallels the bayhead, but more tall hardwoods are mixing in, including hickories and oaks. Passing through a low tunnel of palm fronds, the trail emerges within sight of a massive live oak reaching up and through the canopy. Pause at the bench, halfway through the hike, to reflect on this forest glen.

Circling around the oak, the trail continues into a palm hammock where the dark, rich soil resumes and loblolly bay crowds the edges. The footpath can get damp in this fern-rich stretch. Winding past southern magnolias and holly amid the bounty of ferns, the trail rises to the edge of the pine flatwoods. This last short stretch is in the sun, a mowed path between walls of saw palmetto and gallberry where tufts of wiregrass peep out of open spots. Passing a cluster of saw palmetto with long, healthy trunks, you emerge from the trail to the parking area, between the composting toilet and the picnic pavilion, completing a 0.6-mile walk.

To continue on to the Springs Trail, drive back to US 19. The main entrance is quite prominent along the west side of US 19, 3.4 miles south of FL 52. When you enter there, you'll drive along the park entrance road for 0.5 mile back to the parking area (28.2881, -82.7190).

SPRINGS TRAIL

Pick up a map from the kiosk in the main entrance parking area, and walk around the retention pond to get to its opposite

DEEP SHADE ALONG THE SCENIC DRIVE TRAIL

side. This interpretive trail begins at the SPRINGS TRAIL sign, which lists the named features along the loop and their distance (by the quickest route) from the trailhead. A little beyond that is the first TOILET BOWL SPRING sign. We laughed out loud and walked up along the spring run, past the Little Free Library and picnic area, to the sign marking the spring. The tannic water swirled like a flushed toilet. It does that when the tidal conditions are just right, which is when the other springs are suppressed by the tide. A marsh dense with giant leather ferns is at the upper end of the spring basin.

Walking back along the spring run, rejoin the main Springs Trail and cross the bridge over the run. The CAULDRON SPRING sign draws your attention to the bluff adjoining the run. The spring vent is under the bluff, adding significantly to the flow of this creek. When the tide is high, the spring isn't noticeable. Divers who have mapped this 320-foot-deep spring discovered that the narrow opening goes about 20 feet deep before it opens into a large cavern beneath

the sign on the bluff. However, to enter the cavern, they must pass through "the teeth" formed by stalactites and stalagmites at the cavern entrance, formations that prove that the cavern formed when the Gulf of Mexico was well offshore of where it is today. During the Ice Age, the Gulf may have been as much as 70 miles to the west. Snook swirl around the spring vent as the tide is flowing out.

Continue along the main trail and make the left at the SPRINGS TRAIL sign. The broad path, marked with green arrows, parallels the water along the edge of the pine flatwoods. The creek is just beyond the saw palmettos and young cedars. At a sharp curve in the trail, take one last look down this spring-fed tidal creek from a bench on a bluff overlooking the needlerush marsh. The boardwalk of the Kayak Launch Trail is on the other side of the creek. Returning to the trail, follow it beneath through the lush vegetation, an understory of palms capped with longleaf pines. At a break in this vibrant habitat, you come to an observation

CAULDRON SPRING LIES BENEATH THE BLUFF

point along the tidal creek, which, as it flows out towards the Gulf, joins with Salt Springs Run. You enjoy nice views across the marsh and meet it face-to-face at a boardwalk at 0.3 mile, with coastal panoramas on both sides. Right after the boardwalk ends, there is an observation deck up a short flight of stairs, just enough to provide another perspective on the scenery found here.

The tall, fluffy pines along this next stretch of trail are characteristic of those tapped for turpentine by sailors seeking naval stores along this coastline, although none bear the catface scars seen in more easy-to-reach locations on the Gulf Coast. They provide puddles of shade as the trail stays close to the tidal creek, offering several more stops for scenic views. A thinned palm hammock is home to Otter's Landing, a clearing with a picnic shelter near the water. You may see visitors walking past with pails and fishing poles, as the park has many little coves along the tidal creeks and anglers are welcome to try them all. Once past the picnic spot, you may notice mangroves along the edge of the creek. Leading you through another picturesque stretch of coastal pine flatwoods, the trail reaches a Y intersection. Ignore the arrow and head over to the water's edge instead, following the shoreline over to Fisher's Corner. This little peninsula has a picnic shelter, too, and a great view back towards where the tidal creek merges with Salt Springs Run.

Rejoining the main trail by walking around the picnic pavilion, you come up to an observation deck looking out across the marsh along Salt Springs Run. Pass the trail junction and continue paralleling the marsh through the coastal flatwoods. Stop at the RED SPRING sign. This spring is nestled under a black mangrove canopy. Step to the edge and look down. Tiny fish are swimming through the clear but reddish tannic waters. The footpath continues through a breezy maritime hammock, leading to the end of a peninsula into the open waters of Salt Springs Run, 0.5 mile into your hike. Keep choosing the pathways closest to the water for the best views. Circling back around, it offers a panorama across a needlerush marsh, where a dozen wood storks are roosting in a tall slash pine on the far shore. The trail loops back to Red Spring. Turn left to continue, following the trail up a slight rise to the next junction, this one with a bench facing the return route back to the parking area. You're not done exploring, so don't take that trail quite

yet. Pass the bench and come to a turn at the FIRE LINE TRAIL sign. Skip that side trip on this trek and make the sharp left. You're on your way to see the namesake of this preserve, Salt Spring.

The walk through the pine flatwoods yields to an open mud flat, where it's obvious from the needlerush and the gravel that a high tide can swamp this piece of trail. Cedars and palms edge the cove. Continue straight ahead, where the CAUTION ALLIGATORS sign catches your attention at 0.8 mile. It's there for good reason, as a large alligator has taken up residence near Salt Spring. Don't walk to the edge without looking around first. Salt Spring is just beyond that sign in the tannic water between the mangroves, but at high tide it's impossible to spot. At other times, it's tricky to see. The spring vent is only the width of a manhole cover, but research divers have discovered cavernous rooms beneath the vent, and have explored its plumbing system down to 350 feet, making it one of Florida's deepest springs. The high salt content of these springs led to their use during the Civil War for salt making.

FISHER'S CORNER, WITH JUVENILE
YELLOW-CROWNED NIGHT-HERON

REFLECTION SPRING

These salt works were far enough away from the open waters of the Gulf that the smoke rising from boilers didn't attract Union forces.

Continue past the spring to a bench overlooking the spring run. This is the site of the "tidal waterfall" you saw on the park map and entrance sign, and the farthest karst feature along the Springs Trail. When the Florida Geological Survey assessed this spring in 1960, they noted "the water passes under a 3-foot natural limestone bridge. The water surfaces and flows 75 feet to a second bridge that is about 10 feet long, under which the water flows and discharges in vigorous boils through three holes in Salt Springs Run." This churning of the spring waters is only visible on an outgoing tide. The trail ends around the corner at an overlook on the marsh, where a portable birding stand may be in place.

Leaving this peninsula, walk back across the low-lying marsh and down the straightaway through the pine flatwoods. You have the option of adding the FIRE LINE TRAIL to your hike when you reach the T intersection. It loops less than 0.5 mile through the flatwoods to the property boundary and back again. There are no karst features along it. Staying on the main trail, turn right, and then left at the bench. There is one more spring to visit before you end up back at Cauldron Spring, and it's the one that will wow you the most. Cauldron and Salt may be the deepest, but Reflection Spring is the showiest. Turn left at the REFLECTION SPRING sign.

The short access trail ends at a broad spring basin, where sunlight reflects off the scales of the tiny fish darting near the surface. It almost seems staged, as if it was a garden pond, but the giant leather ferns grew naturally around Reflection Spring. Only the seating area is landscaped. Sit on a bench and enjoy this unexpected oasis. It came to light in 2016, after a 3,000-pound log was hauled out of a stagnant basin. By the very next day, the water flowed clear and fish returned. Divers have not yet explored its depths, so it remains a mystery for now. The log is still sitting off to the side.

Returning to the main trail, turn left. You pass a firebreak road on the left that can also be hiked to add 0.25 mile of walking in a mesic hammock. Straight ahead, the Springs Trail continues through the pine flatwoods to complete its loop, reaching the bridge where Reflection Spring churns at the base of the bluff. Chuckle once more at Toilet Bowl Spring, and walk to the parking lot to finish a 1.3-mile hike.

OTHER HIKING OPTIONS

1. **Eagle Trail.** From the main entrance parking area, the Eagle Trail leads into the pine flatwoods to the south towards the location of an eagle nest, visible in the distance where the trail makes a hard left at a T. The trail ends at the entrance road. An out-and-back walk is 0.6 mile.
2. **Kayak Launch Trail.** Extending less than 0.25 mile from the main entrance parking area to the put-in, this trail begins as a boardwalk adjacent to the canoe rental concession (727-478-3146) and restrooms. It's a scenic 0.5-mile round-trip to the estuary.
3. **Springs Trail Extension.** In addition to the loop described above for the Springs Trail, there are two add-on loops at signs marked FIRE LINE TRAIL that ramble along firebreaks in the pine flatwoods east of the Springs Trail. By taking both loops, extend the hike at the Springs Trail to 1.9 miles. Add in the Eagle and Kayak Launch Trails to do 3 miles of hiking at the main entrance trailhead.
4. **Black Rail Trail** (28.3313, -82.7074). Under development, this birding ramble along the coastal marshes starts at a trailhead at the western end of FL 52. Unless it's been maintained recently, you may only be able to find the first spur trail to a view of the marshes, a 0.2-mile round-trip. In all, it's a mile's worth of wandering along the estuary edge.

CAMPING AND LODGING

Crews Lake Wilderness Park, 16739 Crews Lake Drive, Spring Hill, FL 34610 (727-861-3038, pascocountyfl .net), tents only.

Holiday Inn Express Port Richey, 10619 US 19, Port Richey, FL 34668 (727-868-1900, ihg.com)

Inn on the Gulf, 6330 Clark Street, Hudson, FL 34667 (727-869-0096, innon thegulf.com)

16

James E. Grey Preserve

TOTAL DISTANCE: A 1.3-mile circuit using three of the preserve's trails

HIKING TIME: 45 minutes to 1 hour

DIFFICULTY: Easy

USAGE: Free. Open sunrise to sunset. No pets or bicycles permitted.

TRAILHEAD GPS COORDINATES: 28.236561, -82.700258

CONTACT INFORMATION: James E. Grey Preserve, 6938 Plathe Road, New Port Richey, FL 34653 (727-841-4560, cityofnewportrichey.org)

Hidden in the heart of residential New Port Richey is the 80-acre James E. Grey Preserve, a quiet rural breather along the Pithlachascotee River, known locally as the Cotee. An extensive boardwalk follows the sinuous path of the Cotee, creating the well-shaded Palmetto Loop, which has beautiful overlooks along the river and a large cove on the opposite side. A secondary loop provides a walk through an upland scrub habitat, where roserush and tarflower bloom in abundance.

GETTING THERE

Take FL 54 east from US 19 in New Port Richey for 2.7 miles, until you reach Rowan Road. Turn left and drive north 1.6 miles, past the light at Trouble Creek Road, to the turnoff for Plathe Road on the left. The turnoff for the park has a large sign, and it's on your left after 0.25 mile. Drive in and park in the main parking area to start your hike.

THE HIKE

Between the restrooms and playground adjoining the parking area, a large kiosk showcases the park map, but it's not obvious when you stand here which direction you should go to follow the trails. There is an open area beyond the kiosk, and on the map, it's marked as the Grey Preserve Trail. But it's easiest to start this hike by looking for the paved path that leaves the parking area at the handicapped parking spaces. It guides you through an open area, past a picnic shelter, and across a park access road to start the first of two loops in the park, the Palmetto Loop, which begins as a boardwalk. It's a sturdy structure, built to withstand heavy flooding. It quickly swings through the floodplain forest to

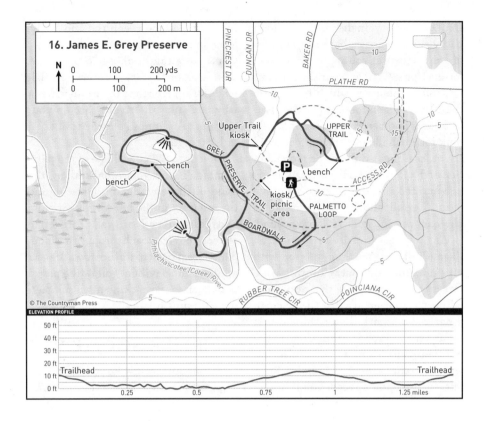

16. James E. Grey Preserve

ELEVATION PROFILE

follow the Pithlachascotee River channel, providing a view of a sluggish waterway and a cove framed by oak branches.

As the boardwalk leaves the cove it meanders through a dense palm hammock, where songbirds fill the air with their calls. The river remains visible through a screen of trees, along with a few residences in view on the far shore. There is a break in the boardwalk at 0.1 mile, with a trail taking off into the forest to connect back to the Grey Preserve Trail. Stay on the boardwalk, and you'll come up to a lake, with the Cotee remaining on your left. When you cross the bridge, it's obvious that the two connect—the lake is a cove off the river, and a large one, lined by lush palm hammocks. The boardwalk winds along the waterway, well-shaded by cabbage palms, with glimpses of water from both

sides. With all of the water surrounding you, there's always a nice breeze, making this a cooler-than-average walk for a summer day.

After 0.25 mile, a side boardwalk leads to an observation deck. The setting is spectacular, with a panorama of the wild river shorelines. It's hard to believe you're in the middle of New Port Richey. Returning to the main boardwalk, turn left. The boardwalk ends, depositing you on a berm surrounded by a forest with ferns thickly carpeting its floor. You're leaving the river now, as the trail keeps close to the shore of the cove. An opening with a bench provides a quiet place to sit and watch herons picking their way through the shallows.

Still in deep shade, the trail narrows, and the footpath becomes gravel. Glimpses of the cove are less frequent through openings in the forest. The footpath broadens again, back to the width of a forest road, as you approach the sign for the Upper Trail at 0.6 mile. Turn left to explore this loop, which focuses on the upland scrub forest near the river and offers two benches for resting. Pale pink roserush blooms in summer amid the grasses. Bear right at the loop junction and follow the wide path as it leads you into the shade of mature sand live oaks. The trail follows what looks like an old road, veering left as it loops around.

As the forest transitions from scrub to sandhill, you reach a junction with a bench. You could stay on this wide forest road to complete the loop, but a left turn at the bench will lead you down a narrow footpath under the oaks. It rejoins the old road within sight of the road you came in on, at a sandy clearing with a prominent cabbage palm. Turn left. In the open spaces, you'll notice gopher tortoise burrows along the way.

By 0.9 mile, you reach the end of the loop as the trail you're on merges in. Continue straight ahead to the kiosk. Take a left on the Grey Preserve Trail. It leads straight back to the trailhead. But why not savor the river again on your way out? An unmarked side trail at 1.1 miles tempts.

Dive into the cool shade of the palm hammock, and you're back along the edge of the cove again, approaching the opening in the boardwalk. Step up and return to the boardwalk. Turn left to retrace your approach through the floodplain forest back to the boardwalk's end at the picnic pavilion. Follow the paved path back to the parking area, completing a 1.3-mile hike.

OTHER HIKING OPTIONS

1. **Scenic Accessible Route.** The paved path leading from the parking area to the boardwalk now enables

TRAIL JUNCTION ALONG THE UPPER TRAIL

PITHLACHASCOTEE RIVER FROM THE BOARDWALK

those with wheelchairs, walkers, or mobility-assistance devices to explore the most scenic portion of the park, a 0.5-mile round-trip to the observation deck and back.

2. **Pasco Palms Preserve** (28.221733, -82.748733). 5.2 miles west of this preserve at the end of Trouble Creek Road, Pasco Palms Preserve is a 116-acre coastal preserve managed by the Pasco County Environmental Lands Division, with a 0.5-mile nature trail. Park at Eagle Point Park or roadside to walk into the preserve.

3. **Jay B. Starkey Wilderness Park** (28.259696, -82.633709). 5.5 miles east of this preserve is the largest trail system in Pasco County, with nearly 20 miles of paved paths and marked forest roads through pine flatwoods and oak hammocks along the watershed of the Pithlachascotee and Anclote Rivers, used by equestrians and cyclists but also popular with hikers. It includes several primitive backcountry campsites. We highlighted it in the first edition of this guidebook.

CAMPING AND LODGING

Quality Inn & Suites, 5316 US 19 N, New Port Richey, FL 34652 (727-847-9005, choicehotels.com)

Seven Springs Travel Park, 8039 Old CR 54, New Port Richey, FL 34653 (727-376-0000, sevenspringsrvpark. com), no tents.

BOARDWALK LEADING TO THE ST. JOHNS RIVER,
BLACK BEAR WILDERNESS AREA

III.

ST. JOHNS
RIVER

17

De Leon Springs State Park

TOTAL DISTANCE: 5.1 miles. The focus of this hike, the Wild Persimmon Trail, is 4.4 miles long. Its trailhead must be accessed by the 0.6-mile paved nature trail loop.

HIKING TIME: 2–2.5 hours

DIFFICULTY: Moderate to difficult

USAGE: $4–6 entry fee. Open 8 AM to sunset. Leashed pets welcome.

TRAILHEAD GPS COORDINATES: 29.1370, -81.3613

CONTACT INFORMATION: De Leon Springs State Park, 601 Ponce de Leon Boulevard, De Leon Springs, FL 32130 (386-985-4212, floridastateparks.org/park/De-Leon-Springs)

When Spanish explorer Ponce De Leon sailed to Florida in 1513, he sought the fountain of youth. He wrote, "We ascended a large river, passing through two small rivers and three lakes, whence we came to a great boiling spring which the Indians call 'Healing Waters.'" Our hike starts at this very spot, where visitors now splash, snorkel, and dive in a first-magnitude spring gushing more than 19 million gallons of slightly sulfuric waters a day to form a broad creek that feeds the St. Johns River.

Accented by layers of human history, De Leon Springs is a fascinating place. Middens and mounds reinforce written descriptions of early encounters with the indigenous Mayaca who lived here until the Spanish settled in. This site became known as Spring Garden, developed into a grand plantation with cotton, corn, and sugarcane. Passing through several owners up through the Civil War, Spring Garden became a destination resort with an upscale 14-room hotel in the 1920s. By the 1950s, it was a roadside attraction called Ponce de Leon Springs, which closed in the early 1970s. It became a state park in 1982. The Wild Persimmon Trail was built soon after by Florida Trail Association volunteers.

Of the park's trails, this is the one for adventure, best visited in winter or under a strong cloud of insect repellent. Wildlife sightings are common, with the occasional Florida black bear reported. If the St. Johns River is above its normal levels, portions of the trail may be flooded, despite the bog bridges provided. If the first bridge is under water, expect an adventuresome wade through the swamp forest, where the "difficult" rating applies.

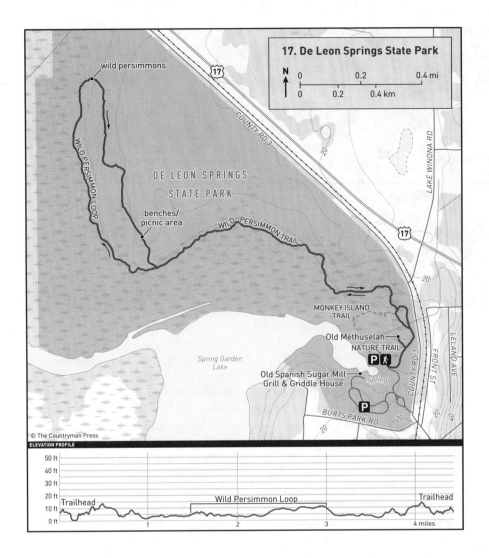

17. De Leon Springs State Park

wild persimmons

WILD PERSIMMON LOOP

DE LEON SPRINGS STATE PARK

benches/
picnic area

WILD PERSIMMON TRAIL

MONKEY ISLAND TRAIL

Old Methuselah

NATURE TRAIL

Spring Garden Lake

Old Spanish Sugar Mill
Grill & Griddle House

spring

BURTS PARK RD

COUNTY RD 3

LAKE WINONA RD

LELAND AVE

FRONT ST

© The Countryman Press

ELEVATION PROFILE

Trailhead — Wild Persimmon Loop — Trailhead

GETTING THERE

The town of De Leon Springs is just north of Deland on US 17. From US 17 in De Leon Springs, turn west onto Ponce De Leon Boulevard. Follow it 0.8 mile. The entrance to De Leon Springs State Park is just after the railroad crossing. You can't miss it—it's an unusually grand entrance surrounded by ornate murals, joined by a reproduction of a very kitschy roadside sign from 1953.

When you stop at the ranger station to pay the entrance fee, let them know you plan to hike the Wild Persimmon Trail. Ask for a map. Turn right at the T intersection to drive to the parking area (29.136952, -81.361309) behind the museum and bathhouse. If this parking lot is full, you'll need to use one on the other side of the park and walk across the causeway between the spring and Spring Garden Run.

SWIMMING AREA AT FIRST-MAGNITUDE DE LEON SPRINGS

THE HIKE

Uphill and northeast of the spring basin, the Nature Trail begins with a kiosk in the middle of a paved path. There are two entrances to it: use the one closer to the parking area by the spring. Constructed for the attraction, the walkway fits neatly into a mature hardwood forest with towering trees. You come to a boardwalk. Follow it into the cypress swamp to see Old Methuselah, a bald cypress estimated to be more than 600 years old. It's an amazing sight, rising more than 150 feet through the understory, and a sobering one—the forests along the St. Johns River were still populated with trees this immense just 200 years ago, before the advent of full-scale logging in the state. As you return along the boardwalk, notice the lush growth of netted chain and royal ferns along the swamp's edge. Turn left, continuing along the paved trail. The views of the surrounding swamp were accented during the roadside attraction era, with

reflection pools, an Oriental bridge, and plantings of azaleas, some of which persist today. Pass an incoming paved path. When the paved trail forks in front of you, keep right. It curves around past a bench, reaching the trailhead sign for the Wild Persimmon Trail after 0.3 mile. This is where the adventure begins.

Blue blazes lead you down the footpath into a transitional zone between floodplain forest, hardwood hammock, and pine flatwoods. Young cabbage palms and loblolly bay crowd the understory; woodlands phlox and dayflower blooms along the grassy sides of the footpath. Hickory trees and longleaf pines tower overhead. Lichen mats cover the roots of a dahoon holly, its splotchy trunk and bright red berries catching your attention. Watch your footing along this trail, as toe-catching roots are common. Soon after passing a bench at 0.5 mile, the trail crosses a footbridge over a trickle of water flowing towards the floodplain. The shiny leaves of Southern magnolia are supplanted by loblolly bay as you draw closer to the floodplain; the footpath gets muddy in several spots before it rises through a corridor flanked by bluestem palm.

Marker 5 is at the beginning of a series of bog boardwalks over an always-wet portion of the floodplain forest, the first one a balancing act nearly 200 feet long, flanked by ferns and reflections. Two more boardwalks follow in quick succession, with muddy spots between them. A clearing sits beyond the tree line where the trail reaches a bench at 0.8 mile. The footpath edges closer to the floodplain. More boardwalks cross the low spots before you cross the bridge at Marker 6. It's here that the trail enters the hydric hammock. It's dark in the forest, even in the early morning light—the broad fronds of the cabbage palms serve well to block out the light, leaving only streamers of sunshine to filter through to the dark soil and tannic water. If the river is high, this area will be very flooded. Continue following the blue blazes if the footpath becomes indistinct. Crossing two more bridges, you come to a third one overlooking a tannic stream snaking its way into the swamp. Speaking of snakes, this is prime habitat for both cottonmouth moccasins and pygmy rattlesnakes. Keep alert as you weave through the cypress knees in the footpath.

The trail briefly skirts the edge of a meadow, where a bench overlooks the opening. It turns back in to the hydric hammock, crossing a bridge over a picturesque stream with sandbanks. You've hiked a mile. Marker 7 sits at the base of a bridge just before the trail gains a little elevation, which changes the landscape. The swamp yields to an oak hammock, with water oaks and laurel oaks, but only briefly. It gets muddy again beyond the next bench, as you're back amid the dense palm fronds and drainages across the trail.

After 1.4 miles, you've reached the beginning of the loop portion of the Wild

BRIDGE ALONG THE EDGE OF THE FLOODPLAIN OF SPRING GARDEN RUN

LEAVING THE PALM HAMMOCK FOR THE WILD PERSIMMON GROVE AT MARKER 10

Persimmon Trail, starting and ending at this bench. Continue past the bench to stay with the floodplain side of the loop. Beyond another bench at the base of a stand of southern magnolia, the trail meets Marker 8, which calls attention to a transition into an oak hammock. The canopy overhead becomes increasingly high; saw palmetto makes up the understory. A pileated woodpecker dives past, flashing its distinctive red crown and black-and-white wings in flight. Rounding a corner of an open area, the trail resumes its canopied route through drier habitats, edged by ancient saw palmetto and bluestem palmetto under loblolly pines, magnolias, and oaks.

As the habitat grows lusher, the live oaks offer even better shade. Bromeliads—air plants—thrive in this humid hammock along the rim of Spring Garden Run's floodplain swamp; oak trunks sprout wild pine-like hair. Long green plumes of goldfoot fern cascade from the soft thatch just below a cabbage palm's fronds. It gets muddy once again as the trail dances in and out of the hydric hammock. Just past a bench at 1.9 miles, there are puddles across the

footpath, the low spot in the forest. Work your way around them. Tannic water covers much of the forest floor. As the trail swings right, it guides you through an immense palm hammock, with the cypresses along the spring run visible in the distance beyond. Fungi thrives in the leaf litter. The thick, arching limbs of live oaks break up the angular feel of the cabbage palm trunks. Bluestem palmetto, sabal minor, thrives in the shade. While it looks similar to saw palmetto, the fronds drape softly; saw palmetto fronds are stiff. There are also no saw teeth on the stems of a bluestem frond. By 2.1 miles, you're immersed in the beauty of the oak and palm hammock, a perfect panorama in every direction, even straight up.

When the cabbage palms thin out, it's time for another habitat change, this time back to the oak hammock. This drier spot signals the end of the trail's traverse along the floodplain, at least until you finish the loop. Just beyond the bench at Marker 9, your surroundings transition from natural habitat into restoration area as the trail emerges into a former open pasture.

Since our first visit here 18 years ago, we've watched the transformation from pasture to meadow to forest. From an aerial view, the old pastures are obvious. They're less so when you're on foot. The same goes for the grove of wild persimmon trees that this trail is named for. Marker 10 points out the location, straight ahead as you leave the oak hammock for an area with tufts of grass and flourishing sweetgum trees. In winter and spring, the wild persimmon trees are indistinct from the surrounding trees. In fall, when their foliage falls off, small orange fruits remain. Pucker up if you pop one in your mouth—wild persimmons are extremely astringent when first picked, but turn sweet when they are allowed to ripen. Raccoons and opossums crave the ripened fruits fallen beneath the trees.

Walking through these woods, you may briefly hear traffic in the distance, since this part of the park is close to CR 3. A grassy aisle through the young forest, the trail skirts around older live oaks and along colorful stands of sweetgum, which sport red and purple leaves in the fall. At 2.5 miles, you pass a bench in a shady oak hammock. The trail curves out of the hammock back to the grassy aisle. Since large trees are few, blaze post markers tipped with blue and topped with arrows are used through the restoration area, since there are many side trails beaten down by deer. Soon after, the trail enters another hammock of oaks and palms, where it's easy to lose the footpath in one spot. Keep watching for the next blue blaze. Emerging back onto the grassy aisle, it passes showy clumps of Carolina jessamine, flowering in winter and spring.

Approaching the next bench, you see a blue-tipped fencepost with barbed wire remaining from the old ranch. The trail turns right down the grassy aisle, meandering into a very open oak hammock briefly before passing a bog. Making a sharp left turn away from going straight into a cypress dome at Marker 12, you follow the grassy aisle beneath the pines towards a marker that says EXIT. Just beyond it is a large sign about Florida black bears. A mature oak hammock with a well-knitted canopy shades the next set of benches, which look like the remnants of a former primitive campsite. In fact, there's a picnic table under the oaks beyond the open area where the benches face each other as if across a fire ring. Take a well-deserved break here. Sit here a while, and you may be rewarded with the appearance of white-tailed deer in the clearing, or the hurried scampering of a flock of wild turkey into the underbrush.

Leaving this clearing, the trail swings right, passing under a stand of live oaks. Short blaze posts guide you up to the tree line of the floodplain forest and into it, completing the loop portion of the Wild Persimmon Trail at a bench at Marker 13. The post next to the bench points left, towards the exit. You've hiked 3 miles. It's time to backtrack through the dense palm fronds and muddy edges of the floodplain. In this direction, you get nice perspectives down the streams in the hydric hammock as you cross each of the bridges again. As you follow the blue blazes, notice the interesting fungi growing at the bases of the trees. By the time you return to the bog bridges, at 3.5 miles, they're a welcome sight. Take your time crossing them, as they may be slippery.

You reach the Wild Persimmon Trailhead at the paved nature trail after 4.4 miles. Continue around the loop, passing the entrance to the Monkey Island Trail. This 0.5-mile diversion (see *Other*

Hiking Options) is worthwhile if you're up for it. Or save it for later, as you have another task to attend to. Stay left at each divergence of the paved trail until you're back to the trailhead kiosk. Continue down to the parking area and spring.

Cross the causeway over to the Old Spanish Sugar Mill Grill & Griddle House, where visitors flock for its renowned and unique meals. Using batter made with grain stone-ground at the old mill, you pour out your own flapjacks on the center of your table, a hot griddle shared with the other people at the table. If bacon and eggs are more your style, try them instead. Breakfast goes on all day, but you might wait 2 or 3 hours for your name to be called. Check when you arrive at the park, and if the wait time is long, you might be able to hike the Wild Persimmon Trail before your name comes up on the roster. They won't hold the table for you, though—we missed ours by 15 minutes—so if you put your name on the list after the hike, you'll have time to visit the museum, cool down in the spring after your hike, and perhaps even take an ecotour cruise down Spring Garden Run.

OTHER HIKING OPTIONS

1. **Accessible Route**. Nearly a mile of paved nature trails, and the boardwalk to Old Methuselah, are fully accessible for wheelchairs and mobility devices. Slow walkers will appreciate the beautiful surroundings, ancient trees, and azalea blossoms in springtime, with numerous benches providing rest stops along the way.

2. **Monkey Island Trail** (29.136733, -81.361467). A 0.25-mile linear spur trail off the paved nature trail, this footpath on a berm through the floodplain forest was called the Audubon Trail when De Leon Springs was a resort and natural theme park. Ending at a bench in the swamp near Spring Garden Lake, it provides a tiny taste of the surroundings found on the Wild Persimmon Trail. Don't miss the short side path to see what remains of Monkey Island, once a stop along the Jungle Cruise.

3. **Lake Woodruff NWR** (29.106825, -81.371012). Head south on Grand Avenue from DeLeon Springs to access the main entrance of this 22,000-acre refuge at 2045 Mud Lake Road. Stop at the visitor center (29.107373, -81.366576) for a map, then follow the road until it ends at the main parking lot. Hike or bike the open levees to Jones Island, where one of the trails leads to Pontoon Landing on the St. Johns River, a 6-mile round-trip. Two shorter footpaths loop through shady hammocks closer to the main parking lot.

CAMPING AND LODGING

Lake Dias Park, 320 SR 11, DeLeon Springs, FL 32130 (386-736-5953, volusia.org), no tents.

Highland Park Fish Camp, 2640 W Highland Park Road, Deland, FL 32720 (386-734-2334, highlandpark fishcamp.com)

Deland Artisan Inn, 215 S Woodland Boulevard, Deland, FL 32720 (386-943-4410, artisandowntown.com)

18

St. Francis Trail

TOTAL DISTANCE: 7.9 miles on a balloon-shaped route

HIKING TIME: 4 hours

DIFFICULTY: Moderate to difficult

USAGE: Free. Open 24 hours. Backpacking permitted, bear bag or bear canister required. Wear bright orange during posted hunting seasons. Leashed pets welcome.

TRAILHEAD GPS COORDINATES: 29.0129, -81.3924

CONTACT INFORMATION: Ocala National Forest, Seminole Ranger District, 40929 SR19, Umatilla, FL 32784 (352-669-3153, fs.usda.gov/ocala)

In the southeast corner of the Ocala National Forest, the St. Francis Trail provides an interesting walk along the floodplain of several side channels of the St. Johns River. Two routes tempt, differing in distance and sights to be seen—a 3-mile trek to a bubbling sulfur spring, or the full 7.9-mile hike to the ghost town of St. Francis. Since this is a national forest, camping is permitted anywhere along the trail, although habitats, water, and terrain limit optimal places to camp to just a few spots mentioned in the narrative. Constructed in the early 1990s as a potential segment of the statewide Florida National Scenic Trail, this popular hike was modified into a loop trail when the Florida Trail took a different route.

GETTING THERE

From US 17 in Deland, follow FL 44 west over the St. Johns River drawbridge. Immediately turn right on CR 42. Drive 0.4 mile to the National Forest sign that says RIVER FOREST GROUP CAMP. Turn right on FR 542. After you pass the River Forest campground, the trailhead parking will be to the left, 0.3 mile from CR 42. Much of the hike is through river hammocks and floodplain forest, so slather on the mosquito repellent before you get out of the car.

THE HIKE

At the trailhead kiosk, pause a moment to learn a little about this forgotten town along the St. Johns River. St. Francis was an early 1900s boomtown built on cypress logging, citrus groves, and farming. As you start walking through the oak hammock, beaten paths lead off in many directions. Stick with the orange blazes as you walk through the

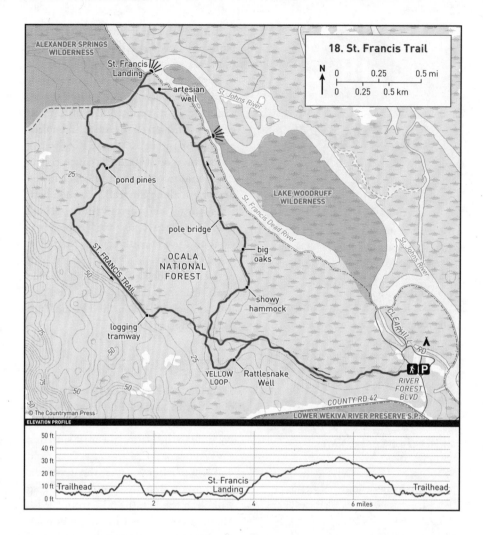

forest of live oak and sweetgum. After the trail veers left, you cross the first of several bridges over waterways flowing towards the floodplain forest along the St. Johns River. A moderate undulation to the footpath is from when this was a plowed watermelon field a century or more ago. By the size of the trees and the rich understory growth, it's hard to imagine the farms that were once here. Now, deer moss and blueberries crowd the understory beneath water oak, laurel oak, and slash pine. Notice the welcome mats—trail maintainers placed indus-

trial black mats in some of the soggier places, hoping to stave off erosion as the footpath drops into a floodplain forest of red maple, sweetgum, and pignut hickory.

At 0.4 mile, you come to the first of many long boardwalks on this trail. Most have slip control built in—a fine mesh of hardware cloth provides traction. Over the next 0.25-mile, a series of boardwalks keep you out of the dark, mucky soil as they bridge together tiny islands in the floodplain. Look for the slender orange fingers of coral fungi, and the many ferns, including royal fern, netted chain, and spleenworts, which swarm across the forest floor. This humid environment encourages riotous growth. Tawny milkcap and violet cort mushrooms rise from the muck. Wild pine and other bromeliads grow in the trees. Shoelace fern drips down the trunk of a tall cabbage palm. Sunlight streams through a cluster of opaque goldfoot fern. Wherever the trail leaves the boardwalk for dry land, the reflective leaves of shiny lyonia dominate the understory.

Leaving the boardwalks behind, the trail rises in elevation slightly, offering views down towards a hydric hammock closer to the river. Cabbage palms and live oaks reach for the sky. The dark earth is damp underfoot. After a mile, you cross a bridge over a small tributary flowing down toward the hidden St. Francis Dead River. As the forest canopy gets higher, it's possible to see the open sky over the river—but only in winter. This is a dense forest, shady and humid, the tree trunks covered with deep, furry coats of sphagnum moss. After you pass a curve in a stream, the water transparent to a sandy bottom but tea-stained with the tannic residue of hickory and oak leaves, you cross another boardwalk.

A prominent trail sign marks the first junction at 1.1 miles. The shorter Yellow Loop leading to Rattlesnake Well turns left. You'll come back that way on the return route. Continue straight ahead along the white blazes of the St. Francis Trail, crossing a bridge over the spring run that flows out of Rattlesnake Well. A grove of southern magnolia and its smaller cousin, the bay magnolia, surrounds the trail, reflecting sunlight off large glossy leaves. The trail rises, the footpath needle-strewn under slash pines. You reach the next trail junction

at 1.4 miles, where the sign says ST. FRANCIS 2 MI. Continue straight ahead. Check out the tall pine right behind the sign—an unusual double-trunked slash pine, rising more than 100 feet over the forest floor.

The footpath turns down a corridor of saw palmetto under large live oaks, then drops into a hydric hammock of tall cabbage palms. As it rises again, it skirts the edge of a pine forest, continuing under a low canopy of oaks. As the trail jogs right, it enters a narrow corridor between saw palmettos, re-entering the hydric hammock. You cross a bridge over a murky side stream and walk along dark, rich earth, where hopping over and around puddles is part of the fun of this hike. Veering left, the trail returns to the oak hammock, within sight of a forest of slash pine. Before this land became a national forest, citrus groves and vegetable fields once blossomed where most of these younger pine forests stand. As you wander through the pines, notice the slender stalks of native bamboo growing along the trail.

The trail crosses a sand road in a deep ditch, then clambers up a bluff onto a levee. Built to allow farmers to flood the fields to grow rice, this levee now provides high ground for the trail. Cross a high pole bridge at 2.4 miles, where guy wires help you maintain your balance. Beyond it, the trail continues almost straight as an arrow under the oaks and palms. A water-filled ditch parallels the levee.

At the next double blaze, take the trail to the right. It's an old railroad tramway that leads to the St. Francis Dead River. When the virgin pines and cypresses in these woods were logged, logging companies built these slightly elevated grades to allow their railcars—first pulled by mules or oxen, then

POLE BRIDGE ALONG THE ST. FRANCIS TRAIL

powered by steam—to reach the inner depths of the forest. This side channel of the St. Johns River is quite beautiful, and the dead-end of the tramway at the river affords views both upstream and downstream. Return to the trail junction and continue straight ahead. You've hiked 3 miles. The tramway leads right to a guardrail and an established forest road; the white blazes guide you to the right just before you meet it. Continue through a dense understory of bluestem palmetto in the palm and oak hammock, skirting more big puddles in the footpath as you walk past several live oaks.

Near one large live oak, you hear the splash of water. An artesian well is piped out of the ground, where it flows into a washtub and overflows into the hammock, encouraging the growth of lizard-tail and water spangles. It has a hint of sulfur but provides a water source for backpackers. If it's not damp, the clearing under the live oak is suitable for setting up camp.

At a T intersection with a graded forest road at 3.6 miles, the double-blaze

directs you left. Turn right instead. This is the wagon road that once connected Paisley to the St. Johns River, and it's the main street of the ghost town of St. Francis. There are no foundations left, no ruins to explore—the buildings, constructed of cypress boards, were recycled for their prize lumber, the remainders plundered by vandals. Imagine the old hotel over there in the opening between the trees, and the livery stable close to the road. A wagon stops at the general store to deliver dry goods. The post office opened in March 1888. Homes and cottages were scattered along the road and throughout the woods.

The road ends at the St. Johns River. If you follow the narrow path at the end of the road, it leads to a point where you can see one piling of the old steamboat dock jutting out of the river. Steamboats would arrive here from Palatka with supplies and head back loaded with fresh fruit and vegetables. In 1886, the new railroad line from Jacksonville opened, coming down the opposite side of the river, missing St. Francis entirely.

When Deland, Orange City, Enterprise, and Sanford started shipping their fruits and vegetables by rail, steamboat traffic ended. St. Francis was doomed. By 1894, deep freezes damaged the citrus groves. A hurricane in the 1920s dealt the final blow. Most of the town suffered considerable damage from flooding.

The last resident of St. Francis left the woods in the 1940s. The land became part of the Ocala National Forest, so you may encounter the hunters and fishermen that use this road to access the river. Walk up the road, passing the incoming trail blazes. This is the southern boundary of the Alexander Springs Wilderness Area, an unbroken forest stretching more than 20 miles to the north. You pass one clearing that might make a suitable campsite, but keep in mind that vehicles drive back here after dark.

At 4.1 miles, a HIKING ONLY marker and a TRAILHEAD 4 MILES sign indicates where the St. Francis Trail leaves the historic road and returns to the woods through a cabbage palm hammock. The landscape yields to tall, straight rows of slash pines, planted many decades ago to reclaim the land from groves and farms. Pine needles form a soft blanket underfoot. Blueberries and cinnamon ferns flourish in the acidic soil, as do scattered loblolly bay trees. Crossing a plank over a murky waterway, the trail meanders into a more open expanse of pine flatwoods, where saw palmettos form a solid understory beneath the pond pines. These flourish throughout the St. Johns River basin. Crooked growth and needles sprouting from the trunks are the telltale features of the pond pine.

Once you cross an old track, the saw palmetto yields to dense thickets of gallberry as the habitat transitions

WHERE THE ST. FRANCIS WHARF ONCE STOOD ALONG THE ST. JOHNS RIVER

PINE FLATWOODS DENSE WITH POND PINES

to scrubby flatwoods. You'll cross several more old tracks before paralleling a bayhead, where plank boardwalks keep you off the soggy ground where water is draining away from the swamp. With a slight change in elevation, the habitat becomes scrub. At 5.3 miles, the trail jogs left to join another logging tramway. A murky duckweed-choked ditch parallels, and thick sphagnum moss carpets the edge of the trail. Ducking under low branches, you must jump over several damp spots. At 5.9 miles, turn left off the tramway as the trail leads you through the pine forest. It crosses several boardwalks through a bayhead.

After 6.3 miles, a familiar sign is at a different location: YELLOW LOOP. You've walked the long loop of the St.

Francis Trail, and now it's time to finish the short one. A bench sits at the junction. Bear right at the fork to follow the yellow-blazed trail towards Rattlesnake Well. Cross a long boardwalk through a low area. You're back in the lush floodplain of the St. Johns River, ducking beneath low-hanging palm fronds and hopscotching around puddles in the footpath.

After a transition into a drier oak hammock, the trail goes down a slope to cross a bridge over a steeply eroded channel. The trail turns left to follow this small creek under a stand of southern magnolia. It crosses several bridges beneath the oaks and palms before it reaches another sharp left turn at the main point of interest on this loop, the spring known as Rattlesnake Well. It

plain forest, finishing the last one after 7.5 miles. After one last bridge, notice the size of the pines in this part of the forest. You emerge at the trailhead kiosk and parking area, completing a 7.9-mile hike.

OTHER HIKING OPTIONS

1. **Yellow Loop**. This is the shorter option from the same trailhead. Follow the hike as described above, but pass the first sign for the Yellow Loop at 1.1 miles. Take a left at the next sign at 1.4 miles. It quickly leads you up to a trail junction with a bench. Turn right to follow the YELLOW LOOP sign here (and the last few paragraphs of the narrative above) for a 3-mile hike from the St. Francis trailhead.
2. **Hontoon Island** (28.9765, -81.3570). The Indian Mound Trail (28.974316, -81.357561) at Hontoon Island State Park, upriver from St. Francis (the St. Johns flows north) and 5.8 miles away by road, provides an immersion in similar floodplain and upland habitats, with the hike terminating at a midden. It's a 3.3-mile round-trip hike, requiring a free ferryboat from the parking area to access the island.

CAMPING AND LODGING

Deland/St. Johns River KOA, 2999 SR 44 W Deland, FL 32720 (386-736-6601, koa.com)

Highland Park Fish Camp, 2640 W Highland Park Road, Deland, FL 32720 (386-734-2334, highlandpark fishcamp.com)

Deland Artisan Inn, 215 S Woodland Boulevard, Deland, FL 32720 (386-943-4410, artisandowntown.com)

bubbles out of the bottom of a small stream, a swirling hole with yellow streamers. A faint aroma of sulfur, like the tips of matches, wafts across the water. After crossing the bridge over the spring run, walk a little closer to the spring on the other side.

As you leave the spring, the trail passes a cleared area under the palms, an ideal place for primitive camping with a group. Continuing beneath the live oak and cabbage palm canopy, the Yellow Loop is a showy corridor between the bluestem palmettos. You reach the end of the loop at 6.8 miles at a familiar T intersection. Turn right to retrace the trail you came in on. Winding through the oak and palm hammock, you start the 0.25-mile series of boardwalks again through the flood-

Black Bear Wilderness Area

TOTAL DISTANCE: 7.1-mile loop

HIKING TIME: 3.5–4.5 hours

DIFFICULTY: Moderate to difficult

USAGE: Free. Open dawn to dusk. Backpacking with free permit. Leashed pets welcome.

TRAILHEAD GPS COORDINATES: 28.833009, -81.353865

CONTACT INFORMATION: Black Bear Wilderness Area, 5298 Michigan Avenue, Sanford, FL 32771 (407-349-0769, seminolecountyfl.gov)

In a most improbable location—a low-lying floodplain forest along a series of languid bends in the St. Johns River, just south of the Wekiva River floodplain—the 1,800-acre Black Bear Wilderness Area offers an extraordinarily wild 7.1-mile loop hike right on the edge of the Orlando metro. When we lived in Sanford and this trail opened, we said, "How?" It seems that in the past, a series of levees had been built along the floodplain for drainage for farming. Add in an major investment in infrastructure—14 sturdy, flood-resistant boardwalks—and the Seminole County Natural Lands Program created what has become one of the most popular hikes in the region.

While it's an easy walk to the river on the most direct route, taking on the full loop is not for the timid. There is no bailout option other than retracing your steps. Wildlife is abundant, and that includes black bears. We've seen four here already. This is by no means a walk in the park: some of the levees are very narrow and sloped, others are rooty or mucky. Bring a hiking stick or two with you—you'll need it for balance. Insect repellent is a must since most of the hike is in deep shade. Most importantly, check on river levels before you take on this hike. Parts of it sit very low and will be inundated if the river rises. If you plan to camp here, call 407-665-2180 in advance to obtain your free permit.

GETTING THERE

From I-4 exit 101C at Sanford, take FL 46 west for 1.5 miles to Orange Boulevard. Turn right. Continue 1.3 miles to New York St on your left. Turn left. Drive 0.5 mile to where New York Street and Michigan Avenue meet. The trailhead is straight ahead of you.

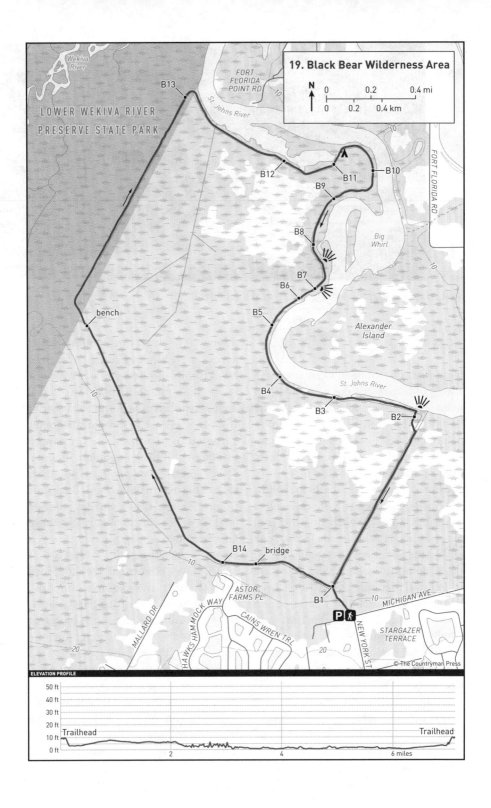

19. Black Bear Wilderness Area

N

| 0 | 0.2 | 0.4 mi |
| 0 | 0.2 | 0.4 km |

LOWER WEKIVA RIVER
PRESERVE STATE PARK

Wekiva
River

FORT
FLORIDA
POINT RD

St. Johns River

FORT FLORIDA RD

B13

B12

B11

B10

B9

B8

Big
Whirl

B7

B6

B5

Alexander
Island

bench

B4

St. Johns River

B3

B2

B14   bridge

ASTOR
FARMS PL

MICHIGAN AVE

B1

STARGAZER
TERRACE

MALLARD DR

HAWKS HAMMOCK WAY

CAINS WREN TRL

NEW YORK ST

© The Countryman Press

ELEVATION PROFILE

50 ft			
40 ft			
30 ft			
20 ft			
10 ft	Trailhead		Trailhead
0 ft			

2   4   6 miles

MAMA BEAR AND CUBS AT THE ENTRANCE TO BLACK BEAR WILDERNESS

THE HIKE

Sign in at the trailhead kiosk and grab a map brochure or take a photo of the map. While it's impossible to lose the route along your hike, being able to pin-point your location by boardwalk number is helpful for gauging your pace. Mile markers also provide a sense of your progress around the loop. Follow the gravel path beneath enormous live oaks. You quickly reach Boardwalk 1, meandering as it leads you into an oak and palm hammock characteristic of the St. Johns River floodplain. If you are committed to hiking the full loop, keep left when you reach the Y intersection in the boardwalk at the Loop Trail sign. Although following the loop clockwise means you're counting down the numbers on both the boardwalks and mileage markers, it's the best way to end your hike with the best views and a cool breeze at your back.

When the boardwalk ends, it drops you onto the first levee. Lined with cabbage palms, some of which grow right out of the middle of the berm, it offers views into the floodplain and across a paralleling canal before the palm fronds swallow you up. Welcome to Florida's jungle habitat. You pass a double-trunked pine. As more pines rise from the levee, the footpath becomes carpeted in pine needles. Crossing a bridge over a dark floodplain channel after 0.6 mile, you see a mile marker sign. These signs are on all Seminole County Natural Lands, with latitude and longitude coordinates to share in case of an emergency. Along this loop, they pop up every 0.5 mile.

This levee is more narrow and sloped than the last and requires dropping down through a drainage area, hopefully dry. Cabbage palms and bluestem palmetto are thick throughout the understory. It's a surprise when you see someone's backyard as you walk up to Boardwalk 14, which crosses a flowing stream. It's the first and final time you'll be near a subdivision on this hike. The trail now follows a forest road, and it's here, near the human interface, that bear sightings are most likely. You'll make your best time along the hike

NARROW FOOTPATH DOWN THE NARROW LEVEE AS YOU APPROACH THE RIVER FLOODPLAINS

while following this old road, which is still deeply shaded. Peer into the leaf litter, and you might notice jelly-leaf, as the perpetual humidity here is perfect for fungi growth. Very old barbed wire adjoins the forest road, blocking access to the canal.

Just past a lichen-dotted and fading NO TRESPASSING sign, the trail breaks into the open at 1.2 miles and crosses a gated access road topped with power lines, used by the water authority to access a riverfront facility you'll encounter closer to the end of the hike. From the looks of the floodgates and walls on the other side of the canal in this next stretch of forest, the water facilities are much older than the Natural Lands Program in Seminole County. The trail continues along the broad forest road, with more sun dappling through the oaks and pines until you reach a bench at 2 miles. The road ends at a grassy clearing. Look for the well-hidden opening onto the next levee, back into the palm hammock.

Here's where the hike gets interesting. Trees crowd the narrow levee. Palm fronds obscure the view ahead. When we stopped for a photo, we stirred up a wasp nest in the footpath. The forest around you is young, speaking to more recent land uses here, but older trees cling to the levee, with massive roots you must pick your way across. Then the footpath starts slipping sideways. Since it's so narrow, you must watch your step or end up sliding off into the swamp. The horizon opens into a marsh. It's filled with the nodding pink blossoms of largeflower hibiscus in late summer and early fall. You've reached the zone between floodplains, the Wekiva River winding its way into the St. Johns to the north. The footpath cants even more, sometimes at a 45-degree angle.

When the levee goes around a slippery curve just past Boardwalk 13, you've reached the St. Johns River, 3.2 miles into your hike. For the next few miles, the trail stays next to the river and its marshes, which is why this is one of the most scenic hikes in the region. The sun sparkles on open water, with marshes to the right. The footpath is still at a challenging angle, and it drops to river level as it approaches Boardwalk

VIEW OF THE ST. JOHNS RIVER FROM THE NARROWS ON THE LEVEE NEAR BOARDWALK 2

12, leading to a tunnel of vegetation. The primitive campsite is at 4 miles. It's a clearing in a level area under cabbage palms and live oaks, with a rain shelter with benches, picnic tables, and a fire ring. Carry enough drinking water in with you, and carry out your trash. We strongly encourage you to bear bag or use a bear canister to protect your food.

After you pass the campsite, boardwalk crossings become more frequent. Each bridges a gap in the riverside levee. A live oak leans low across the trail, which becomes narrow and rooty between Boardwalk 10 and Boardwalk 8, which winds through a pond where tall alligator flags wave in the breeze. Speaking of alligators, they pull themselves up on the slopes of the levee in sunny spots. If you hear a loud splash, you probably spooked one nearby. Past the flag pond, notice the cypress swamp stretching from the canal created from building this berm off into the sun-dappled distance. There are few large trees, as the cypress forests of the St. Johns River were stripped for lumber more than a century ago. Cypress trees grow very slowly, so the only giants in the forest are those left behind because their shapes were too odd to go through a sawmill.

There is an island between the trail and the river as you approach Boardwalk 7, and then you're atop the river bluff with nice views, including one of a long river bend around Alexander Island on the far shore. At 5.1 miles, Boardwalk 6 is long and tall, offering an excellent panorama of passing boaters. Boardwalk 5 is where kayakers can access the trail. A floating platform with a ladder down to it is always at river level. Narrowing once again, the levee is swarmed by tree roots and crowded by cabbage palms. Long and straight, Boardwalk 4 offers a view of a cypress-lined flag pond. Beyond it is a dense collection of cypress knees surrounding mazy channels through the swamp. Before this berm was built, the river's waters rose right through the cypress swamp.

Once you cross Boardwalk 3 at 5.8 miles, you've reached the original trail that we first explored in 2011. This was as far as you could get after crossing the boardwalk built to this river levee. Hurricane Irma took out quite a few trees along this section, which was always narrow and steep. Warning signs point out the narrows on the bluff, which affords great views across the river.

Reaching Boardwalk 2, you've come to the end of your walk along the St. Johns River. This is your last observation point with a river view. Turn right and take the stairs down to follow this boardwalk across the canal, where the reflections of cypress trees make mesmerizing patterns. It continues into the open along a flag pond where red-winged blackbirds flutter. Black vultures often perch on the fence of the water facility where you cross the graveled road that vanishes under the marsh.

After a slight jog, the boardwalk deposits you under the power lines at 6.2 miles, where the well-worn path leads up to the last of the levees. This one heads in a relatively straight line away from the St. Johns River, although you will see an open area with marshes. The sounds of traffic seep in briefly, as I-4 is not far beyond the distant tree line. But the floodplain forest is good at absorbing sound, so you don't notice it for long. As the original trail in the preserve, the footpath down this levee is well-trodden, although you still have to worry about roots and some fire ant nests, especially under the big oaks and cedars. Reflections in the water on both sides are a reminder you're still traversing a swamp. As the levee broadens, you encounter periodic benches placed along this stretch of trail as Eagle Scout projects. When you reach Boardwalk 1, it only takes a moment to seal the 7-mile loop. Continue straight ahead through the palm hammock to walk to the trailhead, concluding your 7.1-mile hike.

OTHER HIKING OPTIONS

1. **River Walk.** When this preserve first opened, the only trail available was along the berm straight to the St. Johns River. Take a right at the loop junction on the boardwalk to follow this direct route, which leads to Boardwalk 2 and views of the river from a small observation deck. A round-trip on this easiest part of the trail system is 2 miles.

2. **Lower Wekiva River Preserve State Park** (28.828370, -81.411167). Adjoining Black Bear Wilderness Area, this state park encompasses more than 18,000 acres of low-lying lands where the Wekiva River meets the St. Johns. Access to the 2.2-mile Sandhills Nature Trail along FL 46 is blocked by a construction zone, but a new connector leads to it from the Katie's Landing trailhead (fee).

3. **Gemini Springs Addition** (28.840028, -81.319691). Across the St. Johns River in Volusia County and slightly downriver, access this complex of more than 5 miles of paved and natural trails through riverfront Lake Monroe Park (28.839718, -81.319855) or the small trailhead just behind that park's campground. The trails extend to Gemini Springs Park (28.867481, -81.311248).

CAMPING AND LODGING

Lake Monroe Park, 975 S Charles Richard Beall Boulevard, DeBary, FL 32713 (386-668-3825, volusia.org)

Gemini Springs Park, 37 Dirksen Drive, DeBary, FL 32713-3707 (386-736-5953, volusia.org), tents only.

Wekiva Falls RV Resort, 30700 Wekiva River Road, Sorrento, FL 32776 (352-383-8055, wekivafalls.com)

20

Spring Hammock Preserve

TOTAL DISTANCE: 3-mile circuit of a network of trails bisected by the paved Cross Seminole Trail. Many other configurations and options possible.

HIKING TIME: 1–1.5 hours

DIFFICULTY: Easy

USAGE: Free. Open dawn to dusk. Leashed pets welcome.

TRAILHEAD GPS COORDINATES: 28.721682, -81.306905

CONTACT INFORMATION: Spring Hammock Preserve, 2985 Osprey Trail, Longwood, FL 32750 (407-349-0769, seminolecountyfl.gov)

Amid a primordial swamp locals once called Devil's Bend, fringing the edge of Lake Jesup—one of the larger lakes in the St. Johns River chain of lakes—Spring Hammock Preserve is the land of the giants. Here, bald cypresses grow to incredible heights, recalling the redwood forests of the Pacific in their sheer majesty. Yet it's not just the cypresses that tower overhead, but sweetgums and red maples, loblolly pines and water hickory, and even basswoods and tulip poplars. More than two-thirds of the nearly 1,500 acres protected as Spring Hammock are swamps draining into the St. Johns River. The preserve is jointly managed by the Seminole County Natural Lands Program and the Seminole County School Board. Established in 1977, the Environmental Studies Center is an environmental education complex for school students, who graduate through their studies to anticipate the Mud Walk that fifth graders experience.

When we lived nearby, this was one of our favorite preserves to hike. There are so many different ways to explore the trail system on the west side of the Cross Seminole Trail, you can come back time after time and never take the same route twice. Many of the trails along the floodplain have closed since the prior edition of our guide, since the infrastructure was difficult to keep up. But you can still immerse in the swamp forest without getting your feet wet. Plans are in the works for a new boardwalk to Lake Jesup to showcase the biggest cypresses. Since the trails will be rehabbed soon, signage may change.

GETTING THERE

From I-4 exit 98, Lake Mary/Heathrow, drive east on Lake Mary Boulevard for 1.6 miles to Longwood–Lake Mary

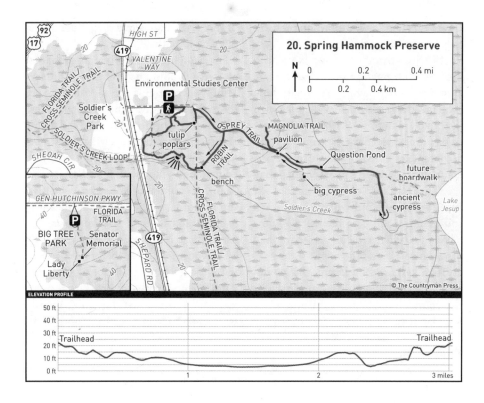

Road. Turn right and continue 2.5 miles to where it ends at Ronald Reagan Boulevard. Turn left at the light and make the first right onto General Hutchinson Parkway. The entrance to Big Tree Park is on your right. Continue down General Hutchinson Parkway through Spring Hammock Preserve to the traffic light at US 17-92. Turn left. After 0.8 mile, make a right at the light onto FL 419. Drive 0.6 miles to the preserve entrance at Osprey Trail, on the left across from the ball fields at Soldier Creek Park. Enter the gates and park in the lot along the road just past the Environmental Studies Center parking area. Gates close at dusk.

THE HIKE

At the east end of the parking area is a small sign that says PINE PAVILLION. It's the first of many small routed wood signs throughout the preserve, especially in the uplands closest to the Environmental Studies Center. While you might encounter students here during the week, the preserve is entirely the domain of hikers and cyclists on the weekends. Follow this short corridor down a pine-needle-strewn path under the oaks and pines. Turn right at the AZALEA TRAIL sign, following the arrow. At the next intersection, turn left. Reaching the CINNAMON FERN TRAIL sign, turn right. The understory is quite dense down this corridor through the uplands, but the trail leads you to the first of the natural wonders of this preserve: a grove of tulip poplars, also known as the tulip tree or yellow poplar (*Liriodendron tulipifera*). An interpretive sign points out the first one. Look up to see the distinct tulip-shaped leaves—except in winter, when they are only on the forest floor.

As you step out of the woods and into the sunlight, past an old FLORIDA TRAIL sign, notice the paved Cross Seminole Trail bisecting the preserve. Look down the paved path to your right: the tallest trees along the corridor are also tulip poplars. They can grow to 100 feet tall. A common tree in the Appalachians, they are at the southern extent of their range here, where they only thrive in the rich soil of hardwood hammocks. We know of very few places in Florida where they grow; this is one of the best.

Turn left and walk up the paved path, passing the trail map kiosk. At the roundabout, turn right and enter the woods to start your walk down the Osprey Trail. It's as broad as a road, but almost entirely canopied, making for a pleasant walk into an ancient hammock. At 0.4 mile, you come to an intersection with the Robin Trail. Stay left to remain on the Osprey Trail. Look to the right and up to make out the shape of a very tall old cypress tree.

As you walk deeper into the woods on the Osprey Trail, ferns swarm along the edges of a paralleling waterway. There is a boardwalk on the other side of the waterway and a picnic shelter. The boardwalk is part of the Magnolia Trail, once a pleasant loop through the floodplain forest but now not easy to follow. It's worth crossing the bridge to the boardwalk and following the trail for a little ways for an immersion in this fern-rich and soggy alluvial forest, where braided streams appear from nowhere and rush across the dark, rich earth under the cabbage palms. Needle palm grows in the shadows; netted chain fern sprouts along a fallen log. Unless the trail has been blazed recently, don't wander too deeply in, as the trail branches in numerous directions without a clear path.

Back on the Osprey Trail, walk past a staircase leading down into the ditch—Mud Walk participants use it to wash off their shoes—and by the picnic shelter. The next two bridges formerly led to the Hydric Hammock Loop, which has been abandoned. If you cross either one, you come face to face with a sign that says TRAIL and points into deep mud. This is the core area for the Mud Walk, and as it is not blazed, it's best to leave the adventuring here for the school groups. Look off to your right after the second bridge with the HYDRIC HAMMOCK LOOP sign. Another enormous cypress is mostly hidden by the dense forest. A boardwalk used to lead back to it, and plans are to restore a portion of that walk in the future.

At times, the answer to Question Pond is obvious: it's a spring. When water levels in the swamp are low, the spring spills aqua blue waters into a run.

TULIP POPLAR AT SPRING HAMMOCK

QUESTION POND

At other times, it's a brownish pond. You've entered a hydric hammock, a swamp dense with cabbage palms and cypresses. Sweetgum and red maple thrive here, their leaves turning shades of crimson and purple in the fall. The canopy of trees presses closer from both sides. When you reach Marker OT-01, you've walked 1.2 miles. You're now at the location where a new boardwalk to Lake Jesup will be built through the mixed hardwood swamp straight ahead. The former boardwalk led to an impressive stand of towering ancient cypress, and we hope the new one will too. Meanwhile, it's up to you whether to continue down the Osprey Trail to try and see those cypresses.

The water level of Lake Jesup dictates if the trail is passable. There are times when the trail simply vanishes beneath the swamp. There are other times when it's perfectly dry. You should turn around if you run into water. Near the end of the Osprey Trail, you'll pass the blocked-off old boardwalk before

emerging in a clearing near Soldier's Creek. Look left to see the cypresses that tower over the tree canopy nearest Lake Jesup. This spot was where the Limpkin Trail once followed the creek west, but it's been washed out with no plans for rebuilding. Turn around and walk back along the Osprey Trail, passing the curve and Question Pond before you take a break at the picnic shelter.

When you reach the Robin Trail intersection, you've hiked 2.2 miles. Turn left. A narrow tunnel with the fronds of bluestem palm and cabbage palm swinging across the footpath, the Robin Trail gains a little elevation as it leaves the swamps of the Osprey Trail behind. The canopy opens, revealing blue skies above the oaks and pines. The trail comes to a sudden end at a bench adjoining Soldier's Creek. Turn right and scramble up to the Cross Seminole Trail. Cross it and continue straight ahead on what was once a segment of the statewide Florida Trail, and still retains that name on some maps.

ALONG THE OSPREY TRAIL

The trees are especially tall here, where the footpath twists and winds to follow the bluffs along Soldier's Creek, sometimes dipping into deep basins to climb right back out again. Watch for tangles of roots underfoot. Pause at a clearing on a bluff to enjoy a curve in the creek. The sand on some of the trail's curves is tossed up here whenever Soldier's Creek overflows its banks. At 2.6 miles, a bench sits on the bluff above the creek.

Loblolly bay trees tower above the forest as you follow the narrow footpath upstream. The habitat transitions to uplands, with oaks and pines dominant again. Passing a trail junction, you continue along the narrowing path on the bluffs until it draws within sight of a railroad trestle. Turn right at this junction, joining the Primary Trail. The path that goes straight ahead under the trestle and highway was built by cyclists, and floods easily after a rain, as it sticks close to the creek. It connects up with Soldier's Creek Loop (see *Other Hiking Options*).

In the upland forest, the Primary Trail quickly comes to a four-way junc-

tion. To the left is a direct route to the Environmental Studies Center. Keep a respectful distance from outdoor classroom activities. Continue straight ahead, passing signs for the SMILAX TRAIL and the BASSWOOD TRAIL. As you meet the AZALEA TRAIL sign, you've come full circle. Go straight up the Azalea Trail to the next junction. Turn right to walk around the picnic pavilion. Keep left to follow the PINEWOODS TRAIL, walking down a narrow corridor of saw palmetto with pines rising high above the oak canopy. Stay left at the next junction to pop out at the paved road you drove in on. Turn left and walk to the parking area to complete a 3-mile loop.

OTHER HIKING OPTIONS

1. **Lake Jesup Trek**. Step over to the paved Cross Seminole Trail from the parking area. Follow it down to the roundabout and junction with the Osprey Trail. Continue down the Osprey Trail, passing the next Y junction and the Mud Walk pavilion and its bridges. Stop at spring-fed Ques-

tion Pond. Continue past it to the curve in the trail at Marker OT-01. If the boardwalk to Lake Jesup has been built, it will extend through the cypress swamp to the lakeshore from here, a 2.4-mile round-trip between the trailhead and the lake.

2. **Soldier's Creek Loop.** Follow the paved Cross Seminole Trail north

LADY LIBERTY AT BIG TREE PARK

and carefully cross FL 419 at the crosswalk. Traffic rarely stops for you, despite state law. When you reach the bridge across Soldier's Creek, take the trail to the left. The sign says SOLDIERS CREEK MOUNTAIN BIKE TRAIL, although in the 1990s it was built and maintained as part of the statewide Florida Trail. The probability of encountering cyclists is high on weekends, but the beauty of this loop is worth the walk. Keeping close to the creek, it stays in deep shade and follows the old orange blazes on the oaks and palms. When it leaves the creek, it emerges at the far side of Soldier Creek Park near the ballfields. Walk across the park to rejoin the Cross Seminole Trail to use the crosswalk. It's a 1.5-mile hike, which can be cut to a 1.1-mile loop by driving across the street and parking at Soldier's Creek Park.

3. **Big Tree Park** (28.720644, -81.331767). At the north end of Spring Hammock Preserve, accessible either by a 4-mile round-trip walk up the paved Cross Seminole Trail or by car, Big Tree Park is home to some incredibly tall trees, including Lady Liberty, a bald cypress thought to be 3,000 years old. The boardwalk to the trees is a 0.25-mile round-trip. Interpretive exhibits pay homage to the remains of The Senator, once Florida's biggest cypress but destroyed in 2012 by an arsonist.

CAMPING AND LODGING

Best Western Plus Sanford Airport, 3401 S Orlando Drive, Sanford, FL 32773 (407-320-0845, bestwestern.com)

Higgins House B&B, 420 S Oak Avenue, Sanford, FL 32771 (407-324-9238, higginshouse.com)

21

Orlando Wetlands Park

TOTAL DISTANCE: 6.2 miles along a route inside a vast network of interconnected trails

HIKING TIME: 3-4 hours, depending on stops for wildlife watching

DIFFICULTY: Easy

USAGE: Free. Open sunrise to sunset. No pets. Bicycles are permitted on the levees but not on the wooded trails.

TRAILHEAD GPS COORDINATES: 28.5696, -80.9964

CONTACT INFORMATION: Orlando Wetlands Park, 25155 Wheeler Road, Christmas, FL 32709 (407-568-1706, cityoforlando.net/wetlands)

Across a chain of wetlands covering more than a thousand acres, wood storks gather sticks for their nests. A flock of roseate spoonbills noses through the mud flats, while moorhens squawk behind a screen of marsh grasses. Limpkins flip over apple snails. In all, more than 150 species of birds have been spotted at Orlando Wetlands Park, from flocks of black-bellied whistling ducks to rare sightings of merlins and indigo buntings. That's why the parking lot is packed on weekends, and why visitors flock here from around the world. This is Florida's original purpose-built wetlands park, the first to prove that wastewater treatment and wildlife habitat could work hand-in-hand. Now more than 30 years old, it's one of the best wildlife-watching sites along the St. Johns River floodplain.

Nineteen miles of berms separate a series of wetland cells that filter water—at a variety of depths—through different natural collections of aquatic plants. Nearly all of these levees are open to hiking, so there are dozens of routes to follow. Ours provides a walk through the natural habitats on the east side of the park before following the most popular loop through the central marshes and to the southwestern corner, where wildlife sightings are at their best. Be sure to use sunscreen and insect repellent, and wear a hat. Most of the hike is out in the open.

Stop by the main pavilion to sign in before your hike and to pick up a trail map. On Fridays and Saturdays from 9-3, the Education Center is staffed by Friends of Orlando Wetlands Park. Inside, you'll find wildlife exhibits and interpretive information. Tram tours are offered when the center is open.

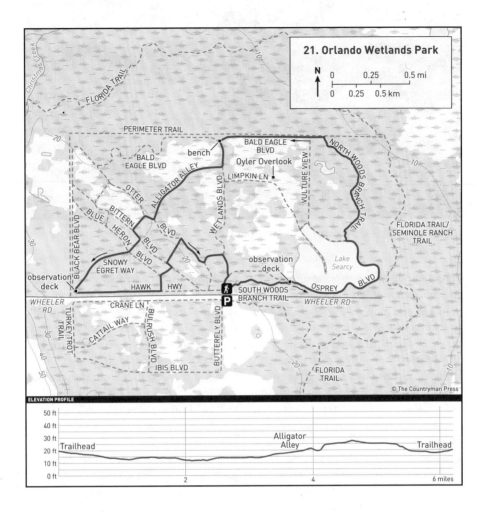

21. Orlando Wetlands Park

N

0   0.25   0.5 mi

0   0.25   0.5 km

Christmas Creek

FLORIDA TRAIL

PERIMETER TRAIL

BALD EAGLE BLVD
bench
BALD EAGLE BLVD
Oyler Overlook
LIMPKIN LN
VULTURE VIEW
NORTH WOODS BRANCH TRAIL

OTTER
ALLIGATOR ALLEY
WETLANDS BLVD

BITTERN
BLUE HERON BLVD
BLVD
BLACK BEAR BLVD

FLORIDA TRAIL/ SEMINOLE RANCH TRAIL

SNOWY EGRET WAY
observation deck
Lake Searcy
OSPREY BLVD

observation deck
HAWK HWY
SOUTH WOODS BRANCH TRAIL

WHEELER RD
CRANE LN
TURKEY TROT TRAIL
CATTAIL WAY
BULRUSH BLVD
IBIS BLVD
BUTTERFLY BLVD
WHEELER RD

FLORIDA TRAIL

© The Countryman Press

ELEVATION PROFILE

50 ft
40 ft
30 ft   Alligator
20 ft Trailhead   Alley   Trailhead
10 ft
0 ft
        2   4   6 miles

GETTING THERE

From I-4 in Orlando, follow FL 408 (toll road) east for 12.6 miles to FL 50 at Union Park. Continue east for 11.3 miles on FL 50 to Fort Christmas Road in Christmas—note the Christmas display on the corner. Alternatively, from I-95 in Titusville, drive west on FL 50 for 10.3 miles through the town of Christmas to the same corner. Turn north on Fort Christmas Road. Continue 2.3 miles, passing Fort Christmas Park, before turning right onto Wheeler Road just before a sharp left curve. Drive 1.5 miles down Wheeler Road to the parking area on the left. If the parking area is full, use the Seminole Ranch parking area across the street.

THE HIKE

After you stop at the main pavilion by the restrooms to sign in, walk across the grassy area between picnic pavilions, passing the bat house, to the big trailhead sign in the distance along the tree line. This is the South Woods Branch Trail, which guides you into a lush hardwood hammock typical of the natural habitats that fringe the man-made wetlands. As this forest lies in the St. Johns

ROSEATE SPOONBILLS IN THE WETLANDS AT THE JUNCTION OF OSPREY BOULEVARD AND WETLANDS BOULEVARD

River floodplain, it can occasionally get soggy underfoot, which is why sweetgum and red maple thrive here among the cabbage palms and live oaks. Numbered signs call attention to the flora; an interpretive brochure can be picked up at the Education Center to follow along. At 0.25 mile, a SEMINOLE CAMPSITE sign points left down a side trail. There is no camping in Orlando Wetlands Park anymore, but there was when this footpath was part of the statewide Florida Trail. Continue straight ahead, following the white blazes past marsh ferns and showy royal ferns as the landscape gets wetter. Past a bench, notice the dark waters of a swamp, which is why a Carolina willow is thriving behind Marker 24.

Reaching a small boardwalk and bridge at 0.5 mile, the trail makes a sharp left to emerge onto the levee at Lake Searcy. Turn left to climb the stairs to the observation deck, which provides a sweeping view of both wetlands and open water. As with all of the water bodies along the levees of this park, Lake Searcy is man-made. Fill for the levee system came from this particular part of the park. Once part of a cattle ranch, this land was purchased by the City of Orlando in the early 1980s to develop

a new method of treating wastewater. With the exception of the swamps and streams along the footpaths on this side of the park, all of the other water bodies were created for treatment purposes. It takes 40 days for wastewater to flow through the wetlands until it reaches a quality where it can be discharged to the St. Johns River through a canal. You'll encounter that canal farther along the hike.

From the observation deck, you start walking around the east end of Lake Searcy by following Osprey Boulevard. All of the levee roads are open to hiking, biking, and equestrian use, and you may encounter equipment working in the wetland cells on weekdays, as they occasionally have to be "mucked out" and rebuilt. The farther you get from the observation deck, the more open the water is. Coots like this end of the lake, and you will see alligators swimming through the open water. You may have noticed the warning signs already: alligators are extremely common here. If you leave the levee to look at blooming wildflowers or waterfowl near the water's edge, be very careful. A rule of thumb is to never get within 20 feet of an alligator. Once in a while, they'll rest on the levee because the limestone is warm.

Enjoy the panoramic views across Lake Searcy as the trail curves around it for the next mile. Notice the dense forest on the opposite side of the levee. Pass by a gate at a property boundary, and an unmarked trail. Soon after, you see the roof of a chickee hut at the base of the levee, around 1.5 miles. It's almost hidden by the forest canopy. Walk down to it to find a sign indicating the start of the North Woods Branch Trail. This is your second opportunity on this hike to enjoy some deep shade. Originally built as part of the statewide Florida Trail several decades ago, the footpath leads you into the forest, starting with a few boardwalks in a spot that's seasonally wet. This trail shows off the natural habitats that surround the man-made wetlands as it slips through uplands with oaks and pines before touching the edge of a swamp forest.

Once you cross a bridge over an ephemeral waterway, the trail enters a beauty spot, a palm hammock where the trunks of the palm trees rise like tall columns to the sky. Beyond the next bridge, you pass the ORANGE MOUND sign, pointing out the former location of another campsite. Continuing through the dense palm hammock, the trail emerges at a bridge with a sign adjoining it. This clearing is the junction with the Wilderness Trail, and the bridge crosses the outflow canal of the wetlands to connect with the current route of the Florida Trail. Don't cross the bridge, but turn left before it. Walk down the shady tunnel of vegetation to pass a water control structure. The trail emerges back into the sun. It's in this area, fittingly perched in a series of dead trees, that black vultures have always gathered. The Wilderness Trail ends here at the junction with Bald Eagle Boulevard and Vulture View, 2.5 miles in, at the next bridge and water structure. Continue straight ahead.

PALM HAMMOCK ALONG THE NORTH WOODS BRANCH TRAIL

For the remainder of your hike, you will be walking along the wetland cells out in the open. Each junction is well marked and has a YOU ARE HERE map. If you need to cut this route short at any point, simply check the map for the most direct route back to the parking area. Along this forested edge of the park, we watched a colony of wood storks gathering sticks to make nests nearby. When you reach the junction of Bald Eagle Boulevard and Wetlands Boulevard, a sheltered picnic bench sits in the shade. After enjoying a break, follow Wetlands Boulevard into the heart of the marshes. The distant tree line marks the edge of the park. The wetlands in the foreground are Wading Bird Marsh, an excellent location to spy herons, bitterns, and egrets, especially along the next portion of the route, Alligator Alley. Make a right off Wetlands Boulevard to follow this curving levee. It's aptly named, as

you're quite likely to see big alligators along this route. As the levee curves, it offers beautiful views across islands of cabbage palms out in the marsh.

Reaching a palm hammock, you come to the junction of Alligator Alley and Otter Boulevard at 3.8 miles. Turn right. A culvert directs water flow beneath the levee here, with the hammock offering shelter for the white-tailed deer sometimes seen in the park. Make a left at the next levee, the aptly named Deer Drive. Marsh grasses are taller here, and water lettuce floats on the surface. You meet Bittern Boulevard at a T. Make a left, and then the next right to walk down Snowy Egret Way. This levee makes a beeline for the southwest corner of the park, where the impoundments are thick with tall cattails and the open water is mainly around the culverts. The reason for going to this corner is the nice observation deck built at the junction of Snowy

A COVE IN THE WETLANDS ALONG NIGHT HERON LAKE

Egret Way with Black Bear Boulevard and Hawk Highway, at 4.6 miles. You'll find it a gathering place for visitors to the park because of the wildlife spotted here. We saw three different snakes—a ribbon snake, a banded water snake, and a red rat snake—and it's not uncommon to find otters in this area. A young alligator surprised us by lounging in the oak hammock behind the deck. If the water looks more scum-covered at this end of the park, that's because the whole process of wastewater treatment starts right here.

Leaving the observation deck, walk along the perimeter levee on Hawk Highway. A screen of trees shields Wheeler Road. Make the next left onto Blue Heron Boulevard, and turn right on Dragonfly Drive. These impoundments tend to be dense with grasses. Make a left on Bittern Boulevard, and a quick right on Warbler Way. It takes you to a T intersection with Otter Boulevard, reached at 5.6 miles. Make a right. At the junction with Night Heron Lane, make a left. The small stretch of woods edges a deeper pool. A bench overlooks a small patch of open water. Cabbage palms rise in the background. By the scuffles in the dirt along the shoreline, it's obvious that alligators enjoy sunning here and crossing the levee to the other impoundment. Be cautious.

When you reach Wetlands Boulevard again, make a right. This takes you past one last open wetland area, where it's not uncommon to see flocks of roseate spoonbills or white ibis pecking away in the shallows. You come to a T intersection with Osprey Boulevard coming in from the left from Lake Searcy. Turn right and walk down past the picnic pavilion and restrooms to the parking area, completing a 6.2-mile hike.

OTHER HIKING OPTIONS

With such an extensive network of trails across the levees, there are dozens of possible ways to explore Orlando Wetlands Park. Check the park map for details. Here are some of our favorites.

1. **South Woods Loop.** For a 1-mile loop, follow the South Woods Branch Trail to the observation deck on Lake Searcy. Loop back to the trailhead using Osprey Boulevard.
2. **Lake Searcy Loop.** Follow the levee system around Lake Searcy on a 3.7-mile loop, with a stop at the Oyler Overlook.
3. **Birding Loop.** Start as in #2 but take the left fork. This marked 2-mile loop focuses on the central marshes with some of the best bird watching.
4. **South Pools.** Cross Wheeler Road to access a 2.7-mile loop around the southernmost wetland cells in the park, which sit off by themselves.
5. **Seminole Ranch Loop.** Using the South Woods Branch, North Woods Branch, and Perimeter Trail, connect to the east of the Florida Trail, adjoining the Seminole Ranch Conservation Area, then hike south and use the blue-blazed trail to the Wheeler Road trailhead to make a 6-mile loop that's mostly in the woods.

CAMPING AND LODGING

Christmas RV Park, 25525 E Colonial Drive, Christmas, FL 32709 (407-568-5207, christmasrvpark.com), no tents.

Lake Mills Park, 1301 Tropical Avenue, Chuluota, FL 32766 (407-665-2001, seminolecountyfl.gov)

Fairfield Inn & Suites, 4735 Helen Hauser Boulevard, Titusville, FL 32780 (321-385-1818, marriott.com)

SUNSET ALONG THE PRAIRIE LAKES LOOP

IV.

ORLANDO METRO

Lake Proctor Wilderness Area

TOTAL DISTANCE: 4 miles in three loops, with shorter and longer options

HIKING TIME: 2 hours

DIFFICULTY: Easy to moderate

USAGE: Free. Open dawn to dusk. Leashed pets welcome.

TRAILHEAD GPS COORDINATES: 28.7266, -81.0991

CONTACT INFORMATION: Lake Proctor Wilderness Area, 920 SR 46, Geneva, FL 32732 (407-349-0769, seminolecountyfl.gov)

You hear them before you see them, as the cries of sandhill cranes rattle across the open marshes and through the forests surrounding Lake Proctor, a meandering, shallow wet prairie where sandhill cranes gather to eat, mate, and raise their young. Protecting 475 acres near the historic rural enclave of Geneva—where their Fourth of July Parade is a slice of Americana you shouldn't miss—Lake Proctor Wilderness Area is one of the best places in Central Florida to watch these graceful birds from the shaded shore of the lake.

GETTING THERE

From I-4 exit 101, Sanford, drive east on FL 46 for 4 miles to downtown Sanford. Turn right, following FL 46 along US 17/92 (South French Avenue) for 1.7 miles. FL 46 then turns left. Continue another 12.1 miles, driving past the Orlando-Sanford Airport and across the St. Johns River into rural countryside. The trailhead entrance is on the left not far past the traffic light for Geneva at FL 426.

THE HIKE

Grab a trail map from the kiosk near the parking lot entrance. Several large loops and many small loops are possible along this trail system; this hike follows the most scenic option. Each loop is blazed using colored markers with arrows. Starting on the Red Trail, it's a pleasant walk down a broad corridor flanked by saw palmetto and shaded by a hammock of sand live oaks with colorful gardens of lichens growing on their trunks and limbs. You very quickly come to a fork with the Orange Trail and a large white sign that says LP-01. This is the first of many such signs you'll

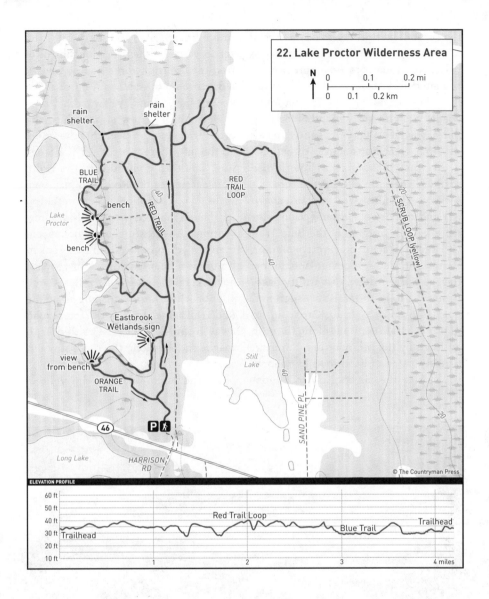

22. Lake Proctor Wilderness Area

N

| 0 | | 0.1 | | 0.2 mi |
| 0 | 0.1 | 0.2 km | | |

rain shelter

rain shelter

BLUE TRAIL

RED TRAIL LOOP

40

RED TRAIL

Lake Proctor

bench

bench

SCRUB LOOP (yellow)

20

Eastbrook Wetlands sign

40

Still Lake

40

20

view from bench

ORANGE TRAIL

SAND PINE PL

46

P

Long Lake

HARRISON RD

© The Countryman Press

ELEVATION PROFILE

| 60 ft |
| 50 ft |
| 40 ft |
| 30 ft |
| 20 ft |
| 10 ft |

Trailhead

Red Trail Loop

Blue Trail

Trailhead

1   2   3   4 miles

find throughout the wilderness areas of Seminole County, installed in recent years to help hikers avoid getting lost. Keep right to follow the red blazes. Sphagnum moss carpets the jagged trunks of saw palmetto that protrude from the footpath.

Making a slight left turn, the trail passes under tall longleaf pines within a sea of saw palmetto. One live oak shows off a bounty of resurrection fern, plump

and green after the prior evening's rain. This is a narrow corridor of oak scrub, transitioning into sand pine scrub with tall sand pines. At a junction with the Orange Trail after 0.25 mile, continue straight ahead on the red trail. The habitat is now firmly sand pine scrub, with myrtle oak and Chapman oak in the understory. At the junction with the Blue Trail, continue straight as the trail loses its shady canopy to the open nature of the scrub. The trail heads down a very long corridor with lots of crunchy myrtle oak leaves underfoot. As it narrows, it's surrounded by young sand pine, soft and fluffy but not tall enough to cast much shade. Walking into a stand of longleaf pines, you face a very old sand live oak with limbs reaching out in all directions.

At what looks like a junction, a marker urges you left. Farther down a scrub corridor, the trail makes a sharp left and reaches a T intersection after 0.9 mile, the junction of the Blue Trail and Red Trail at an interpretive marker. Turn right. Under a power line, follow the red marker down this utility easement. At 1 mile, the trail turns left and goes into an oak scrub. Crossing an unmarked trail, continue along the path outlined by the red markers. Entering a pretty patch of hardwood hammock, you notice the air cool down almost immediately. As you exit into the scrub, you hear the peeps and chirps of frogs as the trail works its way toward a depression marsh at 1.3 miles. It's a beauty spot, edged by saw palmetto.

Scrambling up a slight bluff, the broad trail emerges back into the scrub. To the left, there is a corner of a fence line. The trail continues to the right. This section of the Red Trail may be a little tricky to follow. Keep watching for the red markers, especially at intersections. A seafoam-colored lichen, old man's beard, dangles from the crooked limbs of a rusty lyonia. You reach a covered rain shelter at 1.5 miles. Catch your bearings here. Continue along the Red Trail, which follows the forest road away from the shelter. The Red Trail reaches a fork along the road; stay left to enter the forest.

At the next junction, the yellow-

MARSHES ALONG EASTBROOK WETLANDS

JUNCTION OF TRAILS AT A RAIN SHELTER AT THE NORTH END OF THE LOOP

blazed Scrub Loop heads left toward a bayhead, a marshy area with loblolly bay trees. This trail is an optional add-on for a perimeter hike. While it immerses you into more scrub habitat, a large portion of it is spent following the property line along a fence. Continuing along the red blazes, you enter scrubby flatwoods. At the second junction of red and yellow blazes, turn right. Winding through the diminutive scrub, the trail crosses an access road. Continuing uphill over the next access road, there's a nice view of a wet prairie, where sandhill cranes may be wading. A bench provides a place to rest.

Paralleling the power line, the Red Trail meanders beneath it to a marker that ushers you left towards the parking area. However, the highlight of this trail system is the walk along Lake Proctor, and it's in the opposite direction. Turn right and walk up the power line, passing the Red Trail again to reach the junction.

You return to the main trail junction at 2.6 miles. Continue straight past the shelter, following the Blue Trail as the trail drops toward the lake through the pine forest. At the next rain shelter, follow the blue markers left.

You have your first glimpse of Lake Proctor through the trees as the trail gently descends to the edge of this large, shallow wetland, more wet prairie than lake. A side trail leads to the edge, where leopard frogs sing in the shallows. This is just one little arm of the lake, which the trail now rambles along, beneath the longleaf pines and Southern magnolia. At 2.9 miles, the trail swings right to work its way around a tall wall of saw palmetto, and you have the lake in your sights again. Lily pads drift across the placid surface. Past a depression marsh, the trail makes its way back to the lakeshore at a spot with an interpretive sign and bench.

After another short jaunt along the

lakeshore, the trail emerges on another marshy arm of the lake. A pair of sandhill cranes works its way through the grasses. You see a bundle of yellow move with them—a colt scarcely a month old, herded carefully by its doting parents, who pluck choice morsels for their baby while staying close enough to protect the bundle of fussing feathers. Mating for life, sandhill cranes raise only one or two chicks per year.

Leaving the lakeshore past an ephemeral pond, the Blue Trail meets the Red Trail at 3.3 miles. Turn right. At the picturesque oak just a little ways down the trail, bear right to walk along the Orange Trail, the shortest of the loops. It makes its way down to the marsh edge, where a sign marked EASTBROOK WETLANDS claims the spot for a local school. A tall slash pine has a deep gash in its trunk, a catface speaking to the turpentine industry that was once an important part of the local economy. At 3.7 miles, a bench provides a beautiful view of the wetlands. The trail makes a sharp left. The sound of traffic increases and the forest grows denser as you draw closer to the trailhead, walking uphill through an oak hammock. Keep to the right as you return to the Red Trail, and you emerge at the trailhead after 4 miles.

OTHER HIKING OPTIONS

1. **Wetlands Walk**. Focus on the Orange Trail by taking a left at the first junction with it, and a right twice in quick succession when you meet the Red Trail again. This 0.6-mile hike leads you along the Eastbrook Wetlands, which is the most likely spot to see nesting sandhill cranes.

2. **Lakes and Marshes**. Again, take a left on the Orange Trail to follow it along the scenic shoreline of the Eastbrook Wetlands, a large wet prairie. After rejoining the Red Trail, turn left along it, then left onto the Blue Trail, which slips through some of the most scenic parts of the preserve, including the shoreline of Lake Proctor. Where it meets the Red Trail at a rain shelter, turn right to follow the Red Trail back to the trailhead for a 2.4-mile hike.

3. **Yellow Trail**. Add the Yellow Trail onto your exploration of the Red Trail through the scrub forest on the east side of the powerlines to lengthen your overall hike to 5.6 miles.

4. **Geneva Wilderness Area** (Hike 23) is 3 miles away, so combine both hikes into one trip.

CAMPING AND LODGING

Fort Lane Park, 3301–3367 Fort Lane Road, Geneva, FL 32732 (407-349-9876), reservations required.

Mullet Lake Park, 2368 Mullet Lake Park Road, Geneva, FL 32732 (407-665-2180, seminolecountyfl.gov), tents only.

Danville B&B, 232 N Jungle Road, Geneva, FL 32732 (407-349-5724, danvillebnb.com)

23

Geneva Wilderness Area

TOTAL DISTANCE: 1.9 miles in a loop with several short spur trails

HIKING TIME: 1 hour

DIFFICULTY: Easy

USAGE: Free. Open sunrise to sunset. Leashed pets welcome. Bicycles permitted.

TRAILHEAD GPS COORDINATES: 28.7092, -81.1236

CONTACT INFORMATION: Geneva Wilderness Area, 3485 CR 426, Geneva, FL 32732 (407-349-0769, seminolecountyfl.gov)

Across a palette of pine flatwoods, scrub, and flatwoods ponds, the Geneva Wilderness Area protects 180 acres just outside the suburban creep of Oviedo towards the farms and ranches of Geneva, Seminole County's last truly rural corner. In 1994, Seminole County purchased the land from the Boy Scouts of America to create this preserve, and allowed group camping to continue as a tradition. The South Camp and Chapel date back to Camp Hendricks, the original Boy Scout camp that was here. Two main trails wind through the park. Red blazes designate the Loop Trail, which runs along the edges of the park's many ponds and through a stand of pine forest that once was part of a turpentine camp. The yellow blazes provide a connection to the Flagler Trail, a north-south trail through adjoining Little Big Econ State Forest.

GETTING THERE

From I-4, take exit 94, Longwood. Follow FL 434 for 13 miles east through Longwood and Winter Springs into downtown Oviedo. Turn left at the light, then immediately left on FL 426, following it 6.1 miles west, past the Little Big Econ State Forest trailhead at Barr Street, to the entrance to the Geneva Wilderness Area on the right. The trailhead kiosk (28.708800, -81.123967) is at the south end of the parking area.

THE HIKE

At the kiosk, sign the register and pick up a trail map. The trail enters a forest in miniature—a scrub forest shaded by gnarled sand live oak. Dense foamy clumps of deer moss carpet the forest floor. Where the trail reaches a clearing for a powerline, turn left. A boardwalk

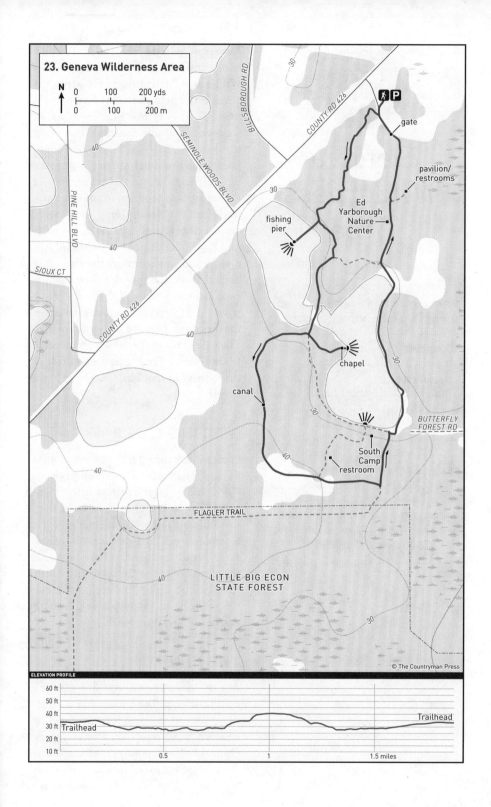

23. Geneva Wilderness Area

N

| 0 | 100 | 200 yds |
| 0 | 100 | 200 m |

BILLSBOROUGH RD

COUNTY RD 426

SEMINOLE WOODS BLVD

PINE HILL BLVD

SIOUX CT

COUNTY RD 426

gate

pavilion/
restrooms

Ed
Yarborough
Nature
Center

fishing
pier

chapel

canal

BUTTERFLY
FOREST RD

South
Camp
restroom

FLAGLER TRAIL

LITTLE BIG ECON
STATE FOREST

© The Countryman Press

ELEVATION PROFILE

| 60 ft |
| 50 ft |
| 40 ft |
| 30 ft | Trailhead | Trailhead |
| 20 ft |
| 10 ft |
| | 0.5 | 1 | 1.5 miles |

FLATWOODS POND ALONG THE LOOP TRAIL

out into a flatwoods pond, a 0.25-mile into your hike, serves as a fishing pier. Walk out on it to watch egrets stalking their prey along the shoreline. Small fish dart beneath the lily pads.

Leaving the boardwalk, turn right and walk up past a building to the next trail marker, which points to the right. This is the start of the Loop Trail, which heads down a causeway between the largest flatwoods ponds in Geneva Wilderness Area. Although both ponds fade to mud during drought, they serve as magnets for wildlife when the waters return. Views are best between the pines as you come up to the marked side trail to the Chapel. Take that trail to stand at the peninsula between the two largest ponds in the preserve.

Back on the Loop Trail, an arrow points away from the ponds and into the forest, curving beneath a canopy of live oaks. Here's where the trail tunnels into

a portion of the preserve that was once a bustling turpentine camp. As the surrounding vegetation becomes denser, the Loop Trail reaches a bench near a narrow but deep cut through the forest. Turn right for a quick side trip along the canal to see several of the longleaf pines that were once regularly tapped for turpentine. Sailors relied on the sap of pine trees for tar, pitch, rosin, and turpentine. These products sealed and protected wooden sailing ships from the harsh effects of salt water.

At the canal's end, near the property fence, notice one tall pine tree with a deep gash running more than 6 feet up the tree from its base. Beyond the fence lie several more tall pines with similar gashes. Called catfaces, these gashes provided the turpentine collector a means of "bleeding" the tree for its resin. A clay cup hung below metal strips set into the gash enabled the resin to pool into a collection basin, which would be emptied into larger containers for transport. Hikers sometimes stumble across these clay cups scattered throughout the woods. If you find one, please leave it be.

Leaving the forest, the Loop Trail pops into the open along the edge of a scrubby flatwoods near the GW 6 sign. There is no shade through this section. At 1.1 miles, an unmarked side trail leads to a rustic restroom at South Camp, the group campsite still used by Scouts and available for group use by reservation. Continue past this turnoff to a trail sign in the distance. The GW 5 sign marks the junction of the Loop Trail and the Flagler Trail. A hike along the historic Flagler Trail, which follows the former route of a branch of the Florida East Coast Railroad, can extend your trek by two hours or more. The trail is named for railroad magnate Henry Flagler. Completed in 1914, the railroad's Kis-

simmee Valley Extension ran down this route from Titusville, crossing the Econlockhatchee River into Chuluota, proceeding to Kenansville and down to Okeechobee. His Chuluota Land Company attempted to sell off 11,000 acres of land in this area with little success. After his railroad line closed, the state bought the right of way to build a highway that was never completed.

Unless you're adding on that extra mileage in Little Big Econ State Forest to the river, turn left at the GW 5 sign to continue your loop around the flatwoods ponds. The next trail junction points out another side trail to the South Camp. Turn right and follow the markers to skirt into the woods away from the marshy edge of the pond, crossing a small footbridge. Stay left at the next junction, following the markers. The path broadens back to the width of a forest road, which it's been throughout most of the preserve, with excellent

NEW PICNIC PAVILION AT THE OLD NORTH CAMP

views of the two ponds. See the Chapel on the distant shore. The shoreline sparkles like rubies when the sunlight catches dewdrops on the carnivorous sundew plants that huddle near the water's edge.

After 1.6 miles of hiking, you reach a trail junction at the GW 3 sign. The Loop Trail has completed its loop. Look for a trail marker pointing to the right, which leads you towards the Ed Yarborough Nature Center. Used mainly for field trips and Scouting outings, this building is open occasionally for public workshops and has a native plant garden. Continue along what was the Boy Scout camp's entrance road. A side trail leads to a picnic pavilion, restrooms, and water fountain at the site of the old North Camp. Trail markers guide you up the road past the caretaker's home, where there is a stile to get around the gate. You end up back at the parking area after 1.9 miles.

OTHER HIKING OPTIONS

1. **Boardwalk Loop**. Take the main trail to the boardwalk, then turn left instead of right at the junction with the Loop Trail. That will bring you back to the parking area via the Ed Yarborough Nature Center and picnic pavilion, a 0.8-mile loop.

2. **Flagler Trail**. Add more mileage by using the Flagler Trail to connect to the trail system in adjoining Little Big Econ State Forest. It's a 2.8-mile round-trip from the GW 5 sign down the Flagler Trail to the Econlockhatchee River to where pilings of the old railroad bridge still stand. You can add on the Kolokee Trail and the Florida Trail for more mileage.

3. **Lake Proctor Wilderness Area** (Hike 22) is 3 miles away, so combine both hikes into one trip.

CAMPING AND LODGING

Lake Mills Park, 1301 Tropical Avenue, Chuluota, FL 32766 (407-665-2001, seminolecountyfl.gov)

Fort Lane Park, 3301–3367 Fort Lane Road, Geneva, FL 32732 (407-349-9876), reservations required.

Danville B&B, 232 N Jungle Road, Geneva, FL 32732 (407-349-5724, danvillebnb.com)

Hal Scott Preserve

TOTAL DISTANCE: 5.9 miles in a loop and three round-trip spur trails

HIKING TIME: 2.5–3 hours

DIFFICULTY: Easy to moderate

USAGE: Free. Sunrise to sunset. Leashed pets welcome. Trails shared with equestrians and cyclists. Backpacking campsites available with free permit.

TRAILHEAD GPS COORDINATES: 28.4861, -81.0954

CONTACT INFORMATION: Hal Scott Preserve, 5150 Dallas Boulevard, Orlando, FL 32833 (386-329-4404, sjrwmd.com/lands/recreation/hal-scott or orangecountyfl.net). Camping reservations: secure.sjrwmd.com/camp

As more and more natural landscapes around the Orlando metro vanish forever under a sea of subdivisions, industrial parks, and apartment complexes, protecting vast landscapes like the ones found at Hal Scott Preserve becomes ever more important. Once common throughout this region, the open pine savannas and prairies found here are a joy to hike through, a place for both expansive panoramas and tiny glimmers of beauty along the trails. More than 9,300 acres provide a buffer of public land along the Econlockhatchee (Econ) River, managed jointly by Orange County and St. Johns River Water Management District.

The trails here are multi-use and popular with equestrians, so don't be surprised to see horse trailers in the lot. Most of this hike is in the open. Slather on the sunscreen and wear a hat.

GETTING THERE

From Orlando International Airport, drive east along toll FL 528 away from the airport, and take Exit 24, Dallas Boulevard. Turn left. Drive 2.4 miles to the preserve entrance on the left. From I-95, follow toll FL 528 west to FL 520. Drive 6.6 miles north to Maxim Parkway. Turn left and continue 1.1 miles to Bancroft Boulevard. Turn right and drive 1.6 miles on Paddock St. Make a left on Dallas Boulevard, and the preserve entrance will be on the right.

THE HIKE

Start at the gap through the fence, walking the narrow strip of grass between the fence line and the firebreak. Pine flatwoods stretch into the distance. On the far side of the gated equestrian parking lot is a large pond edged with cattails.

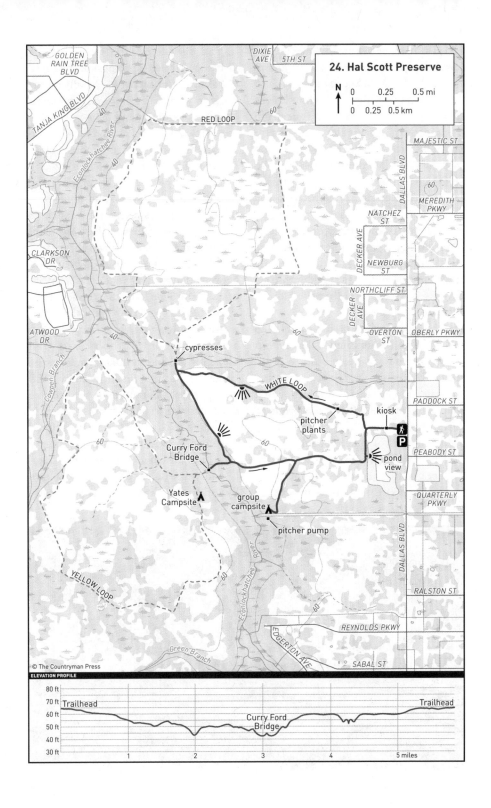

24. Hal Scott Preserve

N ↑

| 0 | 0.25 | 0.5 mi |
| 0 | 0.25 | 0.5 km |

GOLDEN RAIN TREE BLVD

TANJA KING BLVD

DIXIE AVE

5TH ST

RED LOOP

MAJESTIC ST

NATCHEZ ST

MEREDITH PKWY

CLARKSON DR

NEWBURG ST

NORTHCLIFF ST

ATWOOD DR

Cowpen Branch

Econlockhatchee River

cypresses

OVERTON ST

OBERLY PKWY

WHITE LOOP

PADDOCK ST

pitcher plants

kiosk

Curry Ford Bridge

pond view

PEABODY ST

Yates Campsite

group campsite

pitcher pump

QUARTERLY PKWY

YELLOW LOOP

Econlockhatchee River

DALLAS BLVD

DECKER AVE

DECKER AVE

RALSTON ST

REYNOLDS PKWY

EDGERTON AVE

Green Branch

SABAL ST

© The Countryman Press

ELEVATION PROFILE

80 ft						
70 ft	Trailhead					Trailhead
60 ft						
50 ft			Curry Ford Bridge			
40 ft						
30 ft						
	1	2	3	4	5 miles	

Pause at the kiosk to pick up a map. The forest road that serves as the trail continues due west. When it curves left at 0.3 mile, double-diamond white blazes (diamonds are used to mark equestrian trails) call attention to the right turn for you to start following the White Loop into the pine flatwoods. Dew-drenched spiderwebs shimmer in the early morning light. Tall longleaf pines are sparsely interspersed in an unending sea of saw palmetto and wiregrass, a scene described by one Florida naturalist as the "palmetto prairie." Underfoot, the trail is a grassed-over track with fine, delicate grasses, including the blooms of yellow-star grass.

A small but deep ditch parallels the trail. This and other ditches throughout the preserve were likely built to drain the land for cattle ranching, as pine flatwoods retain water. After a rain, you'll find the next mile of the trail prone to scattered muddy puddles. Seepage bogs feed clusters of carnivorous plants. Watch for the curved form of the hooded pitcher plant, a carnivorous plant that is one of Florida's threatened species.

The distant cooling towers of the Orlando Utilities Commission coal-fired generating station appear briefly on the horizon. Pink blooms of pale meadow beauty peek out from between the saw palmetto. After it passes a small hammock with a waterway that comes close to the road, the trail rises in elevation a little and curves right, opening up into excellent views of the open pine flatwoods. Short saw palmettos seem to stretch to infinity on your left. The blanket of palmettos comes to an abrupt halt at a wall of forest—loblolly bay and bald cypress along the meander of a lazy tributary of the Econ River. Scattered purple asters bloom amid the wiregrass.

At 1.9 miles, the White Loop reaches a T intersection. To the right, a trail blazed with red diamonds leads to the tributary. Ramble down to see it. Tall bald cypresses stand over the rush of dark water between their roots. There is no bridge to the Red Loop, an optional northern loop in the preserve, mostly used by equestrians. There is a high likelihood you will see orange blazes here by spring 2019, as the route of the state-

PALMETTO PRAIRIE AT HAL SCOTT PRESERVE

ECONLOCKHATCHEE RIVER AT CURRY FORD

wide Florida Trail is shifting through the Orlando metro and this is one of the public lands it is expected to cross. Turn around and head past the trail junction you came in on, paralleling the river and its floodplain forest. The trail converges with the tree line, offering shade under sweetgum and live oaks. Near the top of a longleaf pine, a pileated woodpecker beats out a steady rhythm. Another outstanding panorama of palmetto prairie stretches to the east. You reach the next T intersection at 2.9 miles, this time with a yellow-blazed trail.

Turn right for a walk down to the Econlockhatchee River. The trail drops into the floodplain forest, with an open understory beneath a canopy of sweetgum, live oaks, and bald cypress. The forest echoes with the screeches and chirps of birds—the blue-gray gnatcatcher, the tufted titmouse, and the wood thrush. Bromeliads cling to the trees. Skirt the deep mud puddles, made messy by the frolic of feral hogs. The lazy meander of the river lies just beyond the cypress knees.

Orlando residents are familiar with Curry Ford Road, but probably not with *the* Curry Ford, this narrow spot in the river near the Curry homestead. Travelers on horseback and stagecoaches crossed here on their way to Titusville until 1924, when the Cheney Highway (now FL 50) opened. On the bridge across Curry Ford, stand over the dark waters and watch them flow through the river swamp. The Yellow Loop starts on the far side of the bridge and is home to the Yates Campsite, 0.25 mile farther. If you've made a reservation in advance, camp there and explore the Yellow Loop tomorrow. Our day hike stays with the White Loop. Turn around and return to the trail junction. Continue straight ahead. The trail drops past a churned-up streambed, where small fish dart in the shallows. Netted chain fern grows in the shadows of the eroded ravine. A worn track takes off into the flatwoods to the right, which stretch on and on.

After 3.8 miles, you reach a major intersection. The campsite sign faces the opposite direction, so you won't see it when approaching this way. Turn right to follow this forest road through the grassy prairie. Stretching into the distance on both sides of the footpath, enveloping the small saw palmettos, shortspike bluestem forms a wheat-colored haze beneath the scattered longleaf pines. The river's floodplain forest defines the edge of the prairie. After crossing several small ditches, the trail rises into a hammock of live oak, where the gnarled branches are covered with a dense skin of resurrection fern and wild pine. Saw palmetto grows taller here, crowding in close to the trail on both sides.

When the view opens to a canal, turn right. You'll pass a portable toilet behind a section of wooden fence. Walk into the oak hammock just beyond it. Several benches are positioned around a fire ring near a picnic shelter. This is the group campsite, a beauty spot for a break. A pitcher pump on the far side of the canal provides non-potable water. The canal ends here, dropping through a spillway into the forest and flowing into the river swamp to meet the Econlockhatchee River. This is your turnaround point. Follow the broad forest road back through the prairie. Look carefully at the center of the trail for tiny but colorful wildflowers and dime-sized carnivorous sundew plants, glistening like drops of strawberry jam.

Rejoining the White Loop 4.8 miles into the hike, pass the campsite sign. Turn right. Tall wormwood grows along the undisturbed ground between the trail and the firebreak. A drainage ditch leads to the right. After you pass the ditch, the prairie yields to flatwoods as thickets of saw palmetto choke out the grasses. Gallberry waves in the breeze, weighed down with a load of purplish-black berries. The forest road sweeps left past a firebreak along the edge of a marshy pond. Follow the curve to find a side path to the shore of the pond.

This portion of the preserve was once a phosphate mine. The preserve's name comes from a former president of the Florida Audubon Society who served as an environmental consultant to mining companies such as IMC Agrico, who named this, their prize-winning reclamation project, after him.

Following the road around the pond, you complete the loop at the white double-diamonds on a post. Turn right to head down the straightaway, passing the kiosk along the way. You reach the parking area after 5.9 miles.

OTHER HIKING OPTIONS

1. **Campsite Ramble.** For a short but interesting walk, follow the White Loop clockwise for a 3.2-mile out-and-back trip to the campsite. We've done this several times at sunset to enjoy the radiance of colors over this panoramic landscape.

2. **River Ramble.** Follow the White Loop clockwise and skip the side trip to the campsite: go directly to the Curry Ford, the other beauty spot in the preserve, for a 3.6-mile round-trip.

3. **White & Red Loops.** Adding the Red Loop to the White Loop makes for an 11.9-mile day hike.

4. **White & Yellow Loops.** Add a walk around the Yellow Loop to the White Loop for a different 11.9-mile hike, either as a day hike or an overnighter.

CAMPING AND LODGING

Hidden River RV Park, 15295 E Colonial Drive, Orlando, FL 32826 (407-568-5346)

Hilton Garden Inn Orlando East/UCF, 1959 N Alafaya Trail, Orlando, FL 32826 (407-992-5000, hilton.com)

25

Prairie Lakes Loop

TOTAL DISTANCE: 11.4 miles in a figure eight loop

HIKING TIME: 5 hours to overnight

DIFFICULTY: Moderate

USAGE: $3 per person (or $6 per vehicle for 2 or more people) parking fee per day. Open 24 hours. Backpacking and tent camping, free permit required. Leashed pets welcome.

TRAILHEAD GPS COORDINATES: 27.9277, -81.1249

CONTACT INFORMATION: Three Lakes Wildlife Management Area, Prairie Lakes Unit, 1231 Prairie Lakes Road, Kenansville, FL 34739 (352-732-1225, myfwc.com/viewing/recreation/wmas/lead/three-lakes)

A broad landscape of prairies and pine flatwoods between three major lakes—Lake Kissimmee, Lake Jackson, and Lake Marian—Three Lakes Wildlife Management Area protects an astounding 63,000 acres in the heart of the Kissimmee River watershed. A little less than 9,000 of those acres comprise the Prairie Lakes Unit, in which the Florida Trail Association built an outstanding trail system soon after the state acquired the land from ranchers and opened it as a state park. Now under management of the Florida Fish and Wildlife Conservation Commission, it remains one of the best places to hike and camp in the region.

The Prairie Lakes Loop has two stacked loops, the North and South Loops, each close to six miles long. They can be hiked individually or together, since there is easy access to the central point where they meet. The route of the statewide Florida National Scenic Trail follows one side of each loop, connecting to additional trails to the north and south in the greater Three Lakes Wildlife Management Area. Check regulations in advance regarding hunting seasons—camping is restricted during general gun season—and always wear bright orange when hiking here during any scheduled hunts. A free permit is required in advance for camping at any of the campsites along this hike; call 352-732-1225 to arrange yours.

GETTING THERE

From US 192 in St. Cloud, which can be reached by Florida's Turnpike, follow Canoe Creek Road south for 25.4 miles. The entrance to Prairie Lakes is well marked. Turn right on Prairie Lakes Road. The Prairie Lakes trailhead is on the right side of the road. Close to the

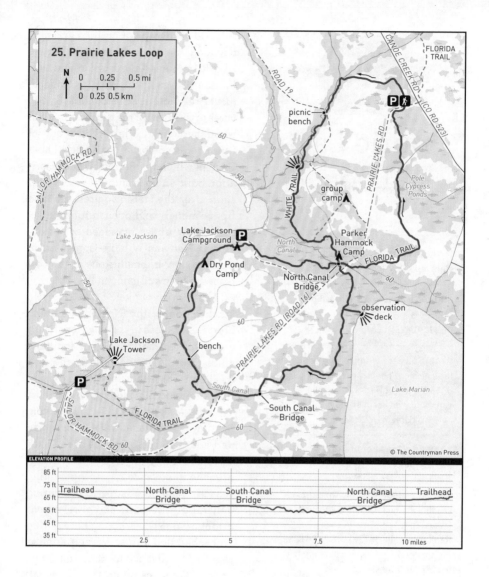

25. Prairie Lakes Loop

N
0   0.25   0.5 mi
0 0.25 0.5 km

ELEVATION PROFILE

© The Countryman Press

meeting point of the North and South Loops, in Parker Hammock, there is a small pulloff suitable for day use parking (27.906468, -81.133955) along Road 16 (Prairie Lakes Road). You may also park in the large parking area at the end of Boat Ramp Road at Lake Jackson (27.910790, -81.149664) to access the west side of the South Loop. Pay your parking fee at an iron ranger at the Prairie Lakes trailhead.

THE HIKE

A figure-eight loop, the Prairie Lakes Loop is blazed in two colors: orange for the official Florida Trail route, and white for the other side of the loop. When you are standing at the Prairie Lakes trailhead, the white-blazed trail immediately catches your attention, heading into the pine flatwoods paralleling Canoe Creek Road. It provides a sweeping view of an open prairie with a cypress dome in its middle. After 0.25 mile, the trail turns away from the highway and the pine forest becomes more dense. You cross a graded road, Road 19. In the oak hammock on the other side of the road, a picnic bench sits on a bluff above the slough. The trail works its way down into the floodplain, balancing on bluffs before leading you through the cypress knees. Along the next set of bluffs, peer down into the slough to see just how tall some of the larger cypress knees are. Giant bromeliads and orchids cling to the live oaks.

Crossing a bridge over the outflow of Pole Cypress Ponds after 1.6 miles, the trail comes to the end of its dance with Parker Slough at a forest road that ends at the waterway. The white blazes jog between saw palmetto down a tree line on the edge of the prairie before emerging briefly along the preserve's boundary fence. Watch for blazes as the trail makes a couple of turns on forest roads before emerging through clumps of saw palmetto into an open area under the oaks. A cove of open prairie sweeps between the oak hammocks, a lone loblolly bay tree rising from the grassland. Expect rough going under the shade of the oaks where hogs have torn up the forest floor. At 2.6 miles, you reach a junction with a blue-blazed trail. It's a 0.5-mile side trail that beelines across the prairie to a group campsite, with picnic tables and a vault toilet.

Soon after the junction, the trail leaves the shade of the oak hammock to enter sun-drenched scrubby flatwoods. In the dense understory, you must be careful not to follow game trails instead of the white blazes. Once the trail returns to the shade of the ancient live oaks, you've entered Parker Hammock, with the first of several camping areas along this loop. Blue blazes lead to a picnic table and pitcher pump; camping is

OPEN PRAIRIE ALONG THE NORTH LOOP

NORTH CANAL, WHERE THE NORTH LOOP AND SOUTH LOOP MEET

in the oak hammock beyond the PARKER HAMMOCKS sign. You've hiked 3 miles. After a zigzag under the oaks, the trail emerges at the south end of the North Loop, the bridge over North Canal. The orange blazes to your left lead back to the Prairie Lakes trailhead. To continue on the figure-eight hike, cross the footbridge and turn left to stay on the white blazes of the South Loop. Walk beneath a bounty of giant bromeliads in the oaks before crossing Road 16 (Prairie Lakes Road). Along this next stretch of trail, the oak hammocks are quite impressive, the limbs of the live oaks laden with resurrection fern. Look for greenfly orchids high up in the trees, and more giant bromeliads clinging to branches and vines.

At 3.6 miles, there's a sign pointing down a side trail to the observation deck at Lake Marian. It's worth the extra 0.25 mile out and back for the view. This side trail is an old road that tunnels beneath a showy oak canopy draped in Spanish moss. Be alert for alligators sunning themselves along the waterway. A ramp leads up to the deck and its panorama of

Lake Marian, the second largest of the Three Lakes at 5,800 acres. With most of its shoreline protected by Three Lakes WMA, it's a beautiful sight.

Back on the white blazes, you round a small grassy cove before returning to the shade of the oak hammocks. It's often hard to determine where the footpath is when the understory under the oaks is so open, so be mindful of the blazes. They lead down a corridor flanked with cabbage palms, before crossing a plank bridge over an ephemeral waterway that flows out of the wet prairie. Tacking between oak trees, the trail offers expansive views of the prairies that make up most of the isthmus between Lake Marian and Lake Jackson.

After a sharp left turn onto an old track, the trail crosses a sometimes-soggy grassland to what was once a ford for cattle crossing the South Canal. The trail crosses the ford on a bridge at 5.4 miles, and turns sharply right to parallel the canal, occasionally jogging away from it to cross a tributary at a drier spot. Wading birds, especially great blue herons, browse through the marshes on the canal's far shore. Reaching Road 16, the trail crosses it and continues through an oak hammock to a footbridge over an often-dry waterway, with a bench on the bluff on the other side. This is the south end of the South Loop, where the white blazes end. It's time to start following the orange blazes back along the opposite side of the figure-eight loop. You've hiked 6 miles. Turn left to go north on the Florida Trail.

Walking beneath streamers of Spanish moss on a berm between two low-lying areas, note how cattle ranching shaped what once was a vast wetland between the lakes into drier prairies drained by ditches and canals. The trail reaches another bench and a footbridge that crosses the paralleling ditch. Turning left, you enter a picturesque hammock of live oaks and cabbage palms, more dense than most of the hammocks you've encountered thus far. Watch for the orange blazes through this maze of tree trunks. It's almost a jolt to leave this ethereal hammock and emerge into the tall prairie grasses. The trail points towards a lone oak in the prairie and passes under its crown before aiming towards the shoreline of oaks rimming the other side of the prairie. Once under the oak canopy, you see more than one sign for the Dry Pond campsite. At 7.6 miles, this backpacker's campsite has a picnic table, pitcher pump, and plenty of flat space for tents under the oaks, with a panorama of the prairie beyond.

Rambling through the oak hammock beyond Dry Pond, you'll notice more giant bromeliads in the trees, looking like chandeliers in green. It doesn't take long to walk right up to the picnic table at Campsite #3 at Lake Jackson, the best of the campsites in this vehicle-accessible camping area. A side trail leads to a vault toilet and the parking area at the end of Boat Ramp Road. Like Lake Marian, the short side trip at this 8-mile mark lets you see the lake from the parking area. A raft of white pelicans floated serenely across the bright blue water on our visit. Watch for alligators along the shoreline. The lake is the water source for the campsite.

Paralleling, then crossing, Boat Ramp Road, the orange blazes lead you into a younger oak hammock, making a sharp turn down a straight corridor. Patches of marsh fern collect under the loblolly bay trees in low-lying spots. The trail turns to enter another lush hammock of palms and live oaks before emerging onto a forest road to cross a culvert over a waterway. Tacking northeast, it draws close to North Canal, providing a view up the steep-sided waterway before it reaches the north junction of the South Loop at the footbridge after 9.1 miles.

You crossed this bridge earlier when you were headed south on the white blazes. Cross it again, this time following the orange blazes up the bluff along the North Canal, with views of the water control structure and floodgates beneath the road. Floodwaters rose so high after Hurricane Irma in 2017 that it was necessary to reconstruct portions of the canal (and replace the footbridge) due to extreme erosion. Although it may not feel like it, the entire Prairie Lakes Loop can get pretty soggy at certain times of year, including having standing water in the palm hammocks.

Passing a bench on the bluff, the trail crosses Road 16 and goes past another bench before turning left into an oak hammock. Younger oaks provide shade, while ferns grow in damp spots. The change in habitat is quite distinct when the orange blazes lead you into the pine flatwoods. Tall longleaf pine dominate this forest, with prairie grasses and saw palmetto making up the understory. You cross a sand road amid the pines before reaching another stretch of mature oak hammock. It's an island in the pine forest, as the blazes lead you under a power line at 9.9 miles and into an impressive panorama of pines. Look carefully at some of the more mature trees, as they bear catface scars from having turpentine tapped from their trunks decades ago. If you look behind you, there is a fire tower not all that far away.

A wall of vegetation marks the edge of the pine forest: a cypress strand and a linear swamp with a stream flowing through it at certain times of year. It's known as the Pole Cypress Ponds, per-

haps from the logging days of long ago. A boardwalk winds through the cypress, providing one final bench along the trail at 10.4 miles. After the trail leaves the boardwalk, the footpath may be mushy underfoot. This is a good spot to look for sundews, tiny carnivorous plants that glisten like globs of raspberry jelly. This final stretch, winding through grasslands between the cypress domes and strands, offers a bounty of wildflowers in spring and fall. Pines are sparse here, offering little shade. Traffic slips by in the distance on Canoe Creek Road. The mowed path winds through the grassland and around a cypress dome before you catch a glimpse of the Prairie Lakes trailhead. Crossing the entrance road, you reach the trailhead after an 11.4-mile hike.

OTHER HIKING OPTIONS

1. **North Loop Day Hike**. Right inside the preserve gate, the 5.4-mile North Loop showcases wide-open prairie, particularly within the first two miles in either direction from the trailhead. The trailhead itself is one of the best places to catch a sunrise or a sunset, thanks to the panoramic view to the south.

2. **South Loop Day Hike**. The 6-mile South Loop begins on the south side of the footbridge over Parker Slough. It keeps largely to the oak and palm hammocks near the lakes, providing sweeping views of prairie from under the shade of the oaks. A side trail leads down to the lakes. At Lake Jackson, a walk between the camp-sites takes you down to the boat ramp area and views along the shore. At Lake Marian, there is an observation deck to perch on for the panorama.

3. **Lake Jackson Tower Trail** (27.891467, -81.173683). Park at the Lake Jackson Tower Trail parking area for a short walk on an old road along the prairie's edge. A nature trail diverges from the road and dives into the palm hammock to add a little variety to this short hike, popping out again onto the blue blazes of a connector to the Florida Trail. Turn left to walk to the Lake Jackson Tower, which offers an expansive view of the lake from several stories up. Follow the old road back to the parking area. The full loop to the tower and back on the three trails is 1.2 miles.

4. **Sunset Ranch Interpretive Trail** (27.904028, -81.098106). South along Canoe Creek Road, this interpretive trail leads through similar habitats as those seen on the Prairie Lakes Loop, but on a much smaller scale, as a 2.2-mile loop hike to an observation point on Lake Marian.

CAMPING AND LODGING

Lake Jackson Campground (27.910790, -81.149664), (352-732-1225), tents only.

Lake Marian Paradise RV Park & Motel, 901 Arnold Road, Kenansville, FL 34739 (407-436-1464)

Middleton's Fish Camp Too, 4500 Joe Overstreet Road, Kenansville, FL 34739 (407-436-1966, mfctoo.com)

VIEW LOOKING NORTH FROM THE LAKE JACKSON TOWER

26

Split Oak Forest Wildlife and Environmental Area

TOTAL DISTANCE: A 6.4-mile loop along the outer perimeter of the preserve

HIKING TIME: 3.5 hours

DIFFICULTY: Moderate

USAGE: Free. Open 8 AM–8 PM during summer months, and 8 AM-6 PM during winter months. A limited number of permits are issued for equestrian use; call 407-254-6840 for details.

TRAILHEAD GPS COORDINATES: 28.3532, -81.2111

CONTACT INFORMATION: Split Oak Forest Wildlife and Environmental Area, 12901 Moss Park Road, Orlando, FL 32832 (407-254-6840, orangecountyfl.net or myfwc.com/viewing/recreation/wmas/lead/split-oak-forest)

It is a haunting cry, the call of the sandhill crane, as the birds glide overhead, casting giant shadows across the prairie. It is an unmistakable cry, a mournful, raspy rattle, naturally amplified through the nostrils of the crane's massive bill. Standing up to 4 feet tall, with a wingspan of up to 7 feet, the sandhill crane is a bird that quickly captures your attention, whether it is soaring overhead or striding through tall grasses. Migrating from the grasslands of Nebraska to the vanishing open prairies of Florida each winter, greater sandhill cranes look for open prairie with wetlands to shelter them from the cold for the season. Split Oak Forest Wildlife and Environmental Area is managed as habitat for both these seasonal visitors and a subspecies, the Florida sandhill crane, which spends all year in the Sunshine State. The South Loop trail circles their habitat, while the northerly trails wind along lakeshores, marshes, and into scrub and sandhill forest critical for gopher tortoise habitat.

These prairies were purchased for conservation in 1994 with funds from a mitigation bank, a program allowing developers to pay the state to preserve habitat in exchange for a green light to destroy similar habitat. It is a sad irony that not only are subdivisions creeping up the entrance road to the preserve, but there is a push to drive an expressway right through Split Oak Forest to open up yet more of this region to development. The preserve is managed jointly by Orange County (via Moss Park) and the Florida Fish and Wildlife Conservation Commission.

GETTING THERE

From the Orlando International Airport, follow FL 528 (Beachline Expressway) east to exit 13. Take CR 15 (Narcoossee

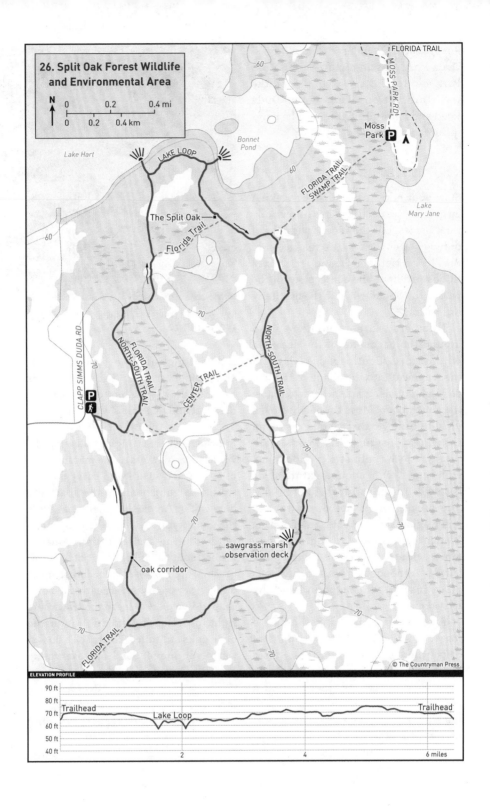

26. Split Oak Forest Wildlife
and Environmental Area

N

0   0.2   0.4 mi
0   0.2   0.4 km

FLORIDA TRAIL

MOSS PARK RD

Lake Hart

LAKE LOOP

Bonnet Pond

Moss Park

The Split Oak

FLORIDA TRAIL/ SWAMP TRAIL

Florida Trail

Lake Mary Jane

60

60

60

70

NORTH-SOUTH TRAIL

CLAPP SIMMS DUDA RD

FLORIDA TRAIL/ NORTH-SOUTH TRAIL

CENTER TRAIL

70

70

70

70

70

70

oak corridor

sawgrass marsh observation deck

FLORIDA TRAIL

© The Countryman Press

ELEVATION PROFILE

90 ft
80 ft
70 ft   Trailhead   Trailhead
60 ft   Lake Loop
50 ft
40 ft

                              2   4   6 miles

Road) south for 7 miles to Clapp-Simms-Duda Road, passing a turnoff for Moss Park and the FL 417 exchange on the way. Turn left on Clapp-Simms-Duda Road and follow it 1.6 miles to the parking area and trailhead.

THE HIKE

Start your hike at the kiosk by picking up a trail map. Each trail has its own distinct blazes, but the recent addition of orange blazes for a future relocation of the Florida National Scenic Trail mixes things up. Since the centerpiece of the park is the Split Oak, hike the northerly trails first.

NEWLY BLAZED FLORIDA TRAIL THROUGH AN OAK HAMMOCK

Numbered green markers lead around the perimeter of the preserve on the North/South Trail. Walk from the trailhead into the shade of the live oaks, and turn left at Marker 2 to follow the North Loop. Moss-draped live oaks yield to turkey oaks as you emerge on the edge of a scrubby flatwoods. Gallberry and saw palmetto predominate, with rusty lyonia adding texture as its crooked branches reach for the sky. The purple blooms of deer's tongue and blazing star add color to the scrub. Watch for tarflower, a fragrant white flower with pink stamens, on the taller shrubs. Although it is not a carnivorous plant, insects get caught on its sticky blossoms.

After a left turn, the trail enters a forest of tall longleaf pines and laurel oaks, where cinnamon ferns rise from the thick cover of needles on the forest floor. Bald cypresses emerge from a cypress dome. After 1.2 miles, you reach the blue-blazed Lake Loop. The orange blazes turn right. Turn left into the pine forest, passing a massive saw palmetto. Deer moss and reindeer lichen cluster under the turkey oaks. An unusual

forked longleaf pine sprouts thick, equal-sized trunks. The trail winds between the saw palmettos into a stand of laurel and live oaks.

You reach the Lake Hart Spur at 1.6 miles. Continue straight, following the white aster markers to the marshy edge of Lake Hart, where wild irises line the trail as it vanishes into the sparkling blue water. An earthy smell rises from the mud. Return to the Lake Loop, turning left at the T intersection. A newly formed split oak is behind a patch of soft grass. Watch for deer in the forest as the understory opens underneath the moss-draped live oaks. Where the trail veers right, go straight, walking under the open oaks at 2 miles. You reach a boardwalk over Bonnet Pond, an observation area. Blue herons wade through the spatterdock and water lilies with broad white blooms drift across the open water.

Return to the lakeshore, turning left to follow the white aster markers back to the main trail. Turn left, walking through an open forest of pines. Scattered clumps of saw palmetto add a touch of green to the earth-toned landscape. Wind whistles through the needles of the longleaf pines. At 2.4 miles, you come to the Split Oak. Before we were born, this centuries-old tree broke under the weight of its own branches, its main trunk falling in two to the ground. Over time, lateral branches grew up as tall and thick as tree trunks, creating an interesting tableau, the splayed trunks thick with resurrection fern and goldfoot fern. This is not an isolated phenomenon—in fact, there are several more nearby—but this tree is a grand one. Its fallen trunk is almost like a cavern inside, yet it clings to life.

Continue along the forest road past the tree. At the next fork, keep left, passing the LAKE LOOP/SPLIT OAK sign. At 2.7 miles, you reach the trail junction for the Swamp Trail, which leads left to Moss Park. To the right is a large oak that appears to be imprisoned by a circle of pine trees. Turn right to walk around it. A forest road comes in from the right as the trail enters the open pine flatwoods. Continue straight ahead along the grassy track. At Marker 14, you reach the junction of the North/South Trail and the Center Trail after 3.3 miles. This is a decision point. While hiking the perimeter of the South Loop provides your best opportunity to see sandhill cranes, it is another 3.1 miles through mostly open pine flatwoods. After a rain, the South Loop will flood up to your ankles in places. If you're happy with a shorter, tamer experience, follow the Center Trail 0.9 mile back to your car. Otherwise, continue straight as the trail veers left.

Wildlife is more prevalent along the South Loop. Watch for wild turkeys in the open prairies, gopher tortoises ambling down the trail, and the tall sandhill cranes. You pass Marker 16 and Marker 17. Young longleaf pines show off various shapes—some look like wiregrass, oth-

SAWGRASS MARSH AT THE SOUTH END OF SPLIT OAK FOREST

THE NAMESAKE OF SPLIT OAK FOREST

ers like bottlebrushes or saguaro cactus. Bracken fern grows densely under the pines. Watch for shards of clay turpentine pots, from the era when this forest served as a turpentine plantation.

At Marker 18, another forest road heads right, just before the ditch. Continue straight ahead. Peer down into the waterway to look for alligators. The forest road becomes deep soft sand, difficult to traverse, as you reach Marker 19. Turn right. The curve leads back into the pine flatwoods. Signs indicate the last occurrence of a controlled burn, a critical part of managing pine flatwoods and scrub so they do not revert to oak hammocks.

The trail reaches a corner of the property boundary at 4.1 miles. Turn right at Marker 21 to follow that boundary, sticking with the grassy track until it merges into the firebreak along the fence line. This section of the trail can be wet since a bayhead swamp sometimes drains across the trail as a tannic stream at Marker 22. As the forest road meets Marker 23 at 4.4 miles, there is an observation deck overlooking the sawgrass marsh. Take a break on the bench, watching for herons and ibises. Returning to the trail, turn right.

The trail leads back into the pine flatwoods. Stay right at the fork. Green markers direct you around the loop. Marker 24 is in a nice patch of pine flatwoods. Marker 25 is at an intersection of forest roads with deep, soft sand. Continue straight ahead. The footing gets much more difficult, as the road is very sandy. The next forest road coming in from the left is the orange-blazed route of the Florida Trail coming in from the south end of this preserve. It joins your route 5 miles into the hike, next to a gnarled sand live oak. For the remainder of the hike, you'll follow the orange blazes. The habitat transitions to sandhills, with turkey oaks dropping their brown leaves. You see a deep burned scar on a pine tree.

Make the sharp right turn at Marker 28 with the double orange blazes. The habitat transitions to pine flatwoods, the understory dense with saw palmetto. Continue straight ahead at the next junction of forest roads, entering an oak hammock. Past Marker 29, the trail is carpeted with pine needles. You enter a long, shadowy corridor under the moss-draped oaks at 5.8 miles. The trail curves left and then right, popping out into an open prairie. Walk softly, watching for sandhill cranes. Consider yourself fortunate to come across sandhill cranes in the throes of their mating dance, as the males leap and prance with wings outspread, bowing and cackling to attract the attention of a mate. Sandhill cranes mate for life, returning to the same nesting site every year. Tall grassy savannas and prairies on the edge of marshes provide their perfect habitat.

From the open space at Marker 31, the parking area is visible. Passing the back of Marker 1, you've returned to the trailhead, completing a 6.4-mile hike.

OTHER HIKING OPTIONS

1. **Swamp Trail**. The Swamp Trail makes a 1.4-mile round-trip to the perimeter trail around Split Oak Forest. Using it to start your hike extends the perimeter hike to 7.8 miles. It starts at Moss Park, a full-service county park with boating and canoe access, picnic pavilions, playgrounds, and a nice roomy campground in an oak hammock. To get to Moss Park, take exit 13 on FL 528 (Beachline Expressway), just east of the Orlando International Airport. Turn south on CR 15 (Narcoossee Road). Drive 2.8 miles to Moss Park Road. Turn left, and follow Moss Park Road 4.5 miles until it ends at the park entrance. A $5 entry fee applies. Inside Moss Park, make the first right and follow the signs for Pavilions 5 & 6, at the far end of the park near the campground. Parking for the trail is across from the tent camping area. Look for the arched entrance and kiosk (28.370524, -81.188611). The Swamp Trail is a long causeway through a marsh, giving you an up-close look at cattails, duck potato, and pickerelweed. After 0.7 mile, it ends at the North/South Trail. Turn left to start hiking the 6.4-mile perimeter loop as outlined above.

2. **Swamp Trail/Lake Loop**. Most visitors are interested in hiking the Lake Loop, the most scenic corner of the preserve. Using the Swamp Trail described above, turn right where it connects to the North/South Trail, visiting the Split Oak along the way. Where the Lake Loop connects at Markers 8 and 9, stay on the North/South Trail until you reach the Lake Loop again. Turn right and follow the hike narrative for the Lake Loop. Return to Moss Park via the way you came in, past the Split Oak and along the Swamp Trail for a 3.5-mile hike with some excellent birding spots and scenery.

3. **Bear Island Trail** (28.3783, -81.1912). At Moss Park, enjoy this 1.2-mile round-trip nature trail along Lake Mary Jane. It's an Eagle Scout project that shows off the ancient saw palmetto and views of the lake.

CAMPING AND LODGING

Moss Park, 12901 Moss Park Road, Orlando, FL 32832 (407-254-6840, orangecountyfl.net)

Orlando SE/Lake Whipoorwill KOA, 12345 Narcoossee Road, Orlando, FL 32832 (407-277-5075, koa.com)

Courtyard by Marriott Orlando Lake Nona, 6955 Lake Nona Boulevard, Orlando, FL 32827 (407-856-9165, marriott.com)

Tibet-Butler Preserve

Hiding just beyond the tourist amenities of Lake Buena Vista, within earshot of the toot of the train whistle at Disney's Magic Kingdom, Tibet-Butler Preserve protects a precious 440 acres of the region's original habitats along the shore of Lake Tibet. A network of well-maintained, family-friendly interpretive hiking trails winds through its forests. Combining a variety of trails, ramble up to 3.5 miles on this loop.

TOTAL DISTANCE: 3.5 miles along a network of short trails

HIKING TIME: 1.5 hours

DIFFICULTY: Easy to moderate

USAGE: Free. Open daily, 8 AM–6 PM. No pets or bicycles permitted.

TRAILHEAD GPS COORDINATES: 28.4428, -81.5418

CONTACT INFORMATION: Tibet-Butler Preserve, 8777 CR 535 (Winter Garden–Vineland Road), Orlando, FL 32836 (407-254-1940, orangecountyfl.net)

GETTING THERE

From I-4, take exit 68, Lake Buena Vista. Drive north on FL 535. Pass the entrance to Walt Disney World/Disney Springs at the first light, turning left at the second light to follow CR 535. The park entrance is 5.3 miles ahead on the right. The entrance road loops around to parking in front of the environmental center, where the trails begin.

THE HIKE

The Vera Carter Environmental Center dominates the entrance to the preserve. Stop and take a look at the displays and pick up an interpretive trail guide, which corresponds to numbers posted along the trails. Restrooms and picnic tables invite you to linger.

Your hike starts behind the building. Sign in at the trail register, then turn right onto Pine Circle. The trail is a low indentation into the pine flatwoods, meandering through tall slash pines, loblolly bay, and saw palmetto. Sphagnum moss creeps along its edges. After passing the Screech Owl Trail, you skirt a damp area with swamp lilies growing under dahoon holly and red bay. The trail rises and becomes sandy underfoot as you approach the intersection with the Palmetto Passage

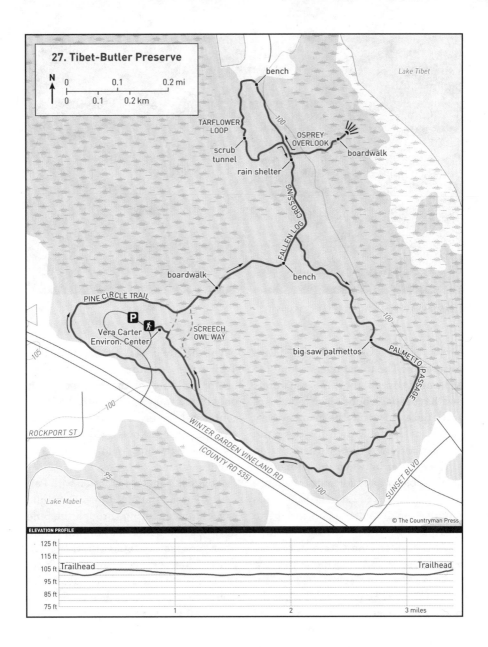

27. Tibet-Butler Preserve

N

0   0.1   0.2 mi
0   0.1   0.2 km

Lake Tibet

bench

TARFLOWER
LOOP

scrub
tunnel

OSPREY
OVERLOOK

boardwalk

rain shelter

FALLEN LOG CROSSING

boardwalk

bench

PINE CIRCLE TRAIL

P

Vera Carter
Environ. Center

SCREECH
OWL WAY

big saw palmettos

PALMETTO PASSAGE

ROCKPORT ST

WINTER GARDEN VINELAND RD
(COUNTY RD 535)

SUNSET BLVD

Lake Mabel

© The Countryman Press

ELEVATION PROFILE

125 ft
115 ft
105 ft Trailhead
95 ft
85 ft
75 ft

Trailhead

1   2   3 miles

Trail, at 0.2 mile. Turn right to stay on Pine Circle.

As the trail rises, the habitat becomes scrubby flatwoods, and the pine canopy thins out. Gallberry, winged sumac, and grasses compete for the understory. Small stands of scrub live oak provide cover. You see the roof of the Environ-mental Center through the trees as you wind down the sandy, narrow passage. Cross the entry road on the crosswalk, making sure to check for cars. The trail enters an oak hammock of gnarled scrub live oaks draped in moss. Like Christmas tinsel, fallen pine needles decorate the branches of the oaks. As the trail

ALONG THE BOARDWALK OF FALLEN LOG CROSSING

circles, you pass an opening filled with royal ferns. The forest opens along the ecotone between the pine flatwoods and bayheads, where slash pines are scattered amid an unbroken understory of saw palmetto. Watch for the palm warbler and the yellow-throated vireo as they flutter between the palmettos. Dense loblolly bay indicates the dampness of the area. You see the roof of the Environmental Center again, now off to the right.

At 0.8 mile, Pine Circle intersects with the Fallen Log Crossing. If you turn right, you'll end up back at the Environmental Center. To enjoy the rest of the preserve, turn left, following Fallen Log Crossing into a bayhead. This marshy forest was once a common sight in Central Florida, where water from the surrounding pine flatwoods drains down into a permanent depression, feeding the roots of damp-loving trees like bay magnolia, sweet bay, red bay, dahoon holly, and loblolly bay. As you walk along the boardwalk, notice the tannic water collecting in the bottom of the

bayhead. You'll pass the Screech Owl Trail again, a hummocky, shady connector trail through the bayhead. Use it only if you want to return to the Environmental Center; otherwise, continue straight along the boardwalk. It ends in the pine flatwoods. Wild iris grows in damp spots.

You reach another junction with Palmetto Passage at 1.2 miles. Continue straight, meandering through the pine flatwoods. Blueberries dominate the open understory beneath the slash pines. After passing a canopied bench, the trail rises into an oak scrub. At the OSPREY OVERLOOK sign, turn right. This spur trail follows the edge of the pine flatwoods along the oak scrub, entering a dense, shadowy forest of oaks and pines. Along the boardwalk to the observation deck, notice the marsh ferns and small pond cypresses with their fernlike needle clusters. The covered deck overlooks a marsh along the edge of Lake Tibet. Watch for purple gallinules picking their way through the duck potatoes, and osprey swooping down from the cypresses to the open waters of the lake in search of fish.

Return to the trail junction, turning right. You are now on the Tarflower Loop, a walk through the preserve's small corner of oak scrub. Head straight at the loop junction. The footpath becomes sugar-white sand, blindingly bright; the oaks are heavy with ball moss and old man's beard, a crispy, grayish-green fungal coating on the oak that can burst into any of several varieties—long, hair-like strands, wiry masses, or tangled fruiting clumps with

VIEW FROM OSPREY OVERLOOK

small plates at the ends of their strands. The last bit of this trail tunnels through a corridor of sand live oaks and rusty lyonia before reaching the end of the loop at 2.1 miles. Turn right and retrace your steps past the Osprey Overlook trail to the Palmetto Passage.

The Palmetto Passage is the most adventuresome trail in this preserve and is often closed due to flooding. If it's closed, continue back along the Fallen Log Crossing to complete a 2.7-mile hike. If it's not too soggy, it is a lot of fun to hike—twisting and turning, ducking and scrambling through a maze of trees. As it starts, it's as well-groomed as the other trails in the preserve. But as it drops into the bayhead swamp that the Fallen Log Crossing crosses on the boardwalk, it can get damp underfoot. Crossing a bridge, you see how one bayhead swamp—a spot where groundwater collects and loblolly bay trees thrive—spills into the next one. Watch for clues as to where the trail goes through this area. Pass a patch of ancient saw palmetto, notable for their long trunks. Roots rise up through the footpath, and you must duck beneath the canopy of trees in several spots. After the trail crosses a forest road, the canopy opens, allowing the sounds of traffic to seep in.

Down a tunnel shaded by loblolly bay trees and cypresses, the trail gains a little elevation and the habitat changes to slash pines and oaks. This well-worn portion of the pathway is near the preserve boundary with the road, so the traffic noise picks up. The Palmetto Passage ends at a T intersection with the Pine Circle. Turn right to continue back past the Screech Owl Trail, ending your hike at the Environmental Center after 3.5 miles. Sign out of the trail register before you leave.

OTHER HIKING OPTIONS

1. **Pine Circle**. The driest of the trails at Tibet-Butler, Pine Circle essentially circles the parking area, staying close to the edge of the bayhead swamps in several places. It's a 0.8-mile loop and the easiest one to jump on and off of from the Environmental Center.
2. **Lake Tibet Stroll**. By far the most popular route in the preserve for families is to follow the Fallen Log Crossing to Osprey Overlook for a look out over the marshes along Lake Tibet. It's a 1.5-mile trip out and back.

CAMPING AND LODGING

Bill Frederick Turkey Creek Park, 3401 S Hiawassee Road, Orlando, FL 32835 (407-246-4486, cityoforlando.net)

Disney's Fort Wilderness Resort, 4510 N Fort Wilderness Trail, Orlando, FL 32836 (407-824-2837, disneyworld.disney.go.com)

Hyatt Regency Grand Cypress, 1 Grand Cypress Boulevard, Orlando, FL 32836 (407-239-1234, hyatt.com)

Palm Lakefront Resort & Hostel, 4840 W Irlo Bronson Memorial Highway, Kissimmee, FL 34746 (407-480-1321, hostelinorlando.com)

Disney Wilderness Preserve

In the early morning stillness, there are no sounds but the drone of cicadas, the cry of a red-shouldered hawk, the flapping wings of a flock of white ibis overhead. Preserved as mitigation (lands preserved in place of lands destroyed for development) for the construction of Walt Disney World on similar habitats, the 12,000 acres of forests and wetlands at the Disney Wilderness Preserve provide room for creatures to roam, and protect one of Florida's rare treasures—a cypress-lined lake.

TOTAL DISTANCE: A 2.5-mile loop and spur. Shorter and longer options are possible.

HIKING TIME: 1.5 hours

DIFFICULTY: Easy to moderate

USAGE: Free, donations appreciated. Open 9 AM–4:30 PM daily, including weekends, November through March. Open 9 AM–4:30 PM on Monday to Friday only, April through October. Closed major holidays. No pets or bicycles permitted.

TRAILHEAD GPS COORDINATES: 28.129015, -81.430470

CONTACT INFORMATION: The Nature Conservancy, 2700 Scrub Jay Trail, Poinciana, FL 34759 (407-935-0002, nature.org)

GETTING THERE

Take I-4 west from Orlando to exit 27, Lake Buena Vista, heading south on FL 535. After 2.9 miles, turn right on Poinciana Boulevard. This southbound road crosses both US 192 and US 17/92. If you are coming from the west on I-4, use exit 24 and head south toward Kissimmee; turn left on US 17/92, then right on Poinciana Boulevard. Make a right at the traffic light at Pleasant Hill Road, immediately getting into the left lane. Make the first left onto Old Pleasant Hill Road, using the left turn lane 0.5 mile down the road. Follow this road for 0.6 mile, turning left onto Scrub Jay Trail, the entrance road for the preserve. It's a slow 1.6-mile drive through the preserve back to the Conservancy Learning Center, where the hiking trails start.

THE HIKE

At the Conservancy Learning Center, look for the hiker check-in and maps before heading out on the trail system. They're along the breezeway near the restrooms. Continue along the concrete path past the butterfly garden to reach the pond. A small sign declares this the HARDEN TRAIL. A line

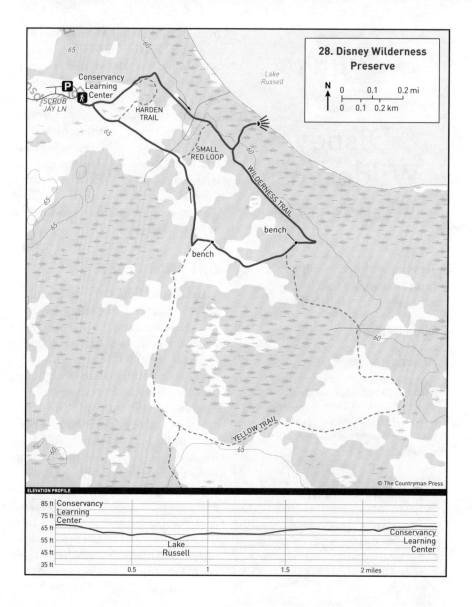

28. Disney Wilderness Preserve

N
| 0 | 0.1 | 0.2 mi |
| 0 | 0.1 | 0.2 km |

ELEVATION PROFILE

of wax myrtle screens the back of the buildings from the paved path, which offers a sweeping view of the pond. American lotuses float on the surface. Surrounded by smooth cordgrass, the viewing platform provides a place for early-morning birding.

After you enter the vast open longleaf pine flatwoods—which are indeed wet, as

are most in Central Florida—the Harden Trail peels off to the right to circle the cypress dome near the pond. Continue straight ahead to meet a T intersection. Turn right to start down a forest road. Wild bachelor's button peeps up along the trail's edge. The trail climbs a slight rise, and a red trail marker confirms you are on the red-blazed Wilderness

ANCIENT CYPRESSES ALONG THE SHORELINE OF LAKE RUSSELL

Trail. Reaching an intersection with a trail to the right, the Small Red Loop, pass it by. Keep walking straight ahead through the flatwoods, and notice the line of cypresses off in the distance to your left. They're getting closer.

At the next trail intersection, turn left to walk down to Lake Russell. This short spur takes you to one of the major reasons to visit the preserve. The trail drops through the floodplain forest of the lake to an open clearing with picnic tables and benches. Fed by Reedy Creek, Lake Russell is truly the jewel of this preserve. Lake Russell drains south through marshes to the Kissimmee River, feeding the Everglades with its northernmost trickle of water. Pause a while to watch the alligators, ibis, and osprey.

Returning along the spur trail to the main trail, turn left to rejoin the Wilderness Trail. The trail climbs into scrubby flatwoods which stretch as far as the eye can see—longleaf pine, saw palmetto, and lopsided Indiangrass. The view is expansive; the saw palmetto short enough that you can see a mile or more in most directions. When naturalist William Bartram wandered through Florida in 1773, he wrote of vast grassy savannas with scattered trees. The dense thickets of saw palmetto we see today in pine flatwoods are not the natural understory, but the result of more than a hundred years of fire suppression in Florida. Cypress domes and strands look like mountains in the distance. For the remainder of the hike, there are only minor variations on this theme, a wraparound landscape of longleaf pine savanna.

At 1.3 miles, turn right at the TRAIL CONTINUES sign. The footpath narrows, with tall grass along a cypress-lined pond. After a straightaway, the trail

FOLLOWING THE HARDEN TRAIL THROUGH PRAIRIE GRASSES

makes a sharp left at a bench, working its way around the pond. The landscape is a little elevated here, as there are no wet spots in the trail. You come to a marker for the Yellow Trail. It once followed a slightly different route but now starts on the west side of the cypress dome. It circles around a vast bayhead swamp and adds 3.6 miles to your hike, should you have the time to hike it.

On this trek, we're sticking with the Wilderness Trail. Keep right at this junction, which is about halfway through your hike. Winding through the saw palmetto, the trail comes to a bench. Look for the next trail marker. You pop out at a T intersection where the Yellow Trail comes back in on a forest road. Turn right. You've walked 1.8 miles. Notice the star-shaped yellow flowers on small bushes scattered between the saw palmetto: St. John's wort, one of the few colorful shrubs in the pine flatwoods, blooming in summer and fall.

This next segment of the trail is lower than the surrounding landscape, so water may gather in sheets across the footpath. Watch the leopard frogs bounce out of your way, and keep alert for water snakes. The savanna opens up more, and you catch a glimpse of the Conservancy Learning Center off in the distance. Meeting up with the Small Red Loop at a bench, the trail jogs left through a drainage area, where standing water is likely. Crossing the savanna, the trail beelines towards the pond, where the Harden Trail joins the route. Circling the pond, the trail meets up with the sidewalk at the kiosk marking the start of the interpretive trail. Turn left to exit, completing a 2.5-mile walk as you reach the parking lot.

OTHER HIKING OPTIONS

1. **Harden Trail**. This 0.5-mile loop around the pond and cypress dome behind the Conservancy Learning Center appeals to young and old, and is easily the most-used trail in the preserve. Benches provide quiet places for birders to sit and watch activity along the pond.

2. **Small Red Loop**. The cypress-lined shore of Lake Russell is the most compelling destination at the preserve. If you don't wish to hike the full Wilderness Trail, backtrack to the red-blazed cross-trail after visiting Lake Russell. It rejoins the other side of the Wilderness Trail at a bench within sight of the pond along the Harden Trail, completing a 1.2-mile trek.

3. **Yellow Trail**. The Yellow Trail follows a good portion of the original Wilderness Trail route around a large bayhead swamp, as we shared in the first edition of this guidebook. Closed for many years, it's reopened for the adventuresome hiker. Adding the Yellow Trail to the hike we describe above expands your loop hike to 6.1 miles.

CAMPING AND LODGING

Palm Lakefront Resort & Hostel, 4840 W Irlo Bronson Memorial Highway, Kissimmee, FL 34746 (407-480-1321, hostelinorlando.com)

Paradise Island RV Park, 32000 US 27, Haines City, FL 33844 (863-439-1350, paradiseislandrvpark.com)

Omni Orlando Resort at Championsgate, 1500 Masters Boulevard, Championsgate, FL 33896 (407-390-6664, omnihotels.com/hotels)

LAKE WALES RIDGE SCRUB AT CROOKED LAKE PRAIRIE

V.

LAKE WALES RIDGE

Crooked River Preserve

TOTAL DISTANCE: 1.7-mile loop along a network of shorter trails

HIKING TIME: 1 hour

DIFFICULTY: Easy

USAGE: Free. Open sunrise to sunset. No pets or bicycles permitted

TRAILHEAD GPS COORDINATES: 28.5079, -81.7504

CONTACT INFORMATION: Crooked River Preserve, Lake County Water Authority, 10272 Lake Louisa Road, Clermont, FL 34711 (352-324-6141, lcwa.org/open-preserves)

Welcome to the northernmost part of the Lake Wales Ridge, a long, slender, ancient ridge that stretches south towards Lake Okeechobee, creating the "spine" of the Florida peninsula. It's home to some of Florida's most ancient landscapes, as it remained an island during periodic immersions of Florida over geologic time. Crooked River Preserve provides a peek into the ancient scrub as well as a pleasant walk along the Palatlakaha River, a winding waterway that connects a chain of lakes through the region.

The high, well-drained, sandy soils of the Lake Wales Ridge were prized by citrus growers, who found them ideal for their groves. At one time, US 27—which follows the ridge, and still gives you a good taste of the hills that make up the middle of Florida's peninsula—was known as the Orange Blossom Highway. When we were kids, riding down that highway with the car windows down meant breathing in the heavenly scent of citrus blossoms during winter and spring. That's no longer true. Since the first edition of this guidebook, the orange groves have transformed into densely-packed subdivisions, apartments, and shopping centers. Crooked River Preserve remains an oasis.

GETTING THERE

From US 27 in Clermont, drive south from its intersection with FL 50 for 1 mile. Turn right on Lake Louisa Road and follow it for 2.7 miles to the trailhead on the left.

THE HIKE

Sign in at the kiosk at the trailhead and pick up a map before starting down the

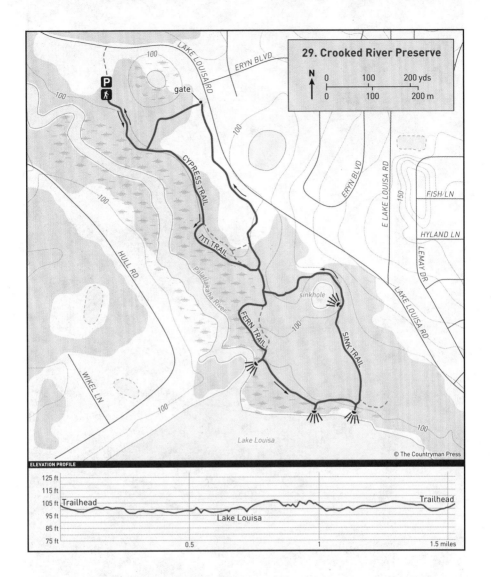

29. Crooked River Preserve

N

| 0 | 100 | 200 yds |
| 0 | 100 | 200 m |

ELEVATION PROFILE

© The Countryman Press

orange-blazed Cypress Trail. Under a canopy of laurel oaks in a second or third-growth forest, the trail is edged by giant mounds of grapevines; the footpath compacted sand. A line of cypresses behind the oaks defines the floodplain of the river. Interpretive markers point out specific plants and trees. In an opening with tall longleaf pines and blueberry bushes, prickly pear cactus and grapevines intermingle as scrub and oak hammock meet.

At an intersection with a yellow-tipped post, turn right on the Titi Trail. It swings closer to the river, affording a shady canopy overhead. It's a crispy, crunchy tunnel of sand live oaks paralleled by a line of cypresses. Palatlakaha River Park is visible on the opposite shore, another public land protecting the watershed of the this little-known river. Rising from the Green Swamp, the Palatlakaha River connects a chain of 11 lakes as it flows from Lake Louisa

PALATLAKAHA RIVER THROUGH CROOKED RIVER PRESERVE

into Lake Minnehaha, Lake Minneola, and Cherry Lake.

Reaching an intersection with the Cypress Trail and the blue-blazed Sink Trail, keep right. You quickly come to another junction of the two trails. Keep right to stay close to the river, following the Fern Trail if it's not flooded. The sparkle of water breaks through the understory as the trail gets within sight of houses on the far side of the sinuous stream.

Tannic but clear, the sand-bottomed Palatlakaha River has ripples across the bottom that make it seem tidal. It's hard to tell, but the river flows north. At 0.5 mile, a picnic bench offers a place to watch for birds and savor the view as Lake Louisa gently pours through a gateway of cypresses into the river. Continue past the picnic bench to join the blue-blazed Sink Trail, a straightaway beneath tall oaks well-draped in Spanish moss and resurrection fern. Bracken fern crowds the understory.

You emerge along the cypresses on the shore of Lake Louisa. The lake is large enough to sport whitecaps when the wind picks up. The far shore is pristine, protected by Lake Louisa State Park, unlike the near shores with their tightly packed lakefront homes. Along this short sandy shoreline, marvel at the oddly shaped, almost bonsai-like bald cypresses, each a short, stout sentinel with a hollow trunk, proclaiming the age and wildness of this place.

Return to the trail and turn right to follow the blue blazes. Southern woods fern rises tall in the shaded understory. It's a fern that prefers dampness, and the humidity from the big lake suits it just fine. At the next junction, the trail straight ahead exits into a neighborhood. Turn left to walk into a sandhill habitat with longleaf pines and turkey oaks. Soon after, the sinkhole, significant in size, comes into view. A pond fills the bottom.

Leaving the sinkhole, turn left at the base of a tall longleaf pine tree—it has its own interpretive marker. The trail sweeps along the rim of the sinkhole. Young longleaf pines shade the path. At 1.1 miles, turn right at the next trail junction. You quickly pass another junction where the Scrub Trail comes in from the left. Keep right at this Y, and you're back on the orange blazes, following the perimeter trail to its other highlight, the ancient scrub.

The scrub of the Lake Wales Ridge

BRIGHT WHITE SANDS OF THE LAKE WALES RIDGE SCRUB

has bright, almost powder-white sand that hosts a variety of woody shrubs and lichens. It is some of the oldest land in the Florida peninsula, teeming with biodiversity and species found nowhere else on earth—which is why this little patch means so much amid the sprawl that surrounds it. In one spot, the sand is covered with sand spikemoss, looking like slender fingers rising from the sand. Notice the SCRUB OLIVE marker, indicating a native olive species that only grows in this well-drained sand. It sports small but fragrant flowers, with fruits larger than those of the wild olive found commonly in Florida.

The hill trends towards Lake Louisa Road, as does the trail, drawing close to the fence line. The sand gets softer and the walking more difficult. A line of cypresses is in the distance after the trail leaves the fence line, where there is an access gate for residents to walk in. The trail makes a sharp left into the scrub. Open patches of scrub with diminutive plants include more patches of sand spikemoss. Reaching the final trail junction at 1.6 miles, turn right to exit down the grapevine-lined corridor. Don't forget to sign out at the trail register.

OTHER HIKING OPTIONS

1. **Scrub Loop**. If you're here to see the ancient scrub atop the Lake Wales Ridge, follow the Cypress Trail along the edge of the ridge and then turn left on the Scrub Trail, a short connector that ends at a T intersection. Turn left at the intersection. Although this orange-blazed route is called the Cypress Trail, it circles the open scrub in the center of the preserve as a 0.8-mile loop.

2. **Scenic Waterways**. Walk out and back along the linear route paralleling the floodplain of the Palatlakaha River to see the riverbend and the shoreline of Lake Louisa on a 1.2-mile round-trip.

3. **Palatlakaha River Park** (28.505575, -81.750494). On the opposite shore of its namesake river at 12325 Hull Road, Clermont, this 18-acre county park has a 0.8-mile loop trail through hardwood hammock and uplands habitats, but offers little in the way of river views for hikers. Just like Crooked River Preserve, it has a launch point into the Palatlakaha Run Blueway Trail.

4. **Lake Louisa Hiking Trail** (28.455807, -81.723799). On the opposite shore of Lake Louisa, Lake Louisa State Park has rental cabins and a 20-mile network of hiking and equestrian trails. The most popular hiking route starts at a trailhead just past the ranger station and continues downhill through restored longleaf pine and scrub habitats to the shore of the lake, for either a 4.1-mile hike to the canoe launch parking area (28.460479, -81.747625) or an 8.2-mile round-trip.

CAMPING AND LODGING

Lake Louisa State Park, 7305 S US 27, Clermont, FL 34714 (1-800-326-3521, floridastateparks.reserveamerica.com)

Holiday Inn Express Clermont, 1810 S US 27, Clermont, FL 34711 (352-243-7878, ihg.com)

Allen David Broussard Catfish Creek Preserve State Park

TOTAL DISTANCE: 3.5 miles on a loop along a network of trails. Shorter and longer loops possible.

HIKING TIME: 2–3 hours

DIFFICULTY: Difficult

USAGE: Free. Open 8 AM to sunset. Leashed pets and equestrians welcome. Bicycles permitted but not recommended due to deep, soft sand. Primitive camping available.

TRAILHEAD GPS COORDINATES: 27.9838, -81.4969

CONTACT INFORMATION: Allen David Broussard Catfish Creek Preserve State Park, 4335 Firetower Road, Haines City, FL 33844 (863-696-1112, floridastateparks .org/park/catfish-creek)

Allen David Broussard Catfish Creek Preserve State Park isn't just "a perfect example of Lake Wales Ridge Scrub." Its 8,000 acres protect a landscape unlike any other you'll find in Florida: a series of tall, steep ridges of sand that sparkles like fresh snow, featuring ascents and descents so steep you'd think you were traversing ski slopes. But this is not a chilly place. Scrub is Florida's desert, and you're in the very heart of it here.

This hike is a physical challenge, even on the shortest possible loop. It has very little shade and many strenuous climbs. Hiking poles are recommended due to the steep slopes and soft sand. Sunscreen, sunglasses, and a hat are a must to protect you from the elements. Get out quickly if a thunderstorm approaches. Equestrian trails share portions of the hiking trails. Prescribed burns manage the diminutive scrub forests, so you may see vast areas burnt to a crisp. But the incredible sweeping views, extraordinary contrasts between "desert" and lakes, bountiful wildlife, strange plants, and physical challenge make this a fascinating destination.

GETTING THERE

From US 27 in Dundee, follow CR 542 east to Hatchineha Road. Turn right and continue 8 miles to Firetower Road. Turn right. Continue 3 miles. The park trailhead (27.983800, -81.496800) is on the left before the FFA Leadership Camp entrance. If you reach their gate, turn around and come back—Firetower Road dead-ends at the camp.

THE HIKE

From the trailhead kiosk, follow the white-tipped blaze posts. The trail is a broad forest road in deep, soft sand,

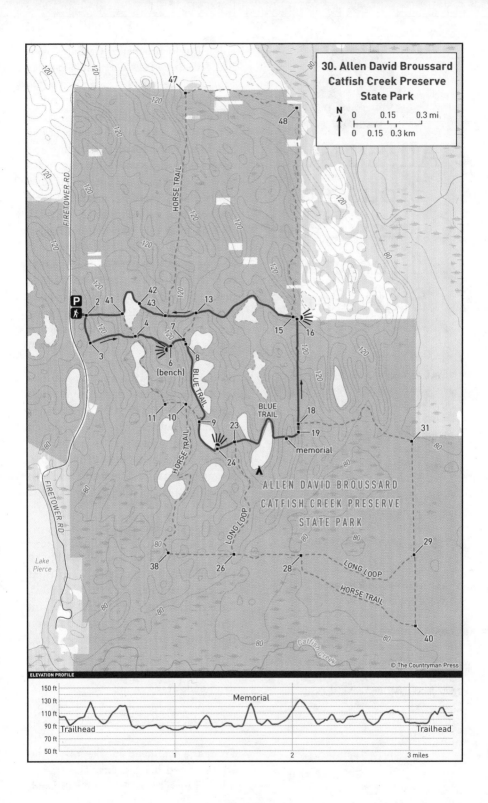

30. Allen David Broussard Catfish Creek Preserve State Park

N

0   0.15   0.3 mi
0 0.15 0.3 km

FIRETOWER RD

HORSE TRAIL

120

P

2 41
42
43
4
7
3
6
(bench)
8
13
15 16
BLUE TRAIL
11 10
9 23
24
18
19
memorial
BLUE TRAIL
HORSE TRAIL
LONG LOOP
31
29
40
38 26 28
LONG LOOP
HORSE TRAIL

ALLEN DAVID BROUSSARD
CATFISH CREEK PRESERVE
STATE PARK

47
48

80

Lake
Pierce

Catfish Creek

© The Countryman Press

ELEVATION PROFILE

150 ft
130 ft
110 ft
90 ft
70 ft
50 ft

Trailhead

Memorial

Trailhead

1   2   3 miles

as this portion is shared with horses. Anywhere the posts are tipped in red or red and white together, equestrians are allowed, and the sand tends to be churned up. A red mailbox says TRAIL MAPS. Stop and get one. Carrying a map, plus a compass or GPS is a smart idea. Markers throughout the preserve are keyed to the map, but there are so many cross-trails between major trails that it's like a giant maze.

Turn right at the trail map box to start walking the Medium Loop (as shown on the park map), moving counterclockwise up a moderate incline along a wall of dense scrub forest. At Marker 3, turn left. You'll find the next climb easiest along the edge of the forest road. Passing Markers 4 and 5 in quick succession at 0.5 mile, you climb to a vantage point at Marker 6, a broad panorama of prairie and open water and a distant gash of sand indicating a trail climbing the ridge on the far side of the next valley. Descend down a very steep slope into this lush prairie. A strong breeze makes the lack of shade more tolerable on a hot day.

At the base of the hill is a T intersection with a blue-tipped post indicating a connector trail at Marker 8. Turn right to follow this connector along a broad prairie studded with interconnecting lakes. The trail follows its well-defined shoreline, with sand less-trammeled and more like a well-packed beach. Lily pads float on the surface. It's a Florida landscape on a grandiose, Big-Sky scale. At a T intersection with a white-blazed trail at Marker 9, turn left. The shoreline swoops to a trail junction at a shady spot with a bench at 1.2 miles. Pass Marker 24 to continue your hike. A Florida scrub-jay lands atop a tall dead tree, seen in silhouette against the blue sky. It's the sentinel of a scrub-jay family, watching out for danger from a high post to warn the others.

At Marker 23, white blazes turn right, and the blue blazes lead straight ahead. Continue straight to ascend steeply to an overlook over a very long and slender prairie, with a shimmering pond and the crests of the ridges beyond. The trail makes a sharp left. At Marker 22, the blue-blazed trail leads left. Continue around this prairie, where you see some of the more unusual plants of the Lake Wales Ridge. The quality of the sand changes—it's extremely white. This was one of the few parts of Florida that protruded from the sea when the state was once underwater. As a result, there's a Noah's Ark of plant species here found nowhere else in the world, including 21 species that are considered endangered due to their rarity. Among those found here are scrub plum (*Prunus geniculata*), scrub morning glory (*Bonamia grandiflora*), and pygmy fringe tree (*Chionanthus pygmaeus*).

An extremely steep ascent faces you, one of the steepest in the Florida Peninsula. Consider making your own switchbacks as you climb to this lofty spot, which lets you survey all of the hiking you've done so far. At 1.7 miles you find a memorial to Allen David Broussard. His family placed quotes on the engraved memorial, and a bronze scrub-jay forever perches on his shoulder, looking out over this incredible panorama.

What goes up must come down. Facing this next slope down off the high ridge, you'll want a toboggan. Keep left at the fork as the descent slides to the next prairie's edge. Reaching Marker 19 at a T intersection, make a left and walk along the prairie. After a few footfalls, you meet the junction of the white and blue trails and the outer combination hiking/equestrian trail at Marker 18. Continue straight. Many lichens and mosses, including patches of sand spikemoss, grow beneath small woody shrubs.

You start a long ascent up the ridge, where the trail kisses the sky. Cloaked in pink blooms, sprays of Ashe's calamint attract bumblebees and butterflies. A deer pauses at the top of the slope before vanishing into a forest only a few feet taller than you. At the crest, don't follow the curvature, which drops into a deep valley. Go straight ahead and meet the outer loop at Marker 16. Turn left to walk downhill to the prairie. At the fork at Marker 15, the horse trail diverges to the right; stay left. Enough shade is cast by a hammock of sand live oaks to encourage you to stop and rest on a bench overlooking this prairie. You've hiked 2.3 miles.

After ascending up and over the ridge, the trail provides you with a panorama of a broad prairie rimmed in saw palmetto. Tall stalks of wheat-colored pinewood dropseed wave in the afternoon breeze. Past Marker 14 is a prairie showcasing the textures of at least seven types of grasses in succession, from sprays of sand cordgrass to tall stands of shortspike bluestem. This is the northern end of the long chain of lakes and prairies. When you reach Marker 13, continue straight to follow the red-tipped posts of the equestrian trail. The sand is more churned up, but this route is worth it. As you climb the hill, look back at the view behind you: across the prairie, framed inside a small oak hammock, you'll see the sweep of a liquid landscape.

The outer equestrian trail joins in

FOLLOWING THE TRAIL ALONG A PRAIRIE POND

from the right at Marker 43, where several scrub plums with weirdly jointed branches flourish. Marker 42 is next to another prairie pond. The main trail skirts around the prairie, where the live oaks arch to provide a spot of shade. The trail turns and follows the prairie rim, where grasses wave in the wind, and climbs steeply uphill past Marker 41. This is the final climb out of the preserve. You complete the loop at the map box at Marker 2 after 3.4 miles. Continue up the footpath to your right into the oak hammock. It ends at the vault toilet and picnic pavilion adjoining the parking area, wrapping up this 3.5-mile loop.

OTHER HIKING OPTIONS

1. **Short Loop**. A 2.5-mile alternative to the above hike, the Short Loop focuses on the first two ridges closest to the trailhead, and the valleys between them. Following a blue-blazed trail between Marker 9 and Marker 7, it leads you along a showy series of flatwoods ponds. Once you're up and over the second ridge, use the trail between Marker 4 and Marker 41 for one last panorama across a wet prairie.

2. **Long Loop**. The 5.5-mile Long Loop veers off the main route just before the steep climb to the statue, adding another partial loop to the hike we describe. It accesses a primitive campsite added since the prior edition of this guidebook. Contact the preserve at 863-696-1112 if you're interested in camping there. A fee must be paid in advance.

3. **Equestrian Loop**. For a real challenge in this soft sand, follow the 8-mile loop blazed with red-tipped posts. It pushes to the edge of the preserve boundaries in most directions and is well-marked on the map. Bring plenty of water for this hike.

CAMPING AND LODGING

Port Hatchineha Campground, 15050 Hatchineha Road, Haines City, FL 33844 (863-438-0228, polk-county .net)

Cherry Pocket Fish Camp, 3100 Canal Road, Lake Wales, FL 33898 (863-439-2031, cherrypocket.com)

Lake Kissimmee State Park

TOTAL DISTANCE: 15.6 miles in two loops along a network of interconnected trails.

HIKING TIME: 7–8 hours

DIFFICULTY: Easy to moderate

USAGE: $4–5 per vehicle. Open 8 AM to sunset; campers have access to trails before the park opens. Leashed pets welcome.

TRAILHEAD GPS COORDINATES: 27.943847, -81.354761

CONTACT INFORMATION: Lake Kissimmee State Park, 14248 Camp Mack Road, Lake Wales, FL 33898 (863-696-1112, floridastateparks.org/park/Lake-Kissimmee)

Hugging the western shore of Florida's third largest lake, Lake Kissimmee State Park provides a weekend's worth of hiking and wildlife sightings galore. Herds of white-tailed deer browse unconcernedly along the entrance road. Sandhill cranes stride through the tall prairie grasses. Alligators bask in the sunshine along a canal filled with colorful purple pickerelweed blooms. The vast prairies and scrub along Lake Kissimmee provided a grazing ground for a scruffy breed of wild cattle known as the scrub cow, descendants of cattle brought to Florida in 1539 by explorer Hernando de Soto. What is now Lake Kissimmee State Park was once a vast cattle ranch. There is evidence of that past along this hike.

Using the park's major trails, we've put together a route that shows off the vast sweep of this landscape. Do any of the loops on their own as an alternative. To enjoy all of the major trails in this park, arrive and set up camp in the full-service campground, hike the Buster Island Loop, and spend the second day tackling the North Loop Trail and Gobbler Ridge Trail. Or plan a backpacking trip: there are two primitive campsites as an overnight option.

GETTING THERE

From the interchange of US 27 and FL 60 in Lake Wales, head east on FL 60 for 9.7 miles, driving through the village of Hesperides before you reach Boy Scout Camp Road. There should be a prominent sign pointing out the turn. Turn left and drive 3.5 miles to Camp Mack Road. Turn right, following this road 5.4 miles to the park entrance on the right. After you enter through the ranger station, the park road twists and winds through the oak hammocks that dominate the North

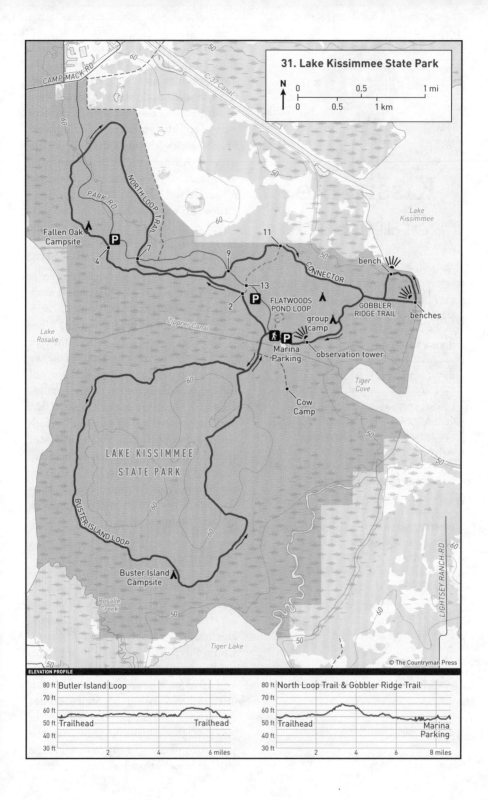

31. Lake Kissimmee State Park

N

0   0.5   1 mi
0   0.5   1 km

CAMP MACK RD

C-37 Canal

60

50

60

Lake
Kissimmee

NORTH LOOP TRAIL

PARK RD

Fallen Oak
Campsite

P

7

4

9

11

CONNECTOR

bench

benches

13

P

2

FLATWOODS
POND LOOP

GOBBLER
RIDGE TRAIL

group
camp

observation tower

Marina
Parking

P

Zipprer Canal

Lake
Rosalie

Cow
Camp

Tiger
Cove

60

50

LAKE KISSIMMEE
STATE PARK

BUSTER ISLAND LOOP

80

80

Buster Island
Campsite

60

Rosalie
Creek

50

Tiger Lake

50

50

60

LIGHTSEY RANCH RD

© The Countryman Press

ELEVATION PROFILE

Butler Island Loop

80 ft
70 ft
60 ft
50 ft   Trailhead   Trailhead
40 ft
30 ft
              2   4   6 miles

North Loop Trail & Gobbler Ridge Trail

80 ft
70 ft
60 ft
50 ft   Trailhead   Marina
40 ft   Parking
30 ft
              2   4   6   8 miles

PINE FLATWOODS ON THE BUSTER ISLAND LOOP

Loop. Continue past the campground and the turnoff to the Cow Camp, reaching the parking area next to the marina. The park's trails radiate from a prominent trailhead here.

THE HIKES

BUSTER ISLAND LOOP

Sign in at the hiker kiosk, which is at the trailhead at the marina parking area. Follow the trail through an oak hammock to a road you passed on the way in—the 1876 Cow Camp. Turn left at the trail junction and follow the road over the bridge. At the fork in the road, the right side leads to the trail; the left side leads to the Cow Camp. Open on weekends, it's a living history encampment of cowmen—never call them cowboys—who show you what it took to live and work in the rough conditions of frontier Florida. A herd of more than 200 scrub cattle roam in the park, a tribute to Florida's frontier history. You may encounter them along this loop.

The blue blazes end as Cow Camp Road ends, so follow the white blazes to continue along the Buster Island Trail. After 0.5 mile, you reach the start of the loop. Turn right into the pine flatwoods to walk it counterclockwise. Thin-needled sprays of wild pine decorate the gnarled branches of live oaks. Comprised of wet prairies, pine flatwoods, oak hammocks, and scrub, Buster Island is an island surrounded by Lake Kissimmee, Tiger Lake, and Lake Rosalie. You can't tell that from the trail since you never see the lakes. Instead, you're on a corridor of high ground. Beyond the cool shade of the live oaks and slash pines is prairie, stretching off into the distance. This trail provides a close-up look at the succession of the pine flatwoods to Florida's climax forest, the live oak hammock. Fire is an integral part of the natural pine flatwoods ecosystem. Prescribed burning and other land management techniques are used to restore the pine flatwoods, so the once-grand oak hammocks on this loop aren't what they used to be. A noticeable number of dead oak trees are obvious throughout the park.

As you cross a forest road at 1.1 miles,

there is an old section of fencing. This land was once farmland owned by the Zipprer family, who sold it to the state in 1969. After walking through a low area of tall grass and ferns, you return to the familiar hammock and pines. For a while, the corridor widens, the prairie disappearing beyond the trees. Watch for signs of the turpentine industry. Although the original pine forest was logged more than a century ago, some of the tall stumps and snags of long-dead pines have the v-shaped catfaces that indicate the pine was tapped for resin.

After 2.2 miles of hiking, you see open scrub. As the trail enters the scrubby flatwoods, it becomes a pine-needle footpath edged by grass. Gallberry swarms the understory. Cross a forest road into an area where the grass creates a chestnut haze beneath the slash pines. At 3.4 miles, the trail turns left at a double blaze, briefly following a forest road before leading you into an oak hammock. Butterfly orchids dangle overhead, catching your eye with their long, grass-like leaves and tall yellow-green flowers with white lips striped purple. The butterfly orchid is Florida's most common wild orchid, blooming from late spring to early fall. It is also a protected species.

Turning left into the pine flatwoods, you hear a distant, constant buzz—airboats on Lake Rosalie. Half-hidden by tall cinnamon ferns, blueberry bushes rise from the needle-carpeted forest floor. A chorus of frogs sings as the trail skirts around a large flatwoods pond, reaching the sign for the primitive campsite. Nestled under live oaks, the campsite has two picnic tables and several fire rings. It's a great place for a break after 3.8 miles of hiking.

Returning to the trail, turn right. The footpath becomes a narrow corridor between dense saw palmettos. Spanish moss drapes over the live oak limbs overhead. You see the prairie, a savanna of tall grass just beyond the tree line. As you walk in deep shade, look for butterfly orchids overhead. A near-seamless canopy of live oak branches shades the trail. After 4.6 miles, the grasslands become more visible as you cross a horse trail. The trail jumps on and off a forest road several times before it makes a sharp left into the scrub.

Short scrub live oak and myrtle oak trees characterize the scrub habitat, with only scattered slash pines. Florida rosemary grows in small clearings between the saw palmettos. A grassy pond sits along the trail. At 5.2 miles, the trail turns right onto a forest road that leads into the pine flatwoods, making a second sharp turn. As you pass another marshy pond, the forest floor gleams green with the needles of hundreds of slash pines taking root. Dark earth gives way to white sand as the elevation increases slightly, bringing you into a sand pine scrub.

After 6.1 miles, the trail enters the vast prairie at the heart of Buster Island, where you cross a forest road. The sweep of the tree line fills the distance, your route through the oak hammock and pine flatwoods in review. You reach the beginning of the white-blazed loop at 6.5 miles. Turn right to follow the blue blazes back to the main trailhead. On the return route, walk down to the Zipprer Canal, which drains Lake Rosalie into Lake Kissimmee, to watch for wading birds and alligators. You reach the marina at 6.9 miles.

NORTH LOOP TRAIL & GOBBLER RIDGE TRAIL

Start at the main trailhead by the marina. Follow the same blue blazes as

FALLEN OAK CAMPSITE, NORTH LOOP TRAIL

for the Buster Island Loop, but this time cross Cow Camp Road. The trail skirts the edge of the prairie along the Zipprer Canal. A large sign confirms your choice of route. Continue straight ahead until you reach the beginning of the yellow-blazed North Loop Trail after 0.4 mile. Turn left, wandering through open cabbage palms and dense gallberry. Entering a tall stand of pines, the trail makes its way to where you see prairie between the trees. A mirror image of the Buster Island Loop, this trail parallels the south edge of the same prairie.

Walk through a stand of young cabbage palms decked out in their full mass of fronds at ground level, growing out before they grow tall. Scattered live oaks and saw palmetto clumps break up the pine forest. A broad ditch, perhaps a seasonal stream, drains into a flatwoods pond. The forest yields to oak hammock, where a damp fur of resurrection fern covers the sprawling limbs of live oaks. Butterfly orchids grow here, too, with several large clusters on the oaks. Saw palmettos with trunks up to 20 feet long sprout near the base of one large live oak. After you cross the for-

est road at Marker 4, the soil becomes a deep cinnamon color, the result of deep layers of decomposing pine needles. Passing another flatwoods pond, the trail reaches the sign for the Fallen Oak Campsite at 1.9 miles. Turn right to check out the campsite, 0.1 mile down a blue-blazed trail. It's a beauty spot under the live oaks, with a picnic table and fire ring.

Continuing along the yellow-blazed loop, the trail veers into the pine flatwoods. Glimpses of open sky show that the prairie isn't far away, but you run out of park. The trail makes a hard right within sight of the fence line, passing through a hammock of sand live oak before it enters the open scrubby flatwoods. Another hard right leads you straight down a long corridor across the park entrance road. A stark but compelling landscape of dense, low saw palmetto and scattered longleaf pines goes on for the next 0.5 mile, broken only by circular wet prairies and one tiny oak hammock. At 3.2 miles, you reach a pen with an unusual occupant—a fire-roasted snag catfaced for turpentine.

Long strands of Spanish moss dangle like beards from the tall longleaf pines. After 4 miles, the forest becomes denser, turning to pine flatwoods that offer well-appreciated shade. Crossing the park road again at Marker 7, you enter a hammock of pines and oaks. Soft pine needles obscure the footpath; watch carefully for the blazes as the trail swings left after the road crossing. Squeezed between the park road and the prairie, this narrow strip of hammock contains both the trail you're on and the trail you've been on, not more than 100 feet apart. Be cautious about stepping off the footpath, as you might step onto the wrong yellow-blazed trail! Skirting a prairie, the corridor narrows through a densely wooded area, becoming damp underfoot. Crossing the park road at Marker 9, you enter another stretch of pine flatwoods beyond a forest road under a power line.

At 5.7 miles is the junction for the blue-blazed connector to the Gobbler Ridge Trail. Continue straight, following this trail out towards Lake Kissimmee. The trail weaves beneath oak hammocks of a sand ridge that is only a few inches high, but high enough to keep the sweeping prairie at bay. Where the

forest ends, the ground is almost desert-like. Clusters of seafoam-colored deer moss sprawl across the blinding white sugar sand.

When the trail reaches a Y intersection with a bench, you're at the Gobbler Ridge Trail. Keep left, reaching the next fork in the trail beneath the oaks at 6.7 miles. Keep right. Traversing a low-lying marsh on a causeway, the trail leads to the tree line on Gobbler Ridge. Once up and over the small ridge, you meet the shoreline of Lake Kissimmee and can see for quite a distance out across the lake. Two benches provide a spot for birding. If the lakeshore has been mowed, it's possible to walk a loop along it to another bench, following the sweep of blue water. Be alert for sunning alligators close to shore. If the water is too high, backtrack the way you came.

At 7.3 miles, the bench on the north end of Gobbler Ridge looks out past a lone cabbage palm to the channel which boaters use to access Camp Mack River Resort, a fish camp not far from the park entrance. The forest road loops back through the marsh, sometimes soggy underfoot, to rejoin the other part of the loop in the oak hammock. Turn right.

VIEW FROM THE OBSERVATION TOWER NEAR THE GOBBLER RIDGE TRAIL TRAILHEAD

Once you've returned to the bench at the junction with the blue-blazed connector to the North Loop Trail, you've hiked 7.7 miles. Turn left to follow the lime-green blazes of the Gobbler Ridge Trail.

A sand road along the prairie's edge, the Gobbler Ridge Trail offers the best wildlife watching in the park. We encountered a pair of bald eagles and a flock of turkeys, two families of sandhill cranes, pileated and downy woodpeckers, two herds of deer, raccoons, an opossum, and several armadillos. The trail curves along the prairie, skirting a round marsh before ducking beneath the splendor of ancient live oaks fuzzy with resurrection fern. It's at the next curve you see picnic tables, a place to stop and take a break if no one is occupying the group camp.

Sweeping over to the prairie rim, the trail leads you to the park's observation tower. If you haven't already climbed it, do so to savor the views. Instead of following the green-tipped posts to the trailhead, stay with the path along the prairie. Let it lead you around the picnic area to the Zipprer Canal. Follow the canal back to the marina parking area to complete this 8.7-mile loop.

OTHER HIKING OPTIONS

1. **Flatwoods Pond Loop**. Directly across the park road from the main trailhead, this 0.4-mile interpretive nature trail is a sampler of the habitats along the longer trail system. True to its name, the trail loops around a small flatwoods pond.
2. **Gobbler Ridge Trail**. A trailhead kiosk at the parking area at the end of the park road marks the beginning of the 3-mile Gobbler Ridge Trail, which is included in the larger cir-

cuit we described above. Follow the lime green blazes through the picnic area and past the playground to the observation tower, then along the forest road on the prairie rim to the junction with the cross-trail to the North Loop. Continue to the right to walk the loop to the shore of Lake Kissimmee. Return along the green blazes.
3. **North Loop Highlights**. The best of the North Loop lies between two small parking areas along the park entrance road. For this 2.2-mile trek, park at the small parking area closest to the campground. Walk along the edge of the park road towards the entrance to meet the trail crossing at Marker 13. Turn left and follow the trail to Marker 2, where you make a right to enjoy the pine flatwoods and oak hammocks that offer glimpses of the wetlands around the Zipprer Canal beyond. When you reach Marker 4, turn right and follow the forest road to the entrance road. Turn right and walk past the second parking area to the trail crossing at Marker 7. Turn right to head back into the woods and stick with the loop as it continues all the way back around to Marker 13. Walk back along the entrance road to where your car is parked.

CAMPING AND LODGING

Lake Kissimmee State Park Campground (1-800-326-3521, floridastate parks.reserveamerica.com)

Camp Mack's River Resort, 14900 Camp Mack Road, Lake Wales, FL 33898 (863-696-1108, campmack.com)

Lake Rosalie Park and Campground, 2859–2925 Rosalie Lake Road, Lake Wales, FL 33898 (863-679-4245, polk -county.net)

Tiger Creek Preserve

TOTAL DISTANCE: 11.8 miles in a network of three loops and the connecting trails between them. Shorter options available.

HIKING TIME: 5–6 hours

DIFFICULTY: Moderate to difficult

USAGE: Free. Open sunrise to sunset. No pets or bicycles permitted.

TRAILHEAD GPS COORDINATES: 27.807983, -81.492050

CONTACT INFORMATION: The Nature Conservancy, 674 Pfundstein Road, Babson Park, FL 33827 (863-635-7506, nature.org)

When the rest of Florida was under a few feet of water, in Miocene times, the long, thin, dune-capped island that is now the Lake Wales Ridge stood well above the waves. It is now one of North America's most diverse biological communities, with the highest concentration of rare and endangered plants in the continental United States. These are also the "mountains" of peninsular Florida, up to 300 feet above sea level. Along this fascinating ridge, The Nature Conservancy provides an outstanding hiking trail system for exploration of nearly 5,000 acres of the Lake Wales Ridge under their care at Tiger Creek Preserve.

Leading you across not just the desert-like scrub but a diversity of habitats sheltered by swales between ridges, the trail network at Tiger Creek Preserve includes a primary connector trail, the Pfundstein Trail, and three loops. Much of the trail system is very dry and open. Take plenty of water along. A hike to and around the hilly Heron Pond Loop via the well-trodden Pfundstein Trail is a 4.2-mile trek. Most hikers looking for a long day hike tackle the Highlands Loop, which is 8.4 miles by going straight out and back along the Pfundstein Trail to the loop. Stretch that to 10.2 miles by tacking on the new Creek Bluffs Loop at the north end of the preserve, or even to 11.8 miles by adding on the Heron Pond Loop on the way, and a stop at Patrick Creek. See *Other Hiking Options*, at the end of this chapter, for more alternatives from a new trailhead for the Wakeford Trail added at the northeast corner of the preserve. Our route follows the full 11.8 miles you can hike from the Pfundstein Road trailhead.

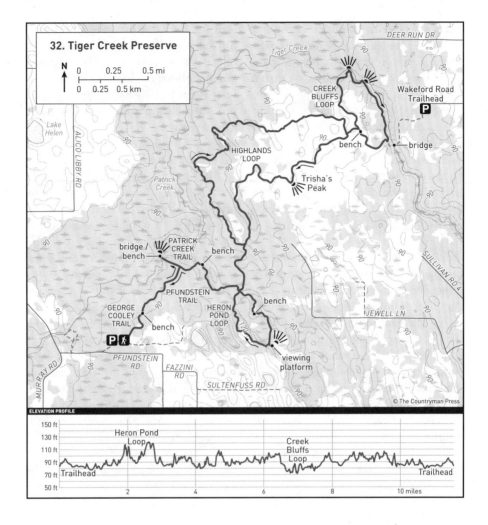

32. Tiger Creek Preserve

N

0   0.25   0.5 mi
0   0.25 0.5 km

DEER RUN DR

Tiger Creek

CREEK
BLUFFS
LOOP

Wakeford Road
Trailhead

P

Lake
Helen

bench

bridge

HIGHLANDS
LOOP

Patrick
Creek

Trisha's
Peak

bridge /
bench

PATRICK
CREEK
TRAIL

bench

bench

PFUNDSTEIN
TRAIL

GEORGE
COOLEY
TRAIL

HERON
POND
LOOP

bench

bench

SULLIVAN RD 4

JEWELL LN

P

PFUNDSTEIN
RD

FAZZINI
RD

viewing
platform

MURRAY RD

SULTENFUSS RD

© The Countryman Press

ELEVATION PROFILE

150 ft
130 ft
110 ft
90 ft
70 ft
50 ft

Heron Pond
Loop

Trailhead

Creek
Bluffs
Loop

Trailhead

2   4   6   8   10 miles

GETTING THERE

Follow US 27 south from Lake Wales to CR 640 east. CR 640 turns into FL 17, passing through Babson Park. Two miles south, turn left on North Lake Moody Road, then left again on Murray Road. The road plunges downhill through orange groves and crosses a railroad track before reaching Pfundstein Road. Turn left and pass the pull-off for the George Cooley Trail before reaching the main trailhead on the left.

THE HIKE

Sign in at the trailhead kiosk. The white-blazed Pfundstein Trail makes a left away from the forest road behind the gate, working its way through a grassy, open scrub. Several low, rounded, natural bowls are cutthroat grass seeps, found nowhere else but Florida. Moisture seeping from the sand feeds the minimal water requirements of this endangered grass. The glistening white sand path is made up of ancient particles of quartzite. It winds through the oak scrub, a forest in miniature. As you walk down the trail, notice how few oaks tower above your head. Myrtle oak, Chapman oak, and scrub live oak thrive here, as do stunted wax myrtle and the pygmy fringe tree. Although the bright white sand reminds you of a desert, this area receives up to 50 inches of rain each year. The well-drained sand soaks up the rain so rapidly that scrub plants barely have an opportunity to use the water. Instead, the oaks and shrubs rely on deep taproots and waxy coatings to maximize their survival.

Where the white blazes lead into the pine flatwoods, wiregrass creates a hazy forest floor under the tall longleaf pines. As the trail climbs over gently rolling hills, you'll notice dead pines in the swales. Extensive flooding along Patrick Creek soaked the roots of those trees for so long that they succumbed to rot. At a junction with a forest road after 0.8 mile, you meet the Patrick Creek Trail. Turn left for a quick ramble to the creek. There is a bench right before the bridge, which provides a primordial scene of cabbage palms forming a backdrop to the marshy creek.

Back at the MAIN TRAIL sign after 1.2 miles, continue along the white blazes. The trail passes a bench beneath the pines, a rest stop with a view of an eagle's nest in the distance. For those returning to this hike after a long absence, as we did, you'll be delighted to discover the trails moved off the forest roads and onto fresh footpaths, especially along the next mile. The exception is where you join a road to walk on gravel through a bayhead swamp to minimize wet feet. After climbing out of the bayhead, watch for the double-blazes into the diminutive scrub forest. Most intersections from this point on have maps to keep you on the correct route. The footpath

leads up the slope of a ridge into sandhill habitat, where longleaf pines stand tall above the turkey oaks. The bayhead swamp follows the base of this ridge to your right, loblolly bay trees making a tall, shimmering green wall. Crossing a sand road, the trail continues into the shade of an oak scrub, where sand live oaks knit a low canopy overhead.

After 1.9 miles, you reach a junction with the Heron Pond Loop. As it's surprisingly hilly, it's best to tackle it while you're fresh. Turn right to follow the red blazes. A small memorial presents the trail in memory of Ken Morrison, a former director of Bok Tower Gardens. He spent decades preserving The Jungle, this landscape between the creeks, as Edward Bok had wished it to be, with the help of The Nature Conservancy.

Keep left at the Y to walk the loop clockwise. Passing through an oak scrub, you'll find it tricky at times to distinguish the red blazes from the red blanket lichen. As the trail gains a noticeable amount of elevation, marshes are visible in the valley below, especially from a peak with a bench. Sandhill habitat with smatterings of scrub covers the hills, which offer views down to the marshy pond. The trail drops to the level of the pond and meets a forest road. Turn right to walk along this road between the marsh and the open water of Heron Pond. On the opposite shore, take a side path to the viewing platform. A shady perch on the shoreline above the open water of the marsh, it's a perfect spot for birding.

Returning to the forest road, make two quick turns, following the double blazes. The trail ascends through a dense understory of saw palmetto and scrub oaks. Views are more pronounced across the marshy pond. Cross a sand road that arcs downhill to the pond. The trail tunnels through oak scrub before

BIRDING PLATFORM ON HERON POND

trail heads uphill as it parallels a large marsh in a swale between the ridges. After crossing a small creek on a bridge, it enters the sandhill forest. Follow the orange blazes from the heights of the sandhill into scrubby flatwoods, dense with saw palmetto and gallberry. You pass a bench where this loop hike used to begin before it was moved off the forest roads.

The desert-like scrub is the highlight on this higher ground, which is the domain of the Florida scrub-jay. The many short scrubby plants with yellow star-shaped flowers are varieties of St. John's wort, some only found in this preserve. The trail is crowded by vegetation in many places, so watch for blazes. In the open scrub, several cabbage palms are growing in a low grassy area—an indicator of a seepage slope where cutthroat grass thrives. Longleaf pines edge an open prairie. Turning left, the trail rises through the scrub, the footpath blinding white sand. Keep alert for a sharp right where the trail climbs beneath the turkey oaks.

After 6.2 miles, you reach a trail junction with a map. This short connector leads to the Creek Bluffs Loop, the northernmost loop in the preserve. It's worth a visit since it offers scenic views of Tiger Creek. The loop begins at a bench atop a ridge, overlooking a wet prairie in a depression. Turn left and climb into the longleaf pine forest. With the sparse scattering of pines and an extremely open understory, views are extensive. Crossing a sand road, the trail continues into a short thicket of scrub forest, with the taller trees in the distance marking the edge of the bluffs along Tiger Creek. Passing swales of prairie grasses between longleaf pines, the trail makes its way to a stand of tall cabbage palms upon the bluffs of Tiger

entering a stretch of sandhills where gopher apple, a favorite food for gopher tortoises, grows densely. Dropping downhill, the Heron Pond Loop leaves your last glimpses of the pond behind as you enter a pine flatwoods and cross a sand road. You reach the end of the loop after 3.1 miles. Pass the memorial and turn right. The trail makes a sharp left onto a forest road to cross a bayhead along the graveled surface of the road. As the road becomes soft white sand, look for the TO HIGHLANDS LOOP sign to the right. Walking between the saw palmetto, you reach an oak hammock where Spanish moss hangs thickly from the tree limbs. Cross a sand road and continue into oak scrub, another delightful tunnel of tangled limbs. Take a moment and pause to listen. One of the most endearing reasons to hike at this preserve is the quiet.

The white blazes of the Pfundstein Trail end, after 3.5 miles, at a clearly marked junction for the south end of the Highlands Loop. Turn left to begin this loop, the largest one in the preserve. Winding through oak scrub, the

Creek. Your first glimpse of the creek is along a showy bend, with the trail providing panoramas in several directions, and a bench for taking in the view.

Beyond this high point, the trail pulls away from the bluffs while providing views of the healthy longleaf pine forest to the west. The next view of the creek is much closer, almost an invitation to cool off in its depths were it not for the massive alligators that call this waterway home. Thanks to The Nature Conservancy, Tiger Creek is one of the last remaining blackwater streams in Florida with a fully protected watershed, and it's along this stretch of trail you realize what that means, in the wild nature of this waterway. Another bench provides a place to enjoy this cool corridor along the creek. After following the edge of a prairie, the trail reaches a tributary flowing into the creek and crosses it on a small bridge.

As you emerge at the CREEK BLUFFS LOOP sign, make a sharp right to stay with the pink blazes of this loop, as the white blazes lead to the Wakeford Trailhead, an alternative access point for these northernmost loops. The trail arcs around a large prairie in a swale, its far edge defined by the longleaf pine forest you first walked through on this loop. You climb out of the scrub and up beneath the pines on this last part of the loop, reaching the bench at the connector trail with the white blazes and the sign TO HIGHLANDS LOOP. By the time you return to the back side of the sign for the Highlands Loop, you've logged 7.9 miles. Turn left to continue along the south side of this loop, which is particularly rugged and scenic. Your ramble beneath the longleaf pines continues, the trail snaking between well-defined clumps of saw palmetto. As the sand grows brighter and softer, the pines retreat where the trail curves through a prairie. The orange blazes briefly lead onto an old sand road. A sharp left leads back to a footpath through an oak scrub at a sign for Tricia's Peak.

Climbing to one of the highest scrub ridges in the preserve, the trail offers a pleasing panorama of the prairies and pines below. A bench honors Tricia Martin, one of the preserve's longtime managers. From this promontory, the trail winds downhill through the sandhills, where the pines are more scattered, offering little shade. A grassy prairie fills a swale at the base of the ridge. Past a statuesque longleaf pine, the footpath leads you through the intimacy of a cluster of sand live oaks. Gopher apple grows densely under young turkey oaks. The trail reaches that line of trees in the distance when it crosses a forest road. Climbing up and over the next ridge, notice the co-mingling of habitats: sand pines and silk bay, usually found in scrub forests, popping up among these sandhills. After the next forest road crossing, Spanish moss drapes in thick curtains from the oak canopy overhead. From a high point, you can see a marsh in the low swale.

Just a little ways past the bridge over the outflow of the marsh, you return to the PFUNDSTEIN TRAIL sign after 9.8 total miles. You've hiked this trail northbound to get here, so now it's time to take it directly south to the trailhead, without any side trips. Turn left and stick with the white blazes, taking advantage of the handful of benches along the way for a break along the next couple of miles. Keep alert where the trail jumps on and off the forest roads to go through the two bayheads. At 10.2 miles, you pass the junction with the Heron Pond Loop, and, at 10.9 miles, the junction with the Patrick Creek Trail. Make a sharp left here to stay with the white blazes as they wind back through the rolling hills above the creek. The last 0.25 mile is mostly open, but the parking area is within sight. You reach the kiosk at 11.8 miles. Sign out before you leave.

PRAIRIE AND SCRUB BELOW TRICIA'S PEAK

OTHER HIKING OPTIONS

1. **George Cooley Trail** (27.806755, -81.498606). This 0.8-mile nature trail along Pfundstein Road provides a quick overview of the habitats found in this preserve. Follow a well-worn path between a set of posts to reach the trailhead kiosk. The Circle Trail is the main loop, with several spurs off it to scenic spots, including along Patrick Creek.

2. **Patrick Creek**. For quite some time, Patrick Creek, a tributary feeding Tiger Creek, rose well above its normal banks and, in doing so, submerged a popular boardwalk loop leading to a giant sand pine. On our visit, the bridge to the loop was still mostly underwater. A hike from the Pfundstein Road trailhead to Patrick Creek and back is 2 miles.

3. **Wakeford Trail** (27.831846, -81.456699). This northern connector to the trail system off Walk-in-the-Water Road enables you to hike to Tiger Creek (1 mile) or do the Creek Bluffs Loop (2.6 miles). If you add on the Highlands Loop, it's a 6.9-mile day hike from this new trailhead.

4. **End to End**. With two cars, leave one at the Wakeford Road trailhead and hike up to it from the Pfundstein Road trailhead. For the best scenic views in the preserve, we recommend you don't skip the Heron Pond Loop, do the south side of the Highlands Loop, and do the north side of the Creek Bluffs Loop. Walking between the two trailheads on this route with a stop at Patrick Creek nets you a 7.3-mile hike.

CAMPING AND LODGING

Lake Wales Campground & RV, 15898 US 27, Lake Wales, FL 33859 (863-638-9011, lakewalescampgroundrvresort.com)

Walk-in-the-Water Primitive Campground, Lake Wales Ridge State Forest (27.783537, -81.447576), (1-877-879-3859, floridastateforests.reserveamerica.com)

Westgate River Ranch Resort, 3200 River Ranch Boulevard, River Ranch, FL 33867 (863-692-0727, westgateresorts.com)

Crooked Lake Prairie

TOTAL DISTANCE: 2.3-mile loop on the perimeter of two interconnected trails.

HIKING TIME: 1–1.5 hours

DIFFICULTY: Easy to moderate

USAGE: Free. Open sunrise to sunset. Leashed pets permitted. Bicycles permitted but not recommended due to soft sand.

TRAILHEAD GPS COORDINATES: 27.8065, -81.5593

CONTACT INFORMATION: Crooked Lake Prairie, 985 Ohlinger Road, Babson Park, FL 33827 (863-534-7377, polknature.com/explore/crooked-lake-prairie)

At Crooked Lake Prairie, the dunes of the Lake Wales Ridge meet showy prairie grasslands along the eastern shore of Crooked Lake. This hike is a refreshing excursion into habitats found on the high hills of the Lake Wales Ridge, a counterpoint to the spreading residential developments replacing scrub forests and orange groves on these high hills. Hiking through this 525-acre preserve provides a pleasant immersion into a healthy scrub forest, and birders will delight in being able to see both green herons and a family of Florida scrub-jays along one short loop. There are two primary trails in the preserve: the Lake View Trail, which loops to a boardwalk on Crooked Lake, and the Scrub Trail, which loops through the heart of the scrub. As the habitats here are very open and desert-like—to be expected of the Lake Wales Ridge—sunscreen, sunglasses, and a hat are a smart idea.

GETTING THERE

From the junction of FL 17 and CR 630 in Frostproof, drive north 3.8 miles to Cody Villa Road and turn left at the sign for Crooked Prairie Preserve. Follow the road for 1.3 miles, making a right onto Ohlinger Road. Look for the left into the parking area.

THE HIKE

Start at the preserve kiosk, which has brochures about the trail. An important note: our map and their map are different. They no longer show the loop that the Lake View Trail makes, although we confirmed that the trails still create a large loop. They may not in the future if the boardwalk is renovated. Following the sign that says SCRUB TRAIL STRAIGHT AHEAD, duck under the oak tree to follow

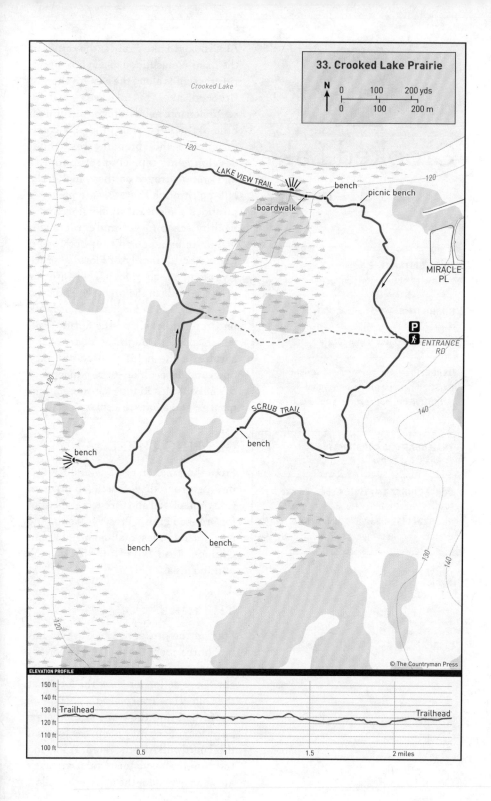

33. Crooked Lake Prairie

Crooked Lake

N

0   100   200 yds
0   100   200 m

LAKE VIEW TRAIL

boardwalk

bench

picnic bench

MIRACLE PL

P

ENTRANCE RD

SCRUB TRAIL

bench

bench

bench

bench

120

120

140

130

140

© The Countryman Press

ELEVATION PROFILE

150 ft
140 ft
130 ft Trailhead   Trailhead
120 ft
110 ft
100 ft
        0.5   1   1.5   2 miles

A PAIR OF SANDHILL CRANES AMONG THE PRAIRIE GRASSES

this narrow corridor into the oak hammock, following a corridor edged by saw palmetto and sand live oaks. You pass a picnic bench tucked away in the shade. The trail corridor is tricky to follow in places, so watch for both signs and a worn footpath. It pops out onto a sand road with views across a prairie. Turn left and look for the next arrow sign and hiker symbol pointing back into the shade of the oaks. An orange arrow sign guides you away from the preserve's perimeter fence with a working orange grove. Making a right turn, the trail crosses the sand road and you see a SCRUB TRAIL sign. Continue walking beneath the shade of sand live oaks along a well-defined path.

As you enter the scrub, things change. There are side trails you need to avoid following, so keep alert for hiker symbols and arrows. The trees are diminutive, with myrtle oak and Chapman oak dominating. You pass under the shade of another oak hammock before emerging into the blinding white sand of the Lake Wales Ridge. Soft and powdery, it's not easy to walk through. The trail continues in soft sand, footprints guiding the way. Islands of short oaks sit amid a sea of sand, with clumps of saw palmetto breaking up the landscape. Crossing another sand road, the trail passes a wooden bench after 0.5 mile.

Snaking through this sandy habitat, keep alert for the arrow markers and faded orange blazes. Take a sharp left at the next SCRUB TRAIL sign. Pay attention to a flutter of blue wings and the *shreep* of a Florida scrub-jay. This preserve is actively managed for the scrub-jay families that reside here. These large, colorful members of the jay family are only found in Florida, their population in decline and severely limited by lack of habitat. Preferring young scrub forests, they don't migrate far.

The corridor narrows again before bursting into an open patch of sand. Mounds of grass look like giant pin-

cushions. Slipping back into an oak scrub, the trail becomes more obvious as it twists and turns between clusters of oaks. Arrows guide the way. You pass a bench in the shade of an oak at 0.75 mile and a bench in the sun soon after. A wander through a shady oak hammock is a welcome break from the sun reflecting off the white sand. A patch of gopher apple is a reminder that this is prime habitat for gopher tortoises.

Navigating your way through the scrub by following the arrows, you come to a T intersection with a VIEWING AREA sign at 1 mile. Turn left to take this short walk to where the scrub meets the shoreline of the lake. It leads through a stand of longleaf pines. Grand sentinels, they are picturesque reminders of the grander forests that once swept across this part of the peninsula. The spur ends at a bench overlooking Crooked Lake.

Return to the trail junction and continue straight, jogging left into the scrub. The corridor tightens between the saw palmetto and scrub oaks. Arrows and posts point the way towards another line of longleaf pines. At 1.5 miles, you reach the pines at a T intersection with a forest road. The Scrub Trail turns right. To stay on the perimeter of the trail system, turn left, catching sweeping views of the cordgrass prairie in the distance. It's easy to miss the next turn: watch for a ditch and oak hammocks just before the landscape opens to barren sand punctuated by thousands of clumps of prickly pear cactus. Around 1.7 miles, the trail turns right and tacks from oak hammock to oak hammock across the ancient sands of the Lake Wales Ridge.

OTHER HIKING OPTIONS

1. **Crooked Lake Sandhill** (27.814114, -81.547776). A little over a mile away, the Turkey Oak Sink Trail is a 0.8-mile loop with both a dip into a deep sinkhole and a climb to a scenic view down to Crooked Lake.
2. **Babson Park Nature Center** (27.841382, -81.533629). At the north end of Babson Park, along Scenic 17, this small Audubon nature center focuses on the Lake Wales Ridge with its easy 0.25-mile Ridge Audubon Trail and Lake Trail.
3. **Black Bear Trail, Lake Wales Ridge State Forest** (27.759989, -81.465249). Off CR 630 east of Frostproof, this 4.8-mile hiking trail system on the ridge leads to two primitive campsites and connects to a larger network of equestrian trails on the Walk-in-the-Water Tract.

CAMPING AND LODGING

Lake Arbuckle Park & Campground, 2600 Lake Arbuckle Road, Frostproof, FL 33843 (863-635-2811, polk-county.net)

Reedy Creek Campground (27.706071, -81.445495) or **Walk-in-the-Water Primitive Campground** (27.783537, -81.447576), Lake Wales Ridge State Forest, Frostproof, FL (1-877-879-3859, floridastateforests.reserveamerica.com)

Westgate River Ranch Resort, 3200 River Ranch Boulevard, River Ranch, FL 33867 (863-692-1321, westgate resorts.com)

Swaying clumps of sand cordgrass rise around you as you reach the berm along Crooked Lake and walk up to the boardwalk. Herons and egrets poke around the edges of the lake, and the view across the marsh is spectacular, with showy sprays of slender grass waving in unison in the breeze and water lilies floating in the shallows.

Leaving the boardwalk, you pass a picnic table at 2 miles. It sits beneath long streamers of swaying Spanish moss under the oaks. The trail leads you through the shade of oak hammocks where sand pine scrub and open prairie meet. Prickly pear cactus rises from the grasses as you come up to the intersection with the Scrub Trail. Turn left to exit, passing a portable toilet on your way to the parking area, completing the 2.3-mile hike.

HILLSBOROUGH RIVER ALONG THE RIVER RAPIDS TRAIL,
HILLSBOROUGH RIVER STATE PARK

VI.

TAMPA BAY

Hillsborough River State Park

TOTAL DISTANCE: 6.7 miles in three linked trails. Other distances and configurations possible.

HIKING TIME: 3–3.5 hours

DIFFICULTY: Easy on the River Rapids and Baynard Trails to moderate/difficult on the Seminole Woods Trail, if it's wet or muddy.

USAGE: $4–6 per vehicle. Open 8 AM to sunset; campers have access to trails before the park opens. Leashed pets welcome, but backpackers may not bring dogs to the primitive campsite.

TRAILHEAD GPS COORDINATES: 28.1491, -82.2273

CONTACT INFORMATION: Hillsborough River State Park, 15402 US 301 N, Thonotosassa, FL 33592 (813-987-6771, floridastateparks.org/park/Hillsborough-River)

One of Florida's oldest state parks, Hillsborough River State Park offers something you don't run across often in Florida—rapids. Limestone boulders create a mild stretch of scenic whitewater along the Hillsborough River, which flows out of the Green Swamp on its lazy way to Tampa Bay. The soothing sound of burbling water is enough for any hiker to make the trek to enjoy this state park, which has a little something for everyone. There are gentle nature trails with boardwalks, accessible paved paths, a dedicated bike path, and footpaths deep into the river bluff forests, one of which leads to a primitive campsite for backpackers. The park's two full-service campgrounds—Rivers Edge and Hammock Circle—cater to tent and trailer campers.

Our hiking route links together three riverside trails—the River Rapids Nature Trail, the Baynard Trail, and the Seminole Woods Trail—to create a loop out and back along the river and its surrounding habitats. Vary the length of this loop according to your interest and time, or start it from a different trailhead. To plan an overnight at the primitive campsite, call ahead to reserve your spot and check in with the rangers at the entrance station. We strongly recommend the use of insect repellent year-round because of the many swamps along the trails.

GETTING THERE

On I-75, take exit 265, Temple Terrace (Fowler Ave/FL 582), and head east to the intersection with US 301. Follow US 301 north for 10.5 miles to the park entrance on the left. After you stop at the entrance station, turn right onto the one-way loop road that circles the park. Pass the interpretive center. Stop at the

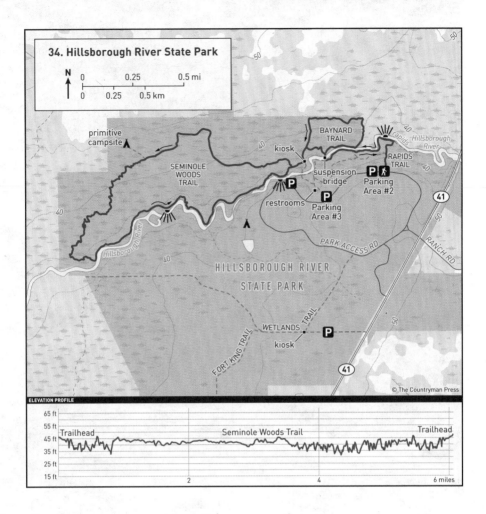

34. Hillsborough River State Park

primitive campsite

SEMINOLE WOODS TRAIL

kiosk

BAYNARD TRAIL

Hillsborough River

RAPIDS TRAIL

suspension bridge

Parking Area #2

restrooms

Parking Area #3

PARK ACCESS RD

RANCH RD

HILLSBOROUGH RIVER STATE PARK

FORT KING TRAIL

WETLANDS TRAIL

kiosk

© The Countryman Press

ELEVATION PROFILE

Trailhead — Seminole Woods Trail — Trailhead

---

next parking area (parking lot #2) with the sign NATURE TRAIL.

THE HIKE

Start your hike at the River Rapids Nature Trail by the PRAYER OF THE WOODS sign. This is a broad, well-maintained interpretive trail ideal for all members of the family. Enter the forest under a canopy of tall live oaks, pignut hickory, laurel oak, and cabbage palms. Oaks are the dominant tree along the river, with surprisingly ancient live oaks along some of the trails. The Native Americans who lived in these woods

called it *Locksa Apoka*, the place for eating acorns. At the first junction, a trail comes in from the left. Continue straight, crossing a small bridge over one of the river's side channels, lined with saw palmettos. The sound of rushing water fills your ears. When you reach the log Civilian Conservation Corps shelter after 0.25 mile, walk to the rapids overlook. The tannic water tumbles over dark red and black boulders, outcrops of Suwannee limestone, creating a small series of rapids. A striking bald cypress rises from its roots in a rocky island, its trunk and branches furry with air plants. As water rushes over the

RIVER RAPIDS AT HILLSBOROUGH RIVER STATE PARK

rocks, frothy bubbles float downstream. Swimming is not permitted in the river, but canoes and kayaks pass by, and families fish along lazy bends in the river. A beaten path leads upstream to another small set of rapids, a brief detour for a nice view.

Follow the trail downstream, where several overlooks provide nice views of the rocks and rapids. Islands sport bald cypress and royal ferns. A large Florida cooter suns on the exposed trunk of a drowned cabbage palm. Meandering under bay magnolias, pignut hickory, and swamp tupelo, the trail passes under an arching live oak thick with wild pine and resurrection fern. At 0.5 mile, cross a high boardwalk over one of the Hillsborough River's many floodplain cypress swamps. This one is tucked into a bend in the river. Stop at the next observation platform to take a look at the now-quiet surface of the river. Pass a side trail that loops back towards the parking area where you started. Fol-

low the most distinct path past benches that look like they date back to the park's opening in 1936.

After 0.8 mile, turn right and cross the lofty suspension bridge. It bounces underfoot as you walk. The original was built by the Civilian Conservation Corps. Since the other footbridge over the river did not withstand the floodwaters of Hurricane Irma in 2017, you'll cross this suspension bridge twice. You come to a marker and kiosk for the Baynard Trail, named for Oscar E. Baynard, the first superintendent of the park. Turn right, passing a cypress floodplain. Curving right, the trail follows the river upstream. A black racer slithers across the path into a saw palmetto thicket.

At 1 mile, the trail turns away from the river, into a tall canopy of cabbage palms and hickory trees, past small clusters of wild citrus trees. There are many side trails created by bicycles. Stay with the distinct path. A few cypress knees poke out of the footpath. Reaching the

VIEW OF THE SUSPENSION BRIDGE FROM THE BAYNARD TRAIL

property line of the park, the trail turns and rises slightly, paralleling a fence on your right. Once the trail takes a sharp left, it becomes grassy underfoot. With a sparse canopy of hickory and sweetgum overhead, it's a tunnel making its way due south. Passing a junction that enables you to loop back on the Bayard Trail after 1.6 miles, you're at a bailout point. To cut your overall hike down to 2.6 miles, turn left and return to the suspension bridge, retracing your steps to the parking area. If you're committed to the longer hike, continue straight ahead through the hardwood forest, crossing a boardwalk, to reach the third named trail of this hike, the Seminole Woods Trail.

A large kiosk shows off a map of the trail. Normally, the trail ahead would lead to a footbridge over the Hillsborough River, but it was in the process of being replaced when we visited. Turn right at the kiosk. Originally called the Florida Trail and established by Florida Trail Association volunteers, the trail has been renamed to avoid confusion with the National Scenic Trail. The orange blazes have been repainted yellow. Numbered posts around the loop have the phone number for the ranger station, in case of emergencies. At the beginning of the loop, turn right. Passing a low swampy area, the trail slips through a sweetgum and hickory forest before edging around the base of a massive pond cypress. Hickory and cypress form the sparse canopy for a while and then are replaced by ancient live oaks.

After crossing a small bridge, the trail wanders beneath tall cabbage palms, their trunks aglow with green and yellow sphagnum moss. A slight elevation drop changes the forest. Sweetgum and elm take over as the ground underfoot becomes damp, dark soil busy

with pennywort. (One thing about this hike: there are seasons when it can get very wet underfoot. If it's uncomfortably so, turn back.) After the next bridge, at 2.5 miles, the trail turns sharply left to follow the creek through a palm hammock. Dark but clear, this tannic creek moves placidly toward the Hillsborough River. Roots and muck can make walking rough as you approach the sign for the primitive campsite. To visit it, follow the blue-blazed trail as it rises from the floodplain forest towards higher ground. A pond serves as a water source; logs may provide a place to sit. The campsite is 2.8 miles from Parking Area #2.

Continuing along the loop, the elevation rises, with white sand underfoot through a mixed oak and palm hammock. Blanketed in ferns, one solitary live oak rises more than 100 feet high. As the trail drops into the dark soil of the palm hammock, notice bright orange polypores on rotting logs. Crossing another bridge, the trail continues under cabbage palms arching overhead. Sunlight glints off the glossy leaves of a southern magnolia. Watch for armadillo holes hidden around fallen logs. As the trail turns back toward the river, you'll discover one of the largest live oaks you've ever seen, a tree easily several centuries old. Its base is a mass of moss-covered knobs; the center has a hollow more than 20 feet tall. Climb the knobs and peer inside. Veering around another grand live oak, the trail emerges on a sand bluff above the river at 4 miles.

The remainder of the loop follows the Hillsborough River upstream. The constant proximity to the river makes this a delightful hike as the trail winds through forests of live oak and cabbage palm, hickory and sweetgum, water oak and holly. The limbs of many old live oaks arch down to the water. The trail

LOOKING DOWNSTREAM ALONG THE HILLSBOROUGH RIVER ON THE SEMINOLE WOODS TRAIL

dips in and out of small hollows created as tributaries drain into the river, winding through a grove of sugarberry trees with shiny dark leaves.

Veering away from the river to skirt a cypress swamp, the trail heads through a corridor of saw palmetto to a bridge over a tributary, at 4.5 miles. The footpath turns to bright white sand around the river bend. Dry floodplain channels parallel the river; the trail walks a narrow path between the two. Crossing another small bridge, clamber up tree roots to the sand bluff. The canopy opens overhead as the forest turns to young hickory and water oak. At the end of the next bridge, sword ferns edge the trail. Dropping down a hill, the trail crosses a bridge into another sugarberry grove. Watch for small details, like tiny, seafoam-colored, star-shaped lichens growing on the trunks of cabbage palms. When you hear children playing, you see the picnic area on the other side of the river.

At the end of the loop after 5.5 miles, continue straight ahead to the T intersection in front of the Seminole Woods Trail kiosk. If the bridge to the right is not open, you'll take the Bayard Trail back. Turn left and backtrack across the boardwalk to the trail junction. Turn right and follow this short connector trail as it climbs over and around swales in the river-shaped landscape, passing a set of benches before it pops out next to the boardwalk that leads to the suspension bridge. Cross the suspension bridge. You've hiked 5.8 miles.

You have two options for the return to Parking Area #2. You can turn right and walk through the picnic area, following the river bluff to the paved path to the restrooms. From there, use the path along the edge of the woods—which passes CCC-built stone picnic benches—

and follow it into the forest to meet the loop section of the River Rapids Trail. Turn right and walk through the shady forest; the footpath can be muddy at times. The trail pops out at a T intersection and bench with the River Rapids Nature Trail. Turn right to exit.

Alternatively, turn left after you leave the suspension bridge and return the way you started your hike, along the river. This lets you enjoy the burble of the rapids as you make your way back to your car. Unless you're looking for variety (or restrooms), the riverside walk is the superior scenic hike. Both routes are the same distance. You reach Parking Area #2 after 6.7 miles.

OTHER HIKING OPTIONS

1. **River Rapids Loop**. The River Rapids Nature Trail is certainly the most compelling hike in the park because of its beauty. Starting at Parking Area #2, follow the hike as above, but turn left when you reach the side trail downstream from the rapids. It loops back through the deep shade of the bluff forest for an easy 1-mile hike.

2. **Wetlands Trail** (28.1433, -82.2298). Accessed from an entirely different trailhead than the rest of the trail system, this 1.6-mile linear trail connects to the Fort King Trail. It's mainly on forest roads in the sun, but shows off how the surrounding habitats were reclaimed from a dairy. It meets the Fort King Trail at 0.7 mile, so it's used as a gateway for cyclists to access that route. The Wetlands Trail turns due west at that point and continues on to the park boundary at a LEAVING HILLSBOROUGH RIVER STATE PARK sign. A walk to the park boundary and back is 3.2 miles.

3. **Fort King Trail**. You saw this 6.7-mile paved trail adjoining US 301. Its northern terminus is at the Wetlands Trail, above. It follows the Old Military Trail between Fort Brooke and Fort King, the same one at Fort Cooper State Park (Hike 11). Here, it's a popular bike path that stretches through the Hillsborough River Wilderness Area.

4. **Fort Foster Tour**. Beginning at the Interpretive Center at Parking Area #1, this tour takes you to Fort Foster State Park on the east side of US 301. This adjacent state park is home to a replica fort used for reenactments and rendezvous, and to tell the story of the Second Seminole War. Once you disembark the tram, there is a good mile to roam in and around the fort and up to the river crossing that the soldiers were defending. The tour is an additional $2 ($1 child) above state park admission and is only held four times a month: the first and third Saturday at 2 PM, and the first and third Sunday at 11 AM.

CAMPING AND LODGING

Hillsborough River State Park (1-800-326-3521, floridastateparks.reserveamerica.com)

Hampton Inn & Suites Tampa East, 11740 Tampa Gateway Boulevard, Seffner, FL 33584 (813-630-4321, hilton.com)

35

Lettuce Lake Park

TOTAL DISTANCE: 1.8-mile loop selected from a network of interconnected trails.

HIKING TIME: 1 hour

DIFFICULTY: Easy

USAGE: $2 per vehicle. Open 8 AM–7 PM, spring and summer; 8 AM–6 PM, fall and winter. Leashed pets and bicycles permitted, but not on boardwalks.

TRAILHEAD GPS COORDINATES: 28.0743, -82.3747

CONTACT INFORMATION: Lettuce Lake Park, 6920 E Fletcher Avenue, Tampa, FL 33637 (813-987-6204, hillsboroughcounty. org/locations/lettuce-lake-park)

Black as midnight, sluggish as molasses, the Hillsborough River laps at the bases of bald cypresses, trapped between the trees in ponds clogged with water lettuce. A series of boardwalks span this backwater, where in times of high water the river cuts itself off at a bend, forming a vast treed swamp: Lettuce Lake. Along the boardwalks through the swamp, canopied and open benches enable you to sit and watch the wildlife. Limpkins plumb the shallows for apple snails, while turtles sun themselves on fallen logs. Canoeists ply the tangle of passageways through the swamp forest.

Located at the north end of Tampa, Lettuce Lake Park protects 240 acres along the Hillsborough River, providing urban residents a quiet place to hike, bike, and picnic. Check at the entrance station about canoe rentals. An open grassy space in the center of the park is ideal for Frisbee or volleyball and has a playground for the kids. Stop in at the Audubon Resource Center, accessed by the paved trail on the opposite side of the parking lot from where you start your hike. Browse through their resource library, examine the natural history exhibits, and take a look in the nature store. Ask about guided hikes and birding workshops, offered regularly for a small fee.

GETTING THERE

From I-75, take exit 266, Temple Terrace, and follow Fletcher Avenue 0.8 mile west to the park's entrance on the right, Lettuce Lake Park Road. Follow the entry road to a T intersection, make a right, then make the first left into the parking area. Your hike starts with the wheelchair-accessible boardwalk between the picnic tables.

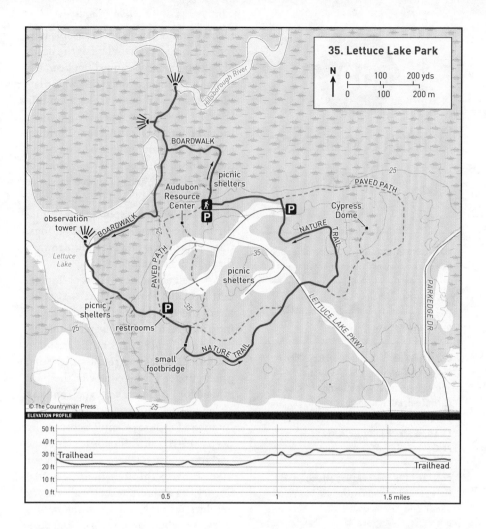

35. Lettuce Lake Park

N
| 0 | 100 | 200 yds |
| 0 | 100 | 200 m |

BOARDWALK

picnic shelters

Audubon Resource Center

PAVED PATH

25

Cypress Dome

observation tower

BOARDWALK

NATURE TRAIL

Lettuce Lake

PAVED PATH

25

35

picnic shelters

PARKEDGE DR

LETTUCE LAKE PKWY

picnic shelters

restrooms

35

NATURE TRAIL

small footbridge

25

© The Countryman Press

25

ELEVATION PROFILE

50 ft
40 ft
30 ft Trailhead
20 ft
10 ft
0 ft
          0.5   1   1.5 miles
                                    Trailhead

THE HIKE

Follow the boardwalk past the covered picnic pavilions and into the blackwater cypress swamp. Scattered red maples show off crimson and gold leaves in the fall. The tall purple blooms of water hyacinths catch your attention. A white heron intently watches the water for the telltale shimmer of fish. At the T intersection, turn right. The boardwalk slips past massive bald cypresses, where duckweed forms a thick blanket over the swamp. You pass a side trail, a boardwalk leading to a canopied bench with a clear view of the open waters of Lettuce Lake. Pause to take in the scene, watching a great blue heron soar overhead. A cottonmouth moccasin swims past, iridescent black scales rippling against the dark water.

Back on the main trail, notice how cinnamon and marsh ferns take advantage of rotting logs to gain a foothold in the slower waters of the swamp. The boardwalk ends at a platform overlooking the narrows of the Hillsborough River, a fast-flowing channel through the cypresses. As a paddler slips by, a flock of white ibises pick between the

LETTUCE LAKE FROM THE OBSERVATION TOWER

cypress knees, searching for insects. Turn around and return to the boardwalk intersection, heading straight. The boardwalk swings out along Lettuce Lake, providing a breezy walk along the open water, then ducks back under the cypresses. Look closely for swamp lilies in the shallows, with their broad grassy leaves and showy star-shaped white blooms.

When you reach a junction where the boardwalk ends, turn right to follow the next boardwalk to return to the river: the left turn leads to the Audubon Resource Center. After 0.8 mile, you reach the observation tower. Climb five stories for a scenic view of the floodplain forest and the Hillsborough River, looking down the length of Lettuce Lake. The boardwalk continues past the junction of Lettuce Lake and the river, sweeping away from the water and into the dense stand of bald cypress. Where the boardwalk ends, two short boardwalks turn right, both leading to picnic pavilions along the river. Follow the sand path through a live oak hammock and up to its junction with the paved, 1.5-mile perimeter loop trail, in front of the restrooms and

water fountain. You've walked a mile. Turn right on the paved trail and follow it into the oak hammock, past an American beautyberry flaunting its brilliant clusters of purple berries.

Turn right at the NATURE TRAIL sign at the split-rail fence, entering the pine flatwoods. Since the nature trail wanders along the edge of the park, traffic sounds carry into the woods. Slash pines tower overhead, dropping a deep carpet of pine needles onto the footpath. Stay to the main trail as you pass a side trail, walking into a shady oak hammock with a dense understory of saw palmetto. Palm warblers scurry between breaks in the saw palmetto, wagging their tails and displaying their yellow breast feathers.

The trail emerges into scrubby flatwoods, open and sunny. Winged sumacs display deep red leaves in the fall. At 1.3 miles, you rejoin the paved trail for a stretch. Turn right, crossing the park entrance road. Soon after, leave the paved path and follow the nature trail as it ducks left into a dense forest of pines and saw palmetto. It drops into a low area with a cypress dome. The trail

FOLLOWING THE BOARDWALK THROUGH THE LETTUCE LAKE SWAMPS

climbs under spreading live oaks and slash pines. Passing a trail to the left, continue straight, making a right at the next fork. You emerge into a parking lot. Cross the parking lot and road to rejoin the paved trail. Make a left, walking along the edge of the cypress swamp to return to where your car is parked near the boardwalk, for a total hike of 1.8 miles.

OTHER HIKING OPTIONS

1. **Short Boardwalk Loop**. Follow the route as outlined above, but when you get to where the boardwalk ends by the Audubon Resource Center, turn left and walk around the center, following the paved path back around to your car for a 0.75-mile walk.
2. **Long Boardwalk Loop**. After the boardwalk ends near Pavilion 5, take a left on the paved path to walk back paralleling the boardwalk in the woods.

You'll pass the Audubon Resource Center, making a 1.1-mile loop.

3. **Paved Loop to Cypress Dome**. Instead of returning to the nature trail once you pass the park entrance, stay on the paved perimeter loop. It extends your overall hike to 2.1 miles, and provides access to a boardwalk into the cypress dome that's seen from the nature trail.

CAMPING AND LODGING

Hillsborough River State Park, 15402 US 301 N, Thonotosassa, FL 33592 (1-800-326-3521, floridastateparks .reserveamerica.com)

Hampton Inn & Suites Tampa North, 8210 Hidden River Parkway, Tampa, FL 33637 (813-903-6000, hilton.com)

Holiday Inn Express Tampa North, 13294 Telecom Drive, Temple Terrace, FL 33637 (813-972-9800, ihg .com)

36

Brooker Creek Preserve

TOTAL DISTANCE: 2-mile loop selected from a network of interconnected trails.

HIKING TIME: 1–1.5 hours

DIFFICULTY: Easy to moderate

USAGE: Free. Hours vary by season but usually run 7 AM to an hour before sunset. No pets or bicycles permitted. Environmental Education Center open Thursday-Saturday, 9 AM–4 PM, Sunday 11 AM–4 PM.

TRAILHEAD GPS COORDINATES: 28.1319, -82.6566

CONTACT INFORMATION: Brooker Creek Preserve, 3940 Keystone Road, Tarpon Springs, FL 34688 (727-453-6800, brookercreekpreserve.org)

Protecting a mosaic of wet pine flatwoods, uplands, and floodplain forests from which Brooker Creek—an important feeder stream to Lake Tarpon—rises, Brooker Creek Preserve covers nearly 8,700 acres in the northeastern corner of Pinellas County. Once characterized by cattle ranches, vegetable farms, and orange groves, the surrounding area continues a march towards being wall-to-wall subdivisions. This is the county's largest preserve and most of it is quite wet. This is largely where the region's water comes from, via surrounding wellfields that feed public utilities in three counties, so the preserve is jointly managed with Southwest Florida Water Management District. While the preserve is made up of several separate tracts, it's the one that's home to the Environmental Education Center that provides miles of hiking trails to roam.

GETTING THERE

From US 19 in Tarpon Springs, exit onto East Tarpon Ave, just north of A. L. Anderson Park. The road becomes Keystone Road as it goes around the north end of Lake Tarpon. Drive 6 miles east along Keystone Road (CR 582). You'll pass a GREAT FLORIDA BIRDING TRAIL sign at Lora Lane, which points to a separate part of the preserve. Pass that and continue another 0.5 mile to the preserve gates on the right. From the Suncoast Parkway (FL 589), exit onto West Lutz Lake Fern Road. Drive west 2.6 miles to CR 587. Turn left. Continue 0.5 mile and turn right onto Tarpon Springs Road. Drive 5.2 miles. The road becomes Keystone Road at the county line. Turn left at the preserve entrance. From either direction, you'll follow the entrance road for the preserve south for a mile before it ends at the parking area.

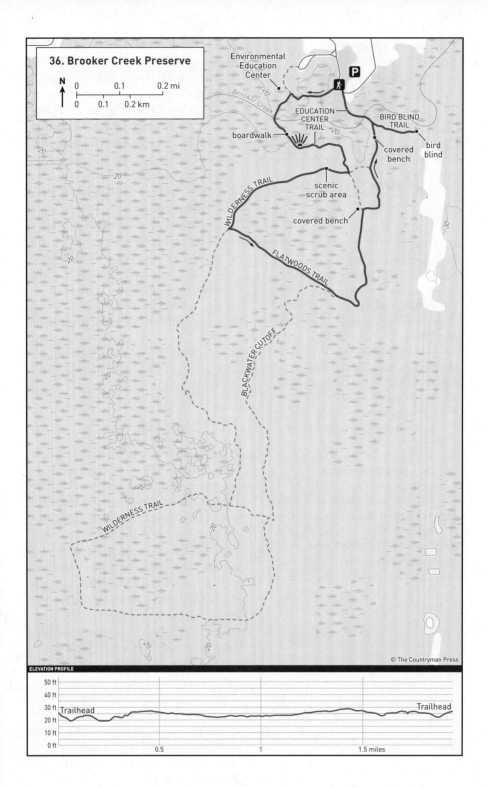

36. Brooker Creek Preserve

N

0   0.1   0.2 mi
0   0.1   0.2 km

Environmental
Education
Center

P

Brooker Creek

EDUCATION
CENTER
TRAIL

boardwalk

BIRD BLIND
TRAIL

covered
bench

bird
blind

WILDERNESS TRAIL

scenic
scrub area

covered bench

FLATWOODS TRAIL

BLACKWATER CUTOFF

WILDERNESS TRAIL

© The Countryman Press

ELEVATION PROFILE

50 ft
40 ft
30 ft   Trailhead   Trailhead
20 ft
10 ft
0 ft   0.5   1   1.5 miles

THE HIKE

Walk up to the shelter that shades the Environmental Education Center entrance. You'll find trail maps and a notice as to the day's closing time for the preserve. This is the beginning of the Education Center Trail, which starts as a boardwalk through a swamp. Cinnamon ferns cluster along the water's edge and red maples show off crimson leaves in winter. Interpretive markers are cleverly hidden under hinged boards, the better to protect them from fading in the sun. In one of the more unusual twists to interpretation, large tags hang off some of the trees, marked as the TRAVELING TREE WALK. Each puts a price tag on a particular species of tree. While we hate to think about having to prove the economic value of forests, we know there are people for whom this is a good teaching tool.

As the boardwalk rises into the uplands, artful sculptures mimick-

INTERPRETIVE STATION ON THE EDUCATION CENTER TRAIL

ing vines arch overhead. You reach a junction at a bench where buildings are tucked into the forest, and signage points in various directions. The Environmental Education Center is straight ahead. If it's open, explore the exhibits about this wild place and its inhabitants, try the hands-on displays, and visit the gift shop. The trail you are following turns at the bench, passing another turnoff to the restrooms and screened picnic area, before it reaches a sign that lists the trails currently open and reminds you of closing time. Trails may close due to prescribed burns or abnormally wet conditions.

The broad boardwalk gently winds through the shade. When it reaches the floodplain forest surrounding Brooker Creek, it adds railings. Along the way, a series of interpretive signs call your attention to the change in habitat. Some look like open books and provide many details about your surroundings, including sketches that identify wildlife and flora you may see. Cypress trees dominate one section of the swamp, and ferns keep the dry spots on the forest floor well-hidden.

After 0.25 mile, the boardwalk ends. The Education Center Trail continues as a footpath, passing a bench as it curves into the woods. As it gains a little elevation, the trail becomes sandy underfoot, passing a white-tipped marker amid a dense understory of young oaks. Myrtle oaks and rusty lyonia appear, signaling a transition to scrub habitat as the trail reaches a four-way junction at 0.5 mile. Turn right to join the Wilderness Trail, blazed with orange-tipped posts and markers. The footpath remains bright white sand as it sweeps around dense stands of saw palmetto punctuated by the fluffy longleaf pines that Pinellas County is known for. When you start

FLATWOODS TRAIL

seeing loblolly bay trees along the sides of the trail, it's a hint that the habitat is going to change for the wetter. Mosses form a carpet across the footpath as you drop into a wet pine flatwoods. The trail is the low spot through this often-damp habitat, so you may see puddles form in places. Some are large, but as evidenced by the well-worn path, can be walked around.

After 0.8 mile, you come to the junction with the Flatwoods Trail, and another reminder of when the park closes. Here's why: if you choose to follow the perimeter loop straight ahead past the WILDERNESS TRAIL SOUTH sign, the hike will take a lot longer than you expect. Wilderness Trail South is not for the timid, as it's a swamp walk most of the year, more wading than walking. We're not sending you that way because we've tried it twice ourselves, and both times had to turn back because of slow going while wading in deep water. Make a left on the

Flatwoods Trail to stay with the loop that most visitors to Brooker Creek Preserve follow.

True to its name, the Flatwoods Trail immerses you in a healthy pine flatwoods, the broad footpath essentially a forest road covered in pine needles from the slash pines, making for easy walking. Blaze posts are tipped green along this route. Some pines are young and skinny, others more mature and stately. Loblolly bay and dahoon holly both appear in this forest, signaling that it can also get soggy underfoot at certain times of year. The trail slowly gains elevation as it approaches the junction with Blackwater Cutoff at 1.1 miles. This is the east side of the Wilderness Trail Loop. Continue past it, following the signs pointing past Signpost 7. As elevation increases, you see clumps of *sphagnum strictum*, a moss that looks like it would enjoy water but which actually prefers drier habitats. Oaks dominate the lower canopy under the pines.

GOPHER TORTOISE ALONG THE FOOTPATH

At a T intersection, a green arrow points left. Walk beneath the towering pines. In fall, you may notice a cluster of the purple, paintbrush-shaped blooms of deer's tongue (*Carphephorus odoratissimus*), also known as wild vanilla. It's a favorite for butterflies to hover around.

As the forest canopy opens to reveal more tall pines, the trail stretches ahead like a hallway between the saw palmetto. At 1.5 miles, you reach a trail junction with a sculpture that looks like a bolt of lightning. It holds an interpretive marker within sight of the Flatwoods

Shelter, a platform for ducking out of the rain. The trail straight ahead returns to the boardwalk near the Education Center. Turn right instead for a ramble through an oak hammock. Live oaks provide a high canopy over a broad open area in the forest, where the Live Oak Shelter sits. An interpretive sign speaks to changes in biodiversity due to human impacts on the land.

Continue straight ahead at the next signposted trail junction, following the PARKING LOT sign. This corridor through the oaks passes an interpretive panel on gopher tortoises, and sure enough, just up the trail, we saw a very large one ambling along, nibbling at grasses near a bench where the TRAVELING TREE WALK tags begin again. You reach a T intersection with the Bird Path. Turn right and walk down this short trail through the edge of the oak hammock. It ends up at a little blind under a power line, with windows looking out over a marsh. Return along the same path, passing the trail junction to reach a bridge over Brooker Creek. We were startled to see a large alligator nestled into the bases of the saw palmetto on the far shore. Beyond the bridge, you reach the back side of signage that greets hikers when they walk this loop clockwise. Continue up to the parking area to wrap up your 2-mile hike.

OTHER HIKING OPTIONS

1. **Accessible Adventure.** For the wheelchair-bound and slow walkers, the boardwalk section of the Education Center Trail is a superb immersion into the spirit of this preserve. It's a 0.5-mile round-trip to the end of the boardwalk and back.

2. **Education Center Trail.** At 0.7 mile, this is the shortest of the loops, focused on the boardwalk and interpretive trails closest to the parking area. Shorten it to 0.5 mile by taking the first left at the junction with the Wilderness Trail.

3. **Wilderness Wander.** The deeper you go into the preserve, the more likely you are to find yourself wading down its trails. Water means very slow going, even if you like to wade. If you can make it to the connector across to Blackwater Cutoff, that extends our route to a 3.5-mile hike. Going all the way around the Wilderness Trail loop makes for a 4.5-mile hike.

4. **The Friends Trail** (28.1294, -82.6706). The first trail built by supporters of Brooker Creek Preserve, The Friends Trail has a separate entrance off Lora Lane, which is pointed out by the GREAT FLORIDA BIRDING TRAIL sign as you head westbound on Keystone Road from the preserve's main entrance. The 1.1-mile loop through the pine flatwoods is more upland than wetland, but there are some soggy spots. For birders, a shorter spur trail leads to a boardwalk overlooking a wet prairie.

CAMPING AND LODGING

Clearwater Lake Tarpon KOA, 37061 US 19 N, Palm Harbor, FL 34684 (727-937-8412, koa.com)

Innisbrook Resort, 36750 US 19 N, Palm Harbor, FL 34684 (1-888-794-8627, innisbrookgolfresort.com)

Vista Hotel on Lake Tarpon, 37611 US 19 N, Palm Harbor, FL 34684 (727-942-0358, vistainnlaketarpon.com)

John Chesnut Sr. Park

TOTAL DISTANCE: 3.3 miles in two distinct loops of 1.8 and 1.5 miles each.

HIKING TIME: 1.5 hours

DIFFICULTY: Easy

USAGE: Free. Open 7 AM to sunset. Leashed pets and bicycles welcome, but neither are allowed on the boardwalks.

TRAILHEAD GPS COORDINATES: 28.0848, -82.7023

CONTACT INFORMATION: John Chesnut Sr. Park, 2200 E Lake Road S, Palm Harbor, FL 34685 (727-582-2100, pinellascounty.org)

When you're walking in the breeze beneath a canopy of towering bald cypresses along the shore of a 2,500-acre lake, it's hard to believe this is an urban hike. Protecting the longest natural shoreline of Lake Tarpon, the largest lake in Pinellas County, John Chesnut Sr. Park has a little something for everyone. There are softball fields and horseshoe pits, and lots of picnic pavilions and playgrounds. You'll even find a dog park near one of the loops. But this 255-acre park is also home to a network of boardwalks and trails that showcase the natural habitats along the lakeshore, with many paths connecting wheelchair-accessible boardwalks.

GETTING THERE

From the junction of FL 60 (Gulf to Bay) and McMullen Booth Road (CR 611) in Clearwater, drive north on McMullen Booth Road. Four miles north of Safety Harbor, it crosses CR 752 (Tampa Road) in Oldsmar on an overpass. Continue north on CR 611, which now changes its name to East Lake Road. Continue another 2 miles. The park entrance is on the left just after you cross Brooker Creek. Once you're inside the park, follow the road to the South Parking Loop to find the trailhead for the Peggy Park Nature Trail.

THE HIKE

SOUTH LOOP/PEGGY PARK NATURE TRAIL

Named after a wildlife officer killed in the line of duty, the Peggy Park Nature Trail introduces you to the floodplain forest along Lake Tarpon and the banks of Brooker Creek. Starting off in a lush pine flatwoods, the trail winds through stands of stately slash pine and cinnamon ferns. It then rises onto

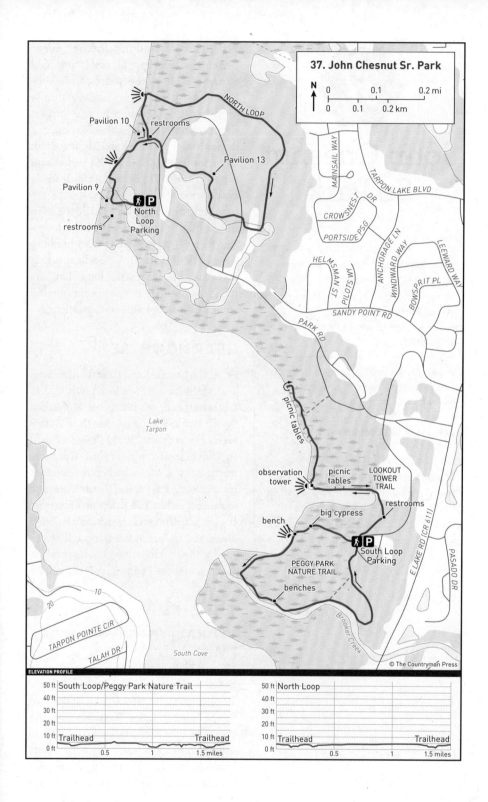

37. John Chesnut Sr. Park

N

0   0.1   0.2 mi

0   0.1   0.2 km

NORTH LOOP

Pavilion 10

restrooms

Pavilion 13

Pavilion 9

North Loop Parking

restrooms

MAINSAIL WAY

TARPON LAKE BLVD

CROW'S NEST DR

PORTSIDE PSG

ANCHORAGE LN

WINDWARD WAY

LEEWARD WAY

HELMSMAN ST

PILOTS WY

BOWSPRIT PL

SANDY POINT RD

PARK RD

Lake Tarpon

picnic tables

observation tower

picnic tables

LOOKOUT TOWER TRAIL

restrooms

big cypress

bench

South Loop Parking

PEGGY PARK NATURE TRAIL

benches

E LAKE RD (CR 611)

PASADO DR

Brooker Creek

20

10

TARPON POINTE CIR

TALAH DR

South Cove

© The Countryman Press

ELEVATION PROFILE

South Loop/Peggy Park Nature Trail

50 ft
40 ft
30 ft
20 ft
10 ft Trailhead   Trailhead
0 ft   0.5   1   1.5 miles

North Loop

50 ft
40 ft
30 ft
20 ft
10 ft Trailhead   Trailhead
0 ft   0.5   1   1.5 miles

a boardwalk through the floodplain forest of cypresses. One stately cypress towers well above the rest. Tannic water—stained the color of tea by the leaves of oaks, red maples, loblolly bays and sweetgums—flows sluggishly below the boardwalk, feeding clusters of giant leather fern. You feel as if you are walking through a prehistoric forest. Elephant ears and royal ferns cluster between the bases of the cypresses.

The boardwalk swings left along the edge of Lake Tarpon, providing your first glimpse of the dark, undulating surface of the lake. Reeds protect the curving shoreline. Soft splashes fill the air as the lake gently laps against the cypress trees. Watch out for mooching gray squirrels along this section of the boardwalk: they will follow you along the railing, begging for a handout. Veering away from the lake, the boardwalk curves through the darkness of the floodplain forest. Both pond cypresses and bald cypresses grow in this part of the swamp. Notice the difference between their needles. Those of the pond cypress sweep upward from the stem, creating a wispy effect. Bald cypress needles spread flat like a hawk's feather. The boardwalk meets Brooker Creek near its discharge into Lake Tarpon. When the boardwalk ends, a trail continues along the placid creek, with many benches along its shore. Crushed white shells create a crunchy footpath under the cabbage palms, slash pines, and live oaks. Look for giant air plants overhead.

After 0.5 mile, you meet a trail junction with a SHORT WAY PARKING AREA sign pointing left. Turn right to follow Brooker Creek through the cypresses, slash pines, and gnarled oaks. As the road noise increases, the trail turns away from the creek, then left again to

loop back toward the trailhead, entering a forest with a tall canopy of laurel oaks and slash pines. Joining up with the shortcut trail, turn right along the shell path, passing several picnic tables as you stroll through the narrow band of oak hammock. At 0.8 mile, you reach the trailhead. Return your interpretive guide to the box.

Continue your hike by walking to the Lookout Tower Trail. Walk away from the Peggy Park trailhead north until you come to a break in the woods, an unmarked trail. Follow this path through the oak hammock past Pavilion 1, curving towards the boat ramp. Walk across the top of the boat ramp to reach the other side and turn left. At 1 mile, the boardwalk starts. Go straight at the trail junction, following the edge of the channel. Benches sit along the channel, and several short boardwalks lead into the cypresses to picnic tables.

Where the channel meets the lake, look down. Although the water of Lake Tarpon looks jet black from a distance, it's clear when you see it in the shallows, cast with a yellow hue. The boardwalk turns to follow the lake, meeting the 40-foot-tall observation tower and its five levels of decks. Take in the view and the stiff, refreshing breeze. Following the lakeshore, the boardwalk sticks to the edge of the floodplain forest. Crimson leaves from red maples flutter into the water. Short boardwalks lead to lakeside picnic tables, a great place to sit and watch for wildlife. The third turnoff is the best, as it overlooks a small cove protected from the main portion of the lake by cattails and reeds.

At the trail junction, continue straight. The boardwalk leads to more platforms along the lake before it hits a dead-end after 1.2 miles. Return the way you came. You pass the boardwalk to the

BOARDWALK ALONG THE NORTH LOOP

left; it leads to the north parking lot and dog park. Enjoy the dappled textures of the shadows from the cypress overhead as you walk back past the tower and turn to follow the boat ramp channel to shore. Retrace your route past Pavilion 1 to return to the south parking lot, completing your 1.8-mile hike.

NORTH LOOP

The northern boardwalk in John Chesnut Sr. Park has no specific name, but it starts within sight of Lake Tarpon at a spot that was once the park's beach. From the marina, follow the park road north 0.7 mile past the dog park and playground. After you cross the bridge, keep left at the fork. Look for the large parking area (28.0950, -82.7098) with the boardwalk to Pavilions 7, 8, and 9. Park near the boardwalk and use it to cross over to the lakefront, which is well-shaded by the forest. To the left is a set of restrooms that is open daily. Turn right

and follow the path up to the lakeshore, where it meets a lakefront boardwalk. This short stretch of boardwalk looks out across the cypress-lined shore of the lake.

At the end of the boardwalk, a sidewalk resumes. Walk past a cypress tree surrounded by its knobby knees, and you see Pavilion 10, probably the nicest of the pavilions in the park thanks to its location along this cove. A crushed-shell path takes off into the woods behind restrooms that are closed on weekdays. Turn left to follow the path. It quickly reaches a low boardwalk in the floodplain, which zigzags to the cove. The pathway turns to dirt briefly as it rounds the bend.

You reach an observation platform after 0.4 mile. Take a moment to savor the view of the cypress-lined lakeshore. Returning to the boardwalk, turn left and follow it as it turns sharply. The cypress swamp here was likely logged out more than 50 years ago, since the cypresses and their knees are small in comparison to the ones seen near Brooker Creek. Highly prized because of their resistance to rot, old-growth cypresses were felled and dragged out of forests along lakes and in swamps throughout Florida to be transported to the nearest sawmill. Carved into boards, the giant cypresses became packing crates for the shipment of citrus fruit, supporting this region's primary industry through the 1970s.

Well-shaded by the forest canopy, the boardwalk is long and narrow. Cabbage palms and cinnamon ferns grow throughout the understory. The boardwalk ends, becoming a crushed-shell path. A park road sits to the right. The trail continues along the ecotone between cypress swamp and pine flat-woods. At 0.2 mile, the next segment of boardwalk begins. It wiggles through a mix of pines and cypresses fighting for control of the forest. A bench overlooks a willow marsh with deeper water, where you might see a young alligator drifting across the open water.

When the boardwalk ends, the trail is a crunchy crushed-shell path as you pass a STAY ON TRAIL sign within sight of a neighborhood behind the trees. Another trail comes in from the left. On the right is a marsh. The next board-walk begins soon after, leading through palms to a bayhead, where frogs kick up a fuss. Older cypress knees rise from the shallows, including one that looks very much like a planter covered in colorful bromeliads.

After 0.9 mile, the boardwalk ends

SHORELINE OF LAKE TARPON ALONG THE BOARDWALK

within sight of a linear man-made waterway. Cross the path and take the footbridge over the small canal. This is one of the many islands providing picnic spots in this part of the park. Turn right to walk along the canal. Turn right again and cross the canal on the wooden park road bridge. Turn left near the PAVILION 13 sign and start following the waterway along the pine duff on the edge of the shoreline, beneath a stand of extremely tall longleaf pines. Note the BEWARE OF ALLIGATORS sign! Continue around this man-made pond, following the shoreline, until an obvious path veers to the right past a picnic spot and you cross the park road towards Pavilion 10. Backtrack along the lakefront boardwalk to Pavilion 9, and the sidewalk and boardwalk back to the parking area. You've completed a 1.5-mile hike.

OTHER HIKING OPTIONS

1. **Peggy Park Nature Trail**. On a quick visit to the park, pick the easiest trailhead for an out-and-back hike to where the Peggy Park Nature Trail ends, about a 0.5-mile round-trip.
2. **A. L. Anderson Park** (28.132223, -82.737629). On the opposite shore of Lake Tarpon, this county park off US 19 also features boardwalks and footpaths that ramble about 0.5 mile along the lake.
3. **Wall Springs Park** (28.106719, -82.771789). Along the marshy shoreline of the Gulf of Mexico in Palm Harbor, Wall Springs Park features more than a mile of paved paths to scenic views, including its namesake spring.

CAMPING AND LODGING

Clearwater Lake Tarpon KOA, 37061 US 19 N, Palm Harbor, FL 34684 (727-937-8412, koa.com)

Innisbrook Resort, 36750 US 19 N, Palm Harbor, FL 34684 (1-888-794-8627, innisbrookgolfresort.com)

Vista Hotel on Lake Tarpon, 37611 US 19 N, Palm Harbor, FL 34684 (727-942-0358, vistainnlaketarpon.com)

Honeymoon Island State Park

TOTAL DISTANCE: 2.5-mile loop, 3-mile route during eagle nesting season.

HIKING TIME: 1–1.5 hours

DIFFICULTY: Easy to difficult

USAGE: $4–8 per vehicle. Open 8 AM to sunset. Leashed dogs permitted but not allowed on any beaches except the designated dog beach.

TRAILHEAD GPS COORDINATES: 28.0681, -82.8304

CONTACT INFORMATION: Honeymoon Island State Park, #1 Causeway Boulevard, Dunedin, FL 34698 (727-469-5942, floridastateparks.org/park/Honeymoon-Island)

Protected by a sand spit called Pelican Point, Honeymoon Island, a barrier island north of Clearwater, guards 80 precious acres of virgin slash pine, a rare sight in Central Florida. Because of the age and the size of the pines, an osprey rookery—another rarity—is going strong in this forest. Also known as a fish hawk, the osprey is a large black-and-white raptor with a 6-foot wingspan. You'll see them hovering and diving into both fresh and salt water to seize fish.

Once known as Hog Island—until a 1940s contest in Life magazine offered a week in paradise here—Honeymoon Island was only accessible by boat until the 1960s. When the city of Dunedin donated its beaches to the state in 1982, the island became Honeymoon Island State Park. It's a bustling place for beachgoers, especially on weekends, so arrive early to enjoy the hike. Insect repellent is strongly recommended for this hike.

GETTING THERE

Drive north from downtown Dunedin along US 19A. Turn left onto Causeway Boulevard (FL 589), and follow it 2.8 miles to the park entrance. After paying your entrance fee, follow the park road to its very end, beyond North Beach. Turn right into the picnic area. Follow the NATURE TRAIL signs to park at the extreme northern end of the picnic area, just after you drive past the trailhead.

THE HIKE

Walk up from the parking area to the OSPREY TRAIL sign. After looking at the map, take the right fork. This is a broad, grassy trail, an easy walking route. Sea grapes cluster under the massive pines,

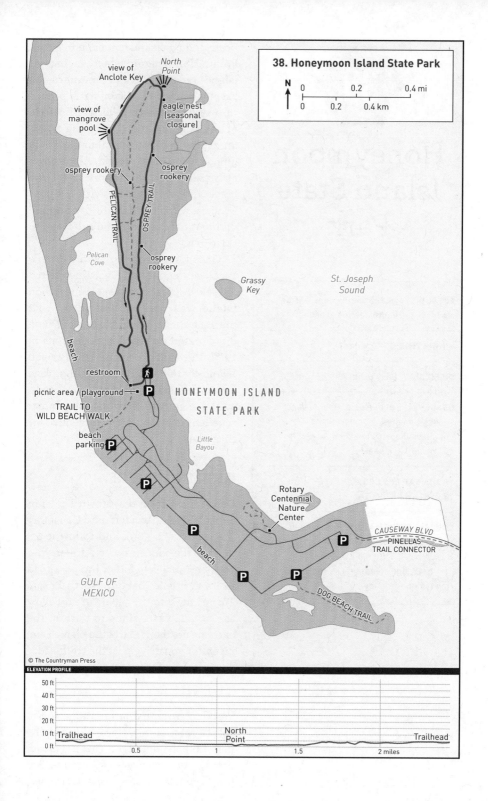

38. Honeymoon Island State Park

N

0   0.2   0.4 mi

0   0.2   0.4 km

view of
Anclote Key

North
Point

eagle nest
(seasonal
closure)

view of
mangrove
pool

osprey rookery

osprey
rookery

PELICAN TRAIL

OSPREY TRAIL

*Pelican
Cove*

osprey
rookery

*Grassy
Key*

*St. Joseph
Sound*

beach

restroom

picnic area / playground

TRAIL TO
WILD BEACH WALK

beach
parking

HONEYMOON ISLAND

STATE PARK

*Little
Bayou*

Rotary
Centennial
Nature
Center

CAUSEWAY BLVD

PINELLAS
TRAIL CONNECTOR

beach

*GULF OF
MEXICO*

DOG BEACH TRAIL

© The Countryman Press

ELEVATION PROFILE

50 ft
40 ft
30 ft
20 ft
10 ft — Trailhead
0 ft

North
Point

Trailhead

0.5   1   1.5   2 miles

OSPREY TRAIL

many of which have strange twists and turns to their trunks. Daisies and yarrow nudge up to the trail's edge. As you hike, take the time to look for osprey nests in the tall bare pine snags. Constructed of loose sticks, the nests look like inverted wigs, and can be up to 5 feet in diameter and several feet thick. Although ospreys will build nests in live pines, they prefer the dead trees because of the ease of landing without dropping a fish.

This is an interpretive trail, with lots of benches, signs, and kiosks along the way. Stay right past the next kiosk. A necklace pod tree catches your attention with its bright-yellow blossoms and seed cases that look like strings of beads. A salt-tolerant species, the blooms of the necklace pod tree provide the fuel for flocks of Florida's ruby-throated hummingbirds, who fill up on nectar before migrating for the winter across the Gulf of Mexico to the Yucatan peninsula.

At the 0.5 mile marker, keep right. A cluster of saw palmettos lifts their strong trunks skyward. If you want to see osprey tending their young, the best time to hike is between December and April. Ospreys mate for life, returning to the same nest every season. The eggs take five weeks to hatch. Although the female sits on the eggs, the male will take over to give her a break to go fishing. After the chicks hatch, the male cares for the family's needs for the next six weeks. Once the chicks are large enough to be left alone, both parents feed them until they are old enough to be taught to fly—and fish.

In addition to the many osprey nests, a pair of eagles returns here year after year. During the winter, when the eagles are nesting, a portion of the Osprey Trail is blocked off. If you find that to be the case, return to the last cross-trail and take it over to the Pelican Trail on the western shore of the peninsula. Or try the unmarked central trail—we found it too wet and mucky to follow to the tip of the peninsula, but it may dry out.

After a mile on the Osprey Trail, you

OSPREY WITH A FRESHLY CAUGHT FISH

reach a kiosk explaining the osprey's fishing behavior. They circle 50 feet or more above the water, scanning for prey, and hover in place as they watch. When an osprey sees its target, it drops from the sky like a rock, hitting the water feet-first. Specially adapted toes allow it to grasp a squirming fish and hold it firmly as it lifts off.

The junction with the Pelican Trail is just after the kiosk. To walk along breezy Pelican Cove, keep right. The narrow trail drops into the mangroves, crossing an old track before it emerges on a windswept beach. The island in the distance is Anclote Key, also a state park. Following the shoreline, the trail continues through the sea oats along the sparkling blue shallows of the cove. Looking left, you see more osprey nests in the trees. You would think the leaping mullet would be a great target for the osprey, but not so. According to John James Audubon's observations in *Birds of America*, the osprey "never attempts to secure its prey in the air," preferring to pluck fish out of the water.

All along the waterfront are benches set as memorials, providing places to perch and watch birds along the shoreline. It's here that the footing gets quite difficult, as it is soft sugar sand underfoot. Black and red mangroves take over the waterfront, forcing the trail several feet back away from the cove. The sand ends as you reach muck. Once you've hiked 1.6 miles, you reach a side trail that allows you to retreat to the Osprey Trail in the drier pine flatwoods, if you choose—a good way out if the trail ahead is flooded.

Continuing along the Pelican Trail, watch for sand fiddler crabs that scuttle out of harm's way as they sense your footfalls. They're responsible for thousands of tiny holes on and around the trail. Grasses and flowers adapted to salty environments thrive here, like the red-tipped glasswort, bristly bulrushes, and thick-leaved sea purslane.

At 1.9 miles, the footpath climbs away from the salt marsh, rejoining the western side of the Osprey Trail. Turn right, following the wide forest road as it becomes a sandy track through the pine flatwoods. At the next trail junction is a PICNIC AREA sign. Keep left. Your trail emerges at the rear of the picnic area, conveniently behind the restrooms. Cross the boardwalk back to the parking area, completing a 2.5-mile loop.

OTHER HIKING OPTIONS

1. **Wild Beach Walk**. Continue along the dirt road that the Pelican Trail followed up to the back side of the picnic area and restrooms. After 0.25 mile, it reaches the beach. Walk north to enjoy the wild shoreline. Or drive directly to the northernmost beach parking area (28.0647, -82.8327) and

OVERLOOK ON PELICAN COVE

4. **Pinellas Trail Connector** (28.0598, -82.8180). Starting outside the park gates, a 2.5-mile paved path parallels Causeway Boulevard, offering scenic views across Clearwater Harbor and St. Joseph Sound. Because shade is limited, it's better for cyclists than walkers. Park at the ferryboat dock to access the path.

5. **Caladesi Island** (28.0598, -82.8180). Featured in previous editions of this guidebook, Caladesi Island State Park lies immediately north of Honeymoon Island. To get there, you must take a ferryboat, 20 minutes each way (adults $14, children $7 for a round-trip ticket). There are miles of beach to roam and 3 miles of marked hiking trails in the interior of the island.

CAMPING AND LODGING

Caladesi RV Park, 205 Dempsey Road, Palm Harbor, FL 34683 (727-784-3622, caladesirvparkpalmharbor.com)

The Blue Moon Inn, 2920 Alt US 19, Dunedin, FL 34698 (727-784-2611, thebluemooninn.com)

The 1910 Inn, 32 W Tarpon Avenue, Tarpon Springs, FL 3468 (727-424-4091, the1910inn.com)

walk north along the beach from there.

2. **Rotary Centennial Nature Center Trail** (28.0601, -82.8228). Park at the Center to access this 0.25-mile loop.

3. **Dog Beach** (28.0578, -82.8212) has an easy 1-mile walk to the tip of the peninsula and back. Extend it by walking farther along the shoreline.

39

Eagle Lake Park

TOTAL DISTANCE: 3-mile circuit of a network of trails. Other configurations and lengths possible.

HIKING TIME: 1.5 hours

DIFFICULTY: Easy

USAGE: Free. Open 7:30 AM to sunset. Leashed dogs and bicycles welcome except in certain posted areas.

TRAILHEAD GPS COORDINATES: 27.9305, -82.7633

CONTACT INFORMATION: Eagle Lake Park, 1800 Keene Road, Largo, FL 33771 (727-582-2100, pinellascounty.org/park)

In the mid-1800s, settlers came to this pine-forested peninsula along Tampa Bay and staked out homesteads for ranching and citrus groves. Pinellas County became known for its citrus. Largo's original nickname was Citrus City, and it was in large part due to the Taylor family. Born in March 1871, John Stansel Taylor is known as the Father of Pinellas County. He was a substantial landowner and citrus grower, the president of the Florida Citrus Exchange, and the first state senator to serve from this county. The Taylor groves and packing plant sustained the local economy for many decades, particularly through the Great Depression. The industry faded after World War II, when servicemen stationed in the region poured in to purchase affordable housing in this tropical setting—housing that was built atop the groves that had sustained the county for so long.

Eagle Lake Park celebrates the legacy of the Taylor family, with an 18-acre remnant of the citrus grove to walk through, picnic pavilions that look like pole barns, and an adorable playground with a citrus theme. Not all of their 163 acres were farmed, so there are natural habitats, including oak hammocks, lakes, and marshes. Old-growth longleaf pine towers over many of the trails. This is truly an urban forest. Although most of the trail system is paved, we acknowledge that urban residents are likely more comfortable on these familiar surfaces, which makes this a great destination for families with small children and people with limited mobility. This hike describes one of dozens of routes to take through the park's extensive trail system.

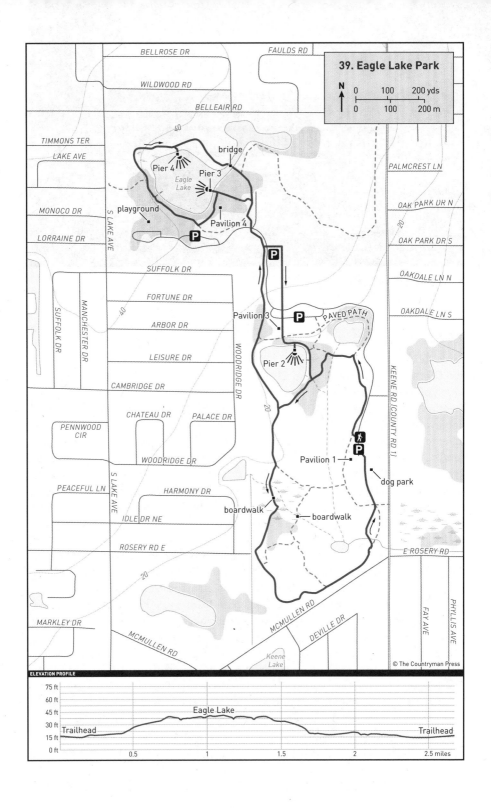

39. Eagle Lake Park

N

| 0 | 100 | 200 yds |
| 0 | 100 | 200 m |

BELLROSE DR

FAULDS RD

WILDWOOD RD

BELLEAIR RD

TIMMONS TER

LAKE AVE

PALMCREST LN

40

bridge

Pier 4

Pier 3

Eagle Lake

OAK PARK DR N

MONOCO DR

playground

OAK PARK DR S

20

S LAKE AVE

Pavilion 4

LORRAINE DR

OAKDALE LN N

P

SUFFOLK DR

OAKDALE LN S

FORTUNE DR

SUFFOLK DR

MANCHESTER DR

40

Pavilion 3

P

PAVED PATH

OAKDALE LN S

ARBOR DR

LEISURE DR

Pier 2

WOODRIDGE DR

CAMBRIDGE DR

CHATEAU DR

PALACE DR

20

KEENE RD (COUNTY RD 1)

PENNWOOD CIR

WOODRIDGE DR

Pavilion 1

P

PEACEFUL LN

HARMONY DR

dog park

S LAKE AVE

IDLE DR NE

boardwalk

boardwalk

ROSERY RD E

E ROSERY RD

20

FAY AVE

PHYLLIS AVE

MARKLEY DR

MCMULLEN RD

MCMULLEN RD

DEVILLE DR

Keene Lake

© The Countryman Press

ELEVATION PROFILE

75 ft				
60 ft				
45 ft		Eagle Lake		
30 ft	Trailhead			Trailhead
15 ft				
0 ft	0.5	1	1.5	2	2.5 miles

OBSERVATION PLATFORM ALONG EAGLE LAKE

GETTING THERE

Eagle Lake Park sits between US 19A and US 19, immediately south of Clearwater, off Belleair Boulevard. From the junction of US 19 and FL 60 (Gulf to Bay Boulevard) in Clearwater, drive west 2 miles to Keene Road. Turn left. Continue south 2.1 miles, crossing Belleair Boulevard, to the park entrance on the right. Inside the park, turn left. Park near the dog park and restrooms.

THE HIKE

From the parking area, face the paved path and make a right. Follow it through the oak hammock. After you pass the main entrance of the park, turn left, meeting a boardwalk around a marshy slough. Turn left again to cross another slough flowing between the marshes. Tall longleaf pines—the reason Pinellas County has its name—rise above. This trail emerges on the outer loop, facing a forest of young longleaf pines. Turn right. Spiderwebs sparkle with dew as they stretch between the pine needles. Following the perimeter of the property, the trail works its way along a pond. A natural surface path comes in from the left.

A fork in the path at 0.5 mile is at the edge of a parking area. Continue straight, passing the parking area and its picnic pavilions with the old orange grove off in the distance. The trail jogs left, slipping around a half-fallen tree and the remnant of an old farm fence line. Passing a crosswalk to the right, where buildings from the Taylor farm sit at the edge of the grove, the path continues up to another crosswalk and to a T intersection. This starts the loop around Eagle Lake. Turn right. Make the first left at the PICNIC PAVILION 4 sign. This path leads to Pier 3, the first of several overlooks on Eagle Lake. Ironically, the signs say NO FISHING, despite this being called a pier. Only certain piers throughout the park may be used to cast a line.

Leaving Pier 3, follow the path around the lake. Spiderwort grows in colorful clusters in a shady spot along the edge of the trail. From the shade of an oak hammock past Picnic Pavilion 5, you see the playground, a fanciful fantasy of a citrus grove complete with a barn. The trail continues around the lake. Keep right, avoiding the trails that branch left, including one that leads to a neighborhood gate. As you emerge from the laurel oaks past Pier 2, the path crosses a small bridge over the outflow of Eagle Lake. Young cypresses have been planted along its banks. The bald eagle nest comes into view in a tall pine just outside the park boundary. Bald eagles build nests of incredible size, which require old-growth longleaf pines for support. There is no mistaking their nest for that of any other bird, since it stands 10 to 20 feet tall, a deep pocket of branches filling the crook of the tree. In springtime, the nest is busy with activity.

As you round the corner, Pier 4 comes into view. Fishing is allowed here. Stop for a moment. Lily pads of American lotuses fill the shallows. A coot fusses as it scurries through the grasses. On the paved path, you cross a sturdy steel bridge, perhaps built atop a frame from when tractors crossed this part of the grove. The bridge crosses a stream flowing into Eagle Lake, a stream so clear you can see fish darting in and out of the aquatic garden below.

After 1.6 miles, you complete the loop around Eagle Lake. Cross the crosswalk again, and make a left at the stop sign. Ramble along the edge of the parking area to where you can see the farmstead, including the historic home and barns. A gravel path leads into the citrus grove. In spring, some trees are laden with oranges, while others are full of fragrant blossoms.

Cross the park road to walk past Picnic Shelter 3 and Restrooms 2, and work your way down to Pier 2. This overlook is great for birding. There is always something going on, from red-winged blackbirds squawking to blue-winged

teals cruising the open water. Follow the boardwalk around to the right between the series of ponds. Past the next pier, make a right, and you're back at the first wetland area you encountered. Now a green heron is hiding in the branches of a wax myrtle. Popping out at the paved perimeter path, take a left this time. A thicket of terrible thistle tempts you over with its big purple blooms.

At 2.2 miles you reach a T intersection under the tall longleaf pines. Turn right. A boardwalk crosses reconstructed marshlands. The longleaf pines are quite old at this end of the park, with oaks making up the understory. This paved trail ends at a pedestrian exit at Rosary Road. Turn left on a crushed-shell path and follow it into the pines. Take the right fork at the Y intersection. In spring, the draping blooms of pawpaw catch your eye as the trail nears the southern boundary of the park. The trail follows the park boundary and the sound of traffic becomes noticeable. Although the park is surrounded by busy roads, there is so much birdsong in the air and so many views to delight the senses that you don't really notice the traffic until you hit this corner, where you see cars rushing by to an intersection with Keene Road. Curving left again, the trail reaches a short boardwalk over a wetland area. Take a peek at the aquatic plants as you continue across a bridge flanked by willows. Lizard-tail grows in the shallows of this natural waterway.

At the next major pedestrian entrance to the park, the Keene Road entrance at 2.8 miles, turn left. A paved path crosses a bridge to the left. Continue straight, since you're now within sight of the parking lot where you started your walk. Passing the dog park, you come up to Picnic Pavilion 1 and its adjoining restrooms, completing a 3-mile walk.

WETLANDS AT THE SOUTHWEST CORNER OF EAGLE LAKE PARK

OTHER HIKING OPTIONS

1. **Wetlands Walk**. The south end of the preserve is circled by footpaths showcasing the restored wetlands. Use the same trailhead as the route above but make a left. Turn right and cross a bridge into the woods. Turn left to leave the paved path to enjoy a sweeping view of the wetlands. Continue along the distinct footpath and take a left at the Y intersection. You'll loop back around to the Keene Road side of the park. Keep left to cross the boardwalk over the wetlands outflow, and left again onto the paved path, which loops back to where you started for a 0.8-mile walk.

2. **Central Birding Loop**. Park near Picnic Shelter 3 (27.9335, -82.7655) and walk down to the boardwalk along the lake. Follow the boardwalk along the lake's edge, and make a left at the T. Continue to the paved path and make a right. Make a right at the next paved path, and you arrive back at Shelter 3 on a 0.5-mile loop.

3. **Eagle Lake Loop**. Park near Picnic Shelter 5 (27.9357, -82.7680). Join the paved path in a clockwise loop around Eagle Lake, stopping at the piers along the way. This 0.8-mile loop is fully accessible.

4. **Grove Trek**. From the above parking area, walk past Shelter 4, visit the pier, and take the trail up to the paved path. Continue north and make the first right. Walk out along the connector to the Bellaire Road pedestrian entrance and return for a 1.5-mile hike.

5. **Largo Central Park Nature Preserve** (27.9127, -82.7746). A 31-acre nature preserve just off East Bay Drive, southeast of Eagle Lake Park, this urban birding location is part wetlands park, part natural floodplain forest. It's looped by a paved trail and crisscrossed by boardwalks, offering more than a mile of hiking.

CAMPING AND LODGING

West Bay Oaks RV Park, 1610 W Bay Drive, Largo FL 33770 (727-586-2440, westbayoaks.com), no tents.

Hampton Inn & Suites Largo, 100 E Bay Drive, Largo FL 33770 (727-585-3333, hilton.com)

Holiday Inn Express, 210 Seminole Boulevard, Largo FL 33770 (727-581-3900, ihg.com)

40

Weedon Island Preserve

TOTAL DISTANCE: 4.6-mile round-trip along a network of trails.

HIKING TIME: 2–2.5 hours

DIFFICULTY: Easy

USAGE: Free. Open 7 AM to sunset daily, except Christmas and the day after Thanksgiving. Daily closing time is posted at the front gate. No pets or bicycles permitted.

TRAILHEAD GPS COORDINATES: 27.8476, -82.6080

CONTACT INFORMATION: Weedon Island Preserve, 1800 Weedon Drive NE, St. Petersburg, FL 33702 (727-453-6500 or 727-582-2100, weedonislandpreserve.org)

For an immersion into the vast mangrove forests that line Tampa Bay, there is no better destination than Weedon Island Preserve. Protecting nearly 3,200 acres along the coast of Florida's largest bay, the preserve is also a world-class birding destination, thanks to its unique perspective on these otherwise tricky-to-reach islands and coves along the shoreline: 178 species of birds, migratory and native, have been documented here. At the various observation platforms and open views across the estuary, you're virtually guaranteed to see flocks of wading birds. What isn't as obvious as you walk the boardwalks and trails is the deep cultural history of this peninsula. Access to the productive waters of the bay made this a place where prehistoric people settled. Archaeologists from the Smithsonian started delving into their secrets in 1923, finding middens, mounds for homes, and a burial mound. Within the past decade, a 40-foot-long dugout canoe was discovered, radiocarbon-dated to 690–1010 AD. But before Weedon Island became a preserve, the peninsula was ditched and dredged for mosquito control and pipelines, planted in orange groves, and even served as an airport.

Before you start your exploration of the preserve, visit the Cultural and Natural History Center. It's open Thursday through Saturday, 9 AM–4 PM and Sunday, 11 AM–4 PM, closed on holidays. Inside, a timeline of the cultural history of Weedon Island compliments detailed information on the flora and fauna of the preserve, with hands-on exhibits that the kids will love. The trail system starts on the back side of the Cultural and Natural History Center, where there are restrooms. The trails are open even when the center is closed.

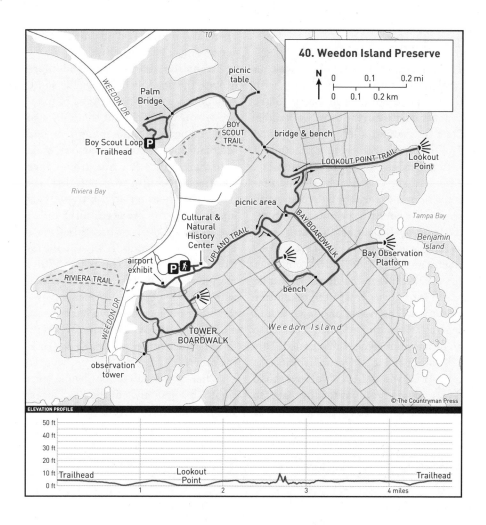

Because mangroves equal mosquitoes, we strongly suggest you apply insect repellent. Take plenty of water with you, too. The trails alternate between sun and shade, but we found ourselves spending more time in the sun than we normally would when hiking thanks to the wildlife watching opportunities and the many scenic views.

GETTING THERE

From I-275 northbound from St. Petersburg or southbound from Tampa, take exit 28 for Gandy Boulevard (US 92) and head east for 2.7 miles, watching the signage, so you stay on the correct road. Turn right onto San Martin Boulevard just past Derby Lane, a large racing/poker facility. Drive a mile and watch for the GREAT FLORIDA BIRDING TRAIL sign pointing left. Continue briefly onto Ridgeway Drive before it becomes Weedon Drive. Drive 1.4 miles, passing a power plant entrance and a small parking area, before you come to the large parking area on the left at the Cultural and Natural History Center.

THE HIKE

The trail system begins behind the Cultural and Natural History Center, with the paved Upland Trail the primary connector between the boardwalk trails. Start by making a left on the Upland Trail to follow it through a pine forest with an understory of dwarf palmetto. After you pass a bench, the habitat transitions into scrubby flatwoods, with scrub oaks beneath the pines. Interpretive signs point out key features, such as fungus found in the preserve. Take a right at another paved trail 0.25 mile into the hike. It meets the Bay Boardwalk, which introduces you to the mangrove forest you'll be traversing for much of the hike. Rounding a corner, it comes to an observation deck with a bench. This saltwater pond is a favorite fishing spot for osprey, which hover well overhead before diving feet first for the water to make their catch. The preserve trails are open to fishing, so don't be surprised to see an angler casting a line, too.

Tunneling deeper into the mangroves, the boardwalk circles the south side of the pond. Three types of mangroves grow throughout the preserve: black mangrove, white mangrove, and red mangrove. To tell them apart, compare their shapes. Red mangroves have a distinct network of prop roots that look like arches holding up the tree. Black mangroves are broader, surrounded by a network of short breathing roots called pneumatophores protruding from the soil under the plant. White mangroves look the most tree-like, with oval-shaped, light green leaves—the other mangroves have dark green, elliptical leaves. White mangroves tend to be farther from the water's edge than the others.

When you reach a boardwalk, turn right. This spur ends at the Bay Observation Platform, where birders tend to

VIEW FROM THE BAY OBSERVATION PLATFORM

flock, watching the flocks of birds. As tides drain Tampa Bay, seagrass and mudflats are exposed. This makes for easy pickings for wading birds, especially the roseate spoonbills, unmistakable thanks to their pink plumage. Notice how they use their unusually shaped bills for sifting through the mud to find a meal. We spotted some glossy ibis here along with the typical white ones, and juvenile ibis in shades of gray and white. They're the wading birds with the curved beaks, once commonly known as curlew. Snowy egrets are especially showy when in their mating plumage. A white bird, they have a contrast of black beaks and yellow feet. Look for great egrets on the flats, too—they're the tallest of the white birds in the distance.

Return along the spur to the main loop and turn right. The mangroves aren't as tall in one spot, so you can see across their canopy, stretching to the blue horizon. There is nowhere else in the United States that mangroves grow other than Florida. When we were kids, they were found no farther north than Central Florida. Today, mangroves have taken root up past Cedar Key on the Gulf Coast and are found on one shore of Dog Island near Tallahassee. On the Atlantic Coast, we've found them spreading northward from St. Augustine. These island-building plants are common throughout equatorial regions worldwide.

When the Bay Boardwalk ends, it's at a junction with the Upland Trail, which also ends at this spot, a picnic grove at 1.1 miles. Turn right at the BOY SCOUT LOOP sign to follow a sand footpath into the forest. From this point on, the trails are natural surfaces and may get wet or mucky in places, especially after a rain. Flanked by dwarf palmetto and cabbage palms, and shaded by oak trees, the sandy footpath winds through the upland forest. Marsh ferns densely cover a low spot. As the trail emerges into the open, the pines are much taller and there are clumps of saw palmetto. At the next sign, turn right to head to Lookout Point. This narrow pathway quickly becomes a berm that tunnels into the mangrove forest, with the mangroves providing deep shade. The pneumatophores of the black mangroves march right up to the edges of the footpath. Ditches parallel the berm; the roots of the red mangroves are a tangled puzzle along them. If you see a small black spot move, it's a mangrove crab. These crabs use the roots and trunks of the mangroves like highways through the forest. Don't be surprised to see a raccoon scurry across the path and vanish into the swamp. Raccoons are adept at fishing and tearing apart shellfish for their meals. Do stay alert, as the splotches of shade across the trail provide natural camouflage for creatures crossing the berm, including alligators.

You pass some pine trees before the straight line of this tunnel curves left. Through gaps between the mangrove roots, an open mudflat is visible, with wading birds browsing along it. Sunlight illuminates the sand underfoot as you draw closer to the end of this peninsula, Lookout Point. A picnic bench sits at the end of the trail. Depending on the tide, you might be able to ease your way through a gap between the red mangroves to the edge of Tampa Bay for a panorama stretching from the Gandy Bridge to MacDill Air Force Base.

Return the way you came, under the shade of the mangrove tunnel. It feels like a much quicker walk on the way back. When you reach the T intersection at 2 miles, turn right to start the Boy Scout Trail in earnest. This trail was

MANGROVE TUNNEL ALONG THE LOOKOUT POINT TRAIL

established in 1984 by George Wysock, an avid volunteer with the Florida Trail Association Suncoast Chapter, at the request of the Florida Park Service. Weedon Island was a state park, and it was called the Weedon Island Trail at the time. Management of the preserve was transferred to Pinellas County in 1999. You'll pass a junction for the Boy Scout Trail as you walk through the pine flatwoods. Stay right at this fork. The trail is broad and sunny here, hemmed in by the understory of saw palmetto. A bench sits just before a bridge over a mangrove-lined waterway.

With a slight elevation gain just past the bridge, the trail is canopied by an oak hammock, a pleasant tunnel in the shade. Red circles with arrows serve as trail markers, but the route through this forest is obvious. When you see marsh ferns and cabbage palms, you know the habitat is about to change. At an intersection, a spur trail leads to the right. It quickly emerges into an open,

fern-filled clearing with stately cabbage palms. Keep going, and you find the treasure at the end of the trail, an island of tropical hammock with a picnic bench. Ancient oak trees shade this forest glen. Return to the main trail and turn right, crossing a bridge over a lazy waterway. At 2.3 miles, you're back in the mangrove forest.

Shaded by the mangroves, the trail is slightly elevated above them on a berm. Open water shimmers through them, where a large expanse is a gathering spot for wading birds. There is no observation deck along this loop, but there are bridges, and a few locations have better views than others. When you cross a broader creek on a wooden bridge, notice it has a name painted on it: Lighter Knot. You may not have seen the names of the bridges up to this point since you'd need to look down. A succession of short bridges traverse little streams in the mangrove forest, joining the berms together into a hiking route. Stay right at the junction after the Palm Bridge to go around the short loop counter-clockwise. Keep following this small loop around, crossing the North Bridge next, and you'll end up back at the Palm Bridge. You've hiked 2.8 miles.

From here you'll backtrack along the route you hiked to this point, skipping the spur trails on the return route. Once you cross the Oak Bridge out of the mangrove forest, the trail leads you back to the 5 Feet Over Bridge, which seems indeed to be that far above the stream below. At the Boy Scout Trail junction, keep left. Skip the turnoff to Lookout Point. At the picnic area where the Upland Trail and the Bay Boardwalk both begin, you're 3.4 miles into your walk. Continue straight ahead along the paved Upland Trail. When you reach the back of the Cultural and Natural History Center, continue past it to tackle one final loop, the Tower Boardwalk. It

starts off at a trail map sign that says PAUL GETTING MEMORIAL TRAIL.

Straight through the mangroves, the boardwalk leads to an overlook on a mangrove-lined pond. The water is clear and shallow, with lots of aquatic vegetation. Oysters cling to mangrove roots along its edge. Ibis pick through the mud. As the boardwalk continues towards Riviera Bay, there is less and less shade. Make a left at the next junction, and you'll immediately see the five-story observation tower at the end of this spur trail. You've hiked 4.1 miles. The boardwalk gently climbs towards the tower, with a view of the fishing pier at the end of Weedon Drive. You also might see a kayaker slip past. You can explore a 4-mile self-guided paddling loop through the preserve with a rental from Sweetwater Kayaks (727-570-4844), just down the road from the parking area towards the pier, or bring your own to launch.

Climb the tower for the panoramic

VIEW FROM THE OBSERVATION TOWER ON THE TOWER BOARDWALK

view of the mangrove forest on Weedon Island, and of Riviera Bay opening onto Old Tampa Bay. The skyline of Tampa is on the north horizon, beyond the sea of mangroves covering this peninsula. The power plant is pretty obvious too. Returning to the boardwalk, make a left when you reach the main trail. The loop continues through the mangrove forest, ending as it meets the Uplands Trail, which curves around the next corner through the pines and palms. In this open area, the vegetation is younger.

Between the trail and the parking area is a fenced-in display of modern archaeology, the showy tiles in the corner speaking to the Art Deco vintage of the control tower of what was once Grand Central Airport. St. Petersburg was the first place commercial airline service began, with regular flights to Tampa in 1914 that continued for several months. This airport was built in 1929 to provide commercial service to Daytona Beach and New York City on Eastern Air Transport, which later became Eastern Airlines. Used for pilot training during World War II, the airport (renamed Sky Harbor in its later years) closed in the 1950s. Except for this unique artifact, all traces of the airport were removed after Weedon Island became a state park.

Continue back along the Upland Trail to the Cultural and Natural History Center to complete your hike. Once you reach the parking lot, you've tallied up 4.6 miles of exploration at this fascinating preserve.

OTHER HIKING OPTIONS

1. **Tower Boardwalk.** For the most expansive view in the preserve, follow the Tower Boardwalk over to the Observation Tower. This 0.8-mile loop gives you a good immersion into the mangrove forest, plus the view of St. Petersburg from the tower.
2. **Boardwalk Loops.** The Tower Boardwalk and the Bay Boardwalk are connected by the Upland Trail, making for an accessible 2.3-mile circuit along the mangrove fringe of Tampa Bay, including the spur boardwalk to the Bay Observation Platform. Both are fabulous for birding. If your time at the preserve is limited, focus on these popular trails.
3. **Riviera Trail** (27.8466, -82.6106). Starting on the opposite side of Weedon Drive, the Riviera Trail makes a 0.75-mile loop out along Riviera Bay.
4. **Boy Scout Trail** (27.8522, -82.6094). A separate trailhead with limited parking lets you just tackle the loops of the Boy Scout Trail. The 0.25-mile loop through the mangroves is an easy scenic walk, but starting here also lets you make the mile-long loop using the return trail that starts on your right after you cross the bridge beyond the picnic area spur. It ends at Weedon Drive; turn right and walk up the road to the trailhead.

CAMPING AND LODGING

Fort De Soto Park, 3500 Pinellas Bayway S, St. Petersburg, FL 33715 (727-582-2267, pinellascounty.org)

St. Petersburg/Madeira Beach KOA Holiday, 5400 95th Street N, St. Petersburg, FL 33708 (727-392-2233, koa.com)

Comfort Inn & Suites Northwest Gateway, 875 94th Avenue N, St. Petersburg, FL 33702 (727-563-9100, choicehotels.com)

Alafia Scrub Nature Preserve

A major tributary of Tampa Bay, the Alafia River rises from tributaries that start as far away as Lakeland, Mulberry, and Fort Lonesome, nearly 30 named waterways feeding a watershed of 335 square miles across southern Hillsborough County. Many public lands—including Alafia River State Park, Alderman's Ford Conservation Park, and Alderman's Ford Preserve—protect portions of the river's 25 mile journey through this heavily populated area. One easily accessed piece of this puzzle is Alafia Scrub Nature Preserve, less than four miles upriver from where the river meets the bay.

Established in the late 1990s, this is a passive recreation site, 79 acres of environmentally sensitive land amid more than 61,000 acres that Hillsborough County manages in order to protect key natural features throughout the region. What's important at this preserve, besides a natural waterfront along a tidal portion of the Alafia River, is the last remaining piece of a scrub ridge that once extended much farther west.

TOTAL DISTANCE: 1.4-mile perimeter loop on a trail network.

HIKING TIME: 1 hour

DIFFICULTY: Easy to moderate

USAGE: Free. Open sunrise to sunset. Leashed pets permitted, but bicycles are not.

TRAILHEAD GPS COORDINATES: 27.8609, -82.3359

CONTACT INFORMATION: Alafia Scrub Nature Preserve, 10243 Elbow Bend Road, Riverview, FL 33578 (813-672-7876, hillsboroughcounty.org/en/locations/alafia-scrub-nature-preserve)

GETTING THERE

From I-75, take exit 250, Gibsonton. Follow Gibsonton Drive east for 0.6 mile. As the curve straightens out, make a left on Hagadorn Road. Turn left after 0.25 mile onto Elbow Bend Road. The trailhead parking area is on the left.

THE HIKE

Starting at the fenced-in trailhead adjoining the power line easement, walk through the gap in the fence and check out the kiosk. It shows a map of this preserve and other ELAPP (Environmental Lakes Acquisition & Protection Program) nature preserves. Red

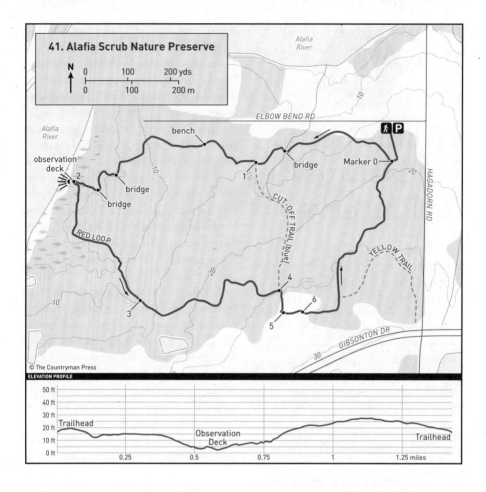

41. Alafia Scrub Nature Preserve

N

| 0 | 100 | 200 yds |
| 0 | 100 | 200 m |

Alafia River

ELBOW BEND RD

bench

Alafia River

observation deck

2

bridge

bridge

RED LOOP

CUT-OFF TRAIL (blue)

bridge

Marker 0

1

YELLOW TRAIL

HAGADORN RD

4

6

3

5

GIBSONTON DR

© The Countryman Press

ELEVATION PROFILE

50 ft					
40 ft					
30 ft					
20 ft	Trailhead				
10 ft			Observation Deck		Trailhead
0 ft					

0.25   0.5   0.75   1   1.25 miles

markers guide you south towards a tree line of oaks. Turn right. You reach the red-blazed loop at Marker 0. The trails here are narrow footpaths, pleasant to walk, and that's what we like about this particular preserve. Fronds of dwarf palmetto lean over the footpath, and sunlight glistens through streamers of Spanish moss hanging from the high canopy of oaks and pines. While the trail briefly draws close to the property boundary fence with Elbow Bend Road, it quickly pulls away from it to immerse you in the forest. A stand of sweetbay magnolia rises in a cluster from the leaf litter of the forest floor.

Crossing a footbridge over an ephemeral waterway, the trail gains a little elevation as you reach Marker 1 at 0.3 mile. It's tipped red and blue to indicate a junction with the blue-blazed Cut-Off Trail that runs down the middle of the preserve to provide a shortcut route. Continue straight ahead, walking through the oak hammock. Clusters of saw palmetto surround a grassy open area where you might spot a gopher tortoise grazing. Winding between the oaks and palms, the footpath is nicely carpeted in oak leaves and pine needles. Past the bench, the trail narrows significantly as the palm fronds crowd the corridor. Expect to push through them in places. Dense draperies of Spanish moss hang overhead. The oaks are taller in this part of the preserve, their limbs curving high overhead. Cabbage palms and dwarf palmetto form a jungle of fronds around you. Along one curve, you spot some dangling orange globes: wild citrus well out of reach. The next short footbridge is amid the palms. An American beautyberry catches your attention with its brilliant purple berries.

At a curve, you catch your first glimpse of the Alafia River basin, and with it, the echoes of traffic from I-75. Stepping over the trunks of saw palmetto in the footpath, you come to the next footbridge. This one crosses a more substantial waterway flowing to the river, fringed with primordial-looking giant leather ferns. The trail climbs a small rise and provides more peeks across the estuary along the Alafia

River, a sea of needlerush on this side of the waterway. Since tides can affect the river, it may be mushy underfoot as you reach Marker 2 after 0.6 mile and climb the stairs to the observation deck. This promontory provides a panorama of the river basin. While the near marshes are natural, the far shore is dotted with residences and crossed by the highway bridge. If the tide is out, you may see ibis and roseate spoonbills on the mud flats.

Leaving the observation deck, turn right to follow the trail along the ecotone between the hammock and the marsh. The understory thickens up with saw palmetto as the trail turns away from the riverfront to start the loop back. The landscape drops off into a large basin filled with palms just before you pass Marker 3. The oaks outnumber the pines in this hammock, but you'll notice more

ESTUARY VIEW ALONG THE ALAFIA RIVER

OPEN SCRUB NEAR MARKER 5

pines towering overhead before the trail reaches a clearing where rust-colored bluestem grass waves above the saw palmetto. This is a transition zone into the scrub ridge. Passing a red-tipped marker near a water oak, you look down and see St. John's wort in bloom. Sphagnum moss edges the footpath as it emerges at a second intersection with the blue-blazed Cut-Off Trail at Marker 4, after 1 mile. Turn right to tack down to the next marker, which is within sight of the property boundary with an apartment complex. Before Hillsborough County bought this land to preserve it, it had already been zoned to be bulldozed for more apartments like those. Make a left at Marker 5 to continue along the trail.

As you walk along this section, it's the bright white sand that makes the scrub ridge obvious. Sand live oaks and myrtle oaks enter the mix of oak trees rising from the clumps of saw palmetto along the footpath. Older saw palmettos arch up on long trunks, lifting well off the forest floor. A slab of concrete is half-hidden by the leaf litter. It's at this spot that an unmarked trail heads to the right. The yellow-blazed trail connects to a pedestrian entrance at the southeast

OTHER HIKING OPTIONS

1. **Short Loop**. Using the blue-blazed Cut-Off Trail, make a loop of less than a mile through upland habitats. The longer loop touches on the best parts of this preserve, however.
2. **Gibbons Nature Preserve** (27.853775, -82.277548). About 4 miles due east along Boyette Road, the Tampa Bay Conservancy manages this 60-acre preserve on bottomlands between Bell Creek and the Alafia River. Limited parking adjoins Ace Golf Driving Range at the nature preserve sign. A loop of more than a mile showcases the natural features of the preserve.
3. **Alderman's Ford Park** (27.865986, -82.146501). The southernmost entrance to this extensive park has a canoe launch and access to a network of several miles of paved bike paths that extend upriver to the park's main entrance off CR 39.
4. **Alafia River State Park** (27.785518, -82.137714). While this park is mainly known for equestrian trails and its classic mountain bike trails through reclaimed phosphate pits in the Alafia River basin, it also has the Old Agrico Hiking Trail, a 1-mile red-blazed loop.

corner of the preserve. Take a short peek down it if you like, but return to the red-blazed trail to continue along the loop.

The oak hammock is more dense and mature through this part of the preserve, with taller laurel oaks and water oaks. The understory is thick with young oaks through one little stretch of trail, before the saw palmetto take over again. Transitioning into pine flatwoods, the trail comes to the close of the loop as you reach Marker 0 again. Turn right to exit the loop, and turn left when you see the fence to return to the trailhead, completing this 1.4-mile hike.

CAMPING AND LODGING

Lithia Springs Park, 3932 Lithia Springs Road, Lithia, FL 33547 (813-744-5572, hillsboroughcounty.org/locations/lithia-springs-park)

Alafia River State Park, 14326 S CR 39, Lithia, FL 33547 (1-800-326-3521, floridastateparks.reserveamerica.com)

Hilton Garden Inn Tampa/Riverview/Brandon, 4328 Garden Vista Drive, Riverview, FL 33578 (813-626-6610, hilton.com)

Little Manatee River Trail

TOTAL DISTANCE: 6.5 miles along the outer loop of the trail system.

HIKING TIME: 3.5–4 hours

DIFFICULTY: Moderate

USAGE: $5 per vehicle. Open 8 AM to sunset. Leashed pets welcome. Bicycles not permitted.

TRAILHEAD GPS COORDINATES: 27.6754, -82.3487

CONTACT INFORMATION: Little Manatee River State Park, 215 Lightfoot Road, Wimauma, FL 33598 (813-671-5005, floridastateparks.org/park/Little-Manatee-River)

An island of natural habitats in an increasingly urban area, Little Manatee River State Park is much the same as when we visited for the first edition of this guidebook, but its setting has changed. Once an oasis of public land amid farms, ranches, and woodlands, it is now edged by subdivisions that press right up to the park boundaries. Fortunately, this is a very large state park, protecting more than 2,400 acres along the Little Manatee River. Rising from swamps in the southeastern corner of Hillsborough County, the Little Manatee River is deeply stained with tannins, earning it the designation of a "blackwater river." It flows a lazy 38 miles before it feeds into Tampa Bay. Since our last visit, a relentless march of development has spilled south along US 301, leaving Little Manatee River State Park as the final buffer for the river and the rural communities that sit just south of it.

With all these new residents in the region, this has become a very busy state park. It's always been popular for paddlers—who can check in at the Canoe Outpost for rentals and shuttles—but now the hiking trails are drawing a crowd, particularly on weekends. That's thanks to a new alignment for the trailhead for the Little Manatee River Trail; it can now accommodate a large number of cars. A primitive backcountry campsite awaits hikers who want to spend a peaceful night under the stars—or use the full-service campground in the main part of the park, and you'll be able to spend a full weekend hiking and canoeing along this outstanding Florida waterway. An iron ranger sits at the entrance to the trail, removing the need for you to visit the main portion of the park before your hike. Pay your fee at the parking lot and off you go.

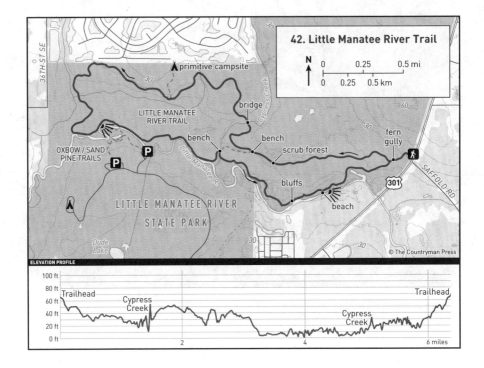

GETTING THERE

From I-75 south of Tampa, take exit 240A, Sun City Center/Ruskin. Drive east on FL 674 through Sun City Center 3 miles to US 301. Head south on US 301 for 2.7 miles to the new trailhead on the right, just before the highway bridge over the Little Manatee River.

THE HIKE

Starting from the trailhead kiosk and iron ranger, walk in on a new linear connector along a fence line. The trail swings left into what was the original parking area, a clearing in the woods. The path narrows just past a WELCOME sign, the yellow blazes leading you into a hardwood hammock lushly carpeted in ferns. You pass an FT sign, a reminder that this trail was built and continues to

be maintained by Florida Trail Association volunteers from the regional Suncoast Chapter. The trail follows a series of boardwalks through this moist hammock, where ferns crowd both sides. Stop and look closely at the many species, including giant sword ferns, marsh ferns, netted chain, and cinnamon ferns.

After 0.25 mile, you reach the beginning of the loop. Turn right. Walk into a dense upland forest, where water oak, yaupon holly, and bay magnolia share the sunlight with the slash pines that leave a thick carpet of needles on the forest floor, encouraging ferns to grow. Damage from feral hogs is evident in the low-lying areas where they root through the soft earth. Rising up through a forest dominated by laurel oaks, the trail crosses an old forest road before reaching a broad bridge over a tannic waterway lined with netted chain fern.

COLORFUL KAYAKS WAITING TO BE LAUNCHED INTO THE LITTLE MANATEE RIVER

Climbing up into an oak hammock, the trail follows a series of boardwalks at 0.6 mile through a thicket of wax myrtle. Signifying seasonal marshy conditions, red maples surround the thicket.

The landscape opens as you pass Marker 12 and enter the pine flatwoods. While the understory is dense, the pines are not. As the footpath becomes sand, the habitat transitions through scrubby flatwoods to scrub, passing through dense thickets of diminutive oaks between patches of open sand with fluffy young sand pines and saw palmetto. An armadillo rustles under the dried fronds, rooting for grubs. Chapman's oak, scrub live oak, and myrtle oak make up the islands of oak. Scrub relies on wildfire to replenish the habitat. When fire happens infrequently, the oaks cluster together tightly, and sand pines grow to the immense heights you see along this section of trail.

After 1.1 miles, you reach a bench and the CROSS TRAIL sign. This is a decision point. If you want a shorter hike, use the cross-trail to make a 3-mile loop. To stay with the outer loop, continue straight ahead into the sand pine forest. The trail soon curves right along the edge of a depression filled with saw palmetto—the floodplain for Cypress Creek. As the trail turns abruptly left at 1.5 miles, you descend steeply down the bluff into the floodplain, crossing a bridge over a side channel. After you scramble up the next rise, Cypress Creek comes into view. Enjoy a few minutes of solitude on the broad bridge over the creek. This is by far one of the most beautiful and serene creeks in Central Florida, where the clear tea-colored water flows gently over rippled sand. Small fish dart through the shallows.

Leaving Cypress Creek behind, the trail ascends up over the bluff through a switchback to return to the sand pine forest. After you cross a small bridge, the forest opens, and you're back in open scrub, out in the bright sunshine, among a broad open sea of scrub palmetto. A pileated woodpecker beats a rhythm against a distant snag as you pass through alternating open scrub and islands of oaks. Taller sand post oaks, laurel oaks, and bracken fern indicate the habitat's shift to sandhill, where oaks dominate and moister conditions make it possible for the bracken to flourish.

After 2.4 miles, you reach the blue-blazed 0.2-mile side trail to the primitive campsite. Even if you're not spending the night, you can take a break at the picnic table. Get a permit from the park office in advance if you plan to camp. There is no water, so you must carry in what you need or filter it at Cypress Creek on the way here. The campsite is surrounded by an oak hammock. If you take this side trip, add 0.4 mile to your overall mileage.

Passing the campsite, the trail continues into an oak scrub, passing briefly under a stand of spreading live oaks. As a radio tower looms in the distance, the trail starts curving left, beginning its route toward the river. The habitat changes to a wet pine flatwoods; damp indentations fill with swamp lilies. After the trail follows a fence line within sight of a subdivision, it swings farther left. Stick with the yellow-blazed trail as it returns to a scrub habitat along the western boundary of the park.

At 3.3 miles, you cross a long boardwalk over a slow-flowing tannic creek. You've finished your trek through the

SCRUB FOREST

VIEW OF THE LITTLE MANATEE RIVER FROM ITS BLUFFS

scrub and pine flatwoods, and are entering the hardwood forests along the Little Manatee River, where cabbage palms and laurel oaks dominate. Not far beyond the bridge, the trail makes an abrupt left—watch the blazes! It's easy to miss this one, as it seems like the trail continues straight ahead. As you walk through the forest, the trail crosses bridges over small channels that feed down into the river. You'll walk along the edges of small marshy ponds, some thick with swamp lilies, others coated with a slimy-looking surface of duckweed. As you approach a tall slash pine in the trail, look for an odd oak tree. The trunk fell over at some point early in the tree's development, leaving the branches to grow straight up—looking like mature trees sprouting out of a long log.

As the trail emerges on a sand bluff, you get a sweeping view of a horseshoe bend in the Little Manatee River. Reaching this point at 3.7 miles, the trail swings left and follows the river upstream for most of the remainder of the hike. Although it jogs around numerous side channels of the river, the trail always returns to the sandy bluffs along the river's edge. Two canoes drift by. It's a gentle paddle, a three-hour trip from the landing just off US 301 on the south side of the river.

The trail then turns sharply left away from the river to skirt a deep floodplain inlet, broadening as it rises from a marshy area into a forest of sweetgum, water oaks, and laurel oaks. Watch for pineapple-sized bromeliads in the trees, particularly when you come up to a large red cedar at 4.3 miles. Soon after, you return to the river's edge, crossing a series of bridges spanning a floodplain channel next to the river. Lilies grow in the thick mud. After you cross another bridge, the trail follows a narrow strip between the river and its floodplain forest, reaching an area where cabbage palms dominate the landscape.

Climbing up a steep bluff, the trail turns to follow Cypress Creek upstream. Look to the right to see where the creek enters the Little Manatee River. The trail sticks to the rugged bluff until it drops to a broad bridge over the creek. This is your last chance to savor this beautiful waterway, so take a moment at the bench. The blue-blazed cross-trail joins in here at 4.8 miles. The yellow blazes swing downstream along Cypress Creek, veering left as the trail winds back through the forest. One palm curves low along the forest floor.

By 5.5 miles, you reach a scenic stretch on the river bluffs, with nice views upstream. The trail clambers up and down little slopes, skirting floodplain forests in old side channels of the river. Pignut hickories dominate the forest. The trail passes through a thicket of wild balsam apple. You briefly emerge back onto the river bluff, hearing the sound of traffic from US 301. Leaving the river, the trail ducks into a scrub oak forest then turns to cross a bridge, returning to the hickory-dominated forest. Look for a beaten path to the right. It leads to a secluded beach at river level. Wild citrus hangs overhead.

After zigzagging along the soft bluffs, you cross a tall bridge over a deep side channel that weaves its way to the river, when it's running at all. Just past it is Marker 2. The trail swings left, where saw palmettos lift their trunks 5 feet and more in the air. The trail emerges into the sunshine in a meadow broken up by smaller live oaks and slash pine. Growing in heaping mounds, smilax provides the ground cover. Your last glimpse of the river is where the wide mowed trail continues through the meadow, where raspberries and daisies fight for space.

After you cross the small bridge in the meadow, the trail heads toward a line of slash pines, then jogs beneath the cool shade of a large live oak. Turning left, you see an old structure in the woods before you walk down a tall corridor of slash pine into an oak hammock. Ferns and sweetbay magnolia appear. After 6.3 miles, you've reached the beginning of the loop. Turn right to exit, walking across the boardwalks through the ferns on the way back to the parking area. When you return to your car, you've completed a 6.5-mile hike.

OTHER HIKING OPTIONS

1. **Cypress Creek Loop**. Use the blue-blazed cross-trail to Cypress Creek to make a very scenic 3-mile loop, following the above directions up to the cross-trail and back from the bench at Cypress Creek. The cross-trail connector is 0.2 mile long and very scenic.
2. **River Trek**. Walk the river side of the loop by following the loop counterclockwise out along the bluffs up to 2.5 miles. When the trail seems to be leaving the river, turn around and either come back the same way, or use the cross-trail to come back to the trailhead along the north side of the loop for a 5-mile hike.
3. **Oxbow Nature Trail/Sand Pine Trail**. From either the main parking area (27.6748, -82.3786) on the south side of the river, or the parking area at the steps to the river (27.6757, -82.3756) inside Little Manatee River State Park, use the Sand Pine Trail to access the Oxbow Nature Trail (27.6767, -82.3790), a 0.6-mile interpretive loop along an oxbow in the river. Using both trails, ramble several miles between picnic area, river steps, and campground. Bikes are welcome on the Sand Pine Trail.

CAMPING AND LODGING

Little Manatee River State Park (1-800-326-3521, floridastateparks .reserveamerica.com)

Canoe Outpost Little Manatee River, 18001 US 301 S, Wimauma, FL 33598 (813-634-2228, thecanoeoutpost.com)

Comfort Inn, 718 Cypress Village Boulevard, Sun City Center, FL 33573 (813-633-3318, choicehotels.com)

OPPOSITE: MARITIME HAMMOCK AT PONCE PRESERVE

VII.

ATLANTIC COAST

43

Tiger Bay State Forest

TOTAL DISTANCE: 4.1 miles in two trails.

HIKING TIME: 1.5–2 hours

DIFFICULTY: Easy to moderate

USAGE: Free at Pershing Highway. $2 per person fee at Indian Lake Recreation Area. Open sunrise to sunset. Leashed pets welcome.

TRAILHEAD GPS COORDINATES: 29.1321, -81.1530 (Pershing Highway), 29.1660, -81.1622 (Buncombe Hill)

CONTACT INFORMATION: Tiger Bay State Forest, 4316 W International Speedway Boulevard, Daytona Beach, FL 32124 (386-985-7815, freshfromflorida.com)

In a land where speed rules, it's refreshing to walk at a slow pace, pausing to smell the wild roses, pondering the choices of butterflies as they flutter from purple asters to sandhill milkweed, and peering across the marshes to figure out where the frog croaks are coming from. Just up the road from the roaring NASCAR engines at Daytona International Speedway, off International Speedway Boulevard, Tiger Bay State Forest protects 27,395 acres along the Tomoka River watershed. In Florida, a bay is an area where water collects—including a swamp forest such as Tiger Bay, vast and impenetrable except along ancient ridges that rise above the tannic waters. Two hiking trails showcase wildly different aspects of this state forest stretching between Deland and Daytona Beach. Sample the swamps of Tiger Bay without getting your feet wet with a hike along the Pershing Highway Interpretive Trail, then head up to Rima Ridge for a walk on the dry side of the forest on the Buncombe Hill Hiking Trail.

GETTING THERE

From exit 261B on I-95, follow US 92 (International Speedway Boulevard) west for 4.3 miles to the light at Indian Lake Road. To access the small trailhead for the Pershing Highway Interpretive Trail, you'll need to continue past the light at Indian Lake Road for another mile and look for a turnout on the left; using the turnout, make a U-turn back onto the eastbound side of US92, and the brown sign marking the trailhead will be on the right. Parking here is limited to just a couple of cars.

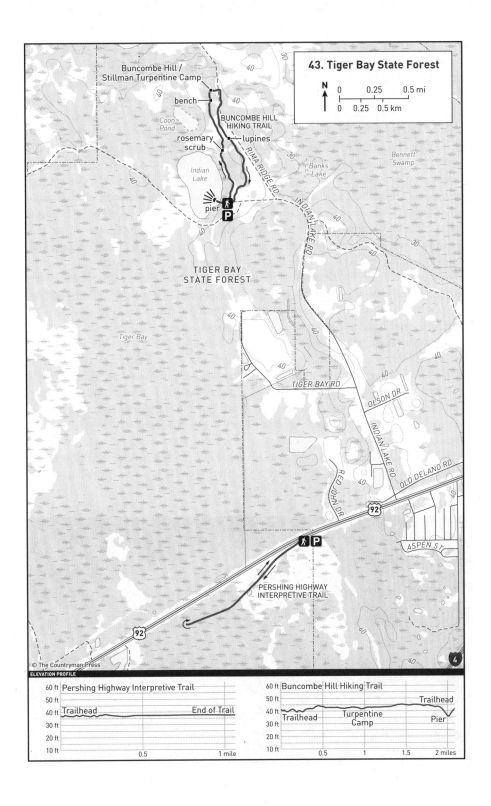

43. Tiger Bay State Forest

N
0   0.25   0.5 mi
0   0.25   0.5 km

Buncombe Hill /
Stillman Turpentine Camp

bench

BUNCOMBE HILL
HIKING TRAIL

Coon
Pond

rosemary
scrub

lupines

RIMA RIDGE RD.

Indian
Lake

Banks
Lake

Bennett
Swamp

pier

P

INDIAN LAKE RD.

TIGER BAY
STATE FOREST

Tiger Bay

TIGER BAY RD.

OLSON DR.

INDIAN LAKE RD.

RED JOHN DR.

OLD DELAND RD.

92

ASPEN ST.

PERSHING HIGHWAY
INTERPRETIVE TRAIL

92

4

© The Countryman Press

ELEVATION PROFILE

Pershing Highway Interpretive Trail

60 ft
50 ft
40 ft Trailhead   End of Trail
30 ft
20 ft
10 ft
        0.5   1 mile

Buncombe Hill Hiking Trail

60 ft
50 ft   Trailhead
40 ft Trailhead   Turpentine
30 ft   Camp   Pier
20 ft
10 ft
        0.5   1   1.5   2 miles

THE HIKES

PERSHING HIGHWAY INTERPRETIVE TRAIL

Starting at a very small trailhead off US 92, this walk is paved, but not in the usual sense. This is a stroll into the past on a surface laid down more than a century ago. In 1903, the Ormond Hotel encouraged early auto owners to gather for a timed racing event along hardpacked Ormond Beach, the world's first automobile time trials. Racing became a regular event in the winter months along the stretch of sand from Ormond to Ponce Inlet. Drivers started finding their way south overland, not an easy task with so few roads—visitors came to Florida by boat in those days. The first driver to make it from New York City to Daytona, as it was known then, arrived in 1907, following the Old Kings Road, an unpaved military trail dating back two centuries. Within the next decade, more trails through this densely wooded Florida coast were improved, usually by widening and grading, to increase automobile access to the region.

It was 1917 when work began on a link between these north-south roads and the Volusia County seat of Deland, which sat not far from the St. Johns River. Named for World War I General John J. Pershing, the Pershing Highway was built across Tiger Bay, curving through extensive marshes, cypress strands, and bayheads. In the heart of the swamp, the 8-foot-wide brick highway was an engineering marvel of its time. It became part of what was later known as the Pershing Triangle, a 63-mile network of roads connecting Deland with Orange City and New Smyrna Beach. And here is a piece of that road, standing the test of time. It stretches off to the horizon into the forest.

When you start your walk, notice that the brick surface is edged by what we know as Chattahoochee stone, a conglomerate of pebbles. Eight feet just wasn't wide enough once traffic picked up, so the brick highway was widened to two narrow lanes by adding this edging, likely in the 1920s. This addition probably helped keep the bricks in place

CENTURY-OLD BRICKS OF PERSHING HIGHWAY

INDIAN LAKE

over the decades. Between the brick and the stone, you can't get lost on this hike. Numerous benches and markers at every 0.25 mile let you easily keep track of your walk. Dayflowers bloom along the grassy sides. Crossing an old culvert over an inky waterway that might be home to an alligator, the road curves gently south around a bend, edged by cabbage palms. The next straightaway is hemmed in by marsh, with red maple resplendent in its red leaves in winter, and Virginia willow leaning out over the pebbled shoulder. Pines on the south side of the road speak to higher ground.

As the highway curves north towards US 92, you come to the end of the interpretive trail after a mile along the bricks. After World War II, it was time to build a better highway. US 92 opened between Deland and Daytona Beach in 1947, and the Pershing Highway was forgotten, reclaimed by the lush swamp forest. A portion of this highway (marked on maps as Old Daytona Beach) was still in evidence north of US 92, near Tiger Bay State Forest headquarters, but this piece vanished from memory until 1998, when it was exposed again by the extensive wildfires that burned across the dried-out swamp during one of Florida's worst droughts. By 2011, a group of Daytona Beach community leaders, along with Scout troops, helped clear this remaining segment of the highway so it could be enjoyed on foot. When you reach the end, turn around and retrace your steps back to the trailhead for a 2-mile round-trip.

After you've visited this trail, drive eastbound on US 92 to Indian Lake Road and turn left at the light. Follow the road through a complex of government buildings. The pavement ends where the state forest begins. Sign in at the kiosk and pick up a map. Continue down the dirt road, following the signs to Indian Lake Recreation Area (29.1660, -81.1622).

BUNCOMBE HILL HIKING TRAIL

Indian Lake Recreation Area is a beauty spot, so it wasn't a surprise to see the new kiosk about its history. What did surprise us was confirmation of the location of the earliest known Boy Scout camp in the Central Florida Council. Photographs show Scouts and their leaders in uniform in the late 1920s, gathered around a rustic lodge with 66-acre Indian Lake in the background; the Scouts are swimming, eating, and posed with a war canoe. This site was also used as a logging camp with a sawmill, as loggers harvested the ancient cypress of Tiger Bay and the tall longleaf pines in the uplands. Commercial use continued until this land was purchased in 1994 to become a state forest.

The trail begins at a prominent kiosk across from the picnic area and iron ranger. Pick up a map at the kiosk. The loop is blazed mint green with green markers that correspond to the interpretive brochure and is best hiked in the suggested direction. The trail starts out as a wide path edged by the sand pine scrub. Although you walk along the edge of a sandhill habitat, sand pines have replaced longleaf as the dominant pine, thanks to aggressive logging of the original forest. As the path narrows, you pass Marker 2, calling your attention to the scrub. Rusty lyonia and silk bay rise from the bright white sand.

At a double blaze, enter an oak hammock, where a split oak splays across the trail. The trail reaches a T intersection. Turn left. Sand live oaks provide a canopy strung with streamers of Spanish moss. Saw palmetto lines the trail corridor. Tall sand pines are interspersed throughout the oaks. The footpath winds through this picturesque forest until Marker 3, where there is a shift in habitat. Here, slash pines were planted by the timber company that owned this forest in the 1990s. While maturing, they stand in rows. Through the empty spaces between them, peek at swamp-loving loblolly bays growing along the marshy rim of Indian Lake.

Rows of slash pine yield to oak hammock after Marker 4, and then you enter the scrub again. This one is different. While the sand pines are everywhere, the understory is taken over by a uniquely Florida landscape, a rosemary scrub. This is a relatively rare habitat, so it's nice to see a healthy one surrounding Marker 6, stretching off in several directions as the understory of this portion of the scrub. These domed woody shrubs, some up to 6 feet tall and almost as wide, are reminiscent of sagebrush. Despite its name, Florida rosemary is not related to the edible herb rosemary, which is in the mint family. To survive in the scrub, a rosemary bush releases a natural herbicide into the sand that inhibit the growth of its seedlings and other plants. That is why the rosemary bushes are so neatly spaced apart. The chemical is stripped from the soil during a fire, so seedlings can then take root.

After 0.5 mile of hiking, you pass Marker 7 at a clump of *Yucca filamentosa*, a native shrub in the same family as agave and Joshua trees. *Cladonia* lichens rise from a patch of bright white sand nearby. The forest is a mix of natural habitat and planted pines, the open understory here evoking the sandhill that once dominated Rima Ridge. The ridge is an old dune line, running north-south and forming an island of

ROSEMARY SCRUB AT MARKER 6

high ground between Bennett Swamp and Tiger Bay. Watch for orange sand, thrown across the white forest floor from the diggings of gopher tortoises. As the habitat shifts to scrubby flatwoods, the trail is surrounded by a massive blueberry patch—a good place to visit in April, when the berries are ripe. In a sand pine forest, a thick carpet of pine needles is underfoot as you pass a bench. The trees are small and slender, packed tightly together, resembling a bamboo grove.

Making a sharp left onto a forest road, you enter a clearing, the site of the Buncombe Hill/Stillman Turpentine Camp at Marker 10. Bedframes, crockery, and the shards of broken Herty cups were on the forest floor when we hiked this trail for the first edition of this guidebook. Now nothing is in evidence, although the echoes of history remain. Booming just after the Civil War, turpentine processing was the state's second largest industry after logging, and

its most infamous, since early turpentine camps relied on cheap labor leased from state prisons in a system that was badly abused. The state's last turpentine camp closed in 1949.

Follow the trail out of the camp, where it goes through an old gate before crossing Rima Ridge Road after 1 mile. It turns right and parallels the road southbound through sandhill forest, which yields to planted pines as you cross to the west side of Rima Ridge Road at FR 706. Clusters of shiny blueberry grow atop the dense mat of pine needles on the forest floor. Past Marker 8, the forest feels more natural and has clumps of wiregrass. In the fall, feathery purple spikes of blooming blazing star attract many varieties of butterflies, including the black swallowtail, the tiger swallowtail, and the southern dogface. Just past the next bench—which sits at a junction with an abandoned forest road—you see Marker 12, beyond the blueberries it indicates.

As you see rusty lyonia and sand pines once again, you know that the trail is headed into the scrub. It pops out within view of power lines on Rima Ridge Road, joining a forest road coming in from the left at a T with a hiker symbol on a green marker at 1.5 miles. It's here that we found the trail ground into a firebreak, which is not the easiest thing to walk on. At Marker 14, it curves past a turkey oak. Just a little farther along, Marker 15 calls attention to the rounded galls that form on young sand pines, caused by a fungus called Eastern gall rust.

Passing an intersection of firebreaks soon after, the trail continues a gradual curve into the scrub forest, emerging along the entrance road to Indian Lake Recreation Area. Turn right and walk past the trailhead kiosk down to the lake. A lengthy pier leads past a picnic pavilion to a panorama of the lake's pristine far shore. Loop back through the picnic area to the parking near the pay station, where a portable toilet sits near the picnic grove under the oaks, to complete this 2.1-mile hike. This is one of the trails in the statewide Florida State Forest Trailwalker Program, so send in your postcard after the hike and add this one to your log.

OTHER HIKING OPTIONS

1. **Rima Ridge North Trails** (29.253178, -81.194532). Just south of FL 40 on Rima Ridge Road, a trailhead provides access to a stacked set of equestrian trails. A hike on the Yellow Trail covers 4.8 miles. Add on the Blue Trail for a total of 6.6 miles. Or drive south on Rima Ridge Road to the Tram Road Equestrian Area (29.228662, -81.183033) to complete a shorter loop of 2.1 miles using the Yellow and Blue Trails. Hikers should yield to equestrians, and keep in mind that it can be tough going in soft sand shared with horses.

2. **Bennett Field Trails** (29.187879, -81.168067). The Bennett Field Campground also provides equestrian trail access, with a 2.4-mile loop on the White Trail. It connects to the North Trails via a 3-mile linear connector, so it's possible to do up to 15 miles along the equestrian trails of Rima Ridge.

3. **Rattlesnake Pond Hiking Trail** (29.085403, -81.169581). At the end of Dukes Island Road, the 0.5-mile Rattlesnake Pond Hiking Trail circles a man-made pond popular with anglers.

CAMPING AND LODGING

Bennett Field Campground, Rima Ridge Road, Tiger Bay State Forest, FL (1-877-879-3859, floridastateforests .reserveamerica.com)

International RV Park Campground, 3175 W International Speedway Boulevard, Daytona Beach, FL 32124 (386-239-0249, internationalrvdaytona .com)

Woodspring Suites Daytona Speedway, 2910 W International Speedway Boulevard, Daytona Beach, FL 32124 (386-333-6512, woodspring.com)

Ponce Preserve

TOTAL DISTANCE: 1.6 miles

HIKING TIME: 1 hour

DIFFICULTY: Easy to moderate

USAGE: Free. Sunrise to sunset. Leashed dogs permitted.

TRAILHEAD GPS COORDINATES: 29.1139, -80.9494

CONTACT INFORMATION: Town of Ponce Inlet, 4300 S Atlantic Avenue, Ponce Inlet, FL 32127 (386-236-2150, ponce-inlet.org)

Stretching between the Atlantic Ocean and the Halifax River south of Daytona Beach, Ponce Preserve is a community park that protects a 40-acre cross section of barrier island habitats. It's one of nature's last stands on the barrier island where auto racing was born. But the primary reason this preserve exists is ancient history. It protects a significant archaeological site: the Green Mound.

Once one of the largest middens on the Atlantic Coast, standing more than 50 feet high, the Green Mound is thought to have been originally built during the late St. Johns culture and was occupied between 500 BC and 1565 AD. It was greatly disturbed prior to 1948 by removal of its materials for road fill. Middens are ancient trash heaps, providing archaeologists clues as to the lives of the people who once lived along Florida's coastlines and rivers. Excavations in this midden uncovered evidence of a village, including fire pits and postholes marking the corners of raised houses

GETTING THERE

From I-95, take exit 256 for Port Orange/Daytona Beach Shores. Drive east on FL 421 (Taylor Avenue), crossing the Intracoastal Waterway onto the barrier island. When you reach A1A (Atlantic Avenue), turn right. Continue 2.5 miles to Wilbur-by-the-Sea. Turn right at Old Carriage Road and drive down to Peninsula Drive, which parallels the Intracoastal Waterway. Turn left. Continue 0.4 mile to the preserve entrance on the left. A new alternative parking area is on Atlantic Avenue (29.1166, -80.9489), but as it provides direct ocean access it tends to stay packed with beachgoers.

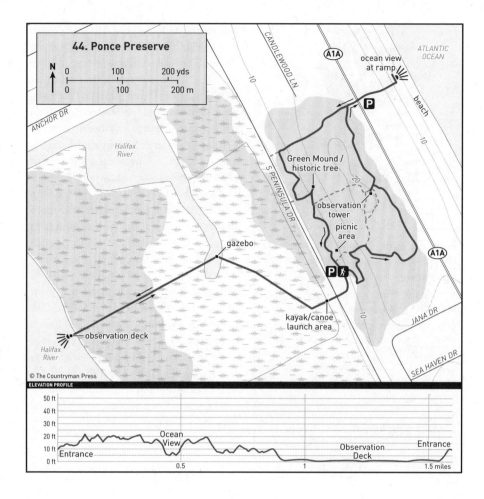

44. Ponce Preserve

N

| 0 | 100 | 200 yds |
| 0 | 100 | 200 m |

CANDLEWOOD LN

A1A

ATLANTIC OCEAN

ocean view at ramp

P

beach

ANCHOR DR

Halifax River

S PENINSULA DR

Green Mound / historic tree

observation tower

picnic area

gazebo

P

A1A

observation deck

Halifax River

kayak/canoe launch area

JANA DR

SEA HAVEN DR

© The Countryman Press

ELEVATION PROFILE

50 ft
40 ft
30 ft
20 ft
10 ft
0 ft

Entrance

Ocean View

Observation Deck

Entrance

0.5   1   1.5 miles

THE HIKE

An inviting sign guides the way into Ponce Preserve from the parking area, leading you through a unique wilderness playground where wooden effigy carvings evoke the spirit of the ancient peoples who once lived on this site. Leaving the playground, you come to a T intersection in a tunnel created by the windswept limbs of sand live oaks in this maritime hammock. Turn right and follow the trail uphill. You see the first of a series of colorful signs at the next junction. These trail maps' key intersections guide visitors to the hot spots inside the preserve. Our hike follows the outer loop counterclockwise, so turn right.

Marked with yellow blazes, the trail is a roller coaster over the midden and ancient dunes beneath a canopy of coastal scrub, with silvery-blue-tinged saw palmetto dominating the understory. Red bay trees and sand live oaks cast corridors of shade, but you do pop in and out of the sunlight while clambering up and down the steep slopes. Despite its short length, this is a rugged little trail. Some fitness stations are installed along it, but don't let those distract you from the beauty of this coastal habitat shaped by salt spray and sea winds.

After serious scrambling on a steep graveled slope, you top out at a sun-drenched high point amid the saw palmetto, where sweet, light scents emanate from the forest below. Power lines betray the presence of the nearby road, Atlantic Avenue (A1A), and while you can't see the cars, you hear them rushing past. From this high point, the trail drops steeply into a sandy bowl, the corridor tightly defined by the saw palmetto. It's a fun scramble, up and down, up and down, over sand ridges. Spikes of gold-enrod create a colorful counterpoint to green surroundings. A variety of wild-flowers grow along this portion of the footpath, including coreopsis, Florida's state flower. The pounding surf of the Atlantic Ocean echoes over the dunes.

Reaching a crest, you see an obser-vation tower. Take this short detour to survey the terrain. The tower provides enough height to let you spy a horizon of blue off to the east. Trails leave the tower in several directions but return to the route you were on. Scrambling up and down across the vegetation-covered dunes, you reach a T intersec-tion after 0.25 mile. Rustic signs point the way: make a right, and you'll soon come across another trail map. There is a crossover on Atlantic Avenue leading to an access point to the ocean, with bright yellow flags provided for you to flag motorists to stop. A reality of walk-ing in Florida: although it is state law to stop for pedestrians at crosswalks, few motorists do.

On the other side of the road, a park-ing area has been added since the last edition of this guidebook, as has an accessible boardwalk to the beach. Fol-low the boardwalk over the dunes and down to the shoreline. This is a rare stretch of oceanfront that isn't crowded with condos or homes. This setting makes it a popular beach, especially with the new parking area. Turn around and head back to Atlantic Avenue, cross-ing carefully back to the trail. You pass the trail you came in on at 0.5 mile. Con-tinue straight ahead. The trail becomes more linear and flat, with softer sand underfoot. Prickly pear cactus sports

ENTRANCE TO PONCE PRESERVE

big yellow blossoms. You enter a long corridor, shaded by red bay. To the left is high ground, part of the midden hidden in the forest. This tunnel trail was the original access point for visitors to the Green Mound.

As you near the light at the end of the tunnel—Peninsula Drive—a historic marker explains the significance of this site. The next set of wooden signs directs you left. The trail snakes its way between large oaks at the base of Green Mound. First noted in accounts of travels in Florida in 1871 as "a pile of oyster shells 30 or more feet high," the mound contains layers of ash, sand, and clay. Between 1914 and 1948, landowners used the mound as a shell pit for fill, not understanding its value in teaching us about ancient peoples. Living in such a bountiful landscape, the people of the Green Mound harvested oysters and clams in the nearby estuary. Mosquitoes breed in the estuary, flocking to this well-shaded portion of the preserve.

The habitat transitions from the cedars and red bay of the maritime hammock to include more tropical vegetation, with wild coffee and acacia growing in the understory. The trail zigzags between the trees, crossing undulating terrain and big roots. On a slope covered in spills of oyster shells from the edges of what remains of the mound, you pass a massive live oak with a sign, DESIGNATED HISTORIC TREE. In 1948, the mound was purchased by local residents to preserve what remained; more than three-quarters of the original mound had already been removed by then. It became a Florida State Park, enabling archeologists to study the structure more fully. Postholes, floors, and pottery shards were discovered during a 1958 dig, with the thickness of deposits convincing the team that this was a heavily occupied site during winter seasons.

Walking down a stately corridor of cabbage palms, you reach a T intersection with Peninsula Drive on the right. Turn left. At the next T intersection, make a left at the GREEN MOUND LIVE OAK sign. It leads you to a bench along the Green Mound, overlooking an ancient live oak, half-fallen and sprawling off the mound, its thick-as-trunks limbs reaching out toward the Halifax River. Photographed by botanist John Kunkel Small in 1924, he described it then as an "old sprawling live-oak (*Quercus virginiana*) growing at the basal edge of Green Mound."

Turn around and follow the pathway in the direction of the PLAY AREA sign. You pass the next signpost at a shortcut trail that leads to the observation tower. Keep going straight ahead to pass a picnic area under a canopy of tropical trees. Once off the mound, the trail winds through a dense forest of wild coffee and yaupon holly, passing another bench and picnic table. It becomes a more substantial path, bolstered by crushed shells underfoot. Passing several more picnic tables, the trail emerges at the parking area as you complete this 0.75 mile circuit on the ancient dunes and midden. Pass the restrooms on the way to the second part of this trek, to the Halifax River. Once again, yellow flags are provided to add visibility when you cross Peninsula Drive to the boardwalk.

The boardwalk is a delightful walk, especially to watch the birds flock in from afar as the sun sets over the river. Winding through a salt prairie, it passes many tidal inlets. When the tide is down, fiddler crabs scurry about, and oysters are uncovered by the receding tide. Look down as well as ahead, so you don't miss the teeming life in the marsh. Two

BOARDWALK TO THE HALIFAX RIVER

observation platforms provide shady birding spots and offer launch points for canoes and kayaks. The farther you progress toward the river, the thicker the mangroves grow together until they create a dense forest along the river's shore. In July, sweet-scented tiny white blossoms cover the black mangroves. Looking down, you see their finger-like pneumatophores, breathing tubes rising from the tidal muck.

Arriving at the final observation deck along the Halifax River after 1.2 miles, you may spot an angler or two. This is a popular place to drop a line, the bounty of the estuary still in fashion after many centuries. Local seafood plays a major role on the menus of local restaurants around Ponce Inlet. Stand here long enough, and you might see a dolphin chasing the wake of a powerboat, or a manatee poking its snout out of the water close to shore.

To finish your hike, walk back along the boardwalk to Peninsula Drive. Pay attention to the rustling of feathers in the mangroves: it's not uncommon to see wading birds like glossy ibis or snowy egrets perched amid this sea of green. Enjoy the sweeping panorama of marsh between the gazebos before you get back to the crosswalk. Once you've returned to the parking area, you've completed a 1.6-mile circuit of Ponce Preserve.

OTHER HIKING OPTIONS

1. **Ponce De Leon Inlet Lighthouse** (29.080657, -80.928782). Climb the second tallest masonry lighthouse on the Atlantic Coast to savor the views. Nature trails wind through the hammock, and history buffs will appreciate the in-depth details on both local history and lighthouse operations. $7 admission. 386-761-1821, ponceinlet. org

2. **Lighthouse Point Park** (29.080740, -80.923527). At the tip of the peninsula, this oceanfront park sits between the historic lighthouse and the sea. Extensive boardwalks crisscross the dunes. Put together a route back and forth across the boardwalks combined with some beach walking. A dog beach is provided.

3. **Dunlawton Sugar Mill Gardens** (29.140788,-81.006202). It's been a working plantation, a roadside attraction called Bongoland, and a botanical garden. Now a 10-acre park, Sugar Mill Gardens offers nods to its past along with 0.5 mile or more of walking among ancient trees and cultivated woodland gardens. dunlawtonsugarmillgardens.org

CAMPING AND LODGING

Nova Family Campground, 4199, 1190 Herbert Street, Port Orange, FL 32129 (386-767-0095, novacamp.com)

Perry's Ocean Edge Resort, 2209 S Atlantic Avenue, Daytona Beach, FL 32118 (1-800-447-0002, perrys oceanedge.com)

Sun Viking Lodge, 2411 S Atlantic Avenue, Daytona Beach, FL 32118 (386-252-6252, sunviking.com)

Doris Leeper Spruce Creek Preserve

TOTAL DISTANCE: 8.2 miles along two separate loops. Longer and shorter options possible.

HIKING TIME: 4–4.5 hours

DIFFICULTY: Easy to moderate

USAGE: Free. Open sunrise to sunset.

TRAILHEAD GPS COORDINATES:
29.0671, -81.0013 (Spruce Creek Bluffs),
29.0945, -80.9723 (Spruce Creek Park)

CONTACT INFORMATION: Doris Leeper Spruce Creek Preserve, 1755 Martin Dairy Road, New Smyrna Beach, FL 32168 (386-423-3300 or 386-736-5953); Spruce Creek Park, 6250 Ridgewood Avenue, Port Orange, FL 32127 (386-322-5133, volusia.org)

With seven separate access points across more than 2,500 acres between Port Orange and New Smyrna Beach, Doris Leeper Spruce Creek Preserve is one of the more extensive landscape-level conservation efforts on this coast. It's not by accident that a drive along US 1 from Port Orange to New Smyrna Beach winds through scenic panoramas: if not preserved, they would have been topped with subdivisions and apartments. From an extensive complex of mounds and middens, it is known that a village sat along this creek as early as 800 AD. In 1768, Andrew Turnbull brought a shipload of indentured servants up the creek to establish the New Smyrna Colony, the first major colonial settlement in the Americas. While mostly abandoned by 1777, it planted the seeds of settlement. It would take more than a century after Turnbull's initial attempt for New Smyrna to grow into a city of commerce.

Selected to contrast two different sides of Doris Leeper Spruce Creek Preserve, both hikes—while not physically connected—share something in common on this sweep of public land: outstanding views of Spruce Creek, which empties into the Halifax River just north of Ponce Inlet. A farsighted effort, started by equestrian Reid Hughes in the 1980s and championed by local artist Doris Leeper in the 1990s, leveraged the national significance of archaeological sites along the creek basin, most importantly the Spruce Creek Mound Complex, to enlist the support of organizations like the Trust for Public Land, the Sierra Club, and the Audubon Society in acquiring lands along the creek. Recreational users now enjoy miles of paddling trails, shorelines for fishing and ramp access for boating, equestrian

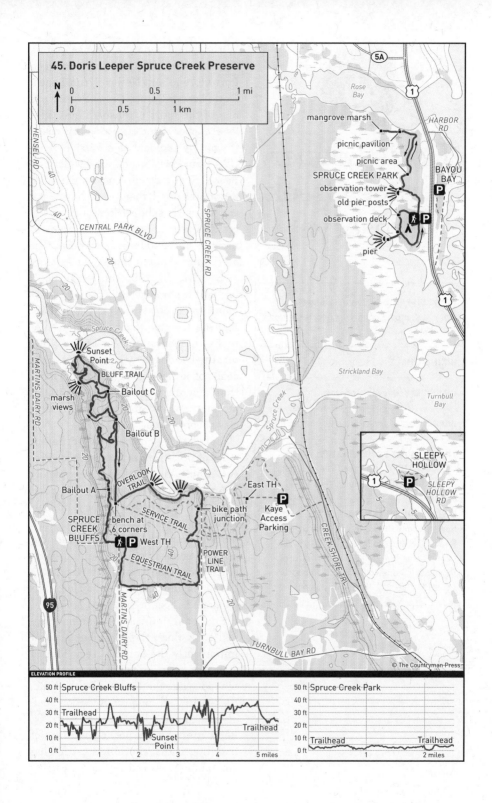

45. Doris Leeper Spruce Creek Preserve

N

0   0.5   1 mi
0   0.5   1 km

5A

Rose Bay

1

HARBOR RD

mangrove marsh

picnic pavilion

picnic area

BAYOU BAY

SPRUCE CREEK PARK

observation tower

old pier posts

observation deck

pier

1

HENSEL RD

CENTRAL PARK BLVD

SPRUCE CREEK RD

40

40

20

Spruce Creek

Sunset Point

BLUFF TRAIL

Bailout C

marsh views

Bailout B

MARTINS DAIRY RD

20

Strickland Bay

Spruce Creek

Turnbull Bay

SLEEPY HOLLOW

1

SLEEPY HOLLOW RD

Bailout A

OVERLOOK TRAIL

East TH

SERVICE TRAIL

bike path junction

Kaye Access Parking

SPRUCE CREEK BLUFFS

bench at 6 corners

West TH

POWER LINE TRAIL

CREEK SHORE TRL

95

EQUESTRIAN TRAIL

40

20

20

40

TURNBULL BAY RD

© The Countryman Press

ELEVATION PROFILE

Spruce Creek Bluffs
50 ft
40 ft
30 ft | Trailhead
20 ft
10 ft
0 ft
        1   2   3   4   5 miles
Sunset Point
Trailhead

Spruce Creek Park
50 ft
40 ft
30 ft
20 ft
10 ft | Trailhead   Trailhead
0 ft
        1   2 miles

and mountain bike trails, and of course plenty of hiking.

GETTING THERE

From I-95 take exit 249, New Smyrna Beach, and drive east on FL 44 for 0.5 mile to Sugar Mill Drive. Turn left and drive 1.3 miles to Pioneer Trail. Turn left and continue 1.7 miles to Turnbull Bay Road. Make a right followed by an almost immediate left onto Martin Dairy Road. The road becomes dirt and can be quite bumpy in places. Follow it for 1.3 miles to where it ends at the preserve. Use care where you park, as portions of the parking area have soft sand.

Spruce Creek Park is along the west side of US 1 in the middle of the marshes, 4.5 miles north of Turnbull Bay Road and just north of the New Smyrna Beach airport. From the entrance road, turn right into the first parking lot, and park near the picnic pavilion.

THE HIKES

SPRUCE CREEK BLUFFS

One of the more outstanding hikes along the Atlantic Coast for scenic beauty, this loop showcases the bluffs above Spruce Creek, rising up to 38 feet above the placid meanders of the waterway. Central to this part of the preserve is a 52-acre complex centered around the Spruce Creek Mound, a massive earthen mound built atop the bluffs. According to an 1885 description of the mound by Andrew E. Douglass, "the mound itself rose to the height of 22 feet above the plain, and the summit plateau was 40 feet in diameter . . . Adjacent to this plateau descended the dug way, and beyond that, the steep bank rose to the summit level of the cliff." The trail system leads you to several overlooks, including one that surveys the mound complex.

Start your hike at the trailhead kiosk,

VIEW OF THE SPRUCE CREEK BLUFFS FROM OXBOW OVERLOOK

where maps are available. The trail system here was built and is well maintained by the Spruce Creek Mountain Bike Association, so you'll find plenty of cyclists here on weekends. All trails, including the equestrian loops, are open to hikers. Our route roughly follows the perimeter trails. Turn left at the kiosk and follow the singletrack up the fence line. A junction provides a side route marked WEST to an entirely different loop; stay with the EAST side. Built for speed and beauty more so than physical challenge, this path meanders gently through a dense bottomland forest, gaining elevation above a blackwater creek drainage below. You reach the BAILOUT A sign after 0.4 mile. This is the first of several crossovers to the park's main path—the Bluff Trail—enabling a more direct loop back to the trailhead. The oaks are tall in the palm hammock that follows. Sword fern covers the forest floor. Sunlight filters through ribbons of Spanish moss as the trail continues its ascent.

Southern magnolia towers over rusty lyonia where a painted plaque says 1 MILE. The gentle curves of this path give you time to focus on the forest. Climbing into scrubby flatwoods, you pass Bailout C. Winding through the oaks, the trail passes a mountain bike obstacle, a series of sideways logs. It sweeps through hardwood forest to Bailout D, the last of the crossovers, at 1.7 miles. Becoming more curvy past this point, it slips beneath a low canopy of oaks until you round a bend and can see light through the forest: the first glimpse of the Spruce Creek basin, a marshy cove. You get a good view of the needlerush marsh around 2 miles. As the trail climbs and curves, you catch sight of open water. *This* is

Spruce Creek. At the top of the bluff, at a fenced clearing called Sunset Point, the panorama is simply superb. Traffic noise filters in from I-95, but it doesn't follow along downstream. Stick with the trail closest to the bluffs.

At 2.3 miles you join the Bluff Trail. This is a primary cross-trail through the preserve, open to all users. The dense understory blocks creek views. Look carefully at the leaf litter, and you might see a cluster of Indian-pipe under the oaks. The path is soft and sandy in places. Curving away from the bluffs, the trail meets a 4-way intersection. On the right is the incoming side of Bailout D, on the left is a meandering mountain bike loop. As it adds mileage without views, pass that junction and follow the broader Bluff Trail. The crossover for Bailout C is just a little downhill. Passing more bike path connectors on the left, you continue downhill to reach 6 Corners, 3.3 miles into this hike. This junction of trails is a decision point. If you follow the path marked West TH, it leads directly back to the trailhead to wrap a 3.7-mile hike. The trail marked East TH leads a couple of miles due east to the Kaye Access trailhead (29.0691, -80.9851), an entirely separate entrance to the preserve with its own set of loop trails.

Turn left to follow the Overlook Trail. It begins a slow ascent through an oak hammock, towards the highest ground in the preserve. When you see a gap between the trees, you've arrived at the bluffs. The mound complex stretches upstream along the bluffs from where this trail turns to lead you downstream. Please stay on marked paths to respect the sanctity of this burial site. Field archaeologists still work in these woods, and their finds sometimes lead to rerouting or permanent closure of trails. At 3.7 miles, the first overlook on Spruce Creek provides a glimpse of a crescent-shaped island topped with needlerush and cabbage palms. Continue along the Overlook Trail to catch views of the creek through the trees. The next overlook offers a closer view of the island. The Oxbow Overlook shows you both the sweep of the island and the bluff on which the Spruce Creek Mounds complex sits. One extremely tall pine, jutting well above the forest canopy from the others, is likely atop the biggest mound.

Although the Overlook Trail technically ends at Oxbow Overlook, the path continues. Along its edges, look for deer moss and other lichens thriving atop the sand pine needles and oak leaves. Passing a junction with a bike path, the trail curves near the power lines; water shimmers beyond them. The trail plunges down the bluff to creek level, the sand soft in places. Sweeping uphill along the edge of the salt marsh, it climbs along a creek under the power line. The sand gets softer once you pass a bridge over the creek at 4.1 miles. The bridge leads to another loop favored by cyclists. At the next intersection, another bridge leads left, partly obscured by the soft sand. That's the more direct route to the Kaye Access trailhead, otherwise posted as East TH on the trail markers. Your car is at West TH, so make a right here instead. Turn left at the next Y intersection to stay on the perimeter trail. There are many small wonders to focus on: orchids clinging to sand live oak branches, the wrinkled leaves of Chapman oak, the sound of an Eastern towhee calling as it scrabbles across the forest floor. Cyclists come around these curves fast, so keep alert. The open area

is a portion of the scrub forest that the county has rototilled for habitat restoration. As evidenced by similar work at Lyonia Preserve (Hike 46), it may take years before the forest grows to a height that Florida scrub-jays prefer.

At 4.3 miles, the trail is bisected by a broader path coming in from the power line. This is the Service Trail, the primary equestrian trail. To the right, it leads directly back to 6 Corners. Cross the Service Trail and past it is another trail marker indicating you're on the correct path to West TH. In the scrub oaks, you'll pass a MILE 5 sign, although you haven't walked that far yet. The understory is dense, with sprouts of young silk bay and shiny lyonia. By 4.7 miles, you're at the southeast corner of the preserve. A directional sign says HORSES and points both to the Power Line Trail on the fence line and into the big open area. This is the last shortcut diagonal along this loop (which is more of a rectangle along the preserve boundary). Cross it. The trail sticks close to the boundary fence briefly before ducking back into the cover of the scrub forest. A long log with a flat top serves as a trail element for cyclists and can be used as a shortcut along a curve. Making a turn as it reaches the fence line along Martin Dairy Road, the trail has another long log to treat like a balance beam. Past the MILE 6 sign, you meet the Service Trail again, on the west side of the big clearing. With occasional peeks to the paralleling road, the trail curves through the scrubby flatwoods, making a loop around the parking area to merge into the Bluff Trail. Turn left to exit, completing a 5.6-mile hike.

To drive to Spruce Creek Park (29.0945, -80.9723) take Martin Dairy Road back to Turnbull Bay Road and

make a left. Follow this winding scenic road for 5 miles to US 1. Turn north and continue 4.5 miles to the park entrance on the left.

SPRUCE CREEK PARK/ROSE BAY

The gentler of the two hikes, the trail system at Spruce Creek Park and Rose Bay is hiking-only and has been around for a couple of decades. Local school students were recruited to create and maintain the trails. Their schools use the trail system as an outdoor education center, so you may encounter students here on weekdays. Start your hike at the picnic pavilion adjoining the interpretive center; it has restrooms and a soda machine. Continue past the playground to the hiker sign, and cross the board-

walk. Make a right on the graded path. It quickly leads to a sturdy boardwalk looking out across a tributary of Spruce Creek, towards the creek itself.

From the boardwalk, it's obvious this is a tidal waterway, where fiddler crabs scramble through the soft mud and black mangroves gain a foothold along the water's edge. The boardwalk ends but the trail continues, passing a sign that explains the Rose Bay Legacy Project and this trail. It's not far to the Bird Observation Tower, one of the primary reasons to tackle this hike. This coastal flatwood does get soggy during high tides, so don't be surprised to find squishy spots between the roots of cedar trees and at the base of the palms along its edge. Roots and muck make for slip-

bench. The benches tell you this is an outdoor classroom. Another aspect of this student-developed trail are a series of signs that enable kids to learn how to use GPS, by providing the latitude and longitude of the location, with the same for the location of the next numbered sign. The trail continues its sweep along the estuary, but the saw palmetto becomes too dense under the oaks to afford any views. Walking beneath this corridor of oaks, smell the salt and feel the breeze.

At a T intersection with a forest road at 0.7 mile, make a left. Honeybees cluster on the purple sprays of deer's-tongue along the edge of this road. A picnic area occupies a large clearing in a palm hammock. Turn right to take a peek between the mangroves at Rose Bay, part of the estuary system into which Spruce Creek drains. Turn back and explore farther down the trail. Here's where it gets tricky—it all depends on the tides as to how far you can walk into the mangrove flats. In this unusual habitat, thousands of mangrove shoots are taking root in the mud. Someday, this will be a wall-to-wall mangrove forest. By the time you turn around and get back to the picnic pavilion, you've walked a mile. Retrace your route, making a right at the next intersection to follow the main trail back to the observation tower. Take the footpath back to the boardwalk to return to Spruce Creek Park. A round-trip hike from the parking area to the mangrove flats is 1.9 miles.

To extend your hike with more scenic views and birding opportunities, stay on the graded path that starts where the boardwalk ends. It's an accessible

pery going between the bridges; the sweep of the Spruce Creek estuary is visible through the trees. The observation tower is around the next bend, 0.25 mile into this hike. Enjoy the panorama of Spruce Creek as it flows towards Rose Bay through a sea of needlerush marsh. It's perpetually breezy up top, but a roof provides cover from the sun.

After you descend the steps, two trails lead northeast. The one closer to Spruce Creek tends to stay wet, so take the one that passes the kiosk. The trail beelines towards the pine flatwoods, then curves left to follow the edge of a marsh, rejoining the other trail. Keep right and follow the curve. You enter a shady tropical glade where giant leather fern peeks out from behind a picnic loop that circles this island, which has a campground—open to nonprofit groups only—in the middle. Walking on this forest road beneath the tall pines and cabbage palms, you reach Spruce Creek, where the remains of an old wooden pier form parallel lines into the marsh. Following the loop through the woods, you pass a picnic table before a signpost for the canoe launch. Open water parts the marshes. Walk out on the boardwalk to survey this big curve in Spruce Creek. Two covered platforms provide breezy spots to watch for eagles winging past. A portion of the creek flows into Strickland Bay beneath US 1. Leaving the boardwalk, look for the hiker sign and follow the forest road around the edge of the campground, passing the canoe storage areas. Check in at the office at the campground entrance about canoe rentals. Popping out at the back side of a hiker symbol sign, you emerge onto the park entrance road. Turn left and follow it to the parking area, completing a 2.6-mile hike.

OTHER HIKING OPTIONS

1. **Sleepy Hollow** (29.0804, -80.9552). South of Spruce Creek Park along US 1, a 0.5-mile loop with several spurs to scenic points offers outstanding views of the estuary and its mangrove islands. Starting near a picnic pavilion, it's a popular destination for anglers.

2. **Bayou Bay** (29.0969, -80.9701). Just north of Spruce Creek Park along US 1, a 0.4-mile loop leads to a linear walk on the old highway route along this mangrove-lined bayou. From a set of benches just south of the loop, you can see the Ponce Inlet Lighthouse across the marshes.

3. **Oxbow Overlook**. Starting at the Martin Dairy Road trailhead (29.0671, -81.0013), follow the Overlook Trail up a well-defined corridor through the oak hammock to the first overlook along the trail for a 1-mile round-trip.

4. **Sunset Bluff**. Follow the Overlook Trail as above until you get to the trail junction at 6 Corners. Turn left onto the Bluff Trail, which goes straight to the farthest viewpoint along the trail system, the best one from which to watch the sunset. This is a direct version of our Spruce Creeks Bluffs hike, a 2.4-mile round-trip.

5. **East Trailhead/Kaye Access** (29.0709, -80.9886). Off Creek Shore Trail north of Turnbull Bay Road, the equestrian trailhead at Kaye Access enables you to connect to the larger trail system off Martin Dairy Road. From here, it's roughly a 4-mile round-trip to hit the overlooks along the Overlook Trail. Park on the south side of the old pasture (29.0691, -80.9851), near the trail kiosk and map, to find a loop to the south. There is another 1-mile loop on the north side of the pasture, and yet another west of the pasture.

CAMPING AND LODGING

New Smyrna Beach RV Park and Campground, 1300 Old Mission Road, New Smyrna Beach, FL 32168 (386-427-3581, beachcamp.net)

The Riverview Hotel, 103 Flagler Avenue, New Smyrna Beach, FL 32169 (386-428-5858, riverviewhotel.com)

Sea Horse Motel, 423 Flagler Avenue, New Smyrna Beach, FL 32169 (386-428-8081, seahorseinnflorida.com)

46

Lyonia Preserve

TOTAL DISTANCE: 2.1 miles along the perimeter of three stacked loop trails. Shorter options possible.

HIKING TIME: 2 hours

DIFFICULTY: Easy to moderate

USAGE: Free. Open sunrise to sunset. No pets or bicycles permitted.

TRAILHEAD GPS COORDINATES: 28.9302, -81.2255

CONTACT INFORMATION: Lyonia Preserve, 2150 Eustace Avenue, Deltona FL 32725 (386-789-7207, volusia.org)

Surrounded by suburban neighborhoods in Deltona, Lyonia Preserve is a Volusia County preserve that's an unexpected delight. Covering 400 acres of relict sand dunes topped with Florida's own desert habitat, scrub forest, it hosts a bird unique to Florida, the Florida scrub-jay. Found only in the Florida peninsula, there are less than 9,500 of these brightly colored birds on earth, their numbers diminishing every year due to predation and habitat loss. This preserve is devoted to their favored habitat. Start your hike in the early morning hours and you may see not just one or two Florida scrub-jays but dozens of them, flitting through the oak scrub in search of breakfast.

GETTING THERE

From I-4, take exit 114, Orange City, and go south on FL 472 (Howland Boulevard) for 2.5 miles. Turn right on Providence Boulevard, turning right again after 0.7 mile onto Eustace Ave. The preserve entrance is immediately on the left. The entrance and parking for the preserve is shared with the Deltona Public Library along with an amphitheater and the Lyonia Environmental Center. Park in the parking lot on the right side of the entrance road, as the trailhead is in the far eastern corner of this complex. The environmental center is worth visiting before your hike, to ground you in understanding the habitats along the trail system, the scrub-jays, and the unique karst aquifer beneath all this white sand.

THE HIKE

Start your hike at the kiosk. Scrub plants are identified beside the short walk along the fence line to a covered

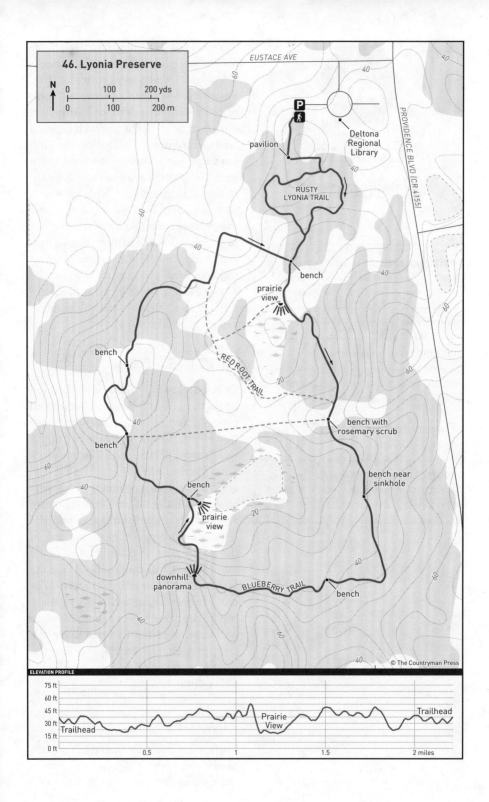

46. Lyonia Preserve

N

| 0 | 100 | 200 yds |
| 0 | 100 | 200 m |

EUSTACE AVE

P

Deltona
Regional
Library

PROVIDENCE BLVD (CR 4155)

pavilion

RUSTY
LYONIA TRAIL

bench

prairie
view

RED ROOT TRAIL

bench

bench with
rosemary scrub

bench

bench near
sinkhole

bench

prairie
view

downhill
panorama

BLUEBERRY TRAIL

bench

© The Countryman Press

ELEVATION PROFILE

75 ft
60 ft
45 ft
30 ft
15 ft
0 ft

Trailhead

Prairie
View

Trailhead

0.5   1   1.5   2 miles

ALONG THE RED ROOT TRAIL

picnic shelter. When you reach the picnic shelter, turn left and follow the broad firebreak behind the nature center and amphitheater to the original entrance to the loop trail system. Turn right to start the Rusty Lyonia Trail, blazed orange. Although many unmarked trails crisscross the stacked trail system of three loops, care has been taken to mark the main loops and intersections well.

Take an immediate left at the first T intersection. The trail rises through a diminutive scrub forest dense with myrtle oak, Chapman oak, and rusty lyonia. Habitat restoration in the past five years has scaled the forest closest to the environmental center down to less than shoulder height on an adult, and taller trees are few and far between. Since scrub-jay families have a sentinel that keeps watch from a high point and alerts the others of intruders, the lack of anywhere for a sentinel to perch means we saw no scrub-jays in this vast swath of extremely short, dense oak scrub.

After 0.2 mile, you reach the upper end of the Rusty Lyonia loop. Continue straight ahead down the scrub-flanked corridor to the intersection with the Red Root Trail, which you now join. Continue straight to keep on the perimeter loop. After you cross a couple of sand roads, used for access to maintain the preserve, the trail reaches a prairie cradled in the scrub, mostly hidden behind a screen of tall bluestem grass with orange stalks. While this was a wetland for a long time, it's now extremely dry.

The trail climbs a tall rise. Young rosemary shrubs grow along both sides of the path in the bright white sand. Silk bay appears along the trail. The leaves are a dark shiny green on top, with silky-haired red undersides. If you crush one, it emits the aromatic smell of bay leaves used in Italian cooking. This tree is a close relative but is endemic to Florida. At the next trail junction, 0.5 mile into the hike, continue straight ahead to walk the perimeter of the Blueberry Trail. The elevation becomes pronounced. Keep alert for the shrill *shreep* of the scrub-jays. Watch for a slight depression, a sinkhole hidden in the pines. Notice the scattered scrub palmetto, a relative of the saw palmetto. They differ in that the scrub palmetto leaf stem is smooth and continues into the leaf, ending in a point. Scrub palmettos also have fine tan fibers growing off their leaves, which the Florida scrub-jay will pull and use to build its nest.

After a mile of hiking, you climb a rise to the trail's high point, looking down on a grassy prairie below. It's a steep downhill to the prairie, which

is rimmed by a handful of tall slash pines and has a pond in its center. As you round the bend at the base of the hill, you may hear the warning cry of a scrub-jay sentinel. The Florida scrub-jay is a curious bird, and when feeling no threat, may draw close to you. Each pair mates for life, raising its family with the aid of helpers, children of the pair who delay their own breeding to help raise a family. Families travel together across a territorial spread of 25 acres. The scrub-jays are large, eight inches tall. As they flit between trees, they are so bright and colorful it's like having a flock of parrots surround you. When the family's sentinel gives another sharp *shreep*, the birds melt back into the scrub, shuffling across the forest floor in search of acorns, insects, and lizards. Like squirrels, each family gathers caches of acorns to feed themselves during leaner times.

Take a short side trip to look over the prairie. While the water has retreated to its very center, it still attracts sandhill cranes. Crossing several more unmarked sand roads, the trail rises out of dense sand pines into taller oaks, with an understory of blueberries and deer moss. More frequent rosemary scrubs occur, creating small openings between the oaks. Headed downhill through a corridor of young sand pines, the Blueberry Trail meets with the Red Root Trail at 1.6 miles. Make a left to continue along that trail's western side. After climbing up and over another sand ridge topped with scrub forest, the Red Root Trail heads steeply downhill to reach a junction at a T intersection after 1.8 miles. Turn left.

You're now back on the entrance trail into the loop system, the Rusty Lyonia Trail. Make a left at the next trail junction to walk the last perimeter trail, the

FLORIDA SCRUB-JAY

other half of the Rusty Lyonia Trail. It scrambles uphill through a dense but short scrub forest of myrtle oak, rusty lyonia, and wax myrtle with scattered blueberries. It reaches the end of its loop at 2 miles. Turn left, facing the back of the environmental center, and walk down to the fence line behind it. Turn left and follow your footprints in the soft, beach-like sand back to the picnic pavilion, and through the tiny stretch of scrub to exit at the trailhead.

OTHER HIKING OPTIONS

1. **Rusty Lyonia Trail**. The shortest possible loop in the preserve is the Rusty Lyonia Trail, the first loop of the three. From the trailhead to the picnic pavilion and around the orange-blazed loop through the diminutive scrub is 0.4 mile. There is no shade along this route.
2. **Red Root Trail**. Hiking only the east side of the Rusty Lyonia Trail to connect to the loop of the Red Root Trail, and following the red blazes around

that trail, nets a 1.6-mile subset of the longer hike.

3. **Prairies and Rosemary Loop**. We've used the unmarked cross-trails of the preserve to ramble into some of the prettier places, including a nice stretch of rosemary scrub just south of the second junction of the Red Root Trail and views of both prairies. That route, using the cross-trails we've marked on the map, creates a 1.8-mile balloon hike.

CAMPING AND LODGING

Blue Spring State Park, 2100 W French Avenue, Orange City, FL 32763 (1-800-326-3521, floridastateparks .reserveamerica.com)

Lake Ashby Park, 4150 Boy Scout Camp Road, New Smyrna Beach, FL 32168 (386-736-5953, volusia.org), tents only.

Highbanks Marina & Camp Resort, 488 W Highbanks Road, DeBary, FL 32713 (386-668-4491, campresort .com)

Merritt Island National Wildlife Refuge

TOTAL DISTANCE: 12.2 miles along a series of six trails ranging from 0.5 to 4.8 miles in length.

HIKING TIME: 5 hours

DIFFICULTY: Easy to moderate

USAGE: Free access to the Visitor Center, Hammock Trails, Scrub Ridge Trail, and Pine Flatwoods Trail. $10 daily per-vehicle fee for Black Point Wildlife Drive and its hiking trails. Open sunrise to sunset, except for the Visitor Center, which is open Monday to Saturday, 8 AM–4 PM.

TRAILHEAD GPS COORDINATES:
28.6415, -80.7357 (Visitor Center),
28.6439, -80.7165 (Hammock Trails)
28.678159, -80.771798 (Cruickshank Trail).
Additional trailhead GPS coordinates found in trail description.

CONTACT INFORMATION: Merritt Island National Wildlife Refuge, 1987 Scrub Jay Way, Titusville, FL 32781 (321-861-5601, fws.gov/refuge/Merritt_Island); Merritt Island Wildlife Association, PO Box 2683, Titusville, FL 32781 (321-861-2377, merrittislandwildlifeassociation.org)

When John Glenn orbited the earth in February 1962, the American space program took a big leap forward. Missile testing was the goal when the first launch pads were built by the Air Force along Cape Canaveral, a spit of land jutting into the Atlantic Ocean along Merritt Island. But after the Russians launched Sputnik in 1957, the race was to prove human spaceflight was possible. In 1963, to expand space support facilities, the federal government acquired all of Merritt Island north of the Air Force station. It was not a wilderness at the time: along CR 3 was a patchwork of citrus groves and farms, waterfront homes, and even the residential communities of Wilson, Allenhurst, and Shiloh, with businesses and schools. Once the footprint of Kennedy Space Center was established—roughly 6,000 acres—the remainder of more than 140,000 acres on Merritt Island was placed under the control of the US Fish and Wildlife Service, becoming Merritt Island National Wildlife Refuge.

As it's been both our big backyard and our family's workplace for the past six decades, we are well acquainted with the density and diversity of wildlife on the refuge. Alligators are commonplace along shorelines and anywhere else they can lie in the sun. Manatees frequent the many shallow coves. We've seen otters and bobcats, and armadillos are common in the denser hammocks. More than 350 species of birds have been identified, with our favorite personal sightings including greater flamingos, reddish egrets, big flocks of white pelicans, small flocks of roseate spoonbills, nesting bald eagles, and numerous families of Florida scrub-jays. Thanks to the ease of birding at the refuge, the Space Coast Birding

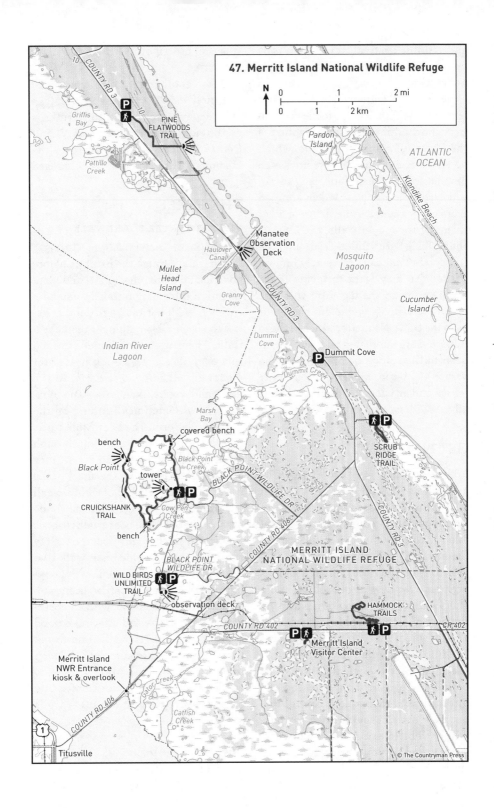

47. Merritt Island National Wildlife Refuge

N

0   1   2 mi
0   1   2 km

COUNTY RD 3
10

Griffis Bay

PINE FLATWOODS TRAIL

Pattillo Creek

Pardon Island

ATLANTIC OCEAN

Klondike Beach

Haulover Canal

Manatee Observation Deck

COUNTY RD 3

Mosquito Lagoon

Mullet Head Island

Granny Cove

Cucumber Island

Dummit Cove

Dummit Cove

Dummit Creek

Indian River Lagoon

Marsh Bay

SCRUB RIDGE TRAIL

COUNTY RD 3

covered bench

bench

Black Point

Black Point Creek

BLACK POINT WILDLIFE DR

tower

CRUICKSHANK TRAIL

Cow Pen Creek

bench

MERRITT ISLAND NATIONAL WILDLIFE REFUGE

COUNTY RD 406

BLACK POINT WILDLIFE DR

WILD BIRDS UNLIMITED TRAIL

HAMMOCK TRAILS

observation deck

COUNTY RD 402

CR 402

Merritt Island Visitor Center

Merritt Island NWR Entrance kiosk & overlook

COUNTY RD 406

Gator Creek

Catfish Creek

1

Titusville

© The Countryman Press

and Wildlife Festival launched in 1997 and remains one of the best of its kind nationwide.

The hiking trails of Merritt Island National Wildlife Refuge focus on birding opportunities, with the exception of the beautiful Hammock Trails, which no visitor should miss. There are seven distinct trails at the refuge, only two of which share a trailhead. We've grouped them by location. Do one, a few, or all of them. Of the longer trails, the Cruickshank Trail, Scrub Ridge Trail, and Pine Flatwoods Trail have extremely limited shade. You may want to tackle these trails earlier in the day. You will also want to have insect repellent handy for all of the trails. No matter which of these trails you are interested in, if you've not been to the refuge before, stop at the Visitor Center for an orientation to the refuge and an easy boardwalk loop that all ages will enjoy.

GETTING THERE

From I-95, take exit 220, Titusville, and follow FL 406 (Garden St) east for 8 miles. It crosses the Max Brewer Bridge to join a causeway to Merritt Island. To get your bearings, stop at the first paved parking area (28.6286, -80.7872) on the right, which provides both an overview of the refuge and a short walk to an observation platform, the first of many that birders stop for. This is where Merritt Island National Wildlife Refuge begins. Narrow dirt roads (such as the one adjoining this parking area) lead to good fishing and birding spots throughout the refuge, but they are not maintained for passenger vehicle use and are generally not marked. If you decide to explore the back roads of the refuge, never go down a road or trail posted AREA BEYOND

THIS SIGN CLOSED or UNAUTHORIZED ENTRY PROHIBITED.

After another 1.5 miles, you reach a turnoff for FL 402. Keep right. The entrance road to the Visitor Center is on the right after 2 miles. If the Visitor Center is closed, skip forward to the Hammock Trails, another 1.2 miles east.

THE HIKES

VISITOR CENTER BOARDWALK

At the Visitor Center (28.6415, -80.7357), take a walk through the exhibits before you pick up maps, checklists, and identification information to help you spot species. Walk out the back door to follow the accessible path onto the boardwalk. There are many benches along this 0.5-mile route, making it easy for visitors of all abilities to enjoy. At the first pond, you're likely to see an alligator or two, sometimes sunning on the wooden platform. The boardwalk turns to follow the shoreline, easing through a butterfly garden behind the Visitor Center before reaching the shore of the next pond. Red-winged blackbirds call out from the cattails. Under the shade of sand live oaks, the boardwalk reaches a junction in the oak hammock. Stay right to come to a side boardwalk that leads to an overlook on a marsh. Looping around, the main boardwalk ends up back at the second pond, with an observation deck at the end offering a good spot for birding. Follow the boardwalk through the oaks to complete the loop portion, and continue straight ahead to wander back to the Visitor Center. Top off your water bottles! The other trails have no facilities.

HAMMOCK TRAILS

Drive 1.2 miles east along FL 402 to the Hammock Trails trailhead (28.6439,

DENSE FOREST ALONG THE PALM HAMMOCK TRAIL

-80.7165) on the north side of the highway. Follow the footpath up to the kiosk. Notice the dense ferns and orange trees? This was the homestead of the Danenburgs, who lived here from 1947 to 1964, growing citrus and gladiolas. When space workers came to the area in 1959, they opened a mobile home park to offer housing, and built a convenience store. Like others who lived in Wilson and nearby Wisconsin Village, they were bought out for the creation of Kennedy Space Center.

Take the right fork to walk through the ferns to start the Oak Hammock Trail. After crossing a bridge over a marshy ditch, you emerge at the railroad line. Continue straight ahead into the woods on the other side, reaching the shade of a giant old water oak. This is the beginning of the loop portion of the hike. Follow the left fork through tall saw palmettos and up to a boardwalk. Turn left at the first intersection for a walk through a laurel oak forest. You'll see some unusual trees—their trunks are bare and smooth, with an orange hue. These nakedwood trees, also known as white stopper, grow profusely along all of the trails in the hammock. The "stopper" part of the name comes from the use of their bark to treat diarrhea.

Parts of this trail can be wet in places, particularly as you reach the boardwalk which rises into the hydric hammock, a dense collection of cabbage palms in the swamp. Islands of ferns break up the dark water. At 0.4 mile, you reach a junction with the boardwalk you turned off earlier. Turn left. The boardwalk soon ends, and the footpath continues through the hammock on a base of ground-up seashells. Wild coffee grows along both sides of the trail: look for its glossy leaves and distinctive reddish-brown beans. A short boardwalk leads to a swamp overlook with wild persimmon trees. The trail veers right, continuing

to the junction under the old water oak. Turn left. When you reach the Hammock Trails kiosk, you've walked 0.7 mile.

To explore the Palm Hammock Trail, continue past the kiosk. It begins in the oak hammock among the ferns, becoming a boardwalk briefly before bursting into an open area edged with grasses and red maples. A small bridge crosses a ditch. Gaining a little elevation, you're back among oaks draped in Spanish moss. Grapevines cover the forest floor and silver-tinged saw palmetto remind you that you're near the coast. Crossing a bridge, you reach the railroad tracks. Beyond it, a boardwalk guides you into the forest over a seasonally wet area to return to the oak hammock. A tightly knit canopy of live oaks provides deep shade, while the understory is dense with cabbage palms and palmettos. The lengthy trunks of some of the saw palmettos speak to their advanced age. You start the short loop section of the trail, 1.4 miles into your hike on the Hammock Trails. As you enter the palm hammock, the cabbage palms rise like columns, the distinct knobby patterns on their trunks standing out in sharp relief.

That rustling in the underbrush is an armadillo. We've seen dozens of them along these two trails, nosing through the leaf litter in search of bugs and grubs. Armadillos are related to anteaters and sloths. Why are there so many armadillos on Merritt Island? The answer may lie with Gus Edwards, the founder of Cocoa Beach. He added a pair of Texas armadillos to his roadside zoo in 1922, and they quickly escaped.

Completing the loop after 0.5-mile of wandering among the palms, you return to the mature oak hammock. Continue along the trail as it snakes its way back to the boardwalk, where tall stems support clusters of the orchid-like blossoms of duck potatoes. Cross the old road and the railroad track, entering the woods on the south side of the railroad. Continue through the red maple marsh to the boardwalk and back to the Hammock Trails kiosk. Turn right to exit, completing a 2.8-mile circuit of the Hammock Trails.

SCRUB RIDGE TRAIL

Continue east another mile along FL 402 to where it meets CR 3. A gate for Kennedy Space Center is to the right, and the road straight ahead leads to Playa-

linda Beach. Turn left and drive north on CR 3 for another 4 miles. Watch for the SCRUB RIDGE TRAIL sign. Turn right and drive 0.4 mile down the dirt road to the trailhead (28.6950, -80.7159). While it's only a mile long, the Scrub Ridge Trail offers the opportunity to see Florida scrub-jays living near the sea.

From the parking area, follow the broad path into the open scrubby flatwoods. The understory is a dense thicket of saw palmetto and scrubby oaks. There is very little shade, since there are few tall pines to provide any, although clusters of cabbage palms do rise above the sea of scrub. This is not a tall ridge, but 4 feet of elevation is enough to make this high ground when surrounded by marshes at sea level. A Florida scrub-

jay lands in a sand live oak, boldly curious at your approach. Merritt Island National Wildlife Refuge and the adjoining Canaveral National Seashore host the state's largest population of scrub-jays. They live in family groups, so when you see or hear one, expect a few more to show up.

The trail, a sandy forest road, is headed straight towards a distant line of tall slash pines. Curving left, it comes to a T intersection with an unmarked trail. Turn left to return along the loop. As you walk back north, views of the Indian River Lagoon open up to the east, the far shore lined with cabbage palms. After 0.75 of a mile, the trail broadens. The scrub closes in for a stretch. When you return to the trailhead, make a short detour to the right for one last view of the lagoon, framed by needlerush and mangroves. You've completed a 1-mile loop.

PINE FLATWOODS TRAIL

From the Scrub Ridge Trail, drive north on CR 3 for 3.5 miles, crossing the Haulover Canal. The trailhead for the Pine Flatwoods Trail (28.7697, -80.7865) is another 3.1 miles north of the canal on the right, north of the radar tower. This is the northernmost trail in the refuge, and one of the least visited, despite the beautiful scenery. While the refuge map showed a loop trail, the signage we found pointed us down a scenic round-trip route with great birding along the way. You are welcome to roam any of the forest roads here as long as they aren't posted.

From the trailhead kiosk, walk east on a forest road. At an intersection with a road to the right, an arrow pointed in that direction, so we followed it. This forest road winds gently through a panorama of pines. A flutter of blue wings caught our attention: a scrub-jay family patrols this part of the trail. A post is half-hidden by the dense understory about 0.25 mile in. This is a very open pine forest, with views stretching off in all directions. One tall pine is home to a pair of osprey that return every season to nest. After 0.8 mile, you reach a T intersection with a forest road. Turn left. As you draw close to a cluster of cabbage palms, a deep green pool is bisected by the forest road. Be cautious: we discovered that an enormous alligator calls it home.

At 1.3 miles, this forest road ends at a sweeping panorama of Mosquito Lagoon. Part of the Indian River Lagoon system, it stretches north to New Smyrna Beach. A dredged channel for boaters enables access by water from Ponce Inlet to the Haulover Canal. You'll rarely see anyone but sport fishermen or kayakers in this lonely spot. To get back to the trailhead, return the way you came. Make the right back into the pine flatwoods up beyond the waterway, walking past the osprey nest again, and a left at the T intersection with the next east-west road. You return to the trailhead after 2.6 miles.

BLACK POINT WILDLIFE DRIVE TRAILS

Return 7.2 miles south along CR 3 to the intersection with FL 405. Turn right. Continue to the well-marked entrance for Black Point Wildlife Drive (28.657522, -80.754546). We've saved this one for last since it's the only place in the refuge with a fee attached to hiking, and the fee doubled to $10 per vehicle in 2018. You're covered if you have a National Parks pass, Federal duck stamp, or Canaveral National Seashore entrance fee receipt. Most visitors drive this scenic one-way limestone road through the impoundments, but you are welcome to bicycle it too. Pick up an interpretive brochure at the pay station. There are many places to pull off along the 6.4-mile road, but two are meaningful for hikers: the Wild Birds Unlimited Trail and the Cruickshank Trail.

At Stop 4, 1.9 miles along Wildlife Drive, you reach a parking area on the right for the Wild Birds Unlimited Trail (28.6564, -80.7771). Park and cross the road to access the trail. Following a levee, it's short, simple, and focused on providing a great birding experience. The open water on your right rises and falls with the levels of the Indian River Lagoon, sometimes exposing mud flats that wading birds flock to for feeding. It's on this side that you'll find the first bird blind, built with slatted sides. It

VIEW FROM THE OBSERVATION TOWER ON THE CRUICKSHANK TRAIL

has a spotter scope to help you see birds congregating on the far shore. At 0.25 mile along the levee, the second observation platform provides a more intimate space, overlooking two small, mangrove-lined coves. Continue back along the levee to the parking area to complete this 0.5-mile walk.

At Stop 9, 3.4 miles along Wildlife Drive, a larger parking area greets you on the left. A composting toilet is provided at the trailhead. This is the starting point for the Allen D. Cruickshank Memorial Trail (28.6780, -80.7718), more commonly known as the Cruickshank Trail. It honors the memory of a nationally known ornithologist who was the official photographer of the National Audubon Society for many years. A local resident at the time that Kennedy Space Center opened, Cruickshank worked with NASA to help establish Merritt Island National Wildlife Refuge.

Stop at the interpretive kiosk for an overview of the trail, the longest footpath in the refuge. This trail follows a levee around several impoundment areas and is the on-foot equivalent of

Wildlife Drive—narrow, surrounded by water, a perfect place for quiet bird-watching. Most visitors who stop here rush over to the nearby covered observation deck, and maybe to the short tower a little farther down the trail. By taking the right fork, you commit yourself to the 4.8-mile loop. The first stop is an observation platform over the marshes to the east, which are less frequented by birds than the man-made impoundments to the west.

Bracken ferns grow in the shade of wax myrtles. Louisiana herons, with their distinctive white bellies and deep blue plumage, wade through the shallows in search of small fry, poking through islands of perennial glasswort swathed in autumn colors—browns, reds, yellows, and greens. At 0.8 mile, it's your first chance to sit and relax on a shaded bench. There are several along the trail. Once you pass the instrumentation station, the trail grows rough. No longer a forest road, it becomes uneven and hummocky, although the park staff keeps the grass trimmed. Expect to walk more slowly for the next 4 miles.

The thick succulent leaves of saltwort peek out of a sea of red-tipped glasswort. White mangroves edge the trail, providing a windbreak against the open waters of the lagoon.

The mangroves part briefly at 1.4 miles for a sweeping view of the lagoon. Tall clumps of big cordgrass grow along the levee's edge. When the wind picks up, the waters of the impoundment area whip to waves. A long, narrow mangrove island creates a canal between the levee and the lagoon. Swamp hibiscus towers up to 10 feet tall, waving its massive pink flowers in the breeze. It's quiet out here: take a moment and listen. You may hear the sudden splash of an alligator into the water, the plop of a jumping mullet, or the creel of an osprey far above. After the trail curves around a small lagoon, another covered bench appears at 2.2 miles. This is Black Point. An opening in the mangroves provides a sweeping view of the north end of Titusville. On the left, NASA's Vehicle Assembly Building comes into view in the distance. It's one of the world's largest buildings, covering eight acres and enclosing 129 million cubic feet of space, and was used for processing rockets and orbiters.

Inside the impoundment, grassy islands give way to more substantial islands anchored by mangroves. The levee arcs back towards Wildlife Drive. Take a moment to look into the water as you veer around the far corner, where tiny fish and seashells are visible against the white sand bottom. The lagoon is stained with tannic acid. At the tip of a small peninsula, a covered bench at 3.6 miles provides a place to perch near the outflow of Cow Pen Creek. The levee follows the creek upstream, zigzagging for the next 0.25 mile, providing views back across to where you walked along the lagoon. As the levee veers right, the marsh on the left resembles an open prairie, with tall cordgrass swaying on each island. Young mangroves struggle to take root. A telephone pole provides a perch for cormorants drying their wings.

Coming around the last curve of the levee, you reach the staircase to the short observation tower. It looks out over the inner marsh and has a permanently mounted set of binoculars, in case you didn't bring your own. Atop it, you can see the full sweep of where you've just walked. We found the salt ponds to be productive during our last visit, with a family of roseate spoonbills, several tricolor herons, some egrets, and an American bittern, all of which we spotted from the smaller covered observation platform right where the trail ends. There were alligators, too, but they appear to prefer the edges of Cow Pen Creek, so keep alert as you walk through this area. Turn right to exit, completing a 4.8-mile walk when you reach the parking area.

One last worthwhile stop on Wildlife Drive is a viewpoint for an eagles' nest, which will be busy with activity in late winter and spring. A volunteer with a spotter scope is usually at this pulloff.

OTHER HIKING OPTIONS

1. **Manatee Observation Deck** (28.7376, -80.7547). An accessible boardwalk provides an overlook over Haulover Canal, frequented by manatees as they migrate along the Indian River Lagoon.

2. **North Haulover Canal** (28.7332, -80.7588). Social trails meander through the hammock and to a beach along the Indian River Lagoon. Access is along a dirt road which leads to a popular put-in for kayak-

ers, especially for night kayaking during the bioluminescent season in summer. On the south side of the canal, Bair's Cove (28.7330, -80.7562) is where boaters put in, and it has restrooms (fee area).

3. **Dummitt Cove** (28.7103, -80.7319). Park near the picnic pavilion and ramble around on the old sand roads to scenic spots along the cove, where anglers have staked out the best spots for fishing. Dummitt Cove is still used as a group campsite for Scout troops, so be respectful of their privacy if you discover a group here, usually on weekends. This is where John's troop camped when he was a kid. Captain Douglas Dummitt established the very first citrus grove along the Indian River Lagoon here in 1807.

4. **Playalinda Beach** (28.6551, -80.6322). The busiest portion of Canaveral National Seashore is just east of the refuge along FL 402. There are twelve large parking areas along the park road; Lot #1 is where locals watch rocket launches, as it sits immediately north of Kennedy Space Center.

Walk up to 4 miles (8 miles round-trip) along the oceanfront, or look into the rugged Klondike Beach Trail, Florida's longest backcountry beach walk.

5. **Coast-to-Coast Trail**. While still in the planning stages, the finale of this state-spanning paved bike path will extend from Parrish Park (28.624144, -80.793839) at the base of the Max Brewer Bridge east along the railroad grade paralleling FL 402 to the north. It will pass the Visitor Center and the Hammock Trails on its way to Playalinda Beach. A segment of the Coast-to-Coast Trail currently runs at least 18 miles north from Titusville (28.619221, -80.820069), past Mims, with more under construction north and west of Maytown.

CAMPING AND LODGING

Titusville/Kennedy Space Center KOA, 4513 W Main Street, Mims, FL 32754 (321-269-7361, koa.com)

Casa Coquina del Mar B&B, 4010 Coquina Avenue, Titusville, FL 32780 (321-268-4653, casacoquina.com)

48

Enchanted Forest Sanctuary

TOTAL DISTANCE: 3-mile loop selected from an extensive network of hiking trails.

HIKING TIME: 1.5–2 hours

DIFFICULTY: Easy to moderate

USAGE: Free. Open 9 AM–5 PM, Tuesday through Sunday. Closed Mondays and holidays. No pets or bicycles permitted.

TRAILHEAD GPS COORDINATES: 28.5326, -80.8023

CONTACT INFORMATION: Enchanted Forest Sanctuary, 444 Columbia Boulevard, Titusville, FL 32780 (321-264-5185, brevardfl.gov)

Topping the Atlantic Coastal Ridge just across the Indian River Lagoon from Kennedy Space Center, the Enchanted Forest Sanctuary is a magical place to explore, a wonderland of big trees and geologic formations with history behind them. This is the flagship conservation project that kicked off Brevard County's Environmentally Endangered Lands program in 1990. Long-time residents were already familiar with the forest and its beauty. By the 1970s, the Apollo Motorcycle Club developed off-road trails up the Atlantic Coastal Ridge from Vero Beach to Titusville, popularizing this area with Enduro riders. John's Boy Scout troop would hike up from Cocoa to overnight here; he later joined others riding mountain bikes on the well-established trails. County acquisition began in 1991, although it took nearly a decade before there was anything more than a dirt parking area and a picnic table, plus the trails that had been in place.

While it's still a destination for recreation, visitors now walk softly through the woods. The Education Center serves not just to interpret the landscape and its history, but also has classrooms for workshops and a small gift shop. Outside, a screened pavilion is a welcome retreat for picnicking during the buggy months and an amphitheater stands for environmental education classes. A native plant garden makes use of massive blocks of coquina to creative effect, and a short paved path, the Enchanted Crossing, extends the accessible offerings of the garden for wheelchair-bound visitors. Regular guided walks are offered along with ongoing workshops as diverse as gardening, outdoor yoga, photography, and storytelling for the kids.

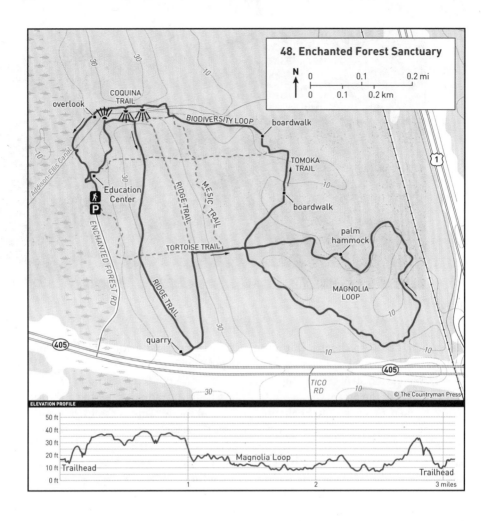

GETTING THERE

From I-95, take exit 215, Titusville, and drive east on FL 50 to the first traffic light. Turn right onto FL 405. Follow it for 4.4 miles to the entrance on the left. If you reach the US 1 overpass, you've gone too far. The entry road is part of the Hernandez-Capron Trail, an old military trail laid out by General Joseph Hernandez and built by his men in 1837, during the Second Seminole War, to link the fortresses at St. Augustine and Fort Pierce. The road persisted as an immigrant trail to South Florida through the late 1800s.

THE HIKE

The Enchanted Forest is a hiker-focused preserve: right in front of the Education Center, there's a Hike Desk for you to sign in and grab a map. While there are several access points to the trail system, the main one is behind the Education Center. Follow the walkway around the building (take advantage of insect spray set out for your use if you didn't already use your own), following the sign that says TRAILHEAD. It points to a map at the first of many trail junctions. The extensive network of trails has eight named trails that crisscross each other

RIDGE TRAIL

like a giant tic-tac-toe board. Our route follows our favorite hike along the perimeter, showcasing all of the habitats and historic sites in the preserve.

At the map, turn left onto Enchanted Crossing. The paved path climbs a gradual incline, with many benches offering spots for slow walkers to rest. Beneath the shade of the cabbage palms and oaks, you see American beautyberry, resplendent with its metallic purple berries in the fall months. An interpretive sign points out a tall Hercules-club tree, also known as toothache tree. You reach a trail junction with the Biodiversity Loop as Enchanted Crossing ends at an overlook. This is your first peek at the Addison-Ellis Canal. Started in 1912, the canal was meant to drain the extensive wetlands between the St. Johns River and the Indian River Lagoon for agriculture and development. A ridge of coquina rock proved too difficult to dig through. This high point above what was dug of the canal, a narrow cut, is one of a handful of overlooks for this failed project along your journey.

Nature heals, and so the cut is filled with vegetation.

Join the Biodiversity Loop and follow it up a gradual rise—the Atlantic Coastal Ridge. This is the high ground along Florida's eastern shore, formed during the late Pleistocene. It outcrops in numerous places along the coast, including showy, rocky shorelines north of Flagler Beach and south of Stuart. Here, the ridge formed a watershed divide until it was sliced through by the canal. Now, rainfall across this preserve makes its way east along the modified waterway. If it were not for the ropes along one side of this trail, you'd forget that the canal is hidden in the forest to your left.

As you reach the junction with the Ridge Trail, turn right. This loop trail circles the high ground of the ridge. The scrub forest atop the ridge is dense but short, with lots of myrtle oak and Chapman oak. Fine orange sand takes its color from the coquina, a sedimentary rock made up of tiny seashells that tend towards orange and pink. Crossing the Biodiversity Loop again at a bench under a longleaf pine, a splash of bright red draws your eyes to a coral bean's blooms. Watch carefully as a Florida scrub lizard vanishes beneath it. This lizard only lives in Florida scrub habitats, dry sandy hilltops like this ridge.

You pass a bench, and there's a tall magnolia tree. Dropping downhill after 0.5 mile, you come to the junction with the Tortoise Trail. To the right it heads to the parking area; to the left, it rises to the highest elevation in this preserve. The ridge tops out around 36 feet, more than double the elevation of the parking area. Continue straight ahead, staying on the Ridge Trail.

Something you may have noticed is air traffic. When you reach the Coquina Quarry Trail, the Space Coast Regional Airport sits across the four lanes of FL 405. It's the closest commercial airport to Kennedy Space Center and home to a collection of vintage warplanes known as the Valiant Air Command. Private pilots make heavy use of the airport on weekends. Take this spur trail down

into an old coquina quarry, shot through with solution holes, formed by the slow drip of water through weak spots in the limestone. This outcropping is part of the Atlantic Coastal Ridge. Quarry walls show the precision scooping of machines that cut the rock for building stone. Retrace your steps and turn right to continue along the Ridge Trail. It loops north along the ridge. Watch for a bigflower pawpaw in bloom during the spring months. The pawpaw is an edible fruit related to the soursop, which is found on Caribbean menus.

At the next junction, there are a couple of benches. Turn right. The Tortoise Trail descends from the scrub into a forest dense with magnolias and oaks. Cabbage palms tower overhead at a junction with the Mesic Trail. Continue straight. The trail ascends and reaches a multitrail junction at a gathering of benches. Turn right to start walking counterclockwise along the Magnolia Loop. A lushly canopied 1.1-mile loop, it passes a large live oak with an unusual curl to its trunk. Wild coffee fills the understory, and cabbage palms rise high overhead. As the trail descends, it winds under southern magnolias more than 100 feet tall, and massive ancient live oaks. A floodplain forest hides behind a screen of trees; in winter, the red seedpods of red maple betray its presence. Wild citrus, including oranges and grapefruit, grow in this forest. The trail passes under a magnificent oak, one that would take quite a few people holding hands to encircle it. Sword ferns, marsh ferns, and royal ferns carpet the deep, rich soil. A thousand shades of green delight the eye.

At 1.9 miles, the trail leads you down a corridor of tall cabbage palms. There's dark earth underfoot, an area that may get damp after heavy rains, with more

LOOKING DOWN INTO THE ADDISON-ELLIS CANAL FROM THE COQUINA TRAIL

massive oaks spreading their thickly knotted root systems across the trail. The swamp within the forest becomes more obvious, bubbles rising to its surface from gases emitted by rotting leaves beneath the water. The trail rises away from it. After you pass a bench, you're back at the clearing where the Magnolia Loop began. Turn right to follow the Tomoka Trail along the outer loop of the trail system. The trail drops through a tunnel of vines, with cabbage palms providing the canopy. A bench sits at the beginning of a boardwalk that works its way through the floodplain forest. Strap ferns sprout from fallen logs like bright green feathers. Open pools of tannic water are edged by ferns. Reaching the Biodiversity Loop junction after 2.7 miles, turn right to stay on the outer loop, joining a boardwalk through more floodplain forest.

Just past the junction with the Mesic Trail, the Coquina Trail veers right. Turn and follow it downhill. The narrow descent leads to a bridge over the Addison-Ellis Canal. The water is tannic but clear. As the trail turns left, it climbs the bluffs. It's a very steep drop—an actual cliff—to the bottom of the canal. Five overlooks along the next 0.25 mile provide different perspectives from the Atlantic Coastal Ridge, rewarding you with excellent views of the geologic formations where the ridge was deeply cut. Strap fern clings to boulders on the rock face.

As the trail descends the ridge, it is soft sand underfoot, much like climbing down dunes. A large gopher tortoise burrow is in the side of the hill. Next to a historic marker, you have one last look at the Addison-Ellis Canal. Vines dangle towards the tea-colored water and giant leather ferns lean over the flow. Before the canal could be dug to a useful width and depth, the consortium went bankrupt. The canal never became usable for commerce or drainage, but remains a feature visible in several spots around Titusville, including beneath US 1, under I-95, and through the Canaveral Marshes along the St. Johns River.

Leaving the woods to approach the gardens surrounding the Education Center, you're back on the old military road. Massive boulders of coquina, shot through with natural solution holes, are centerpieces in a garden of native plants. The look of these rocks evokes moonscapes, appropriate given you're near Kennedy Space Center. Work your way through the garden, with a final stop at the Education Center. Sign out at the Hike Desk on your way out. Returning to your car, you've completed a 3-mile loop around the Enchanted Forest.

OTHER HIKING OPTIONS

1. **Addison Canal Loop.** By far the most interesting trail in the park, the Coquina Trail is the one you should do if your time is limited. Going backward on the above route, walk through the garden and into the woods to the Addison Canal historic marker. Continue around the loop and across the bridge to the T intersection. Turn right and take a piece of the Biodiversity Loop up to where it meets the Enchanted Crossing. Enjoy one last overlook and turn left to follow the Enchanted Crossing to exit, for a 0.5-mile loop around the Addison Canal.

2. **Biodiversity Loop.** True to its name, this east-west loop leads you through a diverse array of habitats. Start east on the trail from the main trailhead. When you reach the Tomoka Trail junction, turn left onto the boardwalk. Follow the loop back west to Enchanted Crossing to exit, for a 0.8-mile loop. Alternatively, use the Coquina Trail to return for a loop that's almost a mile.

3. **Mesic Meander.** Everyone likes a shaded trail, and the Mesic Trail does a nice job of keeping you covered. Use the Coquina Trail to access the north end of the Mesic Trail. Follow it down to the Tortoise Trail, which leads back around to the parking area if you follow it west. This is a 0.9-mile walk; extend it to 2 miles by adding on the Magnolia Loop.

4. **5K Loop.** Follow the signs throughout the trail network to rack up 3.1 miles. This loop is popular with runners and makes good use of the Ridge Trail and Magnolia Loop along with other trails.

CAMPING AND LODGING

Manatee Hammock Campground, 7275 US 1, Titusville, FL 32780 (321-264-5083, brevardfl.gov)

Casa Coquina del Mar B&B, 4010 Coquina Avenue, Titusville, FL 32780 (321-268-4653, casacoquina.com)

49

Maritime Hammock Sanctuary

TOTAL DISTANCE: 2.8-mile circuit of two loops and a connector.

HIKING TIME: 1.5–2 hours

DIFFICULTY: Easy to moderate

USAGE: Free. Open daily, sunrise to sunset. No pets or bicycles permitted.

TRAILHEAD GPS COORDINATES: 27.9564, -80.5028

CONTACT INFORMATION: Maritime Hammock Sanctuary, 6200 S Highway A1A, Melbourne Beach, FL 32951 (321-723-3556, brevardfl.gov)

Bordering and managed by Archie Carr National Wildlife Refuge—the first wildlife refuge in America established to protect sea turtles—Maritime Hammock Sanctuary showcases maritime (coastal) hammock, marshlands, and mangroves along the Indian River Lagoon. It's 150 acres preserved from the residential development that has otherwise spread up and down A1A. According to one interpretive marker, "This is the place where the North meets the South," biologically speaking. Along this hike, you'll discover plant species that are just as comfortable in Naples or Key West as they are here, while you follow a twisting, winding, sometimes soggy footpath. We consider it an excellent adventure, even if there's wet feet in the bargain.

GETTING THERE

From I-95, take exit 180 for Melbourne. Follow US 192 east for 8 miles through downtown and continue over the causeway to Indialantic. When the highway ends at the beach, turn right and follow FL A1A for 10.3 miles, passing a variety of public beaches on the way south to the community of Melbourne Shores. Park at the north trailhead (you'll have to pull across the bicycle path to do so, so watch for pedestrians and bicycles). There is a grassy parking area along the slope above the bike path.

THE HIKE

Stop at the kiosk to pick up a map. The preserve is shaped like a bridge, with an incursion of subdivision in the middle section, although the houses are mostly hidden from view. The trail skirts a large depression that was once filled by an artesian well to create a reservoir for

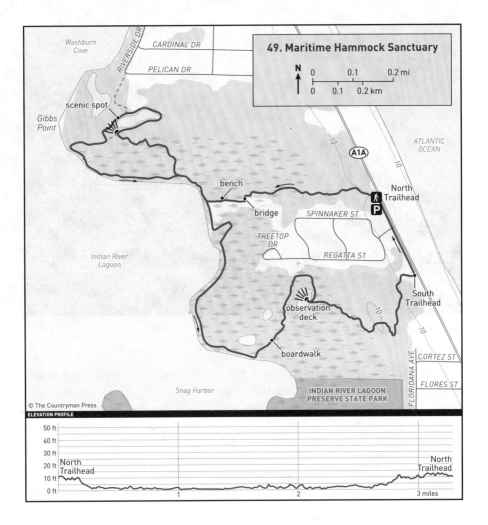

49. Maritime Hammock Sanctuary

N
0   0.1   0.2 mi
0   0.1   0.2 km

Washburn Cove

RIVERSIDE DR

CARDINAL DR

PELICAN DR

scenic spot

Gibbs Point

ATLANTIC OCEAN

A1A

bench

North Trailhead

bridge

SPINNAKER ST

TREETOP DR

REGATTA ST

Indian River Lagoon

observation deck

South Trailhead

boardwalk

FLORIDANA AVE

CORTEZ ST

FLORES ST

Snag Harbor

INDIAN RIVER LAGOON PRESERVE STATE PARK

ELEVATION PROFILE

50 ft
40 ft
30 ft
20 ft   North Trailhead   North Trailhead
10 ft
0 ft
        1   2   3 miles

the Exotica Nursery, which occupied this spot. You may notice some escaped nursery residents like snake plant and Norfolk Island pine growing in the hammocks, but most invasive species have been rounded up.

Snaking around and down, the trail enters a lush hammock. Look up into the high canopy for orchids, which bloom in the summer months. Even off-season, the leaves of greenfly orchid are showy. As the corridor narrows, tropical shrubs like marlberry appear in the understory. A natural archway rises over the trail,

which winds through the dense forest beneath tree limbs outstretched in graceful windswept arcs like ballet dancers. Becoming mushy underfoot, the footpath crosses bog bridges surrounded by pennyroyal and giant leather ferns. After a sharp turn at a fence line, a short spur trail provides a shaded bench from which to see a creek hidden under a tunnel of tropical vegetation.

At the trail junction, the YOU ARE HERE marker provides a map to show where the trail system goes. Turn right to follow the stacked loops on the north

INDIAN RIVER LAGOON AT DUSK, GIBBS POINT

end of the sanctuary. The trail is right behind the mangrove roots along the Indian River Lagoon, and can get wet at times. You encounter your first gumbo-limbo tree after 0.5 mile. The gumbo-limbo is also jokingly called the Tourist Tree due to its distinctive red, peeling bark. This is the northernmost preserve in which we've encountered this tropical tree.

Keep right at the next trail junction, where there is another map. Sprays of shoelace fern and goldfoot fern emerge from the tall cabbage palms. You emerge from the hammock into a beauty spot at the next trail junction, a panoramic view of open marshes along Gibbs Point, framed by cabbage palms and sprays of sand cordgrass. Turn right to circle the marsh. Mounds of coreopsis and aster bloom throughout the open areas. A little blue heron squawks and flies away at your approach. Cormorants crowd the branches of mangroves on a small island in the middle of the marsh.

The breeze off the lagoon across the marsh makes this part of the hike naturally air-conditioned. Pass the side trail to a residential neighborhood and loop around the marsh, crossing it on boards atop a concrete weir. Turn right. After a mile, the trail turns left, and you're along the lapping shoreline of the Indian River Lagoon. Here, the mangroves grow taller. A boardwalk leads through a wet area. Seagrass and oyster shells fill open spots between the mangroves. Bog bridges carry you across damp spots. Complete the upper loop, returning to a junction with a map. Continue forward across the bridge to reach the initial junction at 1.4 miles.

The next part of the trail isn't as interesting as what you've hiked so far. It's a connector between the two preserved hammocks within this sanctuary, skirting the residential area, a long walk along a tall levee next to the mangroves that line the Indian River Lagoon. You may spot ibises in the mangrove limbs,

BOARDWALK THROUGH THE MANGROVE FOREST

and a massive alligator lives at the base of one sharply banked turn in the levee, so don't hike this piece on autopilot. Reaching an interpretive sign about the impoundments, which were created for mosquito control many decades ago, watch for a bridge on the left that gets you off the long dike at 2 miles and back into the tropical hammock.

You encounter benches more frequently as the trail passes through a forest of young gumbo-limbo. Passing an interpretive sign about the tropical plants, the trail is infused with a damp, skunky aroma. Young nakedwood trees are skinny, smooth-barked, and packed densely through this part of the forest, reminiscent of the tropical hammocks of Key Largo. A boardwalk tunnels through the mangroves. A spur trail leads right at 2.3 miles to an observation deck that opens onto a lagoon. If you can tolerate the mosquitoes—which are more intense here than along the rest of the loop—look for wading birds roosting in the mangroves.

Branches curl into bizarre inchworm shapes overhead as the high canopy fills in with red bay and live oak. More shells crunch underfoot as you continue walking in the shade past another bench. At 2.5 miles, the trail turns sharply down a corridor with a scrubby feel. It passes beneath arches of oaks, undulating branches providing shade and shelter for bromeliads and orchids. The footpath gets hilly as if you're climbing up and over middens. Passing an old baffle in a fence, the trail pops out under a power line. A marker points right, where you emerge out on the paved bicycle trail at the South Trailhead. Turn left and walk up the paved trail past Mark's Landing as traffic zips past at high speed along A1A. Reaching the North Trailhead, you complete a 2.8-mile loop.

OTHER HIKING OPTIONS

1. **Barrier Island Sanctuary** (27.903095, -80.471519). Drive 4 miles south on A1A to this lagoon-to-sea preserve with a nature center that welcomes you to learn more about Archie Carr National Wildlife Refuge. A mile-long interpretive loop starts at the beach next to the Center and leads to the lagoon and back.

2. **Coconut Point Sanctuary** (28.011787, -80.531173). Drive 4.2 miles north on A1A and park at Juan Ponce de León Landing to visit this coastal preserve. The habitat diversity is outstanding along a mile loop that takes you to an observation deck on the Indian River Lagoon.

3. **Long Point Park**. Seven miles south on the lagoon side of A1A, this is a popular county campground. Cross the bridge from the campground over to Scout Island (27.873172, -80.471262) to explore a mile of nature trails through the mangroves and uplands.

4. **Sebastian Inlet State Park**. Eight miles south along A1A, this state park spans its namesake inlet. On the north side of the inlet, the Hammock Nature Trail (27.875522, -80.456902) is a 0.5-mile loop through the tropical hammock and mangrove shoreline along the Indian River Lagoon.

CAMPING AND LODGING

Long Point Park, 700 Long Point Road, Melbourne Beach, FL 32951 (321-952-4532, brevardfl.gov)

Sebastian Inlet State Park, 9700 S Highway A1A, Melbourne Beach, FL 32951 (1-800-326-3521, floridastate parks.reserveamerica.com)

50

Turkey Creek Sanctuary

TOTAL DISTANCE: 3.1-mile loop selected from a network of trails and boardwalks.

HIKING TIME: 1.5–2 hours

DIFFICULTY: Easy

USAGE: Free. Open dawn to sunset. No pets or bicycles permitted.

TRAILHEAD GPS COORDINATES: 28.0167, -80.6050

CONTACT INFORMATION: Turkey Creek Sanctuary, 1518 Port Malabar Boulevard NE, Palm Bay, FL 32905 (321-676-6690, brevardfl.gov or palmbayflorida.org)

An oasis in suburbia, Turkey Creek Sanctuary encompasses 133 acres, protecting the gentle bends of Turkey Creek as it carves a deep path through sandy banks on its winding course to the Indian River Lagoon. Manatees graze in the clear tannic waters of the creek in spring and summer, delighting visitors as they swim in search of eelgrass and water lettuce.

Jointly managed by the Brevard County Environmentally Endangered Lands Program and the city of Palm Bay, this preserve sees more visitors than most. As it lies directly behind the Palm Bay Library, it's a popular destination for casual walkers and joggers, as well as families. At the entrance, you'll find a butterfly garden outside the Margaret Hames Nature Center, a great place to take the kids. There are aquariums with turtles and fish, interpretive displays, research materials, and restrooms. Staffed by volunteers, the Nature Center is open most days from 9 AM–4 PM. Call ahead about ranger-led tours, workshops, and educational programs for kids.

GETTING THERE

From I-95 south of Melbourne, take exit 176 and turn left onto CR 516 (Palm Bay Road). Follow it 2.3 miles to Babcock St (CR 507). Turn right, driving 1 mile to Port Malabar Boulevard. Turn left. From I-95 northbound from Vero Beach, take exit 173. Turn right on Malabar Road (CR 514). Make a left onto Babcock Street. Follow it 1.4 miles to Port Malabar Boulevard. Turn right. Drive 1.1 miles down Port Malabar Boulevard to Santiago Dr, just before the park sign. Make a right. Parking is on the right, across from the park entrance and just before the library entrance.

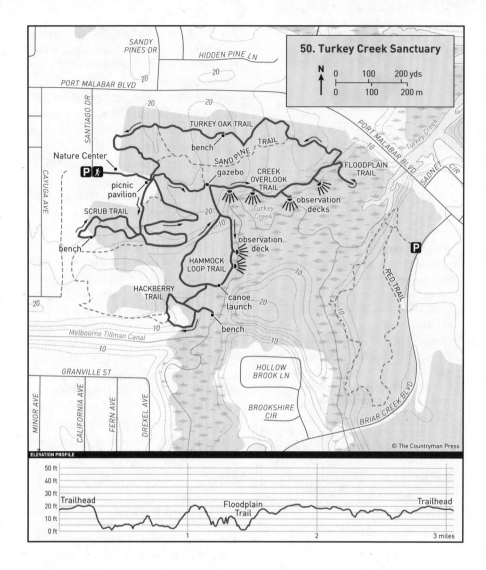

ELEVATION PROFILE

THE HIKE

Your hike starts at the front entrance, with its small butterfly garden. Look for Gulf fritillary butterflies with wide orange wings with white spots below, and zebra longwing butterflies with wide black and yellow wings. Sand pines tower overhead; myrtle oaks and saw palmettos crowd the understory. A kiosk shows off a map of the sanctuary. Visit the Nature Center to pick up a copy

of this map and interpretive information about the park. The trails are well marked, with a miniature version of the map posted at many locations to help you keep track of where you are.

A footpath leads between railings to the gated entrance into the sanctuary, where a list of rules are posted. The path winds behind the public library into the sand pine forest, passing a side trail to a picnic pavilion. At the T intersection with the JOGGING & EXERCISE TRAIL sign, make a left. You're facing the entrance to the Sand Pine Trail. You'll be back at this junction later in the hike. For now, start down the boardwalk, the Creek Overlook Trail. This boardwalk isn't here to keep your feet dry—it keeps the footpath off the habitat, and also enables wheelchair access to the most scenic part of the preserve. It also memorializes residents and visitors who've helped with the construction effort, their names or messages permanently carved in the boards, an interesting distraction as you walk. There is plenty to read along this interpretive trail besides the boards. The boardwalk zigzags through the sand pine scrub. Towering sand pines are thick with ball moss. Greenbrier snakes across open patches of bright white sand. Turkey oaks add a splash of fall color in the lower canopy. Frequent benches make this an easy walk for all ages.

After you pass the first bench, the boardwalk swings left and comes to a gazebo. It's here you reach the second trail intersection: a staircase adjoining the gazebo leads to the Sand Pine Trail, and two boardwalk choices lay ahead of you. Take the one to the right, the Hammock Loop Trail. As it heads downhill, keep left at the fork. You catch your first glimpse of water—Turkey Creek, bordered on the far shore by steep sand bluffs, the remnants of ancient sand dunes. As the boardwalk turns a bend, you enter a hardwood hammock dominated by live oaks, cabbage palms, red maple, and elms. Pignut hickory trees pepper their nuts across the boards. The boardwalk parallels the waterway, with two viewing platforms from which to watch for manatees and gawk at sunning turtles.

As the boardwalk curves along an elbow of the creek, it reaches a canoe landing at 0.5 mile. Visitors are welcome to enter the park by canoe or kayak, paddling up from the Indian River Lagoon or from launch points in Palm Bay, the city boat ramp at Bianca Drive or the hand launch in this park on the east side of Turkey Creek (see *Other Hiking Options*). The canoe landing straddles a side channel of the creek, a floodplain channel hosting wild coffee plants towering up to 7 feet tall. The boardwalk curves away from the creek.

Passing under a power line, you reach a staircase into the woods. Hop off the boardwalk to explore this southern corner of the park on a short loop, the Hackberry Trail. The footpath leads down the power line to a T intersection. Turn left, and stay left at the next junction. As you enter a lush palm hammock, the trail twists and curves across mounds of sand tossed into the woods by the creek overflowing its banks. You see watermarks on the trees. The spur trail ends at a bench on a bluff above the creek, with a view of a small island. Kayakers say there is often a very large alligator lazing in the sun at that spot. Follow the spur trail back to the loop and turn left. You pass another spur to the left with a NO ENTRY sign. Continue around the corner into a sunny, grassy corridor. There is a gopher tortoise burrow near where the trail meets a forest road coming in from the west. Turn right and follow the hiker-symbol sign to continue back into the shade, where wild coffee grows in the understory. Coming back around to the power line, make a left to walk to the Hammock Loop Trail, rejoining the boardwalk after 0.9 mile. Turn left.

Stay on the Hammock Loop Trail as it winds around a sugarberry tree, wandering deeper into the hardwood hammock, a dense canopy of red maples, sugarberry, laurel oak, and black

CREEK OVERLOOK TRAIL ALONG TURKEY CREEK, AS SEEN FROM THE HAMMOCK LOOP TRAIL

it isn't, use the paralleling Sand Pine Trail behind the gazebo to reach the east end of it, which remained open. The Creek Overlook Trail parallels Turkey Creek downstream, providing numerous overlooks from which to watch for manatees. Take the time to stop and savor the views. Above you, sand pines rise to the sky. Deer moss grows in scattered clumps across the pine needles on the forest floor. Each overlook gives you a unique view of the creek. From the first overlook, look back down along the creek's route you traced along the beginning of the Hammock Loop Trail. Set on a high sand bluff, the second overlook provides a sweeping vista of a lazy bend in Turkey Creek. Looking straight down, see that although the water is laced with tannins from oak leaves, the tea color doesn't spoil its clarity. The boardwalk descends down the sand bluff, so the third overlook sits close to creek level, along a sharp bend.

continues. A sign warns that this part of the trail is not wheelchair-accessible—it's a natural footpath defined by logs on the edges. You come to a FLOODPLAIN TRAIL sign. It's worth taking this 0.25-mile spur trail. It switchbacks down the bluff to reach the edge of the Turkey Creek floodplain, where a long boardwalk—an excellent example of an Eagle Scout project—leads you into the marsh to the floodplain forest, ending on a small rise just within sight of the creek. Return the way you came. At the T intersection near the boardwalk, turn right.

You're now on the Sand Pine Trail, which curves through the oak hammock. A gopher tortoise ambles along the side of the trail. If there is one creature there are plenty of in this preserve, this is it. Their burrows, which can be up to 15 feet long, provide shelter for dozens of other species. As the dense oaks and soft sand pines yield to turkey oaks—with leaves that look like turkey tracks—you reach the TURKEY OAK TRAIL sign. Turn right. Sounds of traffic are nearby, muted wherever the forest is dense. Sand live oaks arch over wiregrass. There are many young, skinny sand pines along the footpath, so dense they almost look like bamboo. In spring, look for the showy blooms of skyblue lupine throughout this forest. Not long after you pass a bench, you cross a park road that serves as somewhat of a cross-trail between the Turkey Oak Trail and the Sand Pine Trail. A FIRE EXIT sign points towards Port Malabar Boulevard. Continue straight ahead. The sand pines are taller here and the trail much wider. Passing a bench adjoining a map marking your location, you see that you've looped around behind the Nature Center. You pass a sand live oak with a showy collection of bromeliads growing along its trunk. The trail makes another sharp curve and reaches a junction with the Sand Pine Trail. Turn right.

After 2.2 miles, you're back at the four-way intersection with the Creek Overlook Trail boardwalk. The park exit is to the right, but there is another loop to do to enjoy more of the scrub forest. Continue straight ahead, past the JOGGING & EXERCISE TRAIL sign, and pass the picnic pavilion. Emerging from the sand pine forest into a clearing, you see several cabbage palms, one of which has a strangler fig growing out of its trunk. Cross a park road past a back gate and continue into a shaded corridor of oaks. Just past a trail junction, you come to a SCRUB TRAIL sign and another locator map. Turn right at the sign to follow this short loop clockwise, keeping left at the next junction. Sand pines tower overhead and laurel oaks are in the understory. As the trail gains a little elevation, you're surrounded by a dense oak scrub with short myrtle oaks and Chapman oaks. Sand

live oaks arch over this dense understory. There are gopher tortoises here too. On our hike, we encountered six of them rambling along the trail system.

When you reach the end of the Scrub Trail loop, turn left to exit, then make a right at the map. Make a left at the next T, at 2.6 miles (the trail to the right follows park roads to the Hackberry Trail) to join a shaded corridor edged with sword fern and wild coffee. It's a pleasant, narrow footpath through a dense, hardwood forest, making a sharp right at a T intersection that leads towards the Scrub Trail. This part of the preserve is used by trail runners and joggers, so be alert if someone comes up fast behind you. Bracken fern grows next to the footpath, in the sun under the hickory trees. As this trail loops around, the transition back into the scrub forest becomes obvious.

You pop into a clearing with a fenced building in it. Turn left. Follow this park road to the beginning of the Jogging Trail. At the four-way intersection, turn left to exit. If seeing hundreds of names underfoot on the boardwalks has you wanting to be immortalized too, stop by the Margaret Hames Nature Center and make a contribution to the cause. When you return to your car, you've completed a 3.1-mile hike.

OTHER HIKING OPTIONS

1. **Turkey Creek Boardwalks.** Focus your visit on the easy and accessible boardwalks that have been restored and, in some places, rebuilt entirely after flooding from Hurricane Irma in 2018. There is a short section of level, natural surface between the Nature Center and the start of the Creek Overlook Trail where wheelchairs may require some assistance.

Following both the Creek Overlook Trail (round-trip) and the Hammock Loop Trail (round-trip and loop) nets you a 1.3-mile exploration of the most scenic portion of the preserve along its boardwalks.

2. **Sand Pine/Turkey Oak Loop.** These upland trails start immediately north of the beginning of the Creek Overlook Trail boardwalk and make a 1.1-mile loop. Add on a spur walk to the end of the Floodplain Trail and back for a 1.5-mile hike.

3. **Red Trail** (28.0151, -80.5956). On the east side of Turkey Creek, a popular put-in for kayakers also provides access to a 1-mile loop trail through upland habitats and along a short section of the creek.

4. **Cameron Preserve** (28.0125, -80.5956). Across from the Red Trail, a little south along Briar Creek Boulevard, Cameron Preserve is one of the newer public lands in the south end of Brevard County. Linking together Turkey Creek Sanctuary and Malabar Scrub Sanctuary, it offers many miles of trails to explore, all of which are open to mountain biking. Restrooms and a larger trailhead parking area are at 1400 Marie Street, Malabar, FL 32950. For trail maps, see malabar-trails.org

CAMPING AND LODGING

Wickham Park Campground, 2500 Parkway Drive, Melbourne, FL 32935 (321-255-4307, brevardfl.gov)

Holiday Inn Express Palm Bay, 1206 Malabar Road SE, Palm Bay, FL 32907 (321-220-2003, ihg.com)